# Institutions, Social Norms, and Economic Development

**Fundamentals of Development Economics**

Edited by
**Kaushik Basu**, Cornell University, USA

The **Fundamentals of Development Economics** is designed to help to close the gap between the production of new knowledge and its dissemination. The series will publish leading economists, many of whom have contributed significantly to the current state of the discipline, who will author and edit books which take the reader from the basics to the frontiers of knowledge in particular subfields. In these books the reader will find not just descriptions of what is happening in the real world of development, but also new theorems and new econometric findings in a reader-friendly but authoritative and comprehensive form.

Volume 1 — *Institutions, Social Norms, and Economic Development*
Jean-Philippe Platteau

This book is part of a series. The publisher will accept continuation orders which may be cancelled at any time and which provide for automatic billing and shipping of each title in the series upon publication. Please write for details.

# Institutions, Social Norms, and Economic Development

Jean-Philippe Platteau
Department of Economics, University of Namur, Belgium

Routledge
Taylor & Francis Group
LONDON AND NEW YORK

By Routledge
2 Park Square, Milton Park,
Abington, Oxon, OX14 4RN

Transferred to Digital Printing 2006

---

**British Library Cataloguing in Publication Data**

A catalogue record for this book is available from the British Library.

ISBN: 90-5823-058-9
ISSN: 1562-3440

To Stefan, Corentin, and Alexis

CONTENTS

# FOREWORD

Douglass C. North
*Washington University, St. Louis, USA*

How much do we know about economic development? The output, theoretical and empirical, on the subject over the five decades since World War II would fill a substantial library. But to say that the results have been unsatisfactory is an understatement. Much of that work, indeed, was a retrogression as compared to the insights on the subject of the classical economists (in particular David Hume and Adam Smith) writing more than two centuries ago. The reason is straightforward. The dominant paradigm in the field of economics, neo-classical theory, generated an inappropriate set of tools to deal with the subject. It was concerned with the functioning of markets, not how they evolved. It took for granted polities, demography, and institutions—the necessary building blocks for understanding the process of economic change.

All that is changing now. Not only are some economists widening their horizons in economics, equally essential, they are exploring the links with demography, political science, sociology, anthropology, law, and even cognitive science to attempt to come to grips with the complex issues that make up the subject matter. Understanding economic change entails understanding human beings in the totality of their physical and human environment. That is a tall order and, not surprisingly, we still have a long way to go.

Jean-Philippe Platteau's *Institutions, Social Norms, and Economic Development* is a major step in our progress. It combines the author's sound knowledge of the necessary economic theory with the essential theory of other social sciences enriched by his extensive work in the field. His lengthy bibliography attests to a thorough knowledge of the field work of others as well.

It is easy to state the fundamental dilemma confronting the author. We know a good deal about the sources of productivity growth, the essential underpinning of economic development; yet we do not know how to get economic development. Nor when it does occur are we successful at controlling the undesirable social side effects of economic development. Again, the reason is straightforward. Putting in place the formal institutions that have undergirded the spectacular growth of the developed world does not produce the desired results. That is because the formal rules must be complemented by informal norms of behavior (and enforcement characteristics) to get the desired results. And typically not only are they not forthcoming but we have a very imperfect understanding of their origins and evolution. Drawing inspiration from Ester Boserup's pioneering studies, Platteau makes a convincing case that population density relative to land abundance is the place to begin to understand the sources of norms. The evolution of the informal norms is shaped by a complex of physical and social conditions that he illumines from his extensive field work, particularly in Africa. This study, therefore, makes substantial progress by confronting the fundamental dilemma and providing important insights towards its resolution.

# ACKNOWLEDGMENTS

This book is the outcome of a long reflection process based on my own research as well as on careful and intensive reading of the works of a considerable number of authors who are listed in the bibliography. My greatest debt is to two authors who have continuously inspired me while thinking about this book, Douglass North and Ester Boserup. The former because he provided me with a way of thinking about institutions and institutional evolution, and the latter because her work convinced me of the importance of population density as a clue to understand both institutional phenomena and economic performances. I must also thank my students at the University of Namur who have unconsciously or inadvertently stimulated my thinking while patiently listening to my development lectures and spontaneously raising clarifying questions and critical comments. Finally, I am grateful to all the scholars who have offered me comments and insights, or reacted to my thoughts in the course of private discussions or public seminars during which some chapters of this book were presented (in Stanford, Chicago, Ithaca, Madison, Tokyo, Trivandrum, London, Paris, Oslo, Wageningen, and other places). In particular, I would like to thank Kaushik Basu from Cornell University for the continuous encouragements which he gave to this enterprise; Jean-Marie Baland (who has participated in the writing of parts of Chapter 3) and Frederic Gaspart (for long discussions on Chapters 6 and 7) from the University of Namur; Yujiro Hayami from Aoyama Gakuin University of Tokyo (particularly in connection with Chapter 2); Masahiko Aoki, Kenneth Arrow, Marcel Fafchamps, and Avner Greif from Stanford University; Shem Migot-Adholla and Maurice Schiff from the World Bank; Pranab Bardhan from the University of California, Berkeley; Samuel Bowles from the University of Massachusetts (Amherst); Michael Carter from the University of Wisconsin; Partha Dasgupta from Cambridge University; Karl-Owe Moene from the University of Oslo; Douglass North from Washington University, St. Louis; Keijiro Otsuka from the International Food Policy Research Institute (IFPRI), Washington DC; and Dani Rodrick from Harvard University.

# INTRODUCTION

*No one has a simple answer, and all proposals of panaceas are in a class with millenarian dreams .... A civilization like ours, with its drive to mastery, does not like to be thwarted. It disapproves of discouraging words ...*

David Landes, *The Wealth and Poverty of Nations*

For David Landes, himself an economic historian, economists tend to assume that "every country is destined to develop sooner or later": economic growth "is natural and will occur wherever opportunity and security exist. Remove the obstacles, and growth will take care of itself" [Landes, 1998: 5, 31]. This kind of statement is probably a good reflection of the thinking that prevailed among many economists during the postwar decades, especially during the fifties and the sixties. In those times, indeed, the dominant opinion was that the main problem of many so-called underdeveloped countries lay in the fact that they lacked some essential production factors. If more advanced nations would agree to transfer the missing factors in quantities large enough to trigger off a 'big push' forward (so as to escape low-level equilibrium traps), the recipient laggard countries would be set on the path to self-sustaining growth.

Aggregate production function analyses conducted over a long period of time (in the United States, and in some countries of Europe and Latin America) revealed that the increase in inputs of labour and capital was typically small in comparison with the expansion of gross national product. In other words, the bulk improvements in production and levels of living was attributed to a 'residual factor': its contributory share accounted for as much as 90 per cent of the growth of American output between 1900 and 1960, and for two-thirds of the growth in Norway between 1900 and 1955. In the agricultural sector only, the share of increased output due to the residual factor was 83 per cent for the United States, 62 per cent for Argentina, 45 per cent for Brazil, and 50 per cent for Mexico, considering the period from 1910 (for the first two countries) or 1925 (for the latter two countries) to the middle of the twentieth century [Solow, 1957; Aukrust, 1959; Schultz, 1961—cited from Higgins, 1968: 425–430].

The nature of this residual factor which seems to play such a large role in modern economic growth was, of course, a crucial question. A common answer was that it consisted of "education in the broad sense, including all kinds of technical training, and including also the technological progress that comes from investment in education" [Higgins, 1968: 426; see also Vaizey, 1964]. In his well-known attempt to further break down the sources of American and European growth, Edward Denison (1962, 1967) distinguished the increase in the amount of education from the advance of knowledge as such. The estimates indicate that, even though increase in education, with a generous estimate of its effects, is included in factor inputs, 63 per cent of the increase in output per man-hour in the United States and 80 per cent in Europe are attributed to other factors. A debate ensued about the validity of Denison's estimates, yet the conclusion eventually remained that a significant part of the productivity growth recorded in developed countries cannot be traced back to increases in inputs [Hagen, 1975: 258–60].

The central lesson which was therefore drawn from such exercises is that laggard countries needed to have their technical skills and knowledge enhanced, hence the importance of education programs and technological transfers from rich to poor countries. Looked at from the end of the twentieth century, after the New Institutional Economics has entered the field of development studies, the interpretation of the residual factor advanced by postwar development economists appears as strangely narrow. The inclination today would be, indeed, to construe this factor as reflecting institutional as well as technical dimensions of growth, emphasizing that institutional or organizational features play a non-negligible role in promoting technical progress itself.

Recent, more sophisticated, econometric studies using a cross-sectional framework [Barro, 1991], possibly extended to a panel setup [Barro, 1997], and based on large samples of countries belonging to all the continents, conclude that, in addition to education (years of schooling at the secondary and higher level), birthrates,[1] initial levels of per capita incomes,[2] and some other variables (possibly including regional dummies),[3] institutional factors exert a significant impact on growth rates. This is particularly evident from the fact that better implementation of the rule of law—measuring quality of the bureaucracy, political corruption, likelihood of government repudiation of contracts, risk of government expropriation, and overall maintenance of the rule of law—does significantly and positively affect growth prospects.

Now, once the institutional dimension of development is brought into the picture, the problem of transferring the experience from rich to poor countries appears much more difficult. The fact of the matter is that rules or institutions are much more complicated than goods and services which people buy and sell on the market depending on tastes, technologies, and resource endowments. They are true 'cultural embodiments' in that they reflect the value systems and historical antecedents of the societies in which they prevail and not only the particular parameters of these societies' current economic environment. Hence the enormous difficulties of successfully transplanting institutions which have worked in advanced countries into the terrain of other countries which have different histories. Widely diverging economic performances that are sustained over long periods of time attest that such transplants, which have undoubtedly been tried in the past decades, do not usually fulfil their promise.

The stark truth is, as Paul Krugman put it, that "After all, relative to the hopes of the 1950s and even the 1960s, the performance of most developing countries has been dismal. (Indeed, the polite phrase 'developing country' itself has become an embarrassment, when it must be used in such sentences as 'Per capita income in the developing countries of SubSaharan Africa has declined steadily since the mid-1970s')". Growing disenchantment with aid follows decades of unimpressive results and, even if it would be unfair to blame economists "for more than a small fraction of this failure", the fact remains that "development economists were most often consulted or given positions of influence in connection with the disbursement of foreign aid" and that "the ideas of development economics were too often used as a justification for policies that in retrospect impeded growth rather than helping it along. Where rapid economic growth did occur, it occurred in ways that were not anticipated by the development theorists" [Krugman, 1997: 23–24].

In the concluding chapter of his most recent book *Development Economics—From the Poverty to the Wealth of Nations* (1997), Yujiro Hayami stresses the fact that each country must find its own institutional pattern of development, instead of simply relying on importation of foreign technology and ways of doing:

> Indeed, the traditional culture or value system is an important basis of economic modernization. However, it does not appear that the value system consistent with modernization is limited to a specific culture (such as the

> Protestant ethic)... The forms of organization of modernization are different for different cultural traditions and historical paths, as evident from the contrast between Japan and the West... The historical fact that Japan, Korea, Taiwan, and Thailand, among others, succeeded in getting on the track of sustained economic development, each based on their own unique system and tradition, strongly suggests the possibility that many low-income economies today will be able to achieve modern development in the future, not along a monolithic path, but along multiple paths according to their different traditions [Hayami, 1997: 280, 282].

Upon Hayami's reading, therefore, the predicament of low-income countries suffering from poverty and stagnation today is a temporary situation that will be remedied once these countries have found the way to fit the exigencies of economic modernization into their cultural and social traditions. Yet, Hayami hastens to add: "This is an extremely difficult but not impossible task". In point of fact, "The task required for such a system design is not simply to adapt borrowed technology and institutions to traditionally given culture and value systems. Major efforts should also be made to change people's perception so that economically efficient technology and institutions are acceptable to them" [*ibidem*: 282]. This conclusion is therefore close to the statement of David Landes quoted as an epigraph to this introduction: "No one has a simple answer, and all proposals of panaceas are in a class with millenarian dreams". Countries have to find their own manner of development and, since this may take a lot of time for some of them, one cannot rule out the possibility that those which do not easily find their way will lag behind considerably and for a long time to come. Those are perhaps "discouraging words" which are hard to hear for a civilization like ours, with "its drive to mastery" [Landes, 1998: 5].

The above perspective, which also underlies the present work, seems to be shared by a growing number of economists as attested by the recent contributions of Peyton Young (1998), Masahiko Aoki (forthcoming), and Avner Greif (forthcoming). It runs counter to an important current of development thought dominated by the idea that policy mistakes by ignorant, irresponsible, or corrupt governments are the main culprit for the economic backwardness of many poor countries. As Joseph Stiglitz put it, the underlying orthodoxy is that "countries, if left to themselves, would thus develop to the limit of their capacities and resources; lack of development can only be attributable to lack of resources or (harmful) governmental intervention. Since economic forces naturally lead to economic efficiency, the study of development becomes the study of the political barriers to development. "Lack of development is always and everywhere a political, not an economic, problem" [Stiglitz, 1989: 20].

Of course, misguided policy choices are plentiful in the real world. The problem is that they may not be easily remedied, as too many experts in development or high-level officials in donor agencies and international organizations often seem to assume they will. Such mistakes may actually affect conditions prevailing in a particular country for a long time to come if they are embedded in institutions and systems of beliefs that become self-reproducing. Also, what appear as mistakes by policy-makers may have to be construed as behaviours partaking of a logic of state formation and functioning that requires to be studied on its own. Rent-seeking theory can certainly shed instructive light on many wastes of scarce resources, yet the political processes and the political culture that have allowed rent-seekers to occupy a dominating position in some economies and not in others are still largely ill-understood, at least by economists.

The present book does not want to just argue that institutions are important for development and that they have been shaped by historical antecedents or the "accumulation of precedent" (Peyton Young) crystallized in sets of beliefs, mores and patterns of behaviour. Its originality lies in the adding of a geographical dimension to the institutional-cultural perspective on development. The role of population density as a crucial factor influencing institutional development and market expansion actually provides the clue leading to this peculiar combination of two strands of thought that have so far remained quite separate in the development literature. To give the reader an intuition of how such a combination of approaches can occur, it is useful to start from Adam Smith's essential proposition that economic growth largely depends on the extent of division of labour, and to highlight two different sorts of conditions on which this division hinges.

First, in order that economic specialization can develop, it is important that well-defined property rights are established and that suspicion and fear of fraud do not pervade transactions. Such conditions cannot be created *ex abrupto* by a sort of *deus ex machina* but must somehow evolve within the countries concerned. To be sure, what needs to evolve are not only the suitable practices and rules themselves, but also the public agencies (among which the centralized state is an essential yet not exclusive element) and morality without which generalized trust will be hard to come by. Generalized respect for property rights is an especially vexed issue since no informal network of more or less continuous relationships can easily guarantee it under all the circumstances where detection of violation is costly. The cultural endowment of societies as it has developed over their particular histories is therefore bound to play a major role in this regard. This is one of the central themes running through this book, particularly in Chapters 3 and 4 (devoted to property rights in land) and in Chapters 6, 7, and 8 (devoted to the question of honesty in exchanges).

Division of labour does not only require well-enforced property rights and trust in economic dealings. It is also critically conditioned by the thickness of economic space, itself dependent on population density. Here is the other major theme addressed in the book, which lends to it a definite Boserupean flavour. As a matter of fact, the point can be made that market development, including the development of private property rights, is not possible or will remain very incomplete if populations are thinly spread over large areas of land. This is partly the result of the fact that incentive problems are more difficult to overcome in such circumstances. The difficulties are, of course, compounded if geographical obstacles or wrong macro-economic policies have the effect of inhibiting rather than facilitating transport and communication. Furthermore, public provision of essential services as well as tax collection are impeded by population dispersal. Relatedly, strong states cannot easily thrive in such conditions since people tend to organize themselves into self-subsisting units based on lineage and since class differentiation and an urban–rural divide are prevented from developing. States living on surpluses extracted from rural dwellers are obviously bound to encounter many problems if these dwellers have many exit opportunities available to them thanks to their wide scattering. Chapters 2, 3, and 4 as well as part of Chapter 7 will pay a lot of attention to the role of population density as a crucial factor of growth and development.

In this book, special yet not exclusive reference is made to countries of SubSaharan Africa precisely because they have a long tradition of high land-man ratios and lineage-based systems of social organization (two obviously related features) which, according to the above explanatory scheme, must have a profound impact on their institutional trajectory. In other words, this region of the world, which is also the most disappointing in terms of growth performances, provides us with a unique opportunity to highlight the twin roles of path dependence and population density.

As the reader will be able to make out, specially upon reading Chapters 2 to 5, from the present difficulties of SubSaharan Africa it ought not to be inferred that African societies are stagnant. On the contrary, they do change in response to rising population pressure and to new economic opportunities born of their opening to the outside world. These changes are often so profound that they escape notice from experts or scholars used to looking only at the economic order of things, as reflected in standard economic indicators. On the historical scale, the transformations at work within the body of African societies are undoubtedly rapid. This is certainly apparent on the level of property rights and family structures where SubSaharan Africa has evinced an amazing ability to evolve since the beginning of this century, thus telescoping the long evolution stretching over many centuries that western Europe underwent before the nineteenth century. One may realistically entertain the hope that these changes will gradually prepare the ground for future economic growth at more satisfactory rates than those presently obtaining. Still, that dynamic elements are at work in African societies does not imply that changes are quick enough to enable them one day to match the performances of more advanced countries, including those in the Third World. Particularly worrying in this respect are the weakness of the state structures (see Chapter 7), and the prevalence of strong egalitarian norms that slow down entrepreneurship and capital accumulation (see Chapter 5).

One thing is sure: as suggested in the beginning of this introduction, Africa is in search of her own model of development. What this model will be is still hard to predict—but not much harder than foretelling how Russia or other countries born of the dissolution of the Soviet empire will manage to get out of their present mess (see Chapter 8). Yet, it can be taken for granted that, given the continuing weakness of African states, informal agencies and mechanisms will have a major role to play in the development of SubSaharan Africa. This means, in particular, that communities will remain key actors on the African scene and that, rather than being bypassed or emasculated, they should be considered as unavoidable partners to negotiate with. (This formula would be much more difficult to achieve in Russia where many communities have been destroyed under the communist regime and a tradition of the strong centralized state has prevailed over the country's entire history.) Chapter 4 will bring forward strong arguments to that effect while simultaneously underlining the necessity of mitigating the parochial, indeed even chauvinistic, tendencies present in rural communities or clanic groups.

Note incidentally that the essentials of the analysis proposed in the following pages seem to apply to other regions presenting the same two basic characteristics as SubSaharan Africa, whether they belong to Latin America or to Asia. As a matter of fact, one can only be struck by the economically backward state of many of the regions of the world where sizeable communities live which are thinly spread out over large areas and are socially organized along tribal lines (think of the states of Bihar, Orisse, and Madhya Pradesh in India, of the northern part of Thaïland or huge parts of Burma and Laos in East Asia; or of countries with large Indian communities in Central and South America). Of course, the fact that tribal communities of Asia and Latin America are typically embedded in national entities ruled and dominated by societies with opposite background characteristics is bound to affect their economic and other performances (in terms of health, education, etc.) in a different way from what would obtain in more homogenous tribal societies.

This book, as the title suggests, deals with institutions and social norms in their relation to development. Focus is on the rural sector to which the author's competence is limited. A novelty is that much more stress is laid on the role of social values and norms than is common in studies dealing with institutions that matter for economic growth. Three different kinds of values or social norms will actually retain our attention, namely norms of social identity underlying customary land tenure rights (Chapter 4, partly); norms of income-sharing (Chapter 5); and moral norms (Chapter 7 and 8). Chapters 2 to 4, as well as Chapter 6, address institutional issues, namely property rights in land and other natural resources, and trust-enforcement mechanisms. Chapter 1 serves as a background to the subsequent chapters.

The organization of the book is as follows. In Chapter 1, a brief survey is presented of various strands of thought regarding the role of institutions, norms, and values in economic development as well as of different methodological approaches to this question. After shortly describing the views of leading economists of the 1950s and 1960s, special emphasis is put on the contributions of both the transaction-cost and the principal-agent schools of the New Institutional Economics (which is amply used in Chapters 3 and 4), the evolutionary approach to institutional change (used in Chapter 6 especially), and Ester Boserup (who has inspired Chapters 2, 3, and 4). In addition, economic explanations of social norms are expounded. In all these cases, attention is drawn to limitations inherent in the analytical method adopted.

Chapter 2 specifically deals with the relationship between resource endowments and rural development in the specific context of Sub-Saharan Africa. More particularly, it is argued that low population densities negatively affect the potentialities of growth by precluding the emergence of rural markets or causing pervasive imperfections in them. Unfortunately, such difficulties are compounded by environmental constraints as well as problems of macroeconomic management.

In Chapters 3 and 4, focus is shifted to an institution generally regarded as critical for economic development, namely private property rights. In Chapter 3, the issue addressed is: which factors determine whether a natural resource so far held under some form of communal ownership will be privately appropriated? The issue tackled in Chapter 4 follows from the previous one and concerns the extent of individualization of privately appropriated parcels of land. More precisely, do transfer rights evolve when use rights have been (firmly) established and have they important economic functions to perform? Moreover, should the state intervene, and when, to back up the process of private land rights' consolidation by formalizing and legally sanctioning them through centralized land titling procedures? All these questions will be examined in the light of the contribution of the property rights theorists and their evolutionary followers, taking stock of their typical answers and evaluating them from both a theoretical and an empirical viewpoint. Contrary to Chapter 3 which has a wide empirical coverage, Chapter 4 draws more specific lessons from recent evolutions observed on the African continent.

Chapter 5 is entirely devoted to the task of understanding the impact on capital accumulation and growth of traditional egalitarian norms such as are found to be prevailing in tribal societies. After attempting to explain the rationale of these norms in the specific context of land-abundant countries, this chapter brings to light their negative effects from a growth perspective and, thereafter, taking inspiration from the African experience, it discusses in detail the various ways available to circumvent or overcome them. Contrasts with the situation prevailing in Asia are drawn.

Chapter 6 raises the question of the market order. Can the conditions necessary for an effective functioning of the market system be expected to arise spontaneously when required? What is the role of endogenous institutions for the regulation of market transactions? In other words, is opportunistic behaviour a real danger capable of hampering the market system, or can it be tamed through various informal mechanisms that gradually evolve within modernizing societies? These are the questions which are addressed in this chapter and form the background of the next chapter which argues that neither spontaneous mechanisms nor the rule of law are sufficient to underpin a strong market order.

As a matter of fact, Chapter 7 pursues the inquiry about social norms started in Chapter 5, this time by focusing on moral norms of honesty in private transactions and contracts. A crucial conceptual distinction here is between generalized and limited morality. It is indeed contended that tribal societies as well as caste-based societies are characterized by segmented loyalty feelings that limit the application of codes of honest behaviour to a rather small circle of related people, in fact much the same network as that relevant for redistributive norms. Limited morality restricts the effectiveness of the market by compartmentalizing the market space and thereby preventing many gains from trade and labour division from being reaped. Unfortunately, as Chapter 8 argues and illustrates (using, more particularly, the present predicament of Russia as a reference), there is no solid ground to argue that norms of generalized morality evolve when needed. It is therefore not surprising that some societies are ensnared in low honesty equilibria owing to path-dependent conditions rooted in their history.

## NOTES

1. The results do suggest that an exogenous drop in birthrates would raise the growth rate of per capita output.
2. There is a significant partial relation between growth and the starting level of GDP, thereby confirming the conditional convergence hypothesis.
3. An interesting result is that "much of the positive estimated effect of the investment ratio on growth in typical cross-country regressions reflects the reverse relation between growth prospects and investment". In other words, a positive coefficient on the contemporaneous investment ratio in a growth equation tends to reflect the positive relation between growth opportunities and investment rather than the positive effect of an exogenously higher investment ratio on the growth rate [Barro,1997: 32–33].

# Chapter 1

## THE SUBJECT PUT INTO PERSPECTIVE

### 1.1 RADICALISM VS. GRADUALISM: THE INTELLECTUAL DEBATE OF THE 1950s AND 1960s

During the 1950s and the 1960s, a set of ideas largely shared by social scientists interested in development problems was associated with the so-called modernization approach. The proponents of this approach were sociologists influenced both by the historical experience of industrial transformation in the Western countries and by the tenets of structural functionalism. Talcott Parsons' writings were an important source of inspiration for these scholars, particularly his views that 'the dominant value system, as embodied in culture, shapes everyday role behaviour and interactions' and that 'economic and technical activities are inextricably bound up with and underpinned by the web of social relations and the cultural ethos' [Kennedy, 1988: 136]. A central argument in the modernization doctrine is that traditional societies cannot graduate smoothly into the industrial era because their social structures, personality traits and value systems (which are narrowly interdependent) are inimical to the required kind of changes, in short because their very traditional features are incompatible with modernity. Upon this view, therefore, development cannot occur unless traditional patterns of action, motivations, attitudes and values are previously abandoned [see, e.g., Hoselitz, 1960; Hagen, 1962; Smelser, 1963; Moore, 1963; Eisenstadt, 1966].

The modernization approach has been subject to an intense fire of criticisms, both conceptual and empirical, and the impact of such criticisms was so devastating that the ideas it represented fell into almost total disrepute. The room was then cleared for other views considered to be less biased by Western prejudices, in particular, those which lay more emphasis on the dynamic potential of preindustrial societies and on the adaptability of traditional values and attitudes, or those which explain economic backwardness as a result of unequalizing mechanisms operating through international relations rather than as the outcome of internal inadequacies [see, e.g., Webster, 1990: chap. 34]. It can hardly be denied that the modernization school deserved to be criticized on account of its one-sided approach to the prerequisites of development. Sometimes also, its adherents just seemed to be saying that traditional society does not change because by nature it is resistant to change [Higgins, 1968: 251]. This being said, it may be regretted that the demise of the modernization approach in the field of development studies practically meant an obliteration of the possible role of cultural and institutional factors as a (temporary) brake on change.

Not surprisingly, development economists have lent much less attention to cultural issues than other social scientists. As hinted at in the introduction, their intellectual effort was absorbed into other directions pointing to capital accumulation, education, technical change, and planning. Yet, during the 1950s and 1960s, the most prominent among them have usually mentioned cultural and social aspects of development, albeit shortly, and expressed (sometimes crude) opinions about whether traditional institutions, attitudes and values are likely to block or to promote economic growth. Some of these authors, eager to identify determinants or prerequisites of modern economic growth, have made statements very close to the modernization view. This applies to Walter Rostow (1960, 1963), Stephen Enke (1963), Simon Kuznets (1966, 1968), Henry Bruton (1965) and Benjamin Higgins (1968) who tended to look at development as the result of a 'big push' driving traditional societies out of secular stagnation into the era of self-sustaining growth. What characterizes their writings is a good amount of optimism concerning the pace at which traditional culture and institutions can adjust to the requirements of the new system of growth.

For example, Benjamin Higgins wrote that where 'cultural stability is incompatible with rapid economic growth, the culture will adapt readily and painlessly enough to an economic 'big push'...", and it is important to recognize that 'rapid and complete cultural change is likely to be less traumatic than gradual and partial change'. Hence, 'we end up with a "big push" doctrine in the socio-cultural field as well as in the economic field', and 'development economists should fight tooth and nail any line of argument that might result in a reversion to gradualism as a basis for development policy' [Higgins, 1968: 265–66].

Simon Kuznets agreed that modern economic growth is not possible without a decisive social and cultural breakthrough, yet, contrary to Higgins, he believed that such a break with the old order is bound to be traumatic. As a matter of fact, the changes needed to enter the era of modern economic growth 'do not occur in a vacuum; they are made in societies that usually have a long tradition of the premodern economic organization and social structure, and they must be directed by agents with the power to overcome resistance and incur necessary costs. If agriculture must be changed to permit greater productivity and release labor for other pursuits, the immediate task is to break through the old organizational patterns, to change the relations of man to land (...). It is this dislocation and break with the old order that constitutes the major cost of the transition to modern economic growth' [Kuznets, 1968: 106–7].

As for Henry Bruton, after having pinpointed a series of major cultural obstacles to growth, he concluded that a decisive break is needed to get out of a traditionalistic approach to life: 'This attitude [that it is impossible to exercise control over nature] may be explained by an appeal to religious convictions or a fatalistic philosophy, but perhaps the most satisfactory explanation is simply the mere lack of precedent. Growth has not occurred over such a long interval of time that prevailing opinion has accepted the view that it is impossible. To overcome this pessimistic point of view, obviously the precedent must be broken. To create an attitude that growth is possible, growth must occur. It would appear as simple—and as difficult—as that' [Bruton, 1965: 113].

Other contemporary development economists, however, envisioned institutional and sociocultural change in societies as a much less radical step. Interestingly, their most notable works appeared in the 1950s, such as those of Arthur Lewis (1955)—no doubt, the author who discussed at greatest length the role of cultural (and other institutional) factors in economic development—, Gerald Meier and Robert Baldwin (1957), Peter Bauer and B.S. Yamey (1957), and Alfred Hirschman (1958). In stark contrast to Higgins, for example, Meier and Baldwin adopted a resolutely gradual approach to socio-cultural change: 'Not only must economic organization be transformed, but social organization ... must also be modified so that the basic complex of values and motivations may be more favourable for development (...) To avoid human discontent, [however], changes should be introduced in ways that will disrupt the existing culture as little as possible: the cultural change should be selective (...) more rapid progress will come by utilizing as much as possible existing attitudes and institutions rather than by attempting a frontal breakdown of the culture' [Meier and Baldwin, 1957: 356, 359].

In addition, they explicitly warned against the danger of ethnocentrism in discussions of sociocultural problems: 'In considering the social and cultural requirements for development, a Western student should not make the mistake of ethnocentrism, that is, assuming that, because the West is developed, Western values and institutions are therefore necessary for development ... [*ibidem*: 355]. Yet, in spite of these cautious statements, they did not hesitate to make a rather radical policy recommendation: according to them, indeed, to promote cultural change, investment should be directed to 'projects that break up village life by drawing people to centers of employment away from the village because, by preventing impersonal relations, village life is a major source of opposition to change' [*ibidem*: 357].

Bauer and Yamey recognized that 'Certain social institutions which are appropriate to a subsistence or near-subsistence economy may impede economic growth directly by reducing the rewards of individuals who take advantage of the opportunities presented by wider markets (...) The extended family, sometimes known as the joint family, is an example of an institution which has many advantages in one stage of economic achievement but which may later become a drag on economic development' [Bauer and Yamey, 1957: 64]. Regarding the pace of change, like Meier and Baldwin, they rejected any idea of big pushes or dramatic disruptions: 'Generally, a slow but steady development is likely to create fewer political, social and economic tensions; and it is likely that an attempt to force the pace too strenuously may also be economically wasteful because the social and personal changes may not take place which are necessary to enable individuals or the society to profit from the development and to sustain it' [*ibidem*: 71]. In fact, they did not seem to believe that traditional culture ought to be seriously undermined before growth may become possible. Revealingly, they pointed out that 'the economic history of Japan demonstrates the compatibility of rapid economic change and growth with the preservation of traditional attitudes and social relationships, recast or reemphasized as these may be to suit the needs of a new economic order' [*ibidem*: 68].

As for Arthur Lewis, he certainly shared the view that traditional values, attitudes and institutions may act as a drag on economic development. Nowhere is this more apparent than in the passage where, commenting upon the historical failure of Spain to exploit the economic opportunities presented by the discovery of the New World, he concluded that 'It is possible for a nation to stifle its economic growth by adopting passionately and intolerantly religious doctrines of a kind which are incompatible with growth' [Lewis, 1955: 107]. On the other hand, he was inclined to think that religious beliefs, for example, may evolve and be reinterpreted depending on the economic environment confronting societies. In Lewis's framework, the two views are actually reconciled in the following way: traditional values and attitudes, whenever they are hostile to economic advancement, will eventually adapt themselves to new economic opportunities, yet as this adaptation process may take time, traditional culture is likely to slow down the rate of change and also distort its effects [*ibidem*: 106].

Lastly, in an important section (entitled 'The Idea of Change as an Obstacle to Change') of the first chapter of his book *The Strategy of Economic Development* (1958), Alfred Hirschman argued that there are essentially two types of traditional (purportedly static) societies depending upon whether their members share a 'group-focused' (in corporate or closely integrated societies, such as Indian communities in Latin America) or an 'ego-focused' image of change (in highly differentiated societies, such as *ladino* or *mestizo* societies in the same continent). Both images are inimical to economic development, the former because it strongly discourages exceptional individual performances on the grounds that they can only take place 'at the expense of other members and of the cohesiveness of the group', and the latter because it is harmful to 'the cooperative component of entrepreneurship' (the ability to engineer agreement among all interested parties, to bring and hold together an able staff, to delegate authority, to inspire loyalty, etc.). For Hirschman, the world image congenial to genuine economic development is the so-called 'group- and ego-focused idea of change', that is, the idea that 'the individual can advance at his own speed within an expanding economy' without obstructing the progress of other people. This modern ideology cannot be imposed *ex abrupto* and it 'is likely to be adopted only after a considerable span of experience has convincingly shown the possibility of such a development' characterized by all-round growth and mutual benefits [Hirschman, 1958: 23–24]. In other words, traditional images of change will remain a critical bottleneck of constructive action for economic development until experience modifies them in the appropriate direction.

Two important and obviously interrelated questions emerge from the above discussion: are traditional values, attitudes, and institutions incompatible with modern economic growth and, if yes, how are they to be transformed so as to make such growth possible? Clearly, regarding the latter question, two different views tended to prevail among the above-surveyed authors. On the one side, there are those, like Rostow, Kuznets, Higgins, Enke, Bruton, Meier and Baldwin, who believed that development has to be engineered by an outside (central) agency lest the necessary transformation of institutions, norms and values should not take place. A vicious circle created by the strong compatibility of traditional institutions with low growth performances has to be broken in order to allow rapid growth to occur. On the other side, we find authors like Lewis, Hirschman, Bauer and Yamey, who were more inclined to think that, as the experience of expanding economic opportunities unfolds itself, the traditional social and cultural fabric unavoidably evolves to give way to institutions, rules and values more congenial to modern economic growth. The adjustment process may take time owing to the unavoidable sluggishness of institutional and cultural change, yet the fact that no dramatic break with the old order is necessary to promote growth is good news since such a break involves considerable risks.

Karl Marx, who wrote much earlier than all the authors considered above, marked off an important step in the history of what has become known as the New Institutional Economics: he was indeed the first to raise in an articulated manner the questions which are today at the heart of this new discipline, and he proposed a theory of history which gives pride of place to the material determinants of production relations in society. As shall be seen below, his analysis of the way pre-capitalist societies move forward partly anticipates the thinking of Ester Boserup who was to make a critical contribution to our understanding of the processes of technical and institutional evolution in the agricultural sector. In the next two sections, therefore, attention will be successively drawn to the contributions of Marx and Boserup and to the research programme of the New Institutional Economics.

## 1.2 MARX AND BOSERUP: INSTITUTIONAL DEVELOPMENT AS AN INDUCED MECHANISM

In Marx's theory of history, such as is set forth in the 1859 Preface (to *A Contribution to the Critique of Political Economy*) and elsewhere, the movement of historical progress is caused by the dialectical interplay of two sets of factors, namely the productive forces and the production relations. The former factor—which includes capital goods, raw materials, and labour power with its various attributes such as skill, strength and knowledge—has the primary role since it is the continuous, autonomous expansion of productive forces through technological progress and capital accumulation that drives societies ahead by forcing production relations to eventually adapt so as to make such expansion possible. Foremost among production relations stand property arrangements that are best seen as the legal expression of these relations. And precisely because of their proximity to production relations, property arrangements are the institutional component most heavily influenced by the level of productive forces. It is therefore not surprising that, in Marx's materialistic theory of history (materialist because he ascribes primacy to the capacity of material production as determined by technology and available resources), the core institution is the property right assignment on a key production factor in each stage of economic development—such as slaves in the ancient classical world, land in medieval feudalism, and capital in modern capitalism [Hayami, 1997: 14–16].

A basic tenet in Marx's theory of the rise and fall of modes of production is that, within each mode, the relations of production first 'correspond' to the productive forces, and then enter into a 'contradiction' with them.[1] In Marx's words:

> 'At a certain stage of their development, the material productive forces of society come in conflict with the existing relations of production, or—what is but a legal expression for the same thing—, with the property relations within which they have been at work hitherto. From forms of development of the productive forces these relations turn into their fetters. Then begins an epoch of social revolution. With the change of the economic foundations the entire immense superstructure is more or less rapidly transformed' [Marx, 1859, Preface—cited after McLellan, 1977: 389].

In Marx's view, institutional adjustment is not a smooth process. Such adjustment takes time because it is strongly resisted by the dominant class which opposes any change liable to reduce the social and economic advantages it derives from existing property arrangements. As a result, even though institutions were originally suited to best exploit the productive potential of a society located at a particular stage of its economic development, they tend to be maintained while they have ceased to be consistent with changing material production conditions. The gap thereby created between the institutional setup of a society and its productive potential determined by its level of capital accumulation and rate of technological progress is bound to cause growing tensions and contradictions. These will be ultimately resolved through a political revolution against the economic elite and its vested interests.

When the revolution succeeds, a new set of production relations is established that again 'corresponds' to the level of the productive forces until the latter will have sufficiently expanded to break this 'correspondence' and set off a new chain of tensions and changes. Moreover, changes in the productive forces and the associated production relations (what Marx sometimes calls the infrastructure) are bound to entail changes in the realm of political institutions, ideas, symbolic representations, and values of a society (the superstructure). In brief, the mode of production of material life determines the general character of the legal, political, cultural and ritual components of social life. Marx's materialistic credo is fully evident from the following excerpt of the Preface:

> 'In the social production of their life, men enter into definite relations that are indispensable and independent of their will, relations of production which correspond to a definite stage of development of their material productive forces. The sum total of these relations of production constitutes the economic structure of society, the real foundation, on which rises a legal and political superstructure and to which correspond definite forms of social consciousness. The mode of production of material life conditions the social, political, and intellectual life process in general. It is not the consciousness of men that determines their being, but, on the contrary, their social being that determines their consciousness' [Marx, 1859, Preface—cited after McLellan, 1977: 389].

The independent variable in Marx's scheme of historical evolution is therefore constituted by the productive forces understood as forces that cause an increase in labour productivity. Yet, upon careful reading of his analysis of historical facts, it appears that Marx does not always stick to his theoretical framework. More precisely, it can be argued, following Elster, that productivity-enhancing forces are set to work as an autonomous engine of development only after the capitalist mode of production has been put into place. In fact, 'Marx did not believe that any technical change occurred in precapitalist societies. Hence it is hard to see how these societies could break down as the result of a development of the productive forces, if this is taken in the intensive sense of increased productivity per worker. On the other hand Marx does assert that they broke down because of an increase in population, and in doing so he comes very close to saying that population is a productive force' [Elster, 1985: 250; see also Howard and King, 1975: Chap. 7]. It is this ambiguous understanding of the development of the productive forces—as an extensive process of population growth or as an intensive process of productivity growth per capita, that enabled Marx to bridge, however inconsistently, the gap between the general theory set forth in the Preface and his historical foray into precapitalist societies [*ibidem*: 251].

A striking similarity between Marx's investigation of precapitalist societies and Boserup's theory of agricultural change lies precisely in the role of prime mover assigned to population growth. None the less, this similarity ought not to conceal an essential difference between the two authors. For Marx, indeed, population increase can cause the productivity of labour to rise only under capitalist conditions. Until capitalism arises, population growth only gives rise to a multiplication of production units that are technically and organizationally similar: typically, under the impact of growing land pressure, new agricultural units born of the partition of larger, older units migrate to virgin areas without basically modifying their mode of production. In contrast, Boserup considers that population growth is the source of both technical and institutional change since ancient times. In fact, Boserup (1965, 1981) has challenged the classical theory that population growth leads to a steady decline in the productivity of labour due to the inexorable operation of diminishing returns. Upon her reading, the technological progress and concomitant institutional adjustments induced by population growth help stave off the operation of diminishing returns thanks to gradual intensification of activities involving the use of natural resources. In her view, therefore, 'soil fertility is a dependent variable, responding to the intensity of land use, rather than a determinant of the intensity of land use' [Hayami and Ruttan, 1985: 49]. In the course of intensification, 'both numbers of current operations and the amount of labour used in investment activities to improve the land increase as hunting and gathering is replaced by pastoralism, and then forest, bush and short fallow until eventually annual and multicropping are adopted when population densities become very high' [Booth and Sundrum, 1985: 81; see also Ruthenberg, 1980; Pingali et al., 1987].

The long and detailed story told by Boserup about the evolution of agricultural systems and patterns of land use under preindustrial conditions in both temperate and tropical regions is thus one in which food is produced in increasingly complicated and labour-consuming processes. Such processes, which entail reshuffling of land rights, redefinition of gender roles, and other social and institutional changes, have the effect of enhancing land productivity and preventing labour productivity and standards of living from falling as population pressure rises.[2]

Can given institutions or rules form an obstacle to development in the above schemes? For both Marx and Boserup, the answer is a strongly mitigated yes: institutional resistance against change is likely yet cannot last long given the power of the evolutionary forces at work. This point has been tirelessly emphasized by Marx whenever he insisted that resistance by reactionary social classes in defence of established institutions is bound to end up in defeat at the hands of the progressive elements of society, namely those working in a direction compatible with material conditions (the level of development of productive forces). This holds even more true in the case of Boserup's theory where political and class struggles receive much less attention and inducement mechanisms occupy centre stage of the analysis.

## 1.3 THE NEW INSTITUTIONAL ECONOMICS: A COMPARATIVE STATIC APPROACH PRIVILEGING TRANSACTION COSTS AND RISK CONSIDERATIONS

It can be said of the New Institutional Economics (henceforth designated as the NIE) that it provides bourgeois answers to Marxist questions. Like in Marx's theory of history, institutions that were socially useful at one time become 'fetters' on the further development of the forces of progress and an appropriate evolution of these institutions becomes necessary. However, while the Marxist approach is inspired by the doctrine of methodological collectivism (*supra*-individual entities are posited that are prior to individuals in the explanatory order), the NIE has retained the 'bourgeois' assumption of methodological individualism (all social phenomena are in principle explicable in ways that only involve individuals) and unambiguously belongs to the choice-theoretic tradition of economics. For the NIE, therefore, changes in institutions and rules are seen as the result of the aggregation of the decisions of rational (sometimes boundedly rational), selfish economic agents responding to changes in the underlying parameters of the economic system. A serious problem with Marx's theory of history is precisely that, owing to its lack of microtheoretic foundations, it often falls into the trap of a rather crude type of functionalism and does not provide a satisfactory theory of disequilibrium dynamics outside the long-run equilibria where production relations correspond to the productive forces [Bardhan, 1985, 1989; Elster, 1985: 829; 107–118].

The relationship of the NIE with Boserup's work is more profound than with Marx, not only because Boserup, at least implicitly, follows a microeconomic approach, but also because the impact of population growth she has so strongly emphasized receives a lot of attention from new institutional economists, particularly those concerned with explaining agrarian institutions. Furthermore, some explanations or predictions put forth by the latter bear a strong resemblance to important Boserupean propositions (which is especially obvious in the case of property arrangements). Since these points will be amply illustrated in this book, they need not be probed into here.

The NIE is typically based on the central idea that the existence and transformation of many institutions—understood as rules that structure human interactions by helping people form expectations about each other's conduct and thereby facilitate coordination among them[3]—can be explained only if positive transaction costs, of which information costs form an important part, are posited and risk bearing is treated as an input that must be transacted for. In the most naive version, agents are seen as endeavouring to minimize the sum of transaction costs and production costs by choosing the appropriate contract, rule, or system of property rights. This core idea suffers from two major flaws [Milgrom and Roberts, 1992: 33–39]. First, production and transaction costs generally depend both on the institutional arrangement and on the technology, hence the impossibility to conceptually separate these two types of costs. Second, the notion that efficient institutions minimize transaction costs is troublesome. As a matter of fact, too many different institutional arrangements might be compatible with efficiency for it to be a useful concept. Let us elaborate a little bit on this important point. According to the so-called Value Maximization Principle, an activity or institution which maximizes the total value of the parties concerned is efficient and, for any inefficient institution, there exists another (total value maximizing) institution that all of the parties strictly prefer. The Coase Theorem asserts that, if the parties engage in efficient bargaining and if the above principle applies, efficiency alone determines the choice of activity or institution. The bargaining power of the parties and their initial assets influence only the way costs and benefits are shared.

Yet, this striking result obtains only under a set of highly restrictive assumptions including the absence of wealth effects, costless bargaining, the existence of a solution to the bargaining problem, the ability of the parties to enforce their agreements and to make any required side-payment and, most importantly, the absence of transaction costs resulting from private information, bounded rationality and non-observability of actions [Baland and Platteau, 1996: 49–56].

Economic analysis of institutions using the principal-agent model avoids the difficulties associated with the naive transaction-cost approach and is therefore preferred in many cases. According to this more sophisticated approach using game theory, a principal strives to find a (second-best) efficient contract that provides incentives to the agent so that he complies as best as possible with the principal's objectives. It is in fact the need to provide incentives in a world pervaded by informational asymmetries that makes it impossible to reach anything else than some sort of constrained efficiency. In this perspective, institutions must therefore evolve to ameliorate problems like opportunism either with feasible external enforcement mechanisms or with credible internal ones. For instance, moral hazard problems can be controlled through *ex ante* mechanisms, such as monitoring schemes and incentive-payment contracts, as well as through *ex post* mechanisms, such as auditing and penalties [Dixit, 1996: 55–56].

Instead of being viewed as production functions like in the traditional neoclassical approach, firms are considered as 'networks of contracts', or 'governance structures' which are characterized by various agency relationships in which the principal typically devises a scheme of incentives or penalties such that the agent is prompted to modify his actions in a way that suits the principal's interest [Williamson, 1985].

While in standard neoclassical theory exogenous variables comprise preferences, endowments, technologies, and rule structures or institutions, the NIE is an attempt to endogenize the latter of these four variables as a function of the first three ones [Field, 1981]. In actual fact, changes in endowments propelled by population growth have been regarded as the major source of institutional change, though technological progress (including advances in military technology) and changes in the costs of information are also deemed important [Bardhan, 1989: 1390]. Particularly worth mentioning in this regard is the attempt by Hans Binswanger and his associates to build up a theory in which agrarian institutions and their evolution are largely explained as a function of population density [Binswanger and

Rosenzweig, 1986; Binswanger and McIntire, 1987; Binswanger et al., 1989]. Thus, they incorporate into their analysis 'risk, risk aversion and information problems jointly and simultaneously with the material features of agriculture and the material attributes of its factors of production', including the latter's relative scarcities [Binswanger and Rosenzweig, 1986: 505].

It must be carefully noted that whichever changes are considered tend to get reflected in persistent variations in relative prices and it is these variations, according to the NIE, that create incentives among economic agents to alter existing contractual institutional arrangements. In fact, it is primarily by inducing the development of property rights to the benefit of the owners of scarce production factors that relative price changes fuel the main motive force for institutional change in history [North, 1981; Bardhan, 1989; Nabli and Nugent, 1989a: Chaps. 1–2; Bromley, 1989: Chap. 2; Eggertsson, 1990: Chaps. 4–8; Platteau, 1992: Chap. 2; Baland and Platteau, 1998b]. The method used to understand institutional change is the standard comparative-static approach characteristic of neoclassical economics. An example will illustrate this point. It is taken from a study of contract choice in the case of jeepneys in the Philippines [Otsuka et al., 1986; Hayami and Otsuka, 1993: chap. 8].

Jeepneys are taxis originally converted from the US military jeep after World War II. The relations between owners (the principals) and drivers (the agents) are vulnerable to various kinds of incentive problems and contracts are supposed to be chosen so as to strike a balance between providing work and other incentives (e.g., incentives for proper management of the vehicle) for the driver and lessening his exposure to risk. The inquiry's starting point is the observation of a distinct pattern in the interregional distribution of share and fixed-rental contracts: while the fixed-rental contract is adopted mainly in Greater Manila and neighbouring urbanized areas, the share contract is commonly observed in rural areas away from Manila.

The explanation provided by the authors to account for these geographical variations in contractual forms can be summarized as follows. In rural areas, relationships among people are strongly personalized thereby ensuring an effective circulation of information. As a result, incentive problems are not important and transaction costs (including monitoring costs) are low. Under these circumstances, risk considerations have the edge on incentive considerations and the share contract appears as the most satisfactory contractual form (in a second-best world). In urban surroundings, by contrast, relationships are largely anonymous and information is therefore highly imperfect, giving rise to pervasive and serious incentive problems. High transaction costs come to prevail with the consequence that incentive considerations outweigh risk considerations: as a result, the fixed-rental contract is preferred. In brief, the urbanization drive that typically accompanies economic growth causes transaction costs to increase, which makes existing institutions and rules less satisfactory than alternative arrangements better suited to the new parameters of the economic system. Realizing the potential of these new arrangements, economic agents work towards establishing them (e.g., they change the contractual form).

As the above example shows, the results of principal-agent models are generally valid only relative to the institutional environment in which agents operate, hence the apt remark by Masahiko Aoki that contract theory 'cannot be a complete theory of institutions unless its results are carefully interpreted with respect to their context' [Aoki, forthcoming: chap. 1].

Various criticisms have been raised against the NIE even in its most sophisticated, principal-agent version. One important problem with this theoretical approach is that more efficient (usually second-best efficient) institutions often appear to be automatically evolving simply from the agents's perception of new benefit-cost possibilities. In this way, collective action problems are bypassed that may prevent potential beneficiaries of institutional changes from getting to act together with a view to bringing these changes about. As aptly remembered by Pranab Bardhan, 'an institution's mere function of serving the interests of potential beneficiaries is clearly inadequate in *explaining* it...'. In particular, it is evident that variations in relative prices 'may at most change the costs and benefits of collective action for different classes (creating new opportunities for political entrepreneurs) but cannot predetermine the balance of class forces or the outcome of social conflicts' [Bardhan, 1989: 7–8; see also Langlois, 1986; Basu, Jones, and Schlicht, 1987; Hallpike, 1988; Nabli and Nugent, 1989b].

True, there is a hierarchy of institutions and the NIE is likely to be more appropriate to explain changes in operational rules such as contracts than in predicting adjustments of constitutional rules or more fundamental institutions that are bound to change very slowly because of lock-in effects associated with path-dependent processes (including the mutual reinforcement of complexity and inertia[4]), or of mutually sustaining beliefs, expectations and fears.[5] Thus, for example, Yujiro Hayami and Keijiro Otsuka contend that 'rural people in developing economies make efficient choices from a wide spectrum of contracts taking account their own resource endowments and external conditions surrounding them' [Hayami and Otsuka, 1993: 20]. And, when the observed contractual forms appear to be at variance with the model's prediction, the tendency is often to ascribe the discrepancy not to possible violations of the model's analytical setting but to sociopolitical regulations (e.g., land-reform laws) that result from ill-perception of what efficiency implies or from the lobbying pressures of some population group and that have the effect of arbitrarily restricting the range of choices available to economic agents [see, e.g., Hayami and Kikuchi, 1982; Otsuka, Chuma, and Hayami, 1992].

This said, even socially efficient changes in operational rules may be hard to come by due not only to collective action problems (about the sharing of the costs of bringing about change, or of the benefits resulting from the change) or short-sightedness and opportunism of dominant groups, but also due to particular perceptions about the fairness and legitimacy of alternative arrangements.[6] The neat evolution of Douglass North's thinking towards increasing complexity from his first book with Robert Thomas (*The Rise of the Western World*, 1973) to his *Institutions, Institutional Change and Economic Performance* (1990) and through his *Structure and Change in Economic History* (1981), provides a remarkable illustration of the growing awareness among the most lucid new institutional economists that the efficiency view of institutions is untenable. The possibility of disparities between private incentives of ruling classes and social welfare; the role of ideology, particularly in shaping the perception of opportunities among entrepreneurs in political and economic organizations; and the complex interactions between institutions and organizations (the latter being defined as bodies created to take advantage of the opportunities determined by the former) are all factors that decisively influence the direction of institutional change.

Especially noteworthy is the ample evidence that rules and institutions can be selected for distributive rather than for efficiency reasons, or that institutional change can be redistributive rather than efficiency-improving. Robert Allen (1992) has brought this point forcefully to the fore by showing that the second wave of enclosures in 18th-century Britain came about not because enclosed farming was more efficient than open-field farming but because landowners could expect positive redistributive effects from this reshuffling of land rights [see also Cohen and Weitzman, 1975].

For another thing, many institutions or rules, such as contracts, crystallize through a long period of experimentation with different forms. Eventually, 'one form becomes standard and customary for a given type of transaction (in a given locale), not necessarily because it is optimal, but because it serves the purpose reasonably well and it is what everyone has come to expect. It is now an institution that coordinates behaviors, and to deviate from it would be costly' [Young, 1998: 3–4].

Now, even assuming that efficiency is the relevant criterion to consider, there remains the serious difficulty of working with the same static-allocation objective as that used in standard neoclassical theory. Such an approach has the undeniable advantage of providing a powerful set of analytical tools and equilibrium concepts. Nevertheless, if the NIE is concerned with historical change, the adaptability or dynamic efficiency properties of a rule or institutional arrangement may well prove more important than its optimality properties in a narrow static sense. As stressed by Robert Langlois in the wake of Schumpeter, trade-offs between static efficiency and flexibility considerations are central to many questions of institutional change. For example, 'a firm in a very rapidly changing environment may have very bad transaction-cost properties but be far more efficient—far better able to survive—than a relatively less flexible organizational structure with good transaction-cost properties in equilibrium' [Langlois, 1986: 10–15, 20–21; see also Dixit, 1996: 59, 62]. In other words, adaptability of some sort is often a more pertinent criterion for the survival of an institution than is efficiency in the allocation of resources. In some important cases, fortunately, the potential trade-off does not arise because the institution that scores best in static-allocative terms also appears to be best performing on the ground of dynamic considerations. A striking example is private property of productive assets.

It must finally be noted that, since strategic rationality is a fundamental behavioural assumption of the NIE, classical game theory is a privileged tool of analysis in the hands of new institutional economists. Indeed, the game-theoretic framework has the advantage of making explicit how interacting individuals produce particular institutional forms which will subsequently influence their actions. In other words, in given situations (in given games) institutions emerge endogenously from human interactions to constrain their behaviour in a self-enforcing manner [see, e.g., Greif, 1997, 1998].

Unfortunately, classical game theory suffers from two serious limitations. First, it does not provide selection procedures when several equilibria are possible, a point to which I shall return in the next section. Second, it has nothing to say about the dynamic evolution of institutions and does not take into account the influence of past events and characteristics of a society on its institutional trajectory. As pointed out above, the method to understand equilibrium changes is that of comparative-static analysis: if an exogenous change causes the emergence of a new set of self-enforcing equilibria, no mechanism is specified whereby this new set is possibly influenced by the previous equilibrium. In short, there is no interlinking of successive game situations across time. Evolutionary game theory is precisely an attempt to overcome this important limitation of classical game theory (see *infra*, section 1.5).

## 1.4 SOCIAL NORMS AND FAIRNESS CONSIDERATIONS

If writings in economic development since the seventies have reflected a growing concern about the role of institutions, the analysis of institutional issues has left little room for influences arising from cultural values and social norms or customs. In the NIE, typically, economic agents are supposed to pursue their own material interest and not to care about 'social' goals or values (utilities of contracting parties are assumed to depend on their income and effort). Put in the words of Erich Fromm, there is no room for social controls that so fashion human character that 'people want to act as they have to act and at the same time find gratification in acting according to the requirements of the culture' [Fromm, 1949: 10—cited from Hirschman, 1958: 12].

Overlooked is thus the possibility that social norms—understood as prescriptive rules regarding behavior that are shared among a group of people and that are partly sustained by the approval and disapproval of others [Elster, 1989b: 113]—or principles of equity lead agents to behave in a way that deviates from maximization of selfish material interests. Just consider the example of sharecropping contracts in agriculture. Theory predicts that there should be substantial variability in the crop share depending upon various factors, among which the relative degrees of risk aversion of the landlord and tenant stand foremost. Yet, contrary to such a prediction, empirical evidence shows that crop-sharing rules tend to be remarkably uniform within each agricultural community (but not necessarily between different regions or agro-climatic zones) and, a still more puzzling fact, that the predominant share encountered in all areas and for all crops is 50%–50% (equal division).

As remarked by Joseph Stiglitz: 'Although there have been several attempts to explain this uniformity, none has gained general acceptance'.[7] And he immediately adds: 'I suspect that it is here that a broader social/historical theory is required. Individuals are concerned that in their dealings they are treated fairly. Views of fairness are to a large extent conventionally (historically) determined. It does not pay to treat workers unfairly, for this will reduce their work effort. Hence, if in some society a sharing rule of 50 per cent comes to be accepted, it does not pay for a landlord to deviate from this social convention, even if, at that rate, there is an excess supply of tenants' [Stiglitz, 1989: 22]. In other words, principles of equity based on cultural norms and precedent determine simple sharing rules that apply irrespective of the particular circumstances of each situation. At least, this is true when variations in these circumstances are not too large [see, e.g., Rao, 1971; Bardhan, 1984; Platteau and Nugent, 1992; Dasgupta, 1993: 232–233; Sharma and Drèze, 1996: 18–19]. And even when variations are somewhat substantial, simple norms of equal sharing can be formally or officially maintained provided that corrective mechanisms are discreetly brought into play.[8]

Stiglitz is not the only economic theorist who is attracted by the view that norms embody equity principles and have the effect of improving efficiency. Peyton Young thus believes that 'equity principles are the means by which the parties coordinate on a particular solution given the constraints imposed by economic rationality' [Young, 1994: 81]. He chooses to look at the problem of crop share determination as the outcome of a bargaining process. In such a bargaining framework, the crop share depends on the utility functions of both parties (particularly, on their risk aversion) and on their alternative incomes should they fail to come to an agreement. Therefore, the prediction is again that there should be ample variations in the crop share depending of the particulars of each individual situation (including the size of their farm, soil qualities, etc.). The wide prevalence of the 50%–50% sharing rule is then explained by the fact that 'actors reach agreement, not on the basis of their utility for various allocations, but by coordinating on a prominent or focal solution. Fifty-fifty is certainly the most prominent way to divide a pie into two pieces, and it is easy to justify on grounds of fairness ... [since] nominally fair solutions appear to be very powerful even when the claimants have a lot at stake...' [*ibidem*: 129].[9]

What is important to notice is that in this case the coming into play of fairness considerations does not imply a violation of economic rationality. Indeed, as pointed out by Young, 'a rule like equal division is not economically inefficient as long as the outcome is within the bounds established by the parties' opportunity costs.... In many cases this leaves a wide range of agreements that are economically rational'. By focusing the bargainers' attention on particular outcomes, equity principles or fairness norms perform a useful function since they actually increase efficiency by coordinating people's expectations and reducing the transaction costs of bargaining. In other words, social norms such as fairness norms play a positive role by helping to resolve distributive problems when efficiency by itself yields indeterminate results [Young, 1994: 19, 129, 167].

As is evident from the foregoing examples, economists are typically reluctant to consider norms as exogenously given. Rather than interpreting them as the (given) rules of a social game, they often prefer to construe them as an equilibrium of a game. More exactly, they are inclined to conceive of a social or cultural norm as a selection procedure or set of beliefs that allows choosing among several (sometimes innumerable) equilibria of a game.

This interpretation accords well with the research programme suggested by Roger Myerson who writes: 'From a game-theoretical perspective, *cultural norms* can be defined to be the rules that a society uses to determine focal equilibria in game situations. There may be some situations where people of a given culture might look to equity principles to determine a focal equilibrium (e.g., in bargaining between people of equal and independent status) (...) Thus, the focal-point effect defines both an essential limit on the ability of mathematical game theory to predict people's behavior in real conflict situations and an important agenda for research in social psychology and cultural anthropology (...) On the other hand, the focal-point effect of game theory can offer a useful perspective on the role of culture and perception' [Myerson, 1991: 113–14].

Other economists like Robert Frank (1988), Mathew Rabin (1993) and others have emphasized the positive role of non-rational motives such as emotions also on the ground that they may possibly serve to increase efficiency. Emotions are then seen as springing from fairness considerations, with anger arising from the feeling of being exploited and kindness from that of being fairly or nicely treated. For both Frank and Rabin, the positive influence of emotions is reflected in the fact that, thanks to their operation, actors may be driven to select Pareto-optimal equilibria while a strict pursuit of their own (short-term) material interest would have led them into inefficient Nash equilibria. Here, therefore, the role of culturally-rooted emotions or feelings is even more important than in the previous approach based upon the focal-point effect: indeed, by modifying the preferences of the agents and thereby enlarging the set of possible equilibria, they allow the emergence of new equilibria that are more efficient than those previously existing and thereby create the possibility for the agents to settle at the efficient equilibrium (or at one of the efficient equilibria). Note that the same effect can be produced by social norms that restrict or truncate the players' strategy space (bad behaviour is ruled out because such things are not considered proper to do).

Unfortunately, the so-called fairness equilibria that exist in the psychological games constructed by Rabin, for example, do not necessarily correspond to more efficient outcomes than strict Nash equilibria. On the one hand, fairness may not rule out strict Nash equilibria that are inefficient: thus, in the Prisoner's Dilemma, the strict Nash equilibrium (defect, defect) is also a fairness equilibrium because in this outcome each player is satisfying both his desire to hurt the other and his material self-interest. On the other hand, fairness may rule out strict Nash equilibria that are efficient: in the Chicken game, for example, the worst outcome may arise as a fairness equilibrium because all players may want to hurt each other while in the Pareto-optimal solutions of the game, a player prefers to back down if the other player has chosen to assert his interests.[10]

Clearly, therefore, reference to fairness considerations in game-theoretical frameworks does not necessarily paint cultural norms and the associated emotions in a favourable light. In Rabin's two-player psychological game, whether efficient fairness equilibria will be reached or not depends both on the agents' payoffs and on the beliefs of each agent regarding the other player' strategies and beliefs about his own strategies. Such beliefs may be strongly influenced by prevailing norms. In Chapter 7, however, where fairness considerations of the type considered by Rabin will receive central attention, it will be argued that inefficient outcomes can be avoided if agents adopt attitudes of 'moralistic reciprocity' (Trivers, 1971) whereby they agree to punish non-cooperators even at a positive cost to themselves.

It also bears emphasis that, even in coordination games where agents prefer coordination of their actions to mismatch, cultural or social norms that lead them to select one of the multiple existing equilibria do not necessarily have positive effects in terms of efficiency. This is simply because the equilibrium thus selected may well be Pareto-dominated. For example, in a game of honesty (players have the choice between acting honestly and acting dishonestly) depicted as an assurance game, cultural norms emphasizing mutual mistrust are likely to lead to the Pareto-inferior equilibrium where everyone acts dishonestly [Dasgupta, 1988; Platteau, 1994, 1994b].

Kaushik Basu, George Akerlof, and Timur Kuran make a similar point when they interpret the caste system or oppressive customs as inefficient equilibria into which a whole society can be trapped owing to generalized beliefs supporting such equilibria [Akerlof, 1976, 1984; Basu, 1986b, 1997: 312–14; Kuran, 1987, 1988, 1995: chap. 6–8; see also Naqvi and Wemhoner, 1995]. This outcome directly follows from the fact that it may be rational for an individual to comply with unpleasant rules or to obey a totalitarian regime if there exists an effective (decentralized) network of mutually reinforcing social sanctions against disobedience.[11] As a matter of fact, in a system where each (rational) individual complies lest he should be socially ostracized, potential members of a break-away coalition justifiably fear that a deviant move is doomed to failure. This is all the more paradoxical as deviance is going to be opposed by individuals who actually dislike the rules or system prevailing. By rationally pursuing their interests, they thus contribute to make failure to challenge the system a self-fulfilling prophecy [Bardhan, 1989: 8]. Through the educational system or other socialization processes, dysfunctional arrangements or revolting social customs can thus persist during long periods of history.

Finally, from social choice theory, a new discipline in economics that focuses on the study of rules of distribution and the principles of equity invoked to justify those rules, it is again evident that such principles need not be compatible with efficiency. As a matter of fact, there are well-known instances where the combination of certain normative principles determines sharing rules that are not efficient [see, e.g., Moulin, 1995: chaps. 4–5]. For example, the equity test of resource-monotonicity (everyone should benefit from growth),[12] when combined with the test of equal split (each of the *n* agents considered ought to be entitled to the welfare level resulting from consuming a share *1/n* of the available pie), is not compatible with efficiency in a pure allocation or in a production problem. Furthermore, there is no allocation rule that satisfies simultaneously resource monotonicity and efficiency when these two criteria are combined with Nash-implementability. Nash-implementability is defined as the existence of a cost-sharing or allocation mechanism the Nash equilibrium of which coincides for any preference profile with the considered allocation rule. The latter result is significant in so far as it indicates that societies following the resource monotonicity axiom are likely to be inefficient even when their conception of justice or fairness does not require the test of equal split to be met. As a matter of fact, Nash implementability is an important requirement because any mechanism relying on more intricate equilibrium concepts easily becomes intractable in the sense that the equilibrium may never be reached by agents endowed with human cognitive abilities.

When efficiency is conceived in dynamic rather than in static terms, the possibilities that principles of equity or other cultural values are incompatible with efficiency are tremendously increased. In fact, the incompatibility between resource monotonicity and efficiency (when mechanisms are required to be Nash-implementable) holds *a fortiori* when dynamic rather than static efficiency is considered: the idea that everyone should benefit from economic growth precludes maximum growth. It is not surprising that development economists have been particularly alerted to these incompatibilities since they deal with societies that have precisely to create new productive resources at a rapid pace. Such concerns can certainly be observed in the development writings of the fifties and the sixties, particularly when the authors pointed to the negative impact on economic growth of traditional barriers to mobility (e.g., caste or race barriers) or of customary mechanisms of redistribution (most notably, the extended family system).

As pointed out in the Preface, Chapter 5 will return to this theme and develops it with particular reference to egalitarian norms such as they prevail in African village societies.

## 1.5 THE EVOLUTIONARY APPROACH TO INSTITUTIONS

Before concluding this chapter, it is worth spending some time describing an alternative approach to institutions that has gained increased currency among economists during the last decades. This is the evolutionary theory of institutions which is based on the biological analogy of survival of the fittest.

This theory has an important antecedent since, as early as in the 18th-century, David Hume clearly formulated the idea of spontaneous order which was to be further elaborated two centuries later by Friedrich Hayek (1948, 1960, 1973) and, thereafter, by Richard Nelson and Sidney Winter (1982), and by other economists. For Hayek and Hume, indeed, property, law, and government are the outcome of the evolution of human society (see Chapter 7 for more details). For Robert Sugden, likewise, 'if individuals pursue their own interests in a state of anarchy, order... can arise spontaneously' [Sugden, 1986: vii].

The evolutionary approach to institutions sees the emergence and demise of particular rules or institutional arrangements as the outcome of an organic process of Darwinian natural selection typically equated with the competitive pressures of the market in the works of Hayek and the Austrian school. In an important sense this biological theory is appealing to economists. As a matter of fact, if the *explananda* of Darwinian natural selection are typically located at the level of populations, species and groups, there is no reference to species or group selection, but to individual selection: individual organisms are the units of selection [Vromen, 1995: 92; Binmore, 1996b]. Like in the approach of methodological individualism followed by economists, aggregate phenomena are understood in ways that only involve individuals.

While, as aptly argued by Basu, Jones, and Schlicht (1987), transaction-cost economics is mainly appropriate to explain the persistence of institutions,[13] evolutionary economics is also interested in the origin of the institutions, that is, in the ways institutions are selected. In the words of Langlois: 'A complete explanation may have to suggest not only why a structure is efficient now but why it was efficient throughout its evolutionary history, which means specifying the process by which structure are selected' [Langlois, 1986: 21]. This is precisely where Darwinism seems to be able to help.

After having stressed where evolutionary thinking looks familiar to the economist, points of dissimilarity with standard economic approaches need to be underlined. In particular, the concept of rationality so dear to the heart of neoclassical economists (especially the sophisticated forms of strategic rationality assumed in repeated game theory[14]) is abandoned in favour of limited forms of rationality often labelled bounded rationality. This is an expected feature given that biologists study organisms whose strategies are largely pre-programmed and whose strategy sets are likely to be much more restricted than those of humans. As remembered by Rasmusen, 'the lower animals are less likely than humans to think about the strategies of their opponents at each stage of a game' [Rasmusen, 1989: 121].[15] In fact, rather than explaining how players would rationally pick actions in a given situation, evolutionary theorizing is concerned with understanding how behaviour evolves or persists over time under exogenous shocks including the possibility of odd behaviour caused by occasional mutations [*ibidem*].

While classical game theory requires that the actors' expectations about each other are consistent with the experience that is generated by the resulting actions, evolutionary game theory is based on the idea that agents follow trial-and-error behaviour: what works well for a player is more likely to be used again, whereas what turns out poorly is more likely to be discarded. In the words of Robert Axelrod, 'the analysis of what is chosen at any specific time is based upon an operationalization of the idea that effective strategies are more likely to be retained than ineffective strategies' [Axelrod, 1986: 47–48].

Peyton Young has adopted a strongly polemical tone when he contends that the classical game-theoretical approach is 'a rather extravagant and implausible model of human behavior' that 'represents a peculiar aberration from traditional ways of thinking in economics'. Witness to it is the fact that 'One of the central messages of the pure theory of exchange, for example, is the ability of prices and markets to coordinate economic activity *without* assuming that agents are anything more than naive optimizers acting on limited information' [Young, 1998: 5]. On the contrary, standard game theory assumes that agents are capable of hyper-rational behaviour: 'They know the utility functions of other agents (or the probability that other agents have these utility functions), they are fully aware of the process they are embedded in, they make optimum long-run plans, and so forth'. Is it not more reasonable to posit that agents look around them, gather information and ground their decisions on the basis of fragmentary information, have only an incomplete idea of the way the world in which they operate works, and may not be especially forward looking [*ibidem*: 5–6]?

Another feature that fundamentally distinguishes the evolutionary approach from the classical point of view in economics is the status accorded to equilibrium. While transaction-cost economics relies on the standard concept of equilibrium—describing 'the way the world looks once the dust has settled'—and analyzes institutional change by resorting to comparative-statics, evolutionary economists believe that equilibrium can be understood only within a dynamic framework that explains how it comes about, if it does: they are interested 'in how the dust goes about settling' [Young, 1998: 4].

After having specified the initial proportions of various types of agents (or genotypes in biological terminology) in the whole population, the probabilities of their interactions, and the payoffs associated with every possible pairwise interaction, the evolutionary modeller needs to specify the dynamics by which the proportions of the agents with higher payoffs (or, in biological terminology, with better fitness or reproductive ability) increase in the population. Equilibrium is attained when the proportions of different types of agents able to survive have become stable. The evolutionary approach is thus inherently probabilistic and it often involves non-linear effects that make it impossible to use analytic (deductive) mathematics. Instead, computer simulation techniques are used that allow the researcher not only to identify the equilibrium points but also to reveal the dynamics of the process studied [Axelrod, 1984].

Note that whereas in biology inheritance of parental genes is the replication mechanism (called natural selection) that ensures the survival of the fittest over successive generations (the more effective individuals are therefore more likely to survive and reproduce), in economics replication is often assumed to be effected through imitation and takeover of unsuccessful agents or firms by successful ones. Another possibility is that agents learn by trial and error, retaining srategies that work well and discarding those that do not. In such 'reinforcement' mechanisms, it is thus one's own past payoffs that matter, not those of other agents. The principle is indeed that 'the probability of taking an action in the present increases with the payoff that resulted from taking that action in the past' [Young, 1998: 28]. There is a last adaptive mechanism with an obvious learning aspect that deserves to be mentioned: known as the 'best-reply' mechanism, it implies that agents adopt actions that optimize their expected payoff given what they expect others to do. For example, in the so-called 'fictitious play' models, agents choose best replies to the empirical frequency distribution of their opponents' previous actions. More precisely, 'each person constructs a simple statistical model of what other people are going to do, based on (possibly fragmentary) information about what they did in the past... and then chooses a best reply to the product of these estimated distributions', it being understood that every other player is assumed to choose according to a fixed probability distribution and that these distributions are independent among players [*ibidem*: 28, 30–31].

In all the above mechanisms, it must be stressed, agents are not assumed to be rational since diffusion of more effective strategies does not require that they fully understand the strategic implications of their choices (that is, they are not assumed to have a perfect ability to reason inductively about a feedback mechanism between their own choices and the choices of the other players). Yet, since in most evolutionary models pairs of players are selected randomly from a 'large' population to play the given game once, and are thereafter returned to the population, imitative and learning behaviours that involve strategy changes during the life of an agent are precluded. In learning models *stricto sensu*, by contrast, each player is assumed to interact with many varying opponents with a fixed strategy, modifying his strategy thereafter based on the cumulative experience.[16]

Also noteworthy is that there is absolutely no certainty that optimal rules or institutions will emerge from an evolutionary process. Biologists seem, indeed, to hold the following view: 'Natural selection works on existing genetic material and this material need not include the optimal genetic 'program'. If the optimal program is not available, natural selection cannot lead to optimal adaptation'. Moreover, the fact that gene mutations are blind (their occurrence is assumed to be independent of the needs of organisms) and can represent only gradual variations of existing genotypes precludes them from introducing optimal types in the population [Vromen, 1995: 95–96]. Survival of the *fitter* instead of survival of the *fittest* is clearly the appropriate labelling for Darwin's theory of natural selection.

Consider the famous Hawk-Dove game studied by Maynard Smith (1982). If there are only Hawks (always ready to fight for getting hold of an available resource) and Doves (always bent on withdrawing in case of conflict) in the population, neither type can completely take over the environment. This is not optimal since the world would be better off with Doves only. Now assume that a third type called the 'bourgeois type' appears which respects property rights: it behaves as a Hawk if it arrives first at the resource, and as a Dove if it arrives second (the order of arrival is assumed to be random). It can then be shown that the bourgeois type will invade the population because it will have a higher average expected payoff than the other two types. This is of course a fortunate result since, when the population will be exclusively composed of 'bourgeois', that is, when it will be in an evolutionarily stable equilibrium, no fight will occur any more: the agent first arrived at a resource is considered as the legitimate owner and there is no contender left (the institution of private property rights is universally recognized and enforced).

Has the above theory succeeded in proving that private property rights will eventually emerge to allocate scarce resources? The answer is no. Indeed, if the theory describes the process whereby the 'bourgeois' strategy gets a foothold and spreads itself in the population, it does not say anything about how this particular strategy has actually come about. It is after all a rather sophisticated strategy (requiring something like the order of arrival to decide which of the two players will play Hawk) the discovery of which necessitates a considerable mutation compared to the simple Hawk and Dove strategies.

The same limitation applies to all attempts to look at social institutions as undesigned and unintended regularities of social behaviour that emerge organically (the so-called social conventions), such as are found in the works of Sugden (1986) and Schotter (1981, 1986), for example. In such attempts, institutions or rules are seen as evolving unconsciously and gradually from the pursuit of individual interests as agents repeatedly face the same types of social problems or situations [see Baland and Platteau, 1996: 67–72, for a more complete discussion]. As pointed out by Ken Binmore (1992: 434), however, the results that show up in these works obtain only in so far as attention is artificially restricted to a few strategies, often arbitrarily chosen.[17] No clue is given as to why particular strategies are there while innumerable other conceivable strategies are ignored.

The fact of the matter is that repeated games need some sort of 'friction' to generate predictable outcomes and a form of 'friction' is provided by cultural codes and social norms [Dasgupta, 1988: 70–71]. For this reason, the evolutionary theory cannot claim to be a complete theory of institutional change and, as will be seen in Chapter 7, this conclusion applies to the ambitious research project of Binmore himself.

The analysis of institutional phenomena that aims at deriving cooperative outcomes from non-cooperative (evolutionary) games has always to assume that some initial and unexplained beliefs, conventions or codes of conduct exist for cooperation to occur in a so-called spontaneous way. In other words, some rules must always be presupposed for any economic discourse including the most elementary analysis of market problems [Basu, Jones, and Schlicht, 1987; Field, 1984].

With the help of evolutionary games, on the other hand, it is possible to show that initial conditions may determine different trajectories so that the best trajectory is not sure to be selected. Adjustment processes are path-dependent: evolution can lead to different equilibrium configurations depending on where the process starts and on the sequence of transactions [Young, 1998: chap 1].

All this being said, there is no denying that evolutionary game modelling can provide useful guidance to understand some dynamic processes of institutional evolution [see Young, 1998]. A remarkable illustration of this possibility is Young's (1996) explanation of why in western Europe vehicles drive on the right (a convention that clearly corresponds to one of two possible equilibria in a coordination game). The author shows that the present rule is the result of two distinct processes: an historical and contingent event (the French Revolution) that led to a legal intervention, and a contagion process that unfolded itself in a largely decentralized way. It is the latter process that has been analyzed with the help of an evolutionary game. On the former component of the explanation, economists have nothing to say: the fact that French Revolutionaries chose to impose driving right (rather than left) to symbolize the reversal of the old order was no more rational than keeping on driving left and thereby continuing a convention that was efficient when it was created but had long ceased to be so.[18]

## NOTES

1. For an instructive discussion of the nature of the impact of the productive forces on the relations of production, see Elster, 1985: 30, 267–272; Cohen, 1978. Cohen has argued that the only way of making various Marx's statements consistent is to assume that 'the primacy of the productive forces must be explanatory rather than straightforwardly causal, and that the explanation must be in fact a functional one'. The relations of production must be explained functionally, that is, in terms of their capacity to develop the productive forces. The relations 'obtain because and so long as they are optimal for the development of the forces; they change when and because they no longer are optimal' [Elster, 1985: 268]. However, as persuasively argued by Elster, when Marx refers to the changes in the relations of production that are caused by the productive forces, he does not appear to have in mind changes that are due to new rela-

tions having become optimal. Rather, he seems to refer to more matter-of-fact social impacts of new technologies, that is, to changes that may be required for an *optimal use* of the new technology but not for its *optimal development*.

2. For Boserup, indeed, a significant rise in labour productivity in agriculture cannot occur until there is widespread adoption of science-based technical innovations, such as improved seed varieties and chemical fertilizers. Even then, productivity increases may not match those obtaining in other sectors of the economy. It is only late in the development process when agricultural operations have been mechanized to overcome the constraint of labour scarcity that the productivity of agricultural labour can be expected to rise significantly.
3. In the words of Douglass North, 'The major role of institutions in a society is to reduce uncertainty by establishing a stable (but not necessarily efficient) structure to human interaction' [North, 1990: 6].
4. As pointed out by Matthews, indeed: 'Complex arrangements are difficult to alter radically, so they foster inertia. Inertia makes it easier to respond to changing circumstances and incorporate new institutional ideas by patching up existing institutions and so making them more complicated still rather than by starting again from scratch. As a result, each new step in the process of institutional change is determined by its starting point and itself in turn contributes to shaping later developments. History matters. Since the choice at each step is also likely to be affected more or less strongly by stochastic elements, the process assumes some of the character of a random walk. Institutional change acquires a life of its own' [Matthews, 1986: 915; in a similar vein, see also Basu, Jones, and Schlicht, 1987: 12–19].
5. Thus, socially inefficient institutions may persist not only when selfish or short-sighted rulers find it in their interest to defend them, but also when everybody loses from their existence and therefore wishes their demise. This is because it may be rational for each individual to comply with unpleasant rules or unwanted political regimes due to the existence of a mutually sustaining network of social sanctions (see infra, Section 1.4).
6. Bear in mind that we are not in the Coasian world: negotiating being a costly process and side-payments being practically difficult in many situations, some agents may oppose an institutional change that would be Pareto-improving under Coasian assumptions. It must also be emphasized that only a subgroup of the people concerned might be able to communicate with one another effectively, and that they alone could be in a position to reach and enforce agreements. In this case, 'the interests of people who do not take part in the decision about what choices are made are unlikely to be fully reflected in the choices' [Milgrom and Roberts, 1992: 25].
7. For example, the well-known contribution of Bell and Zusman (1976), based on a bargaining model, holds only because of their restrictive assumption that excludes the option of leasehold contract [Hayami and Otsuka, 1993: 40–1].
8. Thus, I have always been struck by the fact that, in artisanal fisheries, equal shares of the net proceeds of the catch are paid to all adult crew members by the boat captain or owner. None the less, to take account of significant differences in individual productivity, the latter reserves himself the right to pay some additional amount of money to the best crew members. Revealingly, these differential payments are surrounded with secrecy in order to avoid invidious comparisons and jealous feelings which are liable to destroy the team spirit of the whole crew.
9. In a more recent work, Young puts forward the view that particular shares 'appear to be conventions that got an early start through chance events and remain in place because they succeed in conditioning the parties' expectations...Precedents affect present expectations, which determine current actions, which in turn become future precedents' [Young, 1996: 117–18]. According to this view, it is not clear why ?-? would be a prominent focal point when the parties are in obviously asymmetric positions. The explanation for the predominance of this particular sharing rule (different from the fairness argument) is that equal division of the pie is more stochastically stable than other sharing rules: in fact, it can be shown that the fifty-fifty split is the 'unique stochastically stable convention'. In other words, the probability of getting out of ?-? is substantially lower than the probability of getting in, so that the process is much more likely to be in the ?-? convention than in other sharing conventions [*ibidem*: 119–120; see also Young, 1993a, 1993b].

10. A crucial device in Rabin's formalization is the so-called 'kindness function' which captures how much more than or less than player j's equitable playoff player i believes he is giving to player j. The equitable payoff provides a crude reference point against which to measure how generous player i is being to player j. Beliefs play a central role in the model since player i's payoffs do not depend simply on the actions taken, but also on his beliefs about player j's motives. Thus, if player i expects player j to be kind, he will be inclined to reward him for his fairness by playing kindly too. On the contrary, if player i expects player j to be unkind, he will be reluctant to concede to him and will play in an hostile manner. Note that each player's subjective expected utility when he chooses his strategy depends not only on his strategy and beliefs about the other player's strategy choice, but also on his beliefs about the other player's beliefs about his own strategy. If this were not the case, a player would not be able to infer whether the other player is playing kindly or unkindly towards him. A fairness equilibrium is the analog of Nash equilibrium for psychological games, imposing the additional condition that all higher-order beliefs match actual behaviour.
11. Note that, in Kuran's model, a central role is played by the influence on an individual's *private* preference formation of the justification that others give for their *public* preferences for the status quo.
12. See also Young (1994: 78) who uses the expression 'strict monotonicity' of an allocation rule to describe its property that when the amount to be divided increases, everyone gets more.
13. To argue that the NIE provides clues about the origin of institutions is clearly to fall into the functionalist fallacy according to which the origins of institutions can be easily identified by referring to their consequences [Basu, Jones, and Schlicht, 1987: 11; Elster, 1985: 8–22].
14. Underlying repeated game theory are indeed two strong assumptions about human behaviour. On the one hand, agents are supposed to be hyper-rational since they must be able to conceive, implement, and choose among numerous and complex strategies. In particular, they must be able to anticipate all the possible reactions of the other players, even in a distant future, and to decide their current moves accordingly. On the other hand, once they have identified the best strategy, agents never make mistakes, in the sense that they unfailingly act according to this strategy' [Baland and Platteau, 1996: 67].
15. In classical evolutionary models of the biological type, pre-programmation of individual behaviour is total: individuals cannot choose at all. Yet, 'the situation they are in can be said to have a game-theoretic structure in that their results depend not only on their own behaviour but also on the behaviour of the other individuals in the population. To be more precise, their results depend also on what other rules are followed and on the relative proportions of the individuals that follow the different rules in the population'[Vromen, 1995: 136].
16. In both classes of models, the 'fitness' of a given strategy at any stage of the game depends on its average payoff, achieved against the rest of the population. This implies that 'a strategy revision by any single player evokes no response from the other players, as it does not appreciably affect their average payoffs' [Bendor et al., 1994: 2]. Recently, however, economists have paid increasing attention to learning models where the strategy revisions of a given player generate substantial feedback effects by affecting the other players' payoffs, thereby inducing the latter also to revise their strategies subsequently. In all cases, limited rationality is assumed.
17. Thus, for example, Robert Sugden has shown that evolution (in repeated pairwise encounters) tends to favour cooperation. More precisely, a convention of 'brave reciprocity' (start by cooperating and continue to cooperate only if the opponents also cooperate) can be expected to evolve if the agents are allowed to play three strategies: brave reciprocity, the 'nasty' strategy (unconditional defection), and cautious reciprocity (start by defecting and later cooperate if the opponents cooperate). Indeed, even if initially almost everyone defects, cautious reciprocators will gradually emerge and their presence will help to bring about conditions causing brave reciprocators eventually to invade and take over [Sugden, 1986: 118–120].
18. Young actually mentions the fact that left driving was the common practice in many regions of Europe for a long time but without providing an explanation as to why that particular convention was initially chosen. A plausible explanation is that riding left was preferred because of the necessity to quickly draw one's sword or gun in the event of an attack by the passer-by coming from the opposite direction (given that most people are right-handed).

# Chapter 2

## RESOURCE ENDOWMENTS AND AGRICULTURAL DEVELOPMENT

### 2.1 INTRODUCTION

In Sub-Saharan Africa (henceforth denoted by SSA) during the last 25 years, agricultural and food production have largely failed to keep pace with population growth: thus, from a peak in 1975, per capita agricultural (or food) production had by 1993 declined by 20 per cent, with a brief interruption of the downward tendency only during the second half of the 1980s [FAO, 1995: 77]. Since the agricultural sector typically contributes one-third of GDP and employs more than two-thirds of the economically active population, such disappointing performance is necessarily reflected in negative per capita GNP growth rates during the same period. As a matter of fact, the region's cumulative decline in per capita income is 15 per cent over the past twenty years (World Bank estimate). An immediate consequence of this bleak situation is that food imports into the region (mainly from the developed country markets) have soared during the last decades: from $27.9 in 1961–63, per capita food imports have risen to $32.6 in 1975–77 and, more impressively, to $47.7 in 1989–91 [*ibidem*: 44].[1] Today, SSA as a whole seems to be on the verge of shifting from a position of net exporter to that of net importer of agricultural products [FAO, 1995: 211]. Table 2.1 summarizes some of these rather depressing trends.

Recently, echoing warnings issued earlier by Sara Berry (1984), several authors have seriously questioned the reality of a food crisis or of a problem of agricultural development in SSA [see, e.g., Jaeger, 1992a, 1992b; Block, 1994; Wiggins, 1995]. While some are stressing the low quality of Africa's agricultural and food production statistics compiled by the FAO and usually derived from national sources, others prefer to reinterpret the available data (such as the rise of per capita food imports)[2] or to rework them in a way that allows for more optimistic conclusions. The main point to bear in mind here is that there is indeed substantial evidence of serious biases in the reporting of agricultural production data for SSA. The problem is nevertheless that it is difficult to determine the probable direction of these biases and that the village-level case studies upon which more optimistic

Table 2.1: Agricultural growth in Sub-Saharan Africa during the period 1975–90

| Average annual percentage growth rates | 1975–80 | 1981–85 | 1986–90* |
|---|---|---|---|
| Total agricultural production per capita | –2.3% | –2.0% | –1.6% |
| Food production per capita | –2.2 | –2.1 | –1.7 |
| Agricultural exports per capita | –3.6 | –6.0 | –5.7 |

Source UNDP and the World Bank, *African Development Indicators*, 1992, adapted from tables 1–2, 8–3, 8–4, 8–9.

* The terminal year for agricultural exports is 1988.

conclusions are usually based are few, often provide only qualitative evidence about agricultural progress, and are not drawn from a sufficiently large sample of countries and ecological regions or subregions.[3]

Still, there is an important lesson that can be safely derived from such case studies and to which I shall return towards the end of this chapter. It would be wrong to consider that agricultural performance is uniformly poor all over SSA. Rapid agricultural change has actually occurred in a number of areas and some of these localized African experiences have followed a pattern rather similar to Asia's Green Revolution. These limited cases of agricultural transformation, mainly concentrated in the maize belt, make for a highly uneven pattern of agricultural growth. The overall picture therefore remains that depicted by Christopher Delgado when he writes that 'Today most of Africa is clearly at the very early stages of the agricultural transformation and technical change, whereas large parts of Asia and Latin America are clearly in the late stages' [Delgado, 1996: 6].

The major question addressed in the following is therefore why agricultural growth performance in land-abundant Africa has on the whole been so poor relative to that of land-scarce Asia. The abundance of natural resource endowments itself must be a favourable condition for economic growth. Indeed, as the vent-for-surplus theory of Hla Myint (1971) and the staple theory of Harold Innis depicted, exploitation of slack natural resources in response to increased external demands was an engine of economic growth in sparsely populated 'empty lands' under the 19th- to the early 20th-century settings. One reason why post-independent SSA failed to achieve rapid development along the vent-for-surplus model may be relative stagnation in external demands for primary commodities, such as minerals and tropical cash crops, for which SSA has had traditional comparative advantage.

A more decisive factor, however, appears to be the exhaustion of slack natural resources, especially land for cultivation. Major acceleration of population growth in SSA since around the 1920s, which was the highest among the major developing regions, has resulted in rapid exploitation of available land for agricultural production so that further expansion in cultivation frontiers became progressively more difficult. By the 1960s, SSA as a region had reached a stage in which the vent-for-surplus growth was no longer tenable though several exceptional areas with significant resource slack still remained. To sustain growth African agriculture should have switched its growth momentum from expansion of area under cultivation to increase in output per hectare of cultivated area.

This switch is not possible without adequate supply of yield-increasing technologies and inputs such as high-yielding varieties, fertilizers and irrigation. The supply of these inputs requires an institutional and organizational set-up which is entirely different from the system in support of the vent-for-surplus growth. Yet, evolution of necessary institutions and organizations in response to the emerging need is typically slow. It is our basic hypothesis that the deepening agricultural crisis in SSA in the past three decades has been created from a major lag in institutional and organizational adjustments needed for the switch from the vent-for-surplus to the resource-saving growth. Asia has had a unique advantage in this regard since its institutions and organizations had been molded under traditional land scarcity and, therefore, their adjustment for adoption of modern land-saving technology has been relatively modest, requiring relatively little time and strain [Platteau and Hayami, 1999]. In so far as economic policies are not independent of structural characteristics that bear upon the capacity of agricultural producers to form pressure groups aimed at influencing policy-makers, the disadvantage of SSA is also reflected in misguided policies that tend to receive primary (and excessive) emphasis in the literature.

The outline of the core of Chapter 2 is as follows. Section 2 shows how low population density and the scattered pattern of settlement in Africa determine the poor state of existing communication links compared with Asia. This serious problem is actually compounded by macroeconomic mismanagement that results in low rates of utilization of available road infrastructure. In Section 3, the adverse effects of physical isolation on rural market development are highlighted while Section 4 is concerned with the constraints on the supply of public goods that result from such isolation. In Section 5, attention is given to the complicating presence of technological constraints that further limit the range of opportunities available to African agriculture (at least in the medium term). Indeed, in large parts of the African continent the absence of new and sufficiently attractive technological packages tends to make agricultural development difficult even when communications are well-developed. In Section 6, the debate on the aggregate supply response is shortly presented and its conclusions are matched with those of the preceding analysis. Finally, in Section 7, policy implications of the entire analysis are discussed to provide the reader with a broad perspective on African rural development that is enriched by lessons drawn from similarities and contrasts with the Asian experience.

## 2.2 PHYSICAL ISOLATION AND TRANSPORTATION BOTTLENECKS

Relative land abundance and low population density in SSA are associated with small and highly scattered settlements. This section shows how this pattern results in extremely high transportation/communication costs that make isolation and underdevelopment of rural communities inevitable.

### *Low density of road networks*

An immediate consequence of the highly scattered pattern of rural settlement in SSA is a low density of road networks and other communication links. Most African countries thus have but a small fraction of the roads per unit of land area that are found in many countries of Asia and Latin America [Mellor and Delgado, 1987: 4]. The extent of road networks and the percentage of paved roads in twelve African countries and three Asian countries as well as in the United States are shown in Table 2.2 (see also Table 2.3 for additional information). African countries have thus developed road networks to a density of 1 to 11 kilometers of road per 100 square kilometer of land area compared with 30 to 45 kilometers in the Asian countries. In terms of railways and river transports, Asian countries are also much better off than those in SSA. Thus, for example, a country like South Korea has more than 11 miles of rail and road links per 1,000 hectares of cultivated land while Kenya has just about 1 mile and Tanzania 0.09 miles [Ahmed and Donovan, 1992: 6, Table 2].

The comparative disadvantage of SSA (with the exception of Zimbabwe) *via-à-vis* Asia is more pronounced when rail and road mileage is measured per unit of land area than when it is measured per unit of population (as is evident from a comparison of the first columns in tables 2 and 3). This obviously results from the much lower population densities in the former than in the latter continent.

By mid-1991, the density of population was around 131.1 persons per square kilometer in Asia (including South and East Asia and the Pacific, but excluding Central Asia) but only 21.2 persons in SSA. In Africa, population densities can be much lower than 10 persons per

Table 2.2: Road network and incidence of paved roads in selected African and Asian countries and the United States, 1976–78

| Country roads | Density of total road network (kilometer per 100 square kilometer of area) | Percentage of pave |
|---|---|---|
| Botswana | 2 | 9.5 |
| Burkina Faso | 6 | 5.1 |
| Congo | 2 | 6.5 |
| Ethiopia | 3 | 28.0 |
| Kenya | 9 | 9.7 |
| Malawi | 5 | 12.2 |
| Mali | 1 | 11.1 |
| Nigeria | 11 | 40.2 |
| Senegal | 7 | 23.0 |
| Tanzania | 2 | 35.0* |
| Zaire | 6 | 1.5 |
| Zambia | 5 | 13.0 |
| Bangladesh | 35 | 32.0 |
| India | 41 | 38.8 |
| Indonesia (Java) | 41 | 37.2 |
| United States | 67 | 85.0 |

Source Ahmed and Rustagi, 1984: 112; Putterman, 1995: 317.
This percentage applies to trunk roads only.

Table 2.3: Some selected indicators of surface transport for Africa and Asia, 1990

| Region/Country | Rail and road mileage per 1,000 persons | Rail and road mileage per 1,000 ha of cultivated land | No of motorized vehicles per mile of paved road |
|---|---|---|---|
| Africa | | | |
| Benin | 0.17 | 0.36 | 9.0 |
| Kenya | 0.30 | 1.09 | 19.2 |
| Malawi | 0.28 | 1.55 | 17.0 |
| Senegal | 0.44 | 0.60 | 12.2 |
| Tanzania | 0.15 | 0.09 | 14.2 |
| Togo | 0.37 | 1.26 | 13.5 |
| Zimbabwe | 1.09 | 4.11 | 35.7 |
| Asia | | | |
| Bangladesh | 0.07 | 0.75 | 47.5 |
| India | 0.68 | 3.58 | 49.0 |
| Pakistan | 0.73 | 3.71 | 42.5 |
| Philippines | 1.65 | 7.38 | 51.8 |
| South Korea | 0.58 | 11.41 | 67.2 |

Source Ahmed and Donovan, 1992, 6: Table 2.

square kilometer (for example, 7.0 persons in Congo and Mali, 6.2 persons in Niger, 4.5 persons in Gabon and Chad, and around 2 persons in Botswana and Mauritania) and it is only in a few, typically small countries that densities characteristic of the Asian world can actually be found (273.1 persons per square kilometer in Rwanda, 203.6 persons in Burundi, and as many as 550 persons in Mauritius). If big countries in terms of population are considered, one finds that countries like Kenya and Ethiopia have a population density of about 43 persons per square kilometer while Nigeria has one of 107.1 persons. Even the comparatively high density of Nigeria stands in sharp contrast to densities of 209.7 persons in the Philippines, 263.5 persons in India, and 768.1 persons in Bangladesh, but it is not considerably lower than the density of China (120.2 persons), an Asian country with serious communication difficulties [figures computed from World Bank, 1993: World Development Indicators, Table 1].

On the other hand, overall population density in Latin America (23 persons per square kilometer) is close to the density observed in SSA but populations tend to be much more concentrated in Latin America than in Africa where rates of urbanization remain comparatively low (31% as against 74% in Latin America) and rural populations tend to be highly scattered [figures computed from World Bank, 1996, tables 1 and 9].

As far as rural areas are concerned, a recent study shows that a group of 18 countries in the humid and subhumid tropics of Africa for which data are available had only 63 kilometers of rural roads per thousand square kilometers in the early 1990s [Spencer, 1994: 11; for even lower estimates, see Riverson et al., 1991: 4]. The contrast with Asia is again striking as is evident from the fact that this group of African countries would require no less than 388 kilometers of rural roads per thousand square kilometers of land area to bring the rural road infrastructure up to the level of India in 1950, after adjusting for population density differences [Spencer, 1994: 11]. Consider in particular the case of Nigeria which is well above the African average with its network of about 90 kilometers of rural road per thousand square kilometers. This relative performance on the part of a country blessed with huge oil revenues follows a massive investment programme undertaken mostly under the pressure of multi- and bilateral lending agencies: Nigeria's rural road network expanded by 45 per cent between 1985 and 1992 [Howe, 1994: 3]. Yet, based on Indian experience in areas with similar population densities to those in Nigeria, an acceptable 'target' rural road density would be about 730 kilometers, that is, more than 8 times as much as what the Nigeria presently has [Riverson et al., 1991: 4; see also Spencer, 1994: 11].

Given such a low density of rural roads in SSA, it is not surprising that there are usually huge distances between villages and all-weather roads in SSA. Even in a country such as Zimbabwe which has the highest network of (rail and) road mileage per hectare of cultivated land [Ahmed and Donovan, 1992: 6], three-quarters of the farms are situated more than five kilometer away from an all-weather road. This is in sharp contrast with advanced Asian regions (such as the Indian Punjab) where almost all villages are linked through metalled roads to each other and to towns and cities [Sims, 1988].

The above deficiencies may seem surprising given the considerable efforts undertaken by colonial powers to improve the situation by constructing railways and building up roads as feeders to railways from hitherto inaccessible areas. These powers were indeed quite aware that only major investments in modern transport infrastructure could bring about significant acceleration of both internal and external trade in Africa, by promoting mechanized overland transportation and thereby lowering distribution costs. This said, it must be borne in mind that the transport infrastructure developed in the colonial period was heavily biased towards external commerce: thus, two-thirds of the African railways built in that period connected mines to a coastal harbour [Boserup, 1981: 148]. In the words of Ralph Austen: 'African colonial railways are a classical element of what is called a dendritic market system, i.e. a leaflike network emanating from the outlets of international trade to the various regions of the African interior but not linking the latter to one another' [Austen, 1987: 127; see also Boserup, 1981: 148–150].

On the other hand, there is no doubt that in certain cases the communication infrastructure inherited from the colonial period has tremendously decayed in the post-independence period, owing to irresponsibility of national leadership. The most striking example is surely that of Congo (ex-Zaïre): there, the network of usable roads decreased from 88,000 miles in 1960 (at the time of independence) to 12,000 miles in 1985 (with only 1,400 of them paved), that is, a decrease of as much as 75% in twenty-five years! Hence the astonishing reality that between the few points under the effective control of Mobutu regime the only transport was by air [Landes, 1998: 504–505].

*Low quality of the rural road network*

Much more important than differences in sheer availability of rail and road infrastructure are considerable variations in the quality of the existing communication networks between SSA and the other continents. Many African rural roads are just not practicable during the rainy season because they are highly liable to flooding. Moreover, even during the dry season, they are often hardly motorable because they are full of potholes which force slow driving and damage vehicles, thereby causing transport costs to reach abnormally high levels. If African rural roads are in such a mess, it is mainly because they are not properly maintained: about half the rural road network in SSA (350,000 km) has thus been estimated to require 'substantial rehabilitation' [Riverson et al., 1991: 4].

In Tanzania, for example, the percentage of roads found in good condition in 1990 was only 24 per cent for main roads (compared to 50 per cent in Malawi, 40 per cent in Zambia, and 32 per cent in Kenya) and 8 per cent for regional roads. Revealingly, the amount of funds allocated for road maintenance has been less than one-third of the amount required. As a result, the situation was so bad in the 1980s that 'one often preferred to drive over a dirt track than endure the pot-holed remnant of a once-paved highway'. In addition, 'the majority of even paved trunk roads remain dangerously narrow, with fatal accidents an all too frequent occurrence on the busiest stretches...' [Putterman, 1995: 317]. In parts of SSA, existing roads deteriorate at a faster rate than new roads are being constructed, thus causing the stock of roads to actually diminish [Howe, 1992: 8].

The problem arises not only because insufficient budgets are devoted to road maintenance but also because funds earmarked for maintenance are generally spent on improvement and emergency works (such as the repair of damaged bridges) rather than on routine or periodic maintenance [Howe, 1992: 8; Schroeder, 1994: 19]. Such choices result from the fact that political leaders are likely to gain greater recognition from the dramatic improvements associated with newly (re)constructed roads than from the almost imperceptible slowing of deterioration of routinely maintained existing roads [Schroeder, 1994: 19]. As a consequence, 'while Africa is underequipped in relation to its potential it is overburdened by the little infrastructure that it possesses' [Riverson et al., 1991: 5]. Given this state of affairs, although costly, road maintenance makes economic sense. As a matter of fact, the World Bank found that each dollar 'saved' by cutting the maintenance budget would increase the operating costs of vehicles by between $2 and $3 a year. In one case, it even concluded that the extra cost was as much as $22 [The Economist, 1995]. In the case of Tanzania, losses from higher vehicle operating costs due to the bad state of existing roads were estimated at about $150 million a year in 1990, equivalent to about a third of Tanzania's export earnings [Putterman, 1995: 317].

In fact, the problem of road neglect is so serious that some experts consider it futile to try to expand Africa's road network under present circumstances. Investment in new facilities could only be made at the expense of maintenance and rehabilitation of the already overstretched system. In other words, available resources and efforts should rather be concentrated on 'network stabilization' programmes even at the cost of temporarily abandoning significant portions of the existing road system in some countries [Howe, 1994: 3].

*Low rates of road utilization*

The problem with communication facilities in SSA is not only one of insufficient infrastructure and inadequate maintenance but also one of low utilization of whichever road infrastructure is available. As will be seen below, the latter problem is both the outcome of structural handicaps specific to Africa (such as heavy dependence on a restricted range of primary export products for access to foreign exchange, or low human capital in mechanical engineering capabilities) and the effect of mistaken macroeconomic policies and adverse exogenous shocks responsible for the high cost and unreliability of transport services.

To begin with, bear in mind that the number of motorized vehicles per mile of paved road is much lower in Africa than in Asia (see table 3, third column), thus compounding the transport handicap of the former region *via-à-vis* the latter. While there are between 9–20 motorized vehicles per mile of paved road in SSA, figures of 40–50 vehicles are commonly encountered in Asian countries, with South Korea reaching a record of almost 70 vehicles [Ahmed and Donovan, 1992: 6].[4] In many African countries, much of the traffic along the rural roads that exists actually consists of pedestrians or head loaders, hence the appellation 'footpath and headload economy' coined by John Howe.[5]

Restrictive government policies, such as the reliance on parastatal truck fleets for crop transport, or the setting of various limitations on private trading and interregional movements of agricultural goods, have hindered the development of private transporters (and traders) [Riverson et al., 1991: 2; Beynon, 1992; Badiane, 1992]. At the same time, unwise macroeconomic management or the adverse evolution of the international economic environment—particularly, the more or less continuous deterioration of the purchasing capacity of agricultural exports (income terms of trade) since the late seventies [FAO, 1995: 220–23]—have created foreign exchange scarcity, giving rise to lack of spare parts and rationed imports of transport vehicles. This difficult situation has been further exacerbated by inadequate policies concerning pricing and marketing of fuel that contributed to chronic shortages which have drastically curtailed the availability of motorized transport services in rural areas [Riverson et al., 1991: 2].

Transport capacity has been all the more affected by the above factors as, contrary to Asia, many African countries have proven unable to develop intermediate transport technologies that are more suited to the region's factor endowments than the means of transport currently used (often of foreign origin). Reasons behind this situation include, first and foremost, comparatively low capabilities in mechanical engineering[6] and undue pressures from international aid donors (through tied loans, tied aid projects,...). Many hard constraints would therefore be relaxed if appropriate means of transportation intermediate between walking/headloading and cars, pick-ups and trucks could be locally developed and promoted, such as bicycle trailers, handcarts, motorized rickshaws, etc.

A comparative study of long-distance road freight transport in three African countries (Cameroon, Côte d'Ivoire and Mali) and one poor Asian country (Pakistan) sheds considerable light on the magnitude and the varied causes of the above problem of inefficient use of existing road infrastructure in SSA [Hine and Rizet, 1991; Howe, 1992: 22–24]. According to this study, indeed, use of articulated vehicles (tractors and semi-trailers) and trucks is much more intensive in Pakistan than in the African countries considered.

This is mainly due to the three following factors: (i) the annual distance travelled is significantly longer (up to almost four times as long) in the Asian country, because sleeping compartments are generally added so that the vehicle can be operated day and night with two drivers, and because vehicles are usually found to be in better working order; (ii) empty running of vehicles used for the transport of goods is less in Pakistan; and (iii) the average load taken by Pakistanese trucks is much heavier (up to twice as heavy) because they are reinforced upon acquisition (using local engineering capabilities) in order to exceed the payloads for which they were initially designed.

For another thing, running and maintenance (spare parts and repairs) costs are considerably higher in SSA than in Asia—for example, African three-axle vehicles turned out to cost 6.4 times (per t/km) as much as similar Pakistani vehicles—, a difference that is only partly explained by lower road surface quality. At the root of this severe handicap suffered by African countries are also a series of malfunctionings among which the following appear to be the most important: heavy import taxes on spare parts (including tires); insufficient allocation of foreign exchange for fuel, lubricating oil and spare parts (which are often smuggled in, attracting very high black market premiums); uncompetitive environment in the trucking sector; lack of responsibility of African drivers for the different aspects of vehicle running and maintenance.

Unfortunately, some of the problems that impede the effective use of motorized vehicles in SSA also exist for non-motorized vehicles. Thus, only 3.5 per cent of Africa's inhabitants have been estimated to own bicycles compared to 16 per cent in Latin America and near 40 per cent in parts of Asia [Howe, 1993: 7]. One important reason accounting for the comparatively low incidence of bicycle ownership in SSA is that bicycles are not produced locally (an attempt to undertake mass production of bicycles in Nigeria failed) and that imports of bicycles and spare parts have been taxed and surcharged as though they were luxury goods, while agricultural implements have usually been free of such charges. Not uncommonly, the price of bicycles to the purchaser has been several hundred per cent above its landed value at the port of entry [Howe, 1993: 6; 1994: 6].

Perhaps surprisingly, the same problems of maintenance and repair that exist with respect to more sophisticated vehicles also hamper effective use of bicycles in SSA: inadequate repair facilities, dearth of spare parts, or lack of purchasing power in the hands of owners.[7] These dysfunctionings are all the more damaging since bicycles or bicycle trailers, as the Asian experience amply testifies, can significantly increase load-carrying capacity over head, shoulder or back carrying, particularly in rural areas where much travel is for transporting goods.

## 2.3 PHYSICAL ISOLATION AND MARKET UNDERDEVELOPMENT

### *The case of product markets*

High transports costs in SSA, whether due to underdeveloped and ill-maintained communication links, to high cost and unreliability of transport services, or just simply to long distances to travel, get automatically reflected in wide differentials between prices paid by final consumers and those received by primary producers. They moreover result in wide spatial gaps in prices as well as in high price volatility in local markets.

A comparative study of price spreads between Africa and Asia (Kenya, Tanzania, Malawi, Nigeria, and the Sudan for Africa; India, Bangladesh, Indonesia and the Philippines for Asia) has thus shown that African farmers receive a much smaller proportion of the price

Table 2.4: Shares of causal factors in different foodgrain marketing margins between African and Asian countries (Kenya, Malawi, Bangladesh, and Indonesia)

| Explanatory factors | Absolute margin (points) | | | Shares of the factors in the difference (per cent) |
|---|---|---|---|---|
| | Africa | Asia | Difference | |
| Taxes | 3.9 | 0.6 | 3.3 | 9.4% |
| Transport and associated costs | 27.5 | 13.8 | 13.7 | 39.1 |
| Profit | 12.6 | 4.0 | 8.6 | 24.5 |
| Transaction costs (residuals) | 11.0 | 1.6 | 9.4 | 27.0 |
| Total margin | 55.0 | 20.0 | 35.0 | 100.0% |

Source Ahmed and Rustagi, 1984: 114.

paid by final consumers of foodgrains than do Asian farmers. More precizely, the average producer price, expressed as a percentage of the terminal market price, ranges from 75 to 90 per cent in the Asian countries while for African countries the range is only 30–60 per cent [Ahmed and Rustagi, 1984: 115]. The result of the decomposition analysis of marketing margins undertaken by Raisuddin Ahmed and Narendra Rustagin is shown in Table 2.4. Revealingly, differences in transport and associated costs (the absolute transport cost in marketing is about twice as high in Africa as it is in Asia) constitute the largest cause of the different marketing margins between Africa and Asia, accounting for almost 40 per cent of these differentials. Also worth emphasizing is the fact that the import content of marketing costs in Kenya and Tanzania has been found to be about 50 per cent compared with only 17 per cent in Indonesia and Bangladesh [*ibidem*: 112], a huge difference that has much to do with the comparatively sophisticated modes of transport employed in the former region.

In Tanzania, a study about trade in agricultural products conducted in early 1990 reveals that in five of the seven markets surveyed transportation costs alone were higher than the farmgate purchase price of maize. Moreover, transport from the more distant markets exceeded 60 per cent of total marketing costs borne by the traders in Dar es Salaam (covering purchase prices and costs of transport, loading and unloading expenses, market fees, bribes and storage), whereas the proportion still amounted to 25–50 per cent when the produce was purchased from the nearer markets. Prices paid to producers in the more remote Southern Highlands were around half those paid to producers in the more central markets nearer the capital city [Santorum and Tibaijuka, 1992]. A direct implication of transport difficulties and other intermediation costs or bottlenecks is that markets are ill-integrated and it is therefore not surprising that regional price differences are significantly larger in SSA than in Asia [Ahmed and Rustagi, 1984: 114].

A striking illustration of considerable spatial price differentials due to transport problems in SSA is found in the Zambezia province, Mozambique [Stage, 1995]. Prices displayed in Table 2.5 below are consumer prices prevailing at the market places of three different localities situated along the Mocuba-Lugela Sede-Tacuane road in the Lugela district. While the road connecting Mocuba to Lugela Sede is of a good quality, that connecting Lugela to Tacuane has not been rehabilitated: it can however be passed with some difficulties as none of the bridges have been destroyed (by the war) and because it runs through a highland area, it is not flooded during the rainy season. Yet, despite the fact that the road is passable and that the physical distance between Lugela Sede and Tacuane (30 kilometer) is exactly half that separating Lugela Sede from Mocuba (60 hilometer), price differentials between the former two localities are considerably larger than those existing between the latter two localities.

Table 2.5: Spatial price differentials arising from transport problems, Zambezia province, Mozambique (1995)

| | Mocuba | Lugela Sede | Tacuane |
|---|---|---|---|
| Maize per 20 litre tin* | 15,000 Mt | 15,000 Mt | 7,000 Mt |
| Boer beans per 20 litre tin* | 20,000 Mt | 15,000 Mt | 8,000 Mt |
| Banana per unit | 143 Mt | 91 Mt | 33 Mt |
| Big rooster | 20,000 Mt | 15–16,000 Mt | 10–12,000 Mt |

Source Stage, 1995: 10.

* A 20 litre tin contains about 18 kg of maize (or boer beans).
Mt stands for the Metical.

When remoteness, underdeveloped infrastructure and inefficient transport services cause a doubling or tripling of the price of exportables at the African dockside (the f.o.b. price) relative to the farm gate prices and when a similar price rise occurs for importables between their delivery to an African port (the c.i.f. price) and the point of consumption, a large part of the domestic economy is actually insulated from the impact of foreign trade because of a high rate of natural protection [Delgado, 1992: 449, 456; 1996; Jaeger, 1992a: 1636; 1992b: 18]. Most African economies are thus in a semi-closed state: many major consumer items in SSA, particularly traditional starchy staples (millet, cassava, plantains, yams, etc.) which have low value to weight ratios, are non-tradeables on world markets and often even on regional markets. They are non-tradeables only because, at the point of production and consumption, their domestic equilibrium prices fall between widely divergent import and export parity prices for the goods in question. Even in a country like Senegal where the agricultural economy is relatively well developed by African standards, the presence of high transportation and other transaction costs prevents many households from engaging in trading their production.

In such conditions of semi-closed economies, household production and supply response decisions become inseparable from consumption choices and preferences with the result that effective prices are idiosyncratic to the household, reflecting its own internal supply-demand schedule. Strong inter-household variations in the shadow prices of various production factors and products make for rather complex and unpredictable effects which render the assessment of policy impact difficult [Singh et al., 1986; Sadoulet and de Janvry, 1995: chap. 6; de Janvry et al., 1991; Collier and Gunning, 1999; Carter and Wiebe, 1990]. It is also easy to understand that in the same conditions shocks to either domestic supply or demand are not easily dampened by the world market. For instance, bad weather or other natural hazards (e.g., pest infestation) will lead to higher food prices relative to prices of agricultural exports. Given the importance of food in African household budgets, this will in turn lead to higher wage demands according to the Ricardian mechanism that links up labour supply prices with prices of basic foodstuffs. As a result of this exogenous determinant of 'equilibrium' real exchange rates, the competitiveness of African exports will fall [Delgado, 1992: 450–53, 466].

By preventing interregional price equalization, conditions of physical isolation such as they are prevailing in many African countries make them especially vulnerable to famines, as attested by the tragic experiences of Ethiopia and Sudan, for example [see, e.g., Kumar, 1990]. Indeed, to the extent that rainfall outcomes are imperfectly correlated across regions or districts, spatially covariate shocks within one locale are not diluted by opposing movements in other locales. The less integrated the markets the higher price volatility, since price changes cannot be buffered by other markets. In other words, in segmented and isolated markets (generally found in the inland rather than in the coastal areas), little arbitrage takes place and, therefore, seasonality in prices remains high, and inter-year price variability is primarily driven by domestic production levels and local storage [see Dercon, 1995; Badiane and Shively, 1998, for evidence on Tanzania and Ghana, respectively]. To minimize the occurrence of subsistence crises in these conditions of strong market segmentation, farmers tend to excessively focus on food cultivation and subsistence activities at the expense of cash crop production [Fafchamps, 1992]. Furthermore, the fact that shocks are temporally covariate within small areas force farmers to engage in costly strategies of self-insurance, through food storing, diversification of cultivation plots, often separated from each other by long distances, and the choice of relatively reliable crops which reduce the yield variance at the cost of also reducing the expected average income.

It must also be stressed that, in so far as trading takes place, it is likely to be highly non-competitive. For instance, in Madagascar, the probability for a rice farmer living in a rural community to be serviced by more than one buyer increases ninefold, from 6.1 to 54.6 per cent, as one moves from the coastal zones into the Central Highlands where population densities are comparatively high and the infrastructure is relatively well developed [Bernier and Dorosh, 1994—quoted from Barrett and Carter, 1999].

For another thing, since in many African countries the major urban center is also the major sea port, for a substantial fraction of urban consumers the transport costs for imported foods via ocean freight are likely to be considerably lower than the transport costs of domestic foods which are shipped by truck often on poor quality roads [Jaeger, 1992a: 1638]. Therefore, to the extent that urbanization involves migrants who move their residence closer to the source of food imports and farther away from the domestic food-producing region, and provided that imported grains (wheat and rice) are reasonably good substitutes for domestically-produced foodstuffs, rural-urban migration will cause food imports to rise.[8] Per capita domestic production of food will concomitantly decline (aggregate output may still rise due to population growth), a trend that is likely to be reinforced by important preference shifts towards imported foods associated with the urban way of life.

Still another important implication of the existence of high transport and communication costs is the following: inasmuch as large segments of rural economies in SSA consist of non-tradeables—more than half of the 1979–81 total calorie supply of a subset of 28 African countries came from nationally non-traded foods and there is good ground to believe that this estimate represents an upper bound on the tradeability of foodstuffs in Africa [Barrett and Carter, 1999]—a significant share of rural primary resources such as labour and land may remain underexploited. This is true even if policy reform programs are adopted that remove major macroeconomic barriers to trade, such as overvalued currencies and parastatal marketing monopolies. In other words, owing to high transfer costs and considerable segmentation of the economic space, a large part of the rural economy may be demand-constrained: 'Very large shares of household income in rural areas derive from, and very large shares of consumption are devoted to, items that are non-tradeables of the semi-closed economy, such as services, bulky traditional starchy foodstuffs, perishables, and locally processed foods. This means that many people in rural areas can remain underemployed for long periods of time if effective local demand for what they can produce does not rise' [Delgado, 1992: 453; 1996: 8, 15].[9]

Finally, since access to land-use rights is typically easy when population is sparse in relation to land resources, since technology is simple and hired labour is more costly than family labour because of various incentive problems, all households cultivate family plots individually assigned to them by the local community and there is practically no hiring or exchanging of labour among resident farmers during the peak labour season. Together, self-cultivation and geographic isolation imply that, on average, everyone is self-sufficient in food. Moreover, once an output level that sufficiently provides for current household consumption and household storage demand is reached, marginal utility of effort is very low [Binswanger and McIntire, 1987: 76–78].

### *The case of factor markets*

That sparse populations and deficient communication facilities cause rural factor markets to be ill-integrated, highly imperfect, or altogether missing is an essential facet of African rural realities that has drawn the attention of several economists [Collier, 1983; Binswanger and McIntire, 1987; Rosenzweig et al., 1988; Kevane, 1996; Dercon and Krishnan, 1996; Platteau, 1995a, 1996a, 1996b]. The fact has already been mentioned that rural labour markets are generally thin in areas where access to land is easy and technology is simple. In the stylized world of land-abundant economies described by Hans Binswanger, John McIntire and Mark Rosenzweig, it may now be added, a rural credit market cannot develop due to both demand and supply constraints. Demand for credit is low because technology is simple and hiring of labour is rare and supply is hard to come by owing to the absence of good collaterals (land has no sales value).

Moreover, the restricted scope of the output markets makes it impossible to use marketing-credit links as a collateral substitute and, similarly, limitations of the labour market impede the emergence of labour-credit interlinkages towards the same purpose. Also, the constraints on credit supply and demand in land-abundant environments imply that the amounts of loans are small and that consumption is the main purpose for which villagers borrow, with the consequence that loan maturities are short. Finally, the seasonality of demand for credit and the covariance of risks in the localized settings of isolated, small communities imply the absence of financial intermediation (lenders lend out of equity).

In the aforedescribed world, credit is thus not supplied but it is not needed either, so that the absence of a credit market does not raise serious problems. Such is obviously not the case when technical progress becomes possible and necessitates the purchase of new equipments, modern material agricultural inputs and, possibly, the hiring of wage labourers. Under these new circumstances, and considering that villagers are willing to improve their way of living, spatial isolation arising from low population density and high transport costs is responsible for credit market imperfections that are clearly a hindrance to rural economic development.

Just consider the case of isolated and lightly settled areas along the Niger or the Senegal rivers (such as those around Gao and Timbuktu in Mali, or around Matam and Podor in Senegal) which are suitable for irrigated agriculture. Here, tubewells and other mechanical pumping devices are essential for securing control of water and their acquisition requires external financing. Such financing is not likely to be forthcoming because distances between lending agents and farmers make for high administrative costs (whether they arise from loan application, supervision of loan utilization, collection of interests or recovery of loan principal) and seriously aggravate informational asymmetries that are at the root of well-known incentive problems (whether of the moral hazard or adverse selection kinds).[10] As a result, the interest rate that lenders would have to charge in order to make their lending business viable will be so high as to discourage any demand for loans. For the same reasons, collection of bank deposits will prove extremely difficult and depositing money with financial intermediaries will not be attractive to rural households.

In Madagascar, to take another example, it has been estimated that only 2 per cent of rural farm and non-farm enterprises obtain formal credit while informal credit appears to be chiefly short-term, for consumption or seasonal operating expenses [quoted from Barrett and Carter, forthcoming: 21]. Credit constraints also affect traders and limit their operations. Thus, in Tanzania, over 80 per cent of maize traders have no access to credit at all, which prevents them from investing in transportation, storage or processing equipment [Santorum and Tibaijuka, 1992].

In the same conditions of physical isolation, all sorts of rural factor markets, particularly those for the distribution of agricultural inputs (chemical fertilizers, new seed varieties, etc.) and capital goods as well as for the provision of agricultural services, are likely to be missing or highly imperfect. For example, when population is scattered, per unit costs of servicing mechanical equipment (e.g. tractors and tubewells) are inevitably high. Given roughly five to six times higher rural population density per arable hectare in the Punjab than in the arable Sahel, a service center with a given radius of activity would require five to six times as many adoptors per square kilometer in the latter case to be economically viable [Delgado and Ranade, 1987: 134] or, alternatively, it would need to extend its customer area much further away from the place of its location. Due to long distances between customers, the market for mechanical servicing may therefore fail to emerge or, alternatively, natural monopolies may get established with the consequence that farmers are being charged excessively high prices [Platteau, 1995a: 481].[11]

Some of the above-described effects are actually self-reinforcing, giving rise to genuine vicious circles. This is particularly evident in the case of credit market imperfections since they are both the result and the source of high transaction costs. The latter effect arises because, when they are deprived of access to credit, traders or middlemen are unable to effectively link up distant places by using appropriate methods for the transportation, storing and processing of agricultural goods. As a consequence, transaction costs remain high and agricultural marketing channels stay ill-developed and subject to a low degree of competition. Figure 2.1 below summarizes the direct and indirect effects of low population density, including the feedback loop caused by credit market imperfections.

A last remark is in order. As is evident from a number of opinion surveys, African farmers well perceive the lack of good communications as a major obstacle to agricultural development. Thus, in a study aimed at investigating the villagers' subjective valuations of services provided by the state in two different provinces of Kenya (Central and Nyanza), 'road improvements were cited overwhelmingly most frequently as the most useful of government's past services' [Bevan et al., 1989: 236]. In Tanzania, the same study however found that the significance attached to road improvements was greatly reduced compared with Kenya. The authors explain this finding by the fact that Tanzanian peasants are far less integrated into the national economy in a double sense: on the one hand, they are less dependent on good transport facilities to get their produce to market and, on the other hand, they are confronted with serious availability problems which imply a reduced priority on such facilities to bring in inputs and consumer goods [*ibidem*: 241]. To shift from East to West Africa, in

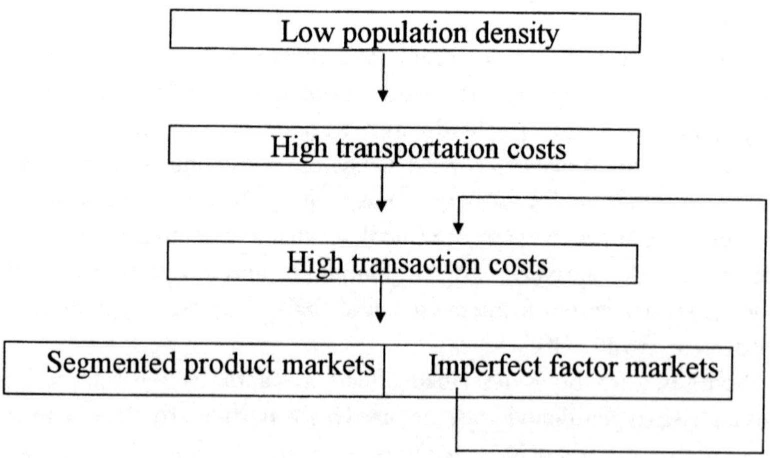


Figure 2.1: The effects of low population density on market development

Ghana and Côte d'Ivoire, the most highly rated priority of villagers consists of rural roads followed by educational needs, health and water supplies [Crook and Manor, 1994: xiii]. Finally, in a review of a World Bank-funded agricultural development project in Nigeria, farmers have been reported as saying that what really encouraged them to produce more was the construction of a road from their village to the market [World Bank, 1990: 270].

### 2.4 PHYSICAL ISOLATION AND CONSTRAINTS ON THE SUPPLY OF PUBLIC GOODS

Underdevelopment of transportation infrastructure does not only hinder the emergence of well-functioning product and input markets that are required by agricultural intensification, it also causes the undersupply of public goods and services in support of agriculture and rural life. The case of information and extension services is especially worth mentioning in this context since it conditions the diffusion of new agricultural techniques. Regarding such services, there are two points that deserve to be added to previous considerations.

First, the cost of providing them is very high not only because African populations are widely dispersed and usually hard to reach, but also because the physical environment for agriculture (and cattle-rearing) in SSA is marked by an exceptional diversity of agroclimatic and soil characteristics, of farming systems and socio-economic conditions [Berry, 1984: 60; Johnston, 1986: 159; FAO, 1986: Annex II, chap. 3; Platteau, 1995a: 319]. These very diverse ecological and socio-economic conditions are found even within individual countries and within small regions or subregions. Standard technical packages have therefore no chance to succeed. Needed are location-specific technical advicing and highly differentiated strategies of soil management and land development that can be successfully implemented only if information is collected, experimentation is undertaken, and diffusion efforts are applied at very decentralized levels.

Second, the fact that agricultural extension is publicly provided and may be heavily subsidized by the state does not eliminate the problems that arise from population dispersal. This is because extension workers are generally reluctant to live in faraway places to and from which they cannot easily move. Moreover, high-level technicians or professionals try their best to evade long and difficult journeys to distant villages. In point of fact, assignment to work in remote rural areas is typically considered as a curse from which one always hopes to escape as soon as possible. Two consequences follow from such a situation: on the one hand, motivation of agricultural experts, extension agents, and local administrative staff tends to be extremely low and, on the other hand, their mobility is often high, thus causing a lot of disruption and frustration among the target rural population.

The same diagnosis actually applies to the provision of education, health and other public goods (such as electricity, drinkable water, sanitation facilities, and family planning services) that are called to play an important role in enhancing the productivity and raising the welfare level of rural people. Thus, for example, the proportion of villages supplied with electricity is very small in SSA and, in many countries, only 3–5 per cent of villages have any electrification. In contrast, in many Asian countries at least 50 per cent of the villages are electrified and, in the most advanced regions (such as the Indian Punjab), electricity is available in every village [Sims, 1988; Ahmed and Donovan, 1992: 5–6]. This is a serious handicap for Africa in so far as lack of electricity constitutes a major impediment not only to use of electricity-powered irrigation facilities but also to development of rural-based industries. For example, in Kenya, Nigeria, Tanzania, and many other African countries most grain milling facilities are located in urban areas. As a result, transport costs for grains are high and the flow of grains from rural to urban areas tends to be erratic, which causes rural and urban prices to be erratic as well. The opposite is true when small-scale milling takes place in rural areas because of rural electrification, such as is observed in India, Bangladesh, Indonesia, and many other Asian countries [Ahmed and Rustagi, 1984: 113].

In another respect, there is substantial evidence that the effectiveness of family planning programmes in many Asian countries must be attributed to the fact that (1) there is a high density of local health services in rural areas and among the urban poor, and that (2) trained health and family planning workers are able to visit households regularly [Caldwell, 1991: 244].

Add to the above shortcomings the fact that, other things being equal, deficient provision of basic public amenities, health and education facilities prompts the younger generations to seek better living conditions in cities even when these are located at considerable distance from their native place. As a result, populations in remote areas tend to diminish, thus causing the per capita cost of providing infrastructure to rise even further. Thus, a vicious circle operates between rural depopulation and under-investment in rural infrastructure [Platteau, 1995a: 479–80; 1996a: 208–9]. Admittedly, this perverse logic can be somewhat mitigated by the aforementioned ineffectiveness of family planning efforts—which, incidentally, can also be traced to complex cultural factors that seem to be characteristic of tribal societies [see Caldwell and Caldwell, 1987, 1990]—as well as by the slow dissemination of values biased towards city life due to shortage of education facilities. Indeed, while in the former case natural population increase in remote areas may be expected to be higher than it would be otherwise, in the latter case outmigration may be less important.

There is another effect of population dispersal that deserves to be brought into light in the context of the present discussion. As a matter of fact, it is not only the cost of providing essential public goods to people that is very high in sparsely settled areas, but also the per capita administrative cost of collecting tax proceeds to finance the related expenses. In this regard, again, sparsely populated Africa is greatly handicapped relative to most Asian countries characterized by much higher population densities. The densely-populated, stably-settled farm population of Asia had traditionally been the convenient basis for rulers to expropriate tax. Since peasants had been the major bearer of the tax burden, a kind of agricultural fundamentalism had developed to regard peasants as the foundation of society. According to this ideology, it is legitimate for a ruler to tax away surplus above peasants' subsistence but he must fulfill the responsibility to maintain their sustenance by providing infrastructure such as flood control, major irrigation and drainage systems [Wittfogel, 1957]. This tradition seems to underlie the Asian development strategy of providing key public goods for agricultural development while taxing farmers for the sake of industrial development [Platteau and Hayami, 1997; Hayami, 1997: chap. 3].

In SSA as in other thinly populated areas, on the contrary, people with their farm in the bush have historically been able to escape attempts by central rulers to impose tributes, tax or labour burdens on them [Hyden, 1983; Mathur, 1991; Binswanger et al., 1995]. It is mainly when the central authority was able to forge narrow ties with local chiefs that it could effectively succeed in extracting surpluses from the commoners. In these instances (such as happened, for example, with the Indirect Rule in many African colonies), indeed, these chiefs became largely unaccountable to their traditional rural constituencies and had therefore few scruples about taxing their subjects, not infrequently in a ruthless and arbitrary manner [see, e.g., Bayart, 1989; Firmin-Sellers, 1996]. To a large extent, the present rulers of Africa are still confronted with this problem today (see also Chapter 7). Taxes are not easily collected from rural communities whether in a direct or indirect form. Thus, when African states imposed low prices for agricultural exports during the sixties and seventies, farmers could often circumvent the implicit taxes thus imposed by smuggling their goods across the border or by retreating into the subsistence economy. Moreover, local-level officials know that customary authorities still wield considerable power and that no fiscal measure imposed from above can be satisfactorily implemented if it has not been previously negotiated with, and somewhat agreed upon, by these traditional authorities presumably acting on behalf of their respective communities.

Finally, by making communication difficult, population dispersal tends to discourage collective action. In particular, it impairs the farmers' ability to organize with a view to lobbying the state for an adequate provision of local public goods. This effect is compounded by the fact that when population densities are low educational services are under-provided (see *supra*), thereby further complicating the task of initiating and organizing pressure groups [see, e.g., Binswanger and Deininger, 1997: 1975–76]. Owing to this comparative disadvantage in bargaining capacity *via-à-vis* the state, whichever public resources are available are likely to be preferentially assigned to non-agricultural sectors, ot to particular, privileged groups within the rural sector (see infra, Chapter 7).

By negatively affecting the ability of agricultural (small) producers to influence policy-making in a direction well-suited to their interests, population dispersal therefore tends to indirectly discourage agricultural growth. For reasons explained above, this link between population density and adverse economic policies is likely to manifest itself more through underprovision of public goods in rural areas than through the celebrated price effects.

## 2.5 THE COMPLICATING PRESENCE OF TECHNOLOGY CONSTRAINTS

A direct implication of the discussion in Section 2.3 is the following: when population density rises the obstacles born of spatial isolation will be mitigated as product and factor rural markets gradually develop to allow various kinds of socially beneficial trading among increasingly specialized agents. Thus, economies of scale for providing infrastructure in more densely settled areas and the concomitant increase in intraregional trade reduce the average cost of infrastructure and permit more specialization in production activities. This reduction of the cost of infrastructural investments helps diffuse covariant risk since it costs less to trade with other nearby areas in bad years. Also, the emergence of output markets prevents marginal utility of effort from declining as fast as under conditions of physical isolation. Credit markets are likely to emerge through both demand and supply effects. On the one hand, demand for credit increases since there are expanding market opportunities both in agricultural and non-agricultural production, technology becomes more complex and the need for working capital is growing (partly because hiring labor becomes increasingly widespread). On the other hand, supply constraints tend to vanish or at least to be reduced because land acquires a sales value and may therefore become an acceptable collateral for willing lenders and because transaction costs diminish concomitantly with the rising density of customers [Boserup, 1965, 1981; Binswanger and McIntire, 1987: 86–90; Rosenzweig et al., 1988: 93–99; Platteau, 1996c].

From an aforementioned survey of fourteen case studies, Steven Wiggins has recently concluded that the Boserupean model of population-induced agricultural intensification is a correct representation of the evolving realities in the African countryside: population growth, the reduction in transport costs and the expansion of markets lead to intensified farming involving such innovations as the introduction of new crops and new varieties of known crops, animal traction, chemical fertilizers, and land improvements (terrace, drainage, fencing, tree planting,...). Moreover, once population density reaches a moderate level, cash crops grown almost exclusively for the market become significant and it is striking that most of these crops are marketed to meet domestic demand [Wiggins, 1995: 830–34]. Other studies have pointed to a similar conclusion as well [Pingali, Bigot, and Binswanger, 1987; Tiffen et al., 1994; Tiffen and Mortimore, 1994].

In the context of this chapter, it bears emphasis that in most of the case studies reviewed by Wiggins, there were significant improvements to roads linking the areas to national and provincial centres of demand. According to the author, 'not only did better roads make marketing traditionally grown products more attractive, but also in some cases farmers seized the chance to market new crops demanded by the towns' [Wiggins, 1995: 831]. In Uganda, likewize, we are told that the presence of roads adjacent to land parcels is strongly correlated with all agricultural investments, especially manuring and terracing [Roth et al., 1994: 195].

The above picture of an unfolding Boserupean sequence based on the efficient working of induced (technical and institutional) innovation mechanisms [see Hayami and Ruttan, 1985] appears far too optimistic, however. This is mainly because it underestimates the power of complex constraining forces, particularly those operating on the technological plane. There are indeed many instances where population density has increased and access to markets has improved and, in spite of those changes, intensification has proceeded at a very slow pace relative to population growth [Smith et al., 1994: 540–41]. The case of Rwanda (but also those of neighbouring Burundi, the Kivu province in Congo, Malawi, and the southwestern part of Benin) is an almost perfect illustration of this distressing possibility: there, population pressure has reached extremely high levels without giving rise to major technical progress susceptible of providing a decent livelihood to the growing number of people living on the land [Andre and Platteau, 1998; World Bank, 1991]. Probably as a result of this lack of profitable investment opportunities, demand for available credit is extremely low.[12] In the Sudanian climatic zone of Burkina Faso (corresponding roughly to the Central or Mossi Plateau), to take another example, high population densities go hand in hand with a series of converging signs of severe agricultural crisis: 'minimal use of purchased inputs, decreased ability of the fallow rotation systems to restore soil fertility due to either the disappearance or reduction of fallow time, decreasing cereal yields, decline and reduced quality of grazing in the communal lands, and decreases in cattle stocks' [Sanders et al., 1990: 6; see also De Haan, 1995, for North Benin]. In Zambia, 'declining productivity measured by falling yields per hectare over time provides a weak indication that soil mining is occurring, and/or that addition of soil supplements and technology growth are not sufficient to offset the natural decline in soil fertility arising from cultivation' [Roth et al., 1994c: 13].

In the whole of the humid and subhumid tropics of Africa, we are told that 'there has been virtually no small farmer adoption of improved soil and crop management technologies recommended by research and extension systems' [Spencer, 1994: 16–17]. Failure of the new seed varieties to yield substantially more than traditional varieties is an important factor behind the reluctance of African farmers to adopt the new varieties. In the Sahel, likewise, the transfer of hybrid sorghum and millet varieties from semi-arid India has failed due to unforeseen problems with dizease, striga weeds and quelea (weaver) birds, variability of rainfall and poor soils [Eicher, 1984: 464; Delgado and Mellor, 1984: 666; Lipton, 1985: 78; FAO, 1986: Main Report, chap. 2; Spencer, 1986: 224].

The fact of the matter is that in SSA the development of prototype high-yielding varieties (or of other prototypes of genetic material) is bound to be especially difficult because many of the cereals (sorghum and millet), many root and tuber crops (cassava, yams, sweet potatoes, banana-plantain) traditionally grown and consumed there are not consumed in the temperate regions. Consequently, the backlog of scientific and technical knowledge accumulated in these regions is of no much use for the African countries. This situation contrasts sharply with that obtaining in Asia and Latin America which could largely benefit from past international accomplishments in modern biogenetic research thanks to the important role of maize, rice and wheat in the local diets and the physical suitability of large chunks of land to these crops [Hayami and Ruttan, 1985: 270, 279]. It is revealing that the areas of SSA which have made most progress in the adoption of modern varieties of foodcrops are those with soils and climate suited for maize cultivation (in East and Southern Africa) and, to a lesser extent, rice (e.g., in Burkina Faso). To these successful cases must be added the technical breakthroughs accomplished in export crops (e.g., cotton, oil palm) as a result of long-sustained adaptive research and experimentation carried out in local institutional networks dating back to the colonial period [Platteau, 1995a: 496–97; Sanders et al., 1990: 17].

A particularly interesting case is that of Nigeria where serious amounts of adaptive research have led to the discovery of hybrid varieties of maize well-adapted to a West African agroclimatic region. The Northern Guinea Savanna (located in northern Nigeria) is a densely settled area which, during the last decades, has seen a rapid expansion of its road system (road mileage within the northern states of the country increased more than fivefold between 1967 and 1980 while feeder roads were simultaneously improved) concomitantly with a major technological breakthrough spurred by the rise of maize as a significant cash and food crop between the mid-1970s and the late 1980s. Over this period, traditional local varieties of maize almost completely disappeared to give way to modern cultivars; (inorganic) fertilizer use increased dramatically; animal traction was widely adopted (for land preparation and weeding); and labour hiring became widespread. It bears emphasis that in this area the state has also been effective in providing support services to farmers in the form of supply centers established through the Agricultural Development Projects [Smith et al., 1994; Goldman and Smith, 1995: 249–57].

In contrast, there are areas in the Northern Guinea Savanna of Ghana which are ecologically highly suited to maize production but where the extremely poor road system prevents maize 'from acting as a catalyst to intensification'. In the other way round, population and road densities are higher in the forest zone of southern Nigeria than in the Northern Guinea Savanna. Yet traditional cultural practices remain predominant despite rapidly declining fallow periods. This is because in this area there is no technological breakthrough in a crop in which the ecosystem has a natural advantage [Smith et al., 1994: 550].

The experience of the Northern Guinea Savanna closely resembles the earlier story told by Mary Tiffen (1976) regarding the situation in Gombe Emirate (North Eastern State, Nigeria), where a wave of agricultural transformation occurred around the rapid expansion of cotton production during the 1950s and 1960s and, in some areas with suitable conditions, around that of rice production. Development of new roads and railway connections greatly facilitated this mini-revolution based on the introduction of new high-yielding cultivars soon followed by increased use of oxplows and chemical fertilizers. The northern portions of the emirate have benefited less because they are more remote from main roads and markets and because they have poorer soils and lower population densities.[13]

An important handicap that slows down technological change in SSA is that investment requirements for developing high-yielding varieties suitable to local environments are much larger in this region than in Asia. Compared with lowlands in Asia, when the green revolution was successfully launched, Africa is characterized by much greater heterogeneity in environmental conditions. Ecology is lowland Asia, especially in irrigated paddy fields, is relatively uniform, because submerged water tends to neutralize variations in soil and many other environmental factors. Consequently, a single rice variety, such as IR 36, could successfully be planted with a similar input package in a very wide area [Otsuka and Delgado, 1995: 371]. Given this environmental homogeneity, national and international efforts could be concentrated on the development of a single technology-input package for wide diffusion. In addition, because the environmental conditions of irrigated paddy fields in tropical Asia are not so greatly different from those of sub-tropical and temperate areas in Asia, modern rice technology accumulated in the latter could be transferred to the former with modest adaptive research. This is more or less the case for the high-yielding varieties of wheat also, which diffused mainly in the irrigated areas of the Indian Subcontinent.

This favourable setup is totally lacking in SSA. Growing conditions for upland crops, both annual and perennial, are very heterogeneous. In the absence of any environmental controller comparable to irrigation water, effective farming systems in dry lands widely diverge for different conditions of soil, rainfall, elevation and slope. No single technology-input package can be applicable to a wide area (see *supra*). Inevitably, the requirement of research investment per unit increment of food output is far larger in Africa than in Asia. The severe limitation of financial capacity and, more critically, the sheer shortage of human capital available for high-powered agricultural research make it impractical to develop suitable technologies for numerous areas with different environmental conditions such as they exist in SSA [Platteau and Hayami, 1999].

Clearly, the main conclusion to draw from the above gamut of experiences is the following: if a Green Revolution of the Asian type is to be one day replicated widely over the African continent, what are needed are significant efforts to build up (or rehabilitate) public infrastructure not only in road and irrigation but also in agricultural research systems highly tuned to the specific characteristics of much varied ecological setups. It thus deserves to be stressed again that the present challenge confronting SSA is all the more serious relative to Asia (and Europe in the past) as low population densities combine their inhibiting effects with the exceptional diversity of Africa's agro-climatic and soil characteristics reflected in highly variable farming systems.

## 2.6 LESSONS FROM THE DEBATE ON THE AGGREGATE SUPPLY RESPONSE

A typical feature of agriculture all over the world is that, while individual crops tend to respond strongly to price factors even in the short run, the short-term price elasticity of aggregate output is very low. This is obviously because the supply of the main factors of agricultural production—land, labour, and capital—is fixed in the short period, with only material variable inputs such as fertilizers being adjustable. In the long run, on the contrary, the response of all agriculture to improvements in the internal terms of trade is expected to be quite large since the constraints on the movements of critical production factors can then be released: more favourable terms of trade will slow down migration out of rural areas and perhaps even prompt reverse migration back to agriculture; moreover, they will increase investment in agriculture and cause land to be reallocated to agricultural uses which was previously put to some non-agricultural use or left idle. A variety of empirical studies actually confirm this expectation that long-term aggregate supply elasticities are quite large relative to disappointingly low short-term elasticities.

It is quite unfortunate that the evidence on SSA is scanty. Yet, a well-known study is that of Bond (1983), which shows low aggregate supply elasticities, both in the short and the long periods, for a sample of nine countries: the average estimated values over the period 1963–81 are 0.18 and 0.21, respectively for the short- and the long-run.[14] In other words, if the short-run supply elasticities for SSA are not lower than for other areas, the same cannot be said of the long-run supply elasticities. A cross-country study carried out by Binswanger and others (1987) also reached the conclusion that short-run supply elasticities for SSA are not statistically different from zero (the estimated elasticity value is only 0.06). As far as long-run elasticities are concerned, the important point has been made that it is not reliable to compute long-run elasticities from time-series data, when countries tend to stick to a given pricing regime for long periods of time with the consequence that the price data tend to reflect mainly short-term variations in price and not stable shifts from one pricing regime to another [Peterson, 1979].

The most theoretically satisfying approach to this difficult problem of estimating long-run price elasticities of aggregate agricultural supply is the general equilibrium approach. As a matter of fact, crucial phenomena on which the long-term aggregate supply response hinges—such as intersectoral labour movements and capital reallocation, adoption of new techniques, etc.—can only be captured in a dynamic general equilibrium framework where intersectoral resource flows in response to price changes can be explicitly modelled. Such an approach has been applied to Chile and Argentina, leading to the conclusion that, if the elasticity of aggregate supply is indeed low in the short-term, it rises quickly after a certain number of years have elapsed.[15] Moreover, compared to single-equation time-series regressions, dynamic general equilibrium models generate large supply responses and there are several reasons to believe that even these higher supply response estimates might be biased downwards [Schiff and Montenegro, 1993: 12–16].

The problem with the above approach is that it is very hard to apply, because it requires a considerable amount of data and the estimating procedure is extremely complex. This is why economists try to get around the difficulties associated with time-series data by undertaking much simpler cross-section studies. Thus, Peterson argued that using cross-section data to estimate long-run aggregate supply elasticities is justifiable on the grounds that different countries tend to pursue different pricing regimes for long periods of time so that their input and output levels have fully adjusted to these regimes [Peterson, 1979; see also Binswanger, 1990: Appendix]. However, as Chhibber has rightly pointed out, this cross-country technique is flawed because it implicitly assumes that the only reason why agricultural output levels differ among the various countries considered is the structure of price incentives (and, in the case of Peterson's study, the volume of research expenditures) [Chhibber, 1989: 60].

To overcome this objection, Chhibber has included a number of non-price variables into Peterson's supply function (estimated from a large sample of 53 countries), so as to measure the impact of some important constraints arising either from the absence or imperfection of markets (availability of credit, fertilizer, and water; transport and communications; geographical and ecological characteristics; etc.). All his experiments caused a significant decline in Peterson's price elasticity estimates, thereby demonstrating the critical importance of structural variables. Furthermore, if all structural differences across countries could be included into the analysis, the aggregate price elasticities of supply initially obtained by Peterson (all in the range of 1.27 to 1.66) would, in all likelihood, undergo a further decline [*ibidem*].

The significant role of non-price factors found in Chhibber's work has been actually confirmed in quite a number of other studies as well. Thus, in a cross-country Cobb-Douglas production function estimated from a combined sample of developed and developing countries and for a sample of developing agricultures alone, Antle (1983) shows that agricultural output is significantly influenced by both the country's research effort and infrastructure. The idea is that, while agricultural research expands the set of technologies from which farmers may choose, their ability to actually use them crucially depends on the country's stock of infrastructure capital and the resulting costs of infrastructural services. And since 'distance seems to be the most important dimension of the infrastructure problem', the effect of transportation and communication services is captured by measuring the amount of spending on these services relative to the country's total land area [Antle, 1983: 611].

Note that the transportation and communication infrastructure variable contributes significantly to the explanation of aggregate agricultural productivity both across the combined sample and the sample for developing countries alone. However, the infrastructure variable's coefficient is larger in the latter regression and the research variable's is smaller, suggesting that agricultural research explains less of the variation in agricultural production in the developing countries than the infrastructure variable [*ibidem*: 617]. Clearly, as pointed out by Chhibber, the omission of these non-price constraints from the estimating equation would lead to overestimation of aggregate supply elasticity with respect to price [Chhibber, 1989: 60].

A host of empirical studies of Asian agriculture also show that appropriate non-price shift variables need to be included in cross-country aggregate supply functions to represent research, irrigation and other infrastructure variables [see Chhibber, 1989: 61, for more details]. In addition, after reviewing two studies of output, fertilizer demand, and draft power investment, one using cross-country data and the other cross-district data from India [Binswanger, et al., 1987; Binswanger, Khandker, and Rosenzweig, 1993], Binswanger reaches the conclusion that 'econometrically, it is easier to show the effect of infrastructure, services, and human capital than it is to show price effects', which does not, however, imply that prices are unimportant [Binswanger, 1990: 244].[16] In this respect, it bears emphasis that the impact of roads on agricultural output is particularly strong. In these two studies, indeed, the density of roads has elasticities of 0.12 and 0.20 for aggregate output and strong effect on demand for fertilizer and tractors. In addition, road quality, as proxied by paving, has a powerful impact on aggregate output [*ibidem*: 247].

Also, irrigation and the stock of human capital (as measured by the adult literacy rate and life expectancy) turn out to have significant influence. Finally, using a Nerlovian model fitted to Indian data (over the period 1954–5 to 1977–8), Chhibber shows that without the inclusion of an irrigation variable (a proxy for non-price variables because of its importance in the use of high-yielding varieties) the aggregate long-run price elasticity of supply is greater than 2. However, when this infrastructure variable is included, the long-run price elasticity is only 0.30 whereas the elasticity of output with respect to irrigation is approximately equal to 1. The conclusion is that the aggregate supply elasticity is much smaller when (non-price) constraints on agricultural production are more binding and the role of publicly provided infrastructure and services is therefore greater [Chhibber, 1989: 65]. From his general review of the empirical literature on the subject, Chhibber draws the following, balanced conclusion:

> ...the long-run aggregate supply elasticity with respect to prices lies in the range 0.3–0.9. It is not greater than 1.0, as is sometimes claimed by those who ascribe primacy to price policy, or as low as zero, according to those who view price policy effects as insignificant. It is higher around 0.7–0.9 in the more advanced land-abundant developing countries. However, in poorer countries with inadequate infrastructure facilities its value is lower, around 0.3–0.5. The supply elasticity with respect to non-price factors is likely to be much higher; around 1.0 in countries with inadequate infrastructural facilities, imperfect markets, and lack of capital and private research organizations. In the more advanced developing countries where farmers do not face infrastructural constraints to the same degree as their counterparts in the more underdeveloped countries, the output effect of additional non-price factors is smaller [Chhibber, 1989: 56].

This conclusion allows us to infer that long-term elasticities of aggregate supply with respect to prices are likely to be low in SSA, a region which is poorly endowed in many infrastructural and other facilities or services. Chhibber has remarked that when such aggregate supply response is low, 'a policy of taxing agriculture through lower farm prices or through overvalued exchange rates and industrial protection policies will generate resources for investment in other sectors of the economy, without significantly affecting agricultural growth' [Chhibber, 1989: 55]. What must be added is that the above evidence about high non-price long-term supply elasticities in countries with inadequate infrastructural facilities, imperfect markets, and lack of capital and private research organizations can be used to advocate an alternative policy consisting of taxing farmers and investing the revenue thereby generated in the production of public goods (such as transport infrastructure and agricultural research systems) capable of increasing the marginal productivity of privately provided agricultural inputs.

The question is therefore to know (i) whether it is more socially efficient to invest state resources in non-agricultural sectors or in agriculture (the general equilibrium approach); and (ii) whether it is better to reduce explicit or implicit taxes on farmers with a view to enhancing their incentives to invest and expand production, or to tax them and devote the proceeds to creating public goods (e.g., rural roads) conducive to higher agricultural productivity (see the Appendix for a formal statement of this second problem). In point of fact, the two strategies available under (ii) can be brought down to the same formulation in price terms. This is because many non-price constraints on the responsiveness of agriculture can be actually expressed in such terms. Thus, for example, the lack or bad quality of roads and transport services lead to high transport costs which have the effect of reducing the farmgate price; or, the absence of extension services raises information costs and contributes to making new technologies prohibitively expensive to most farmers [Jaeger, 1992b: 40]. Clearly, whether it chooses to reduce taxation on agriculture or, say, to build up new roads (or rehabilitate existing ones), the government eventually produces the same effect, which is to raise farmgate prices or to correspondingly reduce production costs for the farmers [see Platteau, 1996a].[17] To what extent the government must follow either policy is a matter that has to be assessed under the peculiar conditions of each country. Needless to say, the optimum strategy will contain a mixture of the two policies.

## 2.7 CONCLUSION AND POLICY IMPLICATIONS

From the discussion in the preceding sections, it is evident that building and maintaining a good network of rural roads as well as developing highly differentiated agricultural research systems are public investments that should have high priority in African countries. This being said, the dilemma remains that if available budgetary resources are spread too thinly over a large number of regions, the impact of such investments is bound to be limited: roads will be of low quality, badly maintained, etc. The case can therefore be made for a concentration of government infrastructural investments and support services in favourable, high-potential areas with the expectation that generation of productive employment and income in high-potential areas will spill over to low-potential areas through migration and specialization according to comparative advantage. More precisely, the point can be made that an escape from the complex interactions of growth-inhibiting forces in which rural SSA has been trapped should be sought in the simultaneous promotion of export cash crops and mini-Green Revolutions in a limited number of food crops. Population growth arising from both natural increase and migratory movements from unfavourable areas will enable the favoured regions to cumulatively benefit from economies of scale in the provision of infrastructure and infrastructure-dependent services.

That such a strategy needs not aggravate interregional income disparities seems to be one of the lessons suggested by Green Revolution experiences in Asia. Indeed, a recent comprehensive study of such experiences by Cristina David and Keijiro Otsuka (1995) shows that the diffusion of modern varieties in ecologically favourable areas did not deteriorate the relative income position of residents in unfavourable areas. Surprisingly, the real labour wage rates in unfavourable areas kept up with increases in those of more favourable areas due to labour migration from the former to the latter as a response to growing labour demand created by the new rice technology. In addition, land use in unfavourable areas shifted from low-valued subsistence crops, such as upland rice and maize, to high-valued commercial crops, such as fruits and vegetables as well as livestock products for which demand increased as a result of higher incomes from rice production in favourable areas [Otsuka and Delgado, 1995: 373–74; Delgado, 1996].

Does there exist any strong reason to suspect that the Asian experience is not replicable in Africa? Schematically, favourable areas in SSA consist of two types: one is favourable in growing export cash crops and another is favourable in growing subsistence food crops, say maize or rice. In many cases, contrary to a widespread view, there is a high complementarity between these two sectors. In the 'semi-closed' economies of Africa with extremely high inland transportation costs from trade ports to rural hinterlands, a major development of the cash crop sector must rely on a concomitant expansion of the domestic food crop sector (rather than imports from abroad). If the food crop sector would fail to fulfill this role, the export crop sector would lose its international competitiveness to the extent that higher food prices cause nominal wage costs to rise relative to prices of agricultural exportables [Delgado, 1992: 450, 466; 1996: 7–8]. On the other hand, unless expansion in food output is matched by an increased demand stemming from the income growth of the cash crop sector, the price of food staples characterized by low demand elasticities may decline sharply enough to choke off incentives to increase food production. In African economies where high transfer costs apply to food imports or where shortage of foreign exchange prevents too rapid an increase of these imports, marketing policies that improve links between high-potential cash crop and food-producing areas are therefore the main vehicle to take advantage of this complementarity between the two areas or sectors [Otsuka and Delgado, 1995: 372–73].

A last point with important policy implications deserves to be made. If rural people respond to the construction of new communication links by spontaneously regrouping along them, the number of points to be accessed by the feeder road system will be smaller and transport costs will be concomitantly reduced. In reality, such movements do sometimes take place, yet perhaps not on anything like the expected scale. The question therefore arises as to whether a government would be well-advised to embark on deliberate policies aimed at prompting such population regroupings. In this respect, the experience of the villagization programme undertaken by the Tanzanian governement in the mid-1970s contains interesting lessons that suggest that gathering rural households into concentration points is not necessarily a blessing and may have ambiguous effects on the ease or difficulty of rural transport [Putterman, 1995: 318].

A direct negative consequence of villagization thus lies in the fact that 'many farmers continue to work land in the more fertile valleys sometimes located several kilometers from their current homes', with the result that there are 'added problems of transporting inputs to the fields and carrying crops back to the homestead'. Furthermore, villagization has accelerated the effects of population growth on the environment in ways that increase domestic transportation burdens. As a matter of fact, 'denser, more permanent settlements more quickly exhaust nearby fuelwood supplies, making the gathering and carrying of wood from more distant points more commonplace' [Putterman, 1995: 318]. The other side of the coin is that, through better proximity to schools and health centers, villagization has eased transportation problems since families reside within moderate distances from facilities located inside the villages themselves.

In the absence of more detailed and extensive evaluations of regrouping experiences such as that which took place in Tanzania and in the light of the aforementioned ambiguous effects in the case of this country, it is probably wise for governments to think carefully before coercing people into gathering along well-established communication links. A sensible approach would consist of letting the people concerned decide by themselves where to put up their residence, or to inform them of the possible advantages of residing near such links and, possibly, to provide material incentives with a view to encouraging them to move into concentration points.

## APPENDIX: OPTIMAL CHOICE OF AGRICULTURAL POLICY MIX

Let the aggregate production function of the agricultural sector be

$$Q = f(p, K_p, K_g), \tag{1}$$

where $Q$ is the aggregate agricultural output, $p$ the price paid to the agricultural producers, $K_p$ and $K_g$, respectively, the stock of private and public capital invested in the agricultural sector.

The budgetary constraint facing the government can be written

$$S = (p - p_w)Q + K_g p_g, \tag{2}$$

where $S$ stands for the externally generated budget which the government has decided to make available to the agricultural sector, $p_w$ is the world market price for the agricultural product—so that $(p - p_w)$ corresponds to the per unit subsidy granted by the government to agricultural producers if the difference is positive and to the per unit tax on the agricultural product if the difference is negative—, and $p_g$ is the unitary cost of public capital (e.g., the cost of one kilometer of rural road). In the particular case where $p < p_w$ (a likely circumstance if the government is not able to generate much revenue from the non-agricultural sectors), the amount of total budgetary resources available to agriculture is increased by $(p - p_w)\ Q$.

Assuming that the government wants to maximize the present value of the future agricultural product flows and to fix the values of its two decision variables once-for-all, that $r$ stands for the discount rate of future incomes and, for the sake of expository convenience, that the public capital has an infinite duration of life, the problem reduces to that of maximizing the following Lagrangian with respect to $p$ and $K_g$:

$$Max\, L = \int_0^{\infty} e^{-rt} f(p, K_p, K_g) - \lambda[(p - p_w) f(p, K_p, K_g) + p_g K_g - S] \tag{3}$$

The two first-order conditions are

$$\frac{\partial L}{\partial p} = \int_0^\infty e^{-rt} f'_p - \lambda[Q + (p - p_w)f'_p] = 0$$

$$\frac{\partial L}{\partial K_g}, = \int_0^\infty e^{-rt} f'_{K_g} - \lambda[P_g + (p - p_w)f'_{K_g}] = 0$$

given that $f'_p$ and $f'_{Kg}$ stand, respectively, for the partial derivatives of $Q$ with respect to $p$ and $K_g$. Note that if, say, the government chooses to expand the rural road network ($K_g$ rises)—see the second FOC above—, since $Q$ increases as a result, a partial effect (assuming a constant differential between $p$ and $p_w$) determines the accrual of more tax proceeds to the government in the case where $p \leq p_w$.

Solving the integrals, we can write these two expressions as follows:

$$\frac{1}{r} f'_p = \lambda$$

The equilibrium condition is then straightforward:

$$\frac{f'_p}{f'_{K_g}} = \frac{Q + (p - p_w)f'_p}{p_g + (p - p_w)f'_{K_g}} \tag{4}$$

The model can be made more realistic by considering that private capital investment in agriculture responds positively to both a price increase and an expansion of public capital. In other words,

$K_p = v(p, K_g)$, so that the maximization problem now becomes:

$$Max\, L = \int_0^\infty e^{-rt} f[p, v(p, K_g), K_g] - \lambda[(p - p_w)Q + p_g\, K_g - S], \tag{5}$$

where $K_p$ has been endogenized.

The FOC of this problem are:

$$\frac{\partial L}{\partial p} = \int_0^\infty e^{-rt} (f'_p + f'_{K_P} \cdot v'_p) - \lambda[Q + (p - p_w)(f'_p + f'_{K_P} \cdot v'_p)] = 0$$

$$\frac{\partial L}{\partial K_g} = \int_0^\infty e^{-rt} (f'_{K_g} + f'_{K_P} \cdot v'_{K_g}) - \lambda[p_g + (p - p_w)(f'_{K_g} + f'_{K_P} \cdot v'_{K_g})] = 0$$

The equilibrium condition which can be derived from these two expressions is obviously more cumbersome than that obtained under the simplified model:

$$\frac{f'_p + f'_{K_p} \cdot v'_p}{[Q + (p - p_w)(f'_p + f'_{K_p} \cdot v'_p)]} = \frac{f'_{K_g} + f'_{K_p} \cdot v'_{K_g}}{[p_g + (p - p_w)(f'_{K_g} + f'_{K_p} \cdot v'_{K_g})]} \tag{6}$$

## NOTES

1. If many African countries can thus purchase far more food than their export sector can afford, it is because the external account gap is covered primarily through financial or food assistance, remittances, and other, more or less reliable, sources of external income or debt alleviation measures [FAO, 1995: 54].
2. Thus, for William Jaeger (1992a), quickly rising food imports do not seem to be a cause of concern because they are essentially the result of preference shifts associated with rapid urbanization. Yet, one has to ask whether high urbanization rates are the result of distortionary policies that discriminate against the rural sector or of more structural tendencies that are not easily changed through policy measures. The answer provided by Jaeger to this last question clearly points towards the first possibility [Jaeger, 1992a: 1640–42] whereas it will be argued here that the second possibility is impossible to ignore. Moreover, Jaeger leaves unanswered the critical question of whether a highly and increasingly import-intensive pattern of food consumption is sustainable and whether it is susceptible of undermining development prospects in SSA. The question is all the more deserving notice as recent trends suggest increasing difficulties for SSA in maintaining its traditional net exporter status in agricultural trade. As a matter of fact, despite the persistently strong agricultural component of its external trade, SSA's share in world agricultural markets has tended to decline since the early 1970s. This is in contrast to the situation of Asia which has been most successful in diversifying its export base away from agriculture and has nevertheless gained share in world agricultural exports since the mid-1970s [FAO, 1995: 210–14].

   Unsustainability of high food imports may result from the fact that heavy food import bills are likely to lead to a shortage of incentive goods if manufactured consumer goods can no more be imported or produced domestically owing to lack of imported intermediate or capital goods. That such a shortage may significantly slow down agricultural growth and thereby give rise to a vicious circle through cumulatively rising dependence on food imports is evident from direct observation of the experience of several African countries (such as Tanzania, Guinea, Guinea-Bissau, and Mozambique) and from a few systematic studies on the subject. Thus, for example, it has been shown econometrically that, in Tanzania during the late seventies and the early eighties, rationing of consumer goods has severely reduced cash crop supply [Bevan et al., 1989: Part III]. On the other hand, using a sample of twelve African countries, Jean-Claude Berthelemy and Christian Morrisson (1987) have been able to confirm the importance of consumer goods rationing. What they show is that the results of the Nerlove model of long-term aggregate food supply are often significantly improved by adding a variable which reflects the supply of manufactures: thus, any 10% increase in the production or import of manufactures raizes agricultural production by 3 to 6%. In addition, the presence of rationing entails lower positive price effects, a result consonant with economic analysis: when manufactures supply is insufficient, the farmers' supply response to an increase in the price of agricultural goods is dampened. Rationing of inputs used in agricultural production or in the transport system have obviously the same effects as rationing of manufactured consumer goods.
3. Steven Block (1994) has estimated total factor productivity growth in African agriculture over the period 1963–88, using wheat equivalents to compare aggregate outputs across countries so

as to eliminate price and exchange rate effects. His conclusion is that 'introducing wheat units as the output aggregate substantially alters the findings regarding African agricultural productivity. In place of a picture of consistent productivity decline painted by the other output aggregates, the wheat units data suggest that after fifteen years of stagnation, African agricultural total factor productivity increased substantially during the mid 1980s, growing at roughly 2% per year from 1983 to 1988' [Block, 1994: 621]. Also, both land and labour productivity rose during the 1980s in all regions except the Sahel, where land productivity grew but labour productivity stagnated. According to Block himself, however, the sustainability of this recovery should not be taken for granted. This is in view of the role of favourable weather in the second half of the decade (quite a number of countries have benefited from exceptionally large harvests in the mid-1980s) and of the one-shot effects of incentive-improving policy reforms [Block, 1994: 622–23].

4. There has in fact been an impressive increase in the stock of motor vehicles in the 1960s and the 1970s in SSA, yet this increase was halted and soon followed by a decrease in the 1980s when the free market in foreign exchange was ended as a result of two successive oil crises. At the end of 1988, only about 1% of households were thought to have access to a private motor vehicle. Regarding Africa's capacity for goods movement, it must be noted that in 1981 SSA received more than 31,000 new trucks of 16 or more tonnes capacity, yet in 1990 this number has reduced to only 6,500 units with a near continuous decline in the intervening period. It is likely that there has been a surge in vehicle imports in a number of countries following market liberalization carried out under structural adjustment policies. However, the volumes appear to be small [Howe, 1994: 3–4].
5. In Tanzania, for instance, the vast majority of transportation in rural areas is accomplished by foot and headloading by women accounts for about 73% of all transportation [Putterman, 1995: 318].
6. Even the manufacturing of spare parts for transport vehicles is not undertaken in many countries, thereby creating heavy dependence on imports and foreign technical assistance.
7. Thus, in Zambia, owing to the high cost of spare parts, 30 to 40% of bicycles have been found to be out of service awaiting repairs [Howe, 1993: 12]. In Zimbabwe, starting in 1980, approximately 5,000 health workers were provided with bicycles at subsidized prices to improve health services in rural areas. A study in one district in 1991 revealed, however, that only 29 out of the original 174 bicycles (that is, only 17% of them) were in working order, the remainder awaiting repair either because of inadequate repair facilities, lack of spare sparts, or because their owners could not afford to repair them [Howe, 1993: 21].
8. Of course, due allowance has to be made for the fact that the price *per calorie* is much higher for imported grains than for domestically produced starchy staples. Poor urban consumers will therefore switch to imported foodstuffs only if the price of domestic staples rises significantly enough as a result of internal transport costs to more than compensate the differential in calorie costs between the two kinds of foodstuffs.
9. The above description fits in well with the vent-for-surplus model used by Hla Myint (who revived a concept originally expounded by Adam Smith) to characterize many 'semi-empty' economies of the Third World that had sizeable surplus productive capacities before they were opened up to international trade in the 19–20th centuries. As a matter of fact, these economies were subsistence economies whose productive capacity was left largely unused owing to insufficient demand resulting from 'the underdeveloped economic organization of an isolated country, particularly the lack of a good internal transport system and of suitable investment opportunities'. Once the opening-up process had got into its stride, these economies with a sparse population in relation to their (valuable) natural resources (e.g., Burma, Malaysia, Côte d'Ivoire, Ghana) expanded rapidly through a process 'which kept itself going by drawing an increasing volume of hitherto unused or surplus resources into export production' [Myint, 1971: 127–9; see also Pingali et al., 1987: 46–48, and Austen, 1987: 138–42]. According to the vent-for-surplus theory, therefore, the effect of trade opening is not to reallocate fully employed resources as in the conventional theories but, rather, to make use of formerly underemployed land and labour resources to produce greater output destined for export markets.

As pointed out by Ester Boserup, the initial expansion of primary production for export in SSA was made possible by the construction of effective communication links in small enclaves of colonial development. Thus, two-thirds of the African railways built in the colonial period connected mines to a coastal harbour since in the sparsely populated areas of Africa railway building was usually uneconomic except when it could be justified by the existence of rich mineral deposits [Boserup, 1981: 148]. With the truck revolution a cumulative bias developed in large parts of the continent in so far as there was little incentive to construct roads in regions without railways to connect them [*ibidem*: 150].

The prevailing organizational form for the production of exportables reflected the wide dispersal of populations as well as the public good nature of infrastructure. As a matter of fact, with the quickly rising demand for tropical products by industrialized countries, the establishment of plantations became a necessity since in regions physically suited for the production of these products there was no significant farmer population that could produce and trade them. In the words of Yujiro Hayami, 'Opening frontier lands for the production of new crops entailed high capital outlays. Virgin lands had to be cleared and developed; and physical infrastructure such as roads, irrigation systems, bridges, and docking facilities had to be constructed ...Labourers were not only imported from the more populous regions but also had to be trained in the production of these crops ... For the investors to internalize gains from investment in infrastructure, the farm size must inevitably be large ... the plantation system evolved not because it was generally a more efficient mode of productive organization than the peasant mode but because it was the most effective type of agricultural organization for extracting the economic benefit accruing from the exploitation of sparsely populated virgin areas' [Hayami, 1997: 8]. The same reasons may go a long way towards explaining the persistence in SSA of large farms (including estate and state farms) that have their own means of transport for delivering products directly to secondary or terminal markets and thus receive a higher market price than is possible for isolated peasants [Ahmed and Rustagi, 1984: 112].

Such large farming units may also help overcome other imperfections that geographic isolation creates in various rural factor markets, including private security forces to protect properties and lobbying and bribing to obtain licences for the import of necessary inputs.

10. Thus, Paul Richards points out that in Sierra Leone, 'loan recovery in distant villages may cost more, in terms of transport and effort on the part of skilled staff, than the value of the amounts outstanding' [Richards,1985: 127].
11. As far as use of farm machinery in rainfed agriculture is concerned, the above difficulty is actually compounded by the fact that annual overhead costs must be amortized over a single and short season spanning only a few months [Delgado and Ranade, 1987: 134].
12. In this regard, the experience of Rwanda is especially instructive since this country has developed an impressive network of savings and credit rural banks known as the *banques populaires*. The density of population is so high that setting up rural branches all throughout the countryside is apparently a sound policy. Yet, it was found that only 9% of depositors borrow money from their local bank and that loans taken for purposes of agricultural production remain few [Gentil and Fournier, 1993: 201–202]. The situation is similar in neighbouring Burundi.
13. None the less, progress was conspicuously absent in neighbouring areas (Zaria, Bauchi, and Sokoto) in spite of favourable conditions in terms of soils and rainfalls, population densities, and road networks. According to Tiffen, the root cause for these regional differences lies in the much stronger dedication to rural development on the part of the local government in Gombe.
14. The long-run elasticity is calculated by using the Nerlove technique which specifies a Bayesian revision of price expectations and an adjustment mechanism. This method, as we know it today, however suffers from some serious technical problems.
15. For references to this (very narrow) literature, see Schiff and Montenegro, 1993.
16. A strength of these two studies is that they combine cross-section and time-series data, and use only the variations within each country or district over time rather than cross-section variations. As a matter of fact, they thus avoid the problem of unobserved variable biases which affects all pure cross-section estimates since it is not possible to measure all the relevant

attributes of agroclimate and public investments and, therefore, explanatory variables (including price) may be correlated with unobserved country effects [Binswanger, 1990: Appendix].

17. In fact, on a standard graph depicting the micro-equilibrium of the individual farm, the impact of infrastructural bottlenecks is either to shift the marginal cost curve upwards (say, because input prices are higher) or, assuming perfect competition, to lower the horizontal price curve (because traders offer lower prices to the producer to take higher transport costs or trade risks into account). In the two cases, the effect is to reduce the equilibrium level of output which the farmer is willing to produce.

# Chapter 3

## PROPERTY RIGHTS IN LAND

### PART I: DIVIDING THE COMMONS

#### 3.1 INTRODUCTION

In the previous chapter, we have seen why low population densities tend not only to block the emergence of rural product and factor markets, but also to make costly the supply of public goods essential for agricultural progress (and the collection of tax proceeds). This situation is not problematic as long as farmers produce mainly for subsistence purposes and remain content with rather low levels of good consumption. Yet, when they begin to aspire to substantial improvements in their standards of living, so that a deepening of their engagement in market-oriented activities becomes inevitable, the aforementioned effects of population scattering turn out to be severe constraints on rural development. As a matter of fact, infrastructural deficiencies and communication problems get translated into higher production costs or lower producer prices with the consequence that production for the market is discouraged. Under these new circumstances, farmers remain confined to the self-subsistence economy out of necessity and no more on their own liking.

If, however, population growth proceeds fast enough, economies of scale for providing infrastructure in more densely settled areas and the concomitant reduction in the average cost of communication will allow trade to increase, specialization to develop and (product or factor) markets to arise and thrive. At least, this will happen in ecologically favourable areas where opportunities for agricultural growth are promising. The question to be addressed now is the following: granting that communication problems lose importance as population grows and tends to concentrate in high-potential regions where the market nexus is likely to be the strongest, will land rights adjust to facilitate market expansion and agricultural development, or will they hamper this process by failing to evolve in the required direction? More precisely, in regions with a long tradition of extensive forms of natural resource use characteristic of land-abundant environments, can we expect that the communal system of land property typical of these conditions will get gradually transformed into land tenure forms more conducive to agricultural practices of the land-saving and yield-increasing kind?

A dominant idea in the new institutional economics literature is that the inevitable evolution of land rights as land assets become more scarce is towards increasing privatization. This idea is cogently put forward by the so-called property rights school: for the authors who refer themselves to that school, private property is not a sacrosanct institution of absolute value as was conceived by the $18^{th}$-century philosophers and the Physiocrats (or so-called 'Economists'), but an arrangement which becomes optimal only in conditions of resource scarcity.[1] There are actually two separate issues involved here which are not always clearly distinguished in current debates. At a first stage, there is the question as to how land assets customarily held under corporate ownership get privatized in the sense of being individually appropriated. At the second stage, once land is divided or shared among individual users, there arises the second question as to what extent property rights need to be individualized. More specifically, do transfer rights evolve when use rights have been (firmly) established and have they important economic functions to perform? The delicate question of whether and when the state ought to intervene to give a legal backing to the emerging land rights is involved here. More precisely, does a spontaneous evolution of land rights need to be supplemented by a formal recognition and sanctioning of private property rights through centralized land titling procedures? And, in particular, is formalization of land rights a prerequisite of land market development?

Note that the first issue arises whether there is a shift in resource use or not. Such a shift actually occurs when, given the growing scarcity of land for cultivation purposes, communally-owned assets so far put to non-agricultural uses are privatized and assigned to a new (agricultural) use. For example, pasture (or forest) lands are partitioned and transformed into individually-owned fields while previously grazing animals either disappear or are brought under the permanent stalling system for intensive cattle-raising inside the farm compound (both possibilities are found in various parts of Rwanda or Burundi today). To turn to the other possibility, no shift in resource use takes place when land areas under an extensive agricultural system (such as the slash-and-burn system) are gradually converted into more individualized plots devoted to intensive forms of cultivation. Or, when vast tracts of pasture land traditionally open to mobile cattle belonging to a community of herders are increasingly brought under private control for intensive exploitation around permanent water points.

In Chapters 3 and 4, I intend to examine in detail these two central questions regarding the transformation of land rights, taking stock of the typical answers provided by institutional economists and evaluating them in the light of both theoretical considerations and empirical evidence accumulated in many countries, more particularly in SSA (for Chapter 4).

In Chapter 3, the discussion proceeds as follows. In a first step, the main thesis of the property rights school and their evolutionary followers is presented in a systematic manner allowing for some complementary precisions and refinements that help make the approach more internally consistent. In the process, an original contribution of the present essay consists of drawing the points of similarity and difference between the property rights theorists and development scholars with an evolutionary approach to property rights, most notably, Ester Boserup and the proponents of the so-called induced institutional innovation hypothesis. All this is done in Section 2. In the next section (Section 3), a number of important limitations of the above approach are pointed out and illustrated. Among these limitations, the neglect of the role of the state and of the distributive impact of efficiency-enhancing institutional changes is given particular emphasis. A final section (Section 4) concludes this chapter and introduces the following one.

## 3.2 THE VIEW OF THE PROPERTY RIGHTS SCHOOL AND THEIR EVOLUTIONARY FOLLOWERS

### *Property arrangements under land abundance*

When a natural resource, say land, is abundant, there is by definition no competition for it. The critical issue is access to labour, not to land.[2] In such circumstances, private property rights in land are not useful nor economically justifiable. Externalities among competing users are indeed unimportant in land-abundant settings since, when people are dispersed over the land, they have little ability to cause a fall in the average income of their neighbours through competition in the joint use of the resource or through ecological spillover effects. In other words, when population densities are low, an open access regime is not inefficient. The conservation of the natural resource is not jeopardized and there is no overcrowding effect through which additional entries can lead to a decline in the income level of existing producers. In the words of a property rights theorist: ‘externalities are of such small significance that it does not pay anyone to take them into account' and 'there is no positive value to society of creating clearly defined property rights in land' [Johnson, 1972: 271].

Access to natural resources does not, however, take place in a social and political vacuum and it is therefore incorrect to speak about an open access regime to describe land tenure rights in land-abundant environments. Even though they may not be precisely defined, territorial boundaries do exist between different communities (lineage-based groups). Thus, in African villages, the operation of territorial delineation actually corresponds to a symbolic gesture by which the head of the founding lineage signifies that there is a privileged association between the delimited portion of the land area and the social group which he represents [Platteau, 1992: 85].

The symbolism of this gesture is twofold. In the first place, an organic link is created with the land which imparts a specific identity feeling to the residents. The event of original demarcation of a portion of land is memorized under the form of a founding myth considered as the starting point of the history of the people concerned. Revealingly, a loosely defined part of the territory known as 'the bush' plays an active role in the social reproduction of the group or lineage. It is believed to be inhabited by supernatural beings which have a strong influence on the life of the people living in the surrounding area. No wonder then that it is deemed a sacred portion of the local resource domain, a part where most rituals take place which serve to strengthen the harmony between living people and the supernatural powers acting on behalf of the dead ancestors, on the one hand, and to foster the unity among these people themselves, on the other hand [Godelier, 1974; Raynaut, 1976; Gruenais, 1986; Laurent, 1995; Laurent et al., 1994].

In the second place, a political act is accomplished whereby a chief establishes himself as an indispensable mediator between the delimited land area and all the people who are going to live in it. Maurice Gruenais has further elaborated this point as follows:

> In this dialectics of the relation between man and his environment which takes us to the very heart of the political sphere, what is at stake is less the land itself than the link tying the people to a local authority... As a matter of fact, land in itself, or its expanse, has no real meaning for the powerful. The 'original' demarcation of a territory expresses the establishment of a privileged relation between the physical environment and a particular political figure. This relation becomes meaningful only in so far as it is being

> recognized. And land is a pertinent object for those in power only when it is peopled by individuals who accept the same relation, which may then become the means through which authority is exercised. It is thus on the basis of a threefold relation—land environment/authority/social group—that a particular territory is formed [Gruenais, 1986: 290–91—my translation].

Clearly, access to communal resources is seldom 'open' but is typically identified with, or mediated through membership in a social group. This relationship is reciprocal: on the one hand, group membership is the basis of social rights and, on the other hand, access to a share of the corporate productive assets serves to validate membership in the group [Berry, 1984: 91]. A guaranteed access to the local resources is a 'general right' granted to all members of the group as distinct from the 'specific rights' to a particular portion of the resource. While the former is 'an inseparable element of the status as member of the tribe' and can only be lost through formal expulsion from the group, the latter can be reshuffled according to circumstances. For instance, in a system of slash-and-burn agriculture, when the period of fallow is so long that all traces of previous cultivation are lost, a household does not automatically return to the same parcel [Boserup, 1965: 79–80]. Specific rights may even be acquired by strangers upon being adopted into the host community, through the establishing of personal links of friendship or godparenthood or through the payment of dues to the local master of land [see Baland and Platteau, 1996: 194–97, for numerous illustrations and references].[3] Communities are therefore largely porous and ethny-, lineage- or community-based identity feelings do not imply any attitude of rigid exclusion *vis-à-vis* strangers.

To sum up, even when they are abundant, natural resources tend to be somehow demarcated and placed under the corporate custody of a given social group or community. None the less, the degree of internal control exercised over local users is extremely low and the flexibility of rules of access conspicuously high in such circumstances.

### *Property arrangements under land scarcity*

*General considerations* When population pressure on the resource intensifies, growing competition causes an increasing incidence of externalities among users. A standard response to this potentially inefficient situation is to restrict outsiders' access to the local resource base [see, e.g., Noronha, 1985; Downs and Reyna, 1988; Bassett and

Crummey, 1993; Laurent et al., 1994]. Thus, for example, in the case of the Orma pastoralist communities of northeastern Kenya, elders responded to increasing land pressure by prohibiting nomadic herders from grazing their herds on the village common pasture. Over the years, they strengthened this prohibition by gradually extending the period during which the local common pasture is made inaccessible to outsiders. Eventually, the restricted zone was declared out of bounds to the outsiders year round. Interestingly, however, Orma villagers continued to use the common pasture as much as they liked and this lack of restrictions applied to insiders was not seen by them as problematic [Ensminger, 1990: 667–9].

Orma villagers thus fought with increasing determination the attempts by Somali and other Orma herders to move into their village resource domain. Interestingly, however, they took no step to impose use restrictions upon themselves in spite of rapid growth of their member population. In other words, communal ownership among the Orma has remained limited to defining and enforcing membership rules. Degradation of pastures quickly ensued. This is the expected outcome when population growth or enhanced exploitation of the resource base following increased market penetration continue unabated and no regulation of resource use is laid down. In the Appendix to the present chapter, the interested reader will find an analytical proof of this proposition: when the number of agreed resource users is very high and no mechanism exists to regulate their use rights, the equilibrium outcome under communal ownership tends towards the Tragedy of the Commons equilibrium.[4]

To prevent efficiency losses and resource depletion, two institutional evolutions are actually available. Either the community takes steps towards regulating the collective use of the resource, or it accepts its division and the consequent emergence of individualized rights. Under some conditions, including the absence of transaction costs, the two solutions are theoretically equivalent and they lead to a Pareto-efficient outcome (see the Appendix for a formal proof). Incidentally, this result illustrates that, absent transaction costs, institutions do not matter such as is the case in the (fictitious) world of standard general equilibrium theory where complete and perfect markets are posited.

The assumption of zero transaction costs is however too strong and the pervasive incidence of these costs in collective regulation is usually considered to tilt the balance in favour of private property. This is the central message of the property rights school which claims that, in many cases, as the scarcity value of a resource increases, a point will be reached where the gains from its privatization exceed the costs [Demsetz, 1967; Davis and North, 1971; Johnson, 1972; Alchian and Demsetz, 1973; North and Thomas, 1973; Barzel, 1989; De Alessi, 1980; Feder and Feeny, 1991; Libecap, 1996].

*Externalities and governance costs under communal ownership* (i) An important part of the gains from privatisation precisely results from the fact that all the so-called governance costs associated with collective regulation are avoided. Such costs include all those incurred to reach a collective agreement and to organize a community of users. They are likely to be higher when the group is larger [Olson, 1965], or when its membership is more heterogeneous [Libecap, 1989a: 22–23, 1989b: 10–13; Milgrom and Roberts, 1992: 295]. Regarding heterogeneity, common property regulation (through taxes, subsidies and quotas) may be expected to be all the more difficult as inequality in wealth is greater [Kanbur, 1992]. In point of fact, it has been demonstrated elsewhere [Baland and Platteau, 1998a, 1999] that wealth inequality tends to make the regulated outcome less efficient and to amplify the distributive effects of regulation, thereby increasing the likelihood that some agents will be hurt in the process. As a corollary to the latter proposition, if we require that the regulated outcome Pareto-dominates the unregulated one, the efficiency gains from regulation decrease with inequality.

In addition, diversity of objectives or interests among users makes co-operation around resource management more difficult to achieve (as exemplified by conflicts between agriculturalists and herders in semi-arid areas, or by conflicts between men and women when they have different uses of the natural resource). Heterogeneity of another type, cultural heterogeneity, also tends to discourage collective regulation. It is especially likely to arise when the boundaries of the resource concerned do not coincide with a particular village or homogeneous group of villages [see Ostrom, 1990]. Thus, it has been argued that one reason behind the relative success of the West Bengal state (India) in local forest management lies in the existing topography that allows each forest unit to coincide with one village, or group of villages [Saxena, 1997].

Moreover, governance costs are enhanced by the opportunistic tendencies of rights-holders not only to violate or circumvent collective rules but also to eschew efforts to create collective mechanisms of decision-making and enforcement. Costs arising from such proclivities are also dependent on the size of the user group: they are lower if the number of resource users is smaller and, at the limit, they are nil when there is a single user. (Note that the impact of wealth inequality cannot be determined a priori, as shown in Baland and Platteau, 1997, 1999). There are actually several reasons why incentives to free ride on others' efforts diminish with group size [Baland and Platteau, 1996: 75–78].

First, when a group is small, it is less vulnerable to the problem of free riding as users internalize a larger share of the benefits of their individual action. This is the well-known incentive dilution argument put forward by Olson (1965, 1982). Indeed, free riding is a strategy whereby an individual trades a reduction in his own effort, from which he alone benefits, for reductions in the income of the whole group, which are shared among all members. As the size of the group increases, the terms of exchange become increasingly favourable to the free rider (since shares are diluted), and the opposite is true when the size of the group decreases. Therefore, the cost of free riding rises (falls) when the size of the group is reduced (increased) while the benefit remains constant.

Second, when groups are small, members are better informed about each other's behaviour and, through reputation effects, repeated interactions may significantly reduce the attractiveness of opportunistic behaviour [Sethi and Somanathan, 1996]. As we know from game theory, when the length of a Prisoner's Dilemma game is infinite or indeterminate, cooperation is a possible equilibrium outcome [see, e.g., Gibbons, 1992: 88–102]. Moreover, communication is relatively easy when members are few and, as experimental social psychology has shown, communication facilitates collective undertakings not only by allowing verbal exchanges but, more importantly, by encouraging the formation of identity feelings that drive people to better internalize the consequences of their own behaviour on others [Frank, 1988: 223–25; Dawes and Thaler, 1988: 194–95; Ostrom et al., 1994].

Finally, members of small groups are often involved in multiple relationships and tightly intertwined interests which make violation of rules of use with respect to natural resources liable to entail sanctions in other walks of social life [Ellickson, 1991: 55–56]. To put it in theoretical terms, the game played out in resource management is not an isolated game but is linked up with another 'social' game being played simultaneously. Defection in the former game is punishable by the exclusion from the latter. If the present value of individual costs of being excluded indefinitely from social goods (mutual aid in times of stress, participation in religious rituals and social events, etc.) is far greater than the current cost of contributing to these goods, then it may become incentive compatible for each family to be cooperative in the resource game. On the other hand, it is incentive compatible with other village members to ostracize the defector in the resource game from the social game, if the cost of sacrificing his individual contribution to the social goods is less than the damage done by him on the economic value of the resource system. Under these conditions, the threat of exclusion is credible and cooperation in the resource game can become a subgame-perfect equilibrium outcome, even if there is strong incentive to free ride in this game. Masahiko Aoki refers to the expectation of punishment in the social game in the event of noncooperation in the resource game as the community norm [Aoki, forthcoming: Chap. 3].

(ii) Now, it needs to be stressed that regulation often remains imperfect as it is difficult to eliminate all the inefficiencies arising from a collective mode of exploitation. The remaining inefficiencies must therefore be considered as genuine costs of maintaining the commons. In other words, regulation is necessarily imperfect and a fully efficient outcome cannot be expected to result from the joint exploitation of a natural resource.

The classical rent-dissipating externality which follows from the uncoordinated and joint use of a resource is probably the problem most easy to solve through regulation (e.g., by means of taxes or quotas). There are, however, two other negative external effects which are more difficult to remove through concerted action. On the one hand, in the absence of such action, investment incentives regarding resource improvement and conservation are blunted for the well-known reason that any single user contemplating investment will have to bear all the related costs (including the cost of forebearance to preserve the resource) while the benefits are shared with other users. Unfortunately, while simple coordination of harvesting efforts, for example, can presumably be collectively implemented (e.g., by means of quotas), cooperation in investment undertakings (including forebearance to preserve the resource) usually requires a more sophisticated organization and a genuine ability to foresee, and to agree upon, the likely effects of different courses of action on the state of the resource.

Relatedly, as long as membership involves access to the resource, a demographic externality arises as the costs of an increased number of children are spread over the whole group of rights-holders [Dasgupta, 1995: 1896]. Conscious attempts to control this externality seem to be rare, probably because they would imply a great extent of foresight on the part of the resource users as well as an ability to enforce delicate control measures. Exceptions nevertheless exist. The regulation system reported by McKean in her thorough study of three Japanese villages during the Tokugawa period provides a clear illustration. According to her, indeed, equal rights of access to communal resources were allotted on a household basis so as to avoid giving advantages to large families and thus discourage population growth. To make this system effective, the formation of a branch household from the main family was subject to approval by village authorities. The latter 'recognised that creating an additional household would enlarge the number of claimants on the commons without enlarging the commons' and were therefore reluctant to grant such a permission. In some villages, 'no new household were permitted unless an old one died out for lack of heirs' [McKean, 1986: 551–53].

A similar system was in force in the Canton of Zürich (Switzerland) during pre-industrial times. We are thus told that in this region 'the general right of using the common property and being a member of the community was the strongest obstacle for the entry and the settlement of newcomers...'. Also, 'the *numerus clausus* of these rights was used as legitimation for setting up regulations that no new house could be built either in the village settlement or outside, unless an old one was torne down. These regulations prevented an uncontrolled expansion from within too' [Braun, 1978: 299].

A direct implication of the foregoing discussion is that people's ability to cooperate in the management of common access resources determines the relative profitability of these resources and those that are individualized and, therefore, affects the allocation of resources held by households to one use or the other. It has thus been shown that in Mexico, when cooperation fails in the management of collectively grazed pastures, more land is allocated to crops than under successful cooperation and less to pastures, while the stocking rate on pastures is increased. This results in too much land in extensive crops and too many animals per hectare of pasture [McCarthy et al., 1998].

(iii) The efficiency losses resulting from the three aforementioned types of externalities obviously grow with the value of the resource. This explains the frequent emphasis in the literature on the unit value of natural resources as one of the main determinants of its privatization (division) [Dyson-Hudson and Smith, 1978; Cashdan, 1983; Levine, 1984; Wade, 1988: 215; Libecap, 1989a: 21; Dasgupta, 1993: 288–89; Noronha, 1997: 49]. For example, in his classical study of the Swiss Alps, Netting contrasts the lowlands of the valley which are fertile and therefore tend to be privately appropriated with the more arid highlands which are used as communal (summer) pastures under the authority of the village council [Netting, 1972, 1976, 1981, 1982]. Likewise, in Bangladesh, low-quality water bodies tend to remain common properties of local fishermen communities whereas high-quality bodies are privately appropriated [Toufique, 1997].

Population pressure bears upon the efficiency gains of division in two different ways. For one thing, by increasing the number of users per unit area, it creates more room for external effects and, thereby, the governance costs and the inefficiencies involved in the joint exploitation of the resource rise. For another thing, by making the resource increasingly scarce, population pressure enhances its value and therefore makes for increased aggregate losses from collective exploitation. In other words, the amount of the rents foregone by not dividing the resource tends to increase with population. This is especially true when population pressure involves a transformation of the pattern of resource use, such as a shift from extensive to intensive agricultural or grazing practices. As a matter of fact, such intensive practices have the effect of increasing the potential value of the resource per unit area and, therefore, to enhance the gains of private property.

Market penetration and the ensuing commercialization of products from primary activities is another critical determinant of the relative profitability of private property. It is by enhancing the realizable value of natural resources that growing integration of rural communities into developing market networks increases the benefits of resource division. Thus, in many developing countries, dramatic increases in prices for fuelwood or fresh fish as a result of a rapid expansion of urban markets have prompted rural inhabitants to intensify the exploitation of many forest and fish resources during the post-independence period. Significant efficiency losses have resulted from the growing pressure on these resources and the rising incidence of negative external effects that accompanied it [see, e.g., Baland and Platteau, 1996: 262–70].

The advantages of private property appear all the more decisive as it enables users to internalize the above-discussed externalities without involving any governance costs. This is because this regime establishes a one-to-one relationship between individual actions and all their effects: 'A primary function of property rights is that of guiding incentives to achieve a greater internalization of externalities...' [Demsetz, 1967: 348]. As pointed out earlier, the advocates of the property rights approach however stress that the benefits of private property ought always to be weighted against the costs of privatization and it is only when the pressure on a resource becomes acute that the argument in favour of private property rights gains force. It is now time to examine the cost-side of the balance sheet.

*Direct costs of privatization* The direct costs of private property have to be distinguished from its opportunity costs. In the first category, primary attention is drawn to transaction costs, including the costs of negotiating, defining and enforcing private property rights [for a classical exposition, see Eggertsson, 1990: 262–71]. The usual argument is that such costs are increasing with the physical base of the resource. Thus, the more spread the resource base (or the less concentrated the resource) the higher the costs of delimiting and defending the resource 'territory'.[5]

To illustrate the point, consider a resource domain having the shape of a square with surface $S$. Transaction costs incurred for the delimitation and protection (say, fencing or surveillance costs) of the undivided resource, $C_u$, are a linear function of the length of the frontier set up towards these purposes. Normalizing the unit cost of fencing to one, we get that $C_u = 4\sqrt{S}$. If, alternatively, the resource is equally divided into $n$ agents, the fencing cost of the partitioned resource is easily shown to be $C_d = 2(\sqrt{n}+1)\sqrt{S}$, bearing in mind that contiguous parcels are protected by only one fence. The cost per agent of dividing the resource is then $\frac{C_d}{n} = 2\sqrt{S}(\frac{\sqrt{n}+1}{n})$, which is decreasing in $n$ but increasing in $S$.

The latter result means that the more spread the resource base the higher the individual cost of partitioning. In other words, for a given individual benefit of partitioning, the individual cost increases as the density of the resource (measured by the inverse of $S$) falls. Finally, the extra cost entailed in the division of the resource is given by $C_d - C_u = 2(\sqrt{n}-1)\sqrt{S}$, which is also decreasing in its density. This short example illustrates the 'density argument' put forward by Dasgupta and other authors [Netting, 1976, 1981; Dasgupta, 1993: 288–89; Noronha, 1997: 49] according to which private property rights tend to be instituted on resources characterized by high density while low density resources remain common property.

For many natural resources, the costs of dividing the resource domain appear prohibitive under the present state of the technology. For example, the open sea—or, more exactly, the fish stock contained into it—presents insuperable difficulties for private appropriation. As a matter of fact, the enforcement of exclusive property rights to individual patches carved up in the ocean would be infinitely costly. This is especially evident when fish species are mobile and move over large water spaces, since exclusive rights are too costly to establish and enforce whether over the resource or on the territory in which it moves. Such a situation is in contrast to that which sometimes obtains in inshore maritime waters or, more often still, around islands or in inland fisheries: in the latter areas, indeed, fishing spots can be more easily demarcated and safeguarded, particularly for sedentary species such as shellfish and seaweed [Eggertsson, 1990: 265]. Under these circumstances, fishing sites are not infrequently assigned for exclusive use to private users [see, e.g., McEvoy, 1986: 34; Cruz, 1986: 123; Cordell and McKean, 1986: 92; Ruddle, 1987: 46; Acheson, 1989: 367; Fay, 1990b: 224–5].

To take an example from the forestry, in the tropical forests of East Kalimantan (Borneo), the great diversity of species of trees, of which only some are economically valuable and the fact that they are largely dispersed throughout the forest prohibited individual appropriation. However, birds' nests caves which are concentrated and therefore more easily watched and guarded are often controlled as private property by individuals and families [Jessup and Peluso, 1996].

Note that, as emphasized by North (1981), the direct costs of resource division may fall with technological progress. For example, the introduction of modern borehole drilling facilitates the privatization of common grazing areas (see infra, the example about Botswana). It is therefore not only the factors which enhance resource value but also those which reduce direct costs of partitioning that may favour private appropriation of natural resources.

Finally, the costs of resource division depend on the extent of formalisation of private property rights. As shall be argued in Chapter 4, there is good ground to limit such formalisation and leave informal mechanisms substitute for costly titling procedures. Other things being equal, the less codified the private land rights the higher the profitability of privatization.

*Opportunity costs of privatization: scale economies* Let us now turn to the opportunity costs of resource division. There are indeed various instances in which an undivided resource produces benefits that are necessarily foregone in the process of division. Among these benefits is the presence of scale economies. Thus, in the case of hunting, wild animals require large territories to survive and reproduce. Under such circumstances, division of a hunting domain into smaller parcels would imply the destruction of the resource. Resources offering multiple products are also subject to scale economies to the extent that they form part of an overall ecosystem. This multiple product character of the resource is a reason often mentioned to argue against the parcelling out of forest areas into individual holdings.

When discussing the role of scale economies, it is important to bear in mind that they may be present not in the resource itself but in complementary factors. The obvious advantage of co-ordinating the herding of animals so as to economize on shephard labour in extensive grazing activities is probably the best illustration of the way scale economies in a complementary factor may prevent the division of a resource domain [see, e.g., Dahlman, 1980; Netting, 1981; Binswanger et al., 1989; Bromley, 1989: 16; Nugent and Sanchez, 1993]. Livestock is extremely vulnerable to the risk of asset mismanagement, which explains why collective ownership of animals is not observed even in communities specialized in cattle-raising. To exploit the scale economies in herding, the collective management of individually-owned herds therefore appears as the best solution. Regarding the ownership status of the grazing lands, it can then be argued that, even irrespective of the fact that wide tracts of land are required as pastures under extensive grazing practices (see infra), the private apportioning of grazing spaces would entail few advantages compared to the costs involved: in this case, it is the need to monitor the individual herds collectively that seems to determine common ownership of the pastures.

Another illustration can be taken from fisheries (marine or inland). Indeed, in many cases the guarding of privately apportioned fishing spaces is subject to strong scale economies. As a consequence, it may make sense for several individuals or families to get together to enforce a *de facto* right of collective property over a given fishing ground. This is actually what many traditional fishing communities have done in the past when competition around scarce fish resources began to develop, particularly in inland fisheries.

Relatedly, a resource can be impossible to divide because of its symbolic value rather than its physical characteristics. In this case, there are economies of scale in the intangible benefits derived from 'consuming' the resource: divided, the resource would lose all its symbolic value for the owners. A typical example is provided by territories that are considered sacred by their inhabitants because they are earmarked for certain ritual functions or ceremonies and serve as burial places (see *supra*). Thus, for instance, the Bijogos in Guinea-Bissau regard some of their islands (in the Bijogos Archipelago) as sacred portions of their land domain where key rites of passage are performed. As a consequence, they are eager to keep the sacred islands whole since their social identity as Bijogos is strongly associated with the physical integrity of these territories. In Tanzania, to take another example, Barabaig herders have sacred sites which they use as places of worship: it is there that they make offerings and call on God's blessings through the medium of their ancestors. It is not surprising, therefore, that they strongly reacted when a development project initiated by CIDA (Canadian International Development Agency) with a view to establishing several 4,000-hectare highly mechanized wheat farms in northern Tanzania had the effect of destroying these sacred sites or of rendering them inaccessible [Baland and Platteau, 1996: 40].

*Opportunity costs of privatization: risk-reduction under common property*
When returns to a resource are highly variable across time and space, the need to insure against such variability is yet another consideration that may militate against resource division [McCloskey, 1976; Dahlman, 1980; Runge, 1986; Dasgupta, 1993: 288–89]. When a resource has a low predictability (that is, when the variance in its value per unit of time per unit area is high), users are generally reluctant to divide it into smaller portions because they would thereby lose the insurance benefits provided by the resource kept whole. In the words of Nugent and Sanchez: 'the lower the quality of land or the more variable the weather, the more important it is that the land be held in communal, that is, tribal form' [Nugent and Sanchez, 1993: 107].[6]

For instance, herders (fishermen) may need to have access to a wide portfolio of pasture lands (fishing spots) insofar as, at any given time, wide spatial variations in yields result from climatic or other environmental factors. Assuming that the probability distributions are not correlated too much across spatial groupings of land or water and that they are not overly correlated over time, a system offering access to a large area within which rights-holding users can freely move appears as highly desirable from a risk-reducing perspective. For example:

> in the tropical and subtropical rangelands of the Sahel and East Africa rainfall varies considerably from year to year. But, more importantly, rainfall is unevenly distributed over an area in any given year. Rain is usually produced in this region by individual storms creating narrow rainfall paths with inter-storm areas remaining quite dry...in parts of Kenya,...as a result of this pattern of rainfall, a traveller on horseback during a single day in the rainy season can easily pass through several spots that are saturated with water and full of grass and others that have not received any rainfall. The proper utilization of such pastures requires that livestock producers have the freedom to move animals over a large area in order to efficiently use available forage resources. Masai herders in East Africa must have access to between 120,000 and 200,000 hectares of rangeland to be able to cope with this situation [Gilles and Jamtgaard, 1981: 132–33; see also Netting, 1976, 1981; Wiessner, 1982; Cashdan, 1985; McCloskey, 1972; Binswanger et al., 1989; Low, 1990; Nugent and Sanchez, 1993; Wilson and Thompson, 1993: 305–6].

It must nevertheless be remarked that private property rights over portions of the resource could apparently solve the predictability problem. Consider the case of extensive grazing again. Due to the unpredictability of rain-induced growth of grasses within any small region, what is important for herders is to be able to move over large ranges of land and rapidly change locations when the need arises. By holding exclusive ownership rights over widely dispersed patches of pasture lands, they would therefore achieve their objective of risk-reduction. Clearly, to account for the maintenance of communal property, one needs to appeal to transaction cost considerations. In actual fact, it is because it would be prohibitively costly to enforce exclusive rights over widely dispersed and infrequently visited ranch patches that the division of the resource domain turns out to be infeasible. The same situation actually obtains in many fisheries. For instance, in the case of lobster fishing territories in Maine (United States), 'it would be very difficult or impossible to divide the entire coast into small territories owned by single individuals. If a person is going to fish year-round or even most of the year, he needs access to a large and diverse area. The costs of defending such a territory would be prohibitive' [Acheson, 1972: 61].[7] We are therefore back to the argument emphasizing the high exclusion costs of a spread resource base.

In terms of the simple example used above to illustrate the impact of a resource's physical base, it is easy to define formally the cost of dividing a common property resource, it being understood that its insurance function must be preserved. Assuming that $n$ continues to stand for the number of resource users while $m$ represents the total number of portions into which the resource domain is divided, and bearing in mind that $n < m$ because of the low predictability of the resource, we have that the total fencing cost of dividing it is equal to $C_d = 2(\sqrt{m}+1)\sqrt{S}$. The individual cost of division for each agent is

$\frac{C_d}{n} = 2\sqrt{S}(\frac{\sqrt{m}+1}{n})$, which is increasing in $S$ (see *supra*), increasing in $m$ (the lower the predictability of the resource or the more diversification needed to insure a given number of users against its variability, the higher the per agent cost of dividing it), and decreasing in $n$. The extra individual cost resulting from the necessity to guard against the low predictability of the resource is therefore equal to

$$\Delta_{ins} = 2\sqrt{S}(\frac{\sqrt{m}+1}{n}) - 2\sqrt{S}(\frac{\sqrt{n}+1}{n}) = 2\sqrt{S}(\frac{\sqrt{n}}{n})(\sqrt{\alpha}-1), \quad with\, \alpha = \frac{m}{n} > 1.$$

It is thus evident that the extra cost of insurance, $\Delta_{ins}$, is inversely related to the density and the predictability of the resource (as measured by the inverse of $S$ and the inverse of $a$, respectively), and to the number of users.

Finally, it is worth noting that growing demographic pressure resulting in higher population densities may encourage the emergence of new ways of insuring against income variations, whether through diversification of income-earning opportunities or through the development of rural credit markets (see Chapter 2). As a consequence, agents are no more compelled to use the costly method of plot diversification and a strong argument in favour of keeping the resource undivided vanishes. This shows once again that, as population density rises and markets develop, division of CPRs may become more profitable not only because benefits increase but also, possibly, because some costs fall in the process.

### *The indeterminacy of institutional evolution*

To sum up the above discussion of the views of property rights theorists, when population density and market integration have increased enough to make natural resources a scarce asset, private property is generally desirable on efficiency grounds. It is also their contention that private property constitutes an institutional innovation that is expected to emerge spontaneously under the combined impact of population growth and market development.[8] Thus, Demsetz writes: 'It is my thesis... that the emergence of new property rights takes place in response to the desires of interacting persons for adjustment to new benefit-cost possibilities... property rights develop to internalize externalities when the gains of internalization become larger than the cost of internalization' [Demsetz, 1967: 350]. Arthur Lewis also had no doubt about the inevitability of the commons' demise under the pressure of evolutionary forces: 'Communal tenures worked passably in Africa as long as populations were very small in relation to land, but population pressure everywhere causes such tenures to destroy the land. Investment apart, communal tenure is a handicap to innovation... These are the reasons why communal tenures are disappearing rapidly in places where they flourished fifty years ago. Many people regret their passing for sentimental reasons, but there is no reason to doubt their incompatibility with economic development' [Lewis, 1955: 121].

Unfortunately, property rights theorists provide few clues as to what happens when privatization is too costly and is bound to remain so for a long time to come (like in the case of open-sea fisheries). In fact, the precise characteristics of communal ownership which they use as a counterfactual in their argument remain largely undefined: the degree of regulation in this property regime is left unspecified, or the potential for regulation in village communities is considered to be hopelessly low. For instance, Feder and Feeny write that, when population increases and land becomes scarce, village communities become larger with the consequence that 'the mechanisms for imposing restrictions on individuals' land use patterns which are harmful to the group's interest' are increasingly deficient [Feder and Feeny, 1991: 140]. In contrast with this view of communities as rather static agencies, a number of scholars have stressed their capacity to adapt to changing circumstances. In conformity with the induced institutional innovation hypothesis [Kikuchi and Hayami, 1980; Ruttan and Hayami, 1984; Hayami and Ruttan, 1985; Binswanger and McIntire, 1987; Hayami, 1997], these authors thus argue that collective regulation of a resource may evolve under (moderate) population growth when its privatization remains prohibitively costly.

Thus, Hayami and Kikuchi point out that, under these circumstances, 'the social structure becomes tighter and more cohesive in response to a greater need to co-ordinate and control the use of resources as they become increasingly more scarce....rules defining rights and obligations among people on the use of the resource as well as rules to settle possible conflicts' then emerge. As scarcity increases and competition is intensified, such rules are defined more clearly and enforced more rigorously [Hayami and Kikuchi, 1981: 22]. Thus, in premodern Tokugawa Japan, because population growth was gradual, 'there had been sufficient time for village communities to develop the organizational capacity for mobilizing communal labour to build and maintain local irrigation facilities' [Hayami, 1997: 92]. Inasmuch as environment determines which resources are scarce, which are difficult to privatize and which are relatively easy to handle at village level, environmental conditions are 'a critical variable in the formation of village structure' [Hayami and Kikuchi, 1981: 21–22].[9]

Close to Hayami and Kikuchi is the position taken by Wade on the basis of detailed village studies in South India (1988). According to him, indeed, 'villagers will deliberately concert their actions only to achieve intensely felt needs which could not be met by individual responses', that is, 'they will straightforwardly come together to follow corporate arrangements' whenever 'the net material benefits provided to all or most cultivators are high' [Wade, 1988: 185–88, 211]. Wade is actually confident that when no other, more decentralized alternative is available, villagers will somehow succeed in overcoming the incentive problems associated with collective action. Lawry reaches a similar conclusion when he writes that 'collective action is more likely to result where the common resource is critical to local incomes and is scarce', and where privatization appears unfeasible or too costly [Lawry, 1989b: 7–9]. This is again the position espoused by Boserup when she writes in general terms that 'when grazing opportunities become scarce, rules are likely to be laid down concerning the number of animals a cultivator family is allowed to have and the amount of straw the cultivator is allowed to remove with the harvest.' [Boserup, 1965: 85].

The above view, it must be noted, is espoused by those political scientists for whom leadership and rules arise within social groups in response to the need to regulate the allocation of resources under conditions of scarcity [see, e.g., Tyler, 1990: 66–67].

According to the evolutionary doctrine, the ways societies adjust to new environmental conditions go much beyond the mere creation or strengthening of regulatory mechanisms. They involve deep changes in the social structures, norms and standards of behaviour: 'The cohesion and solidarity of the village community are based on the norms and moral principles sanctioned by tradition and ingrained in the minds of the villagers. They do change in response to change in the relative scarcity of resources, but the change takes a very long time, often several generations' [Hayami and Kikuchi, 1981: 23]. In terms of the above framework, such changes are directed towards minimizing internal governance costs.

Adjustment along this evolutionary path may also involve decentralization or reorganization of societies around smaller and more homogenous social groups or communities, delegating to them as much regulatory power as possible [see, e.g., Smith, 1959; McKean, 1986; Jayaraman, 1981; Easter and Palanisami, 1986; Tang, 1991, 1992, 1994; Weissing and Ostrom, 1991; Gregersen et al., 1989; Kaul, 1996]. An excellent illustration of this possibility is given by Wilson and Thompson (1993) in their analysis of the transformation of the *ejidos* in Mexico. As a matter of fact, owing to the excessive size of herding groups, pastoral management at community level (the *ejido*) proved to be a failure. In a significant number of cases, this led to the formation of grazing coalitions within smaller groups where co-operation is assured and benefits are enjoyed under very severe ecological conditions. It is noteworthy that the most effective of these (smaller) grazing associations are based upon the extended family. They practise intensive grazing management with short grazing periods and hoof action contributing to a more sustainable and productive range resource. Outside these short periods, interestingly, multiple families combine their livestock into one large herd (200–600 animals) and move the entire grazing operation to range camps situated in remote areas less subject to population pressure [Wilson and Thompson, 1993: 300, 310–12].

## 3.3 LIMITATIONS OF THE (QUALIFIED) PROPERTY RIGHTS APPROACH

### *The questionable view of efficiency as the engine of evolution*

Thus qualified, the property rights approach to institutional change is more satisfactory because it is more coherent and complete. None the less, it remains problematic in so far as it assumes a priori that the main force behind institutional evolution is the search for a more efficient utilization of (natural) resources [for a general critique of this view, see chap. 1]. There are two main problems with such an approach to institutional change. First, on the empirical level, evolutionary accounts based on historical evidence suffer from an important methodological problem. This problem is the selection bias that unavoidably arises when attention is focused on resource systems and societies that have persisted. Experiences that turned into failures, precisely for this reason, tend to be forgotten and to become unobservable in the long run. To illustrate this point, suppose that institutions (including private property) evolve in a completely haphazard manner. In the long run, the analyst would observe only those arrangements which survived because they were better adapted (that is, more efficient). To infer from those observations that institutions always adjust in the direction of more efficient use of the resources would clearly be unwarranted. This is at least true if evolution and adjustment of human societies mean something more than just the survival of the fittest as a result of competitive forces acting upon randomly formed types of institutions.

Second and relatedly, the range of evolutionary patterns considered remains too narrow. In particular, the possibility of degeneration into an open-access regime owing to a lack of adaptability of the society concerned is overlooked: there is always an happy outcome available to cancel threats to resource survival. In this manner, the theory makes itself unable to properly account for the oft-observed cases of chronic resource degradation. Suboptimal evolutionary patterns actually reflect the fact that other forces than efficiency may be at work in human societies. Three such forces come to mind, which are possibly interdependent: the influence of cultural and social norms, the distributive consequences of institutional change, and the role of the state. They will be the focus of attention in the rest of this chapter.

Before probing into these alternative determinants of evolution, it deserves to be stressed that users are not necessarily aware of the efficiency advantages of privatization and this may lead them to inexorably degrade their resources. Witness to it is the fact that in some instances privately appropriated resources continue to be overexploited owing to a poor understanding of the causal relationship involved. For example, in the Kgatleng district of southeastern Botswana, privatization of grazing lands through private ownership of boreholes did not have the effect of preventing overgrazing. Tswana people were eager to maintain or expand their cattle herds and 'they continued to consider that the cause of overgrazing was the lack of rain, which forced concentration of cattle around scarce water.' [Peters, 1994: 82]. The solution for them lay in the digging of new boreholes and not in the enforcement of stock limits such as could be achieved through the spacing of water points. It is therefore not surprising that 'most ranches have had no better record in herd and range management than the typical cattle-post system—and sometimes the record has been worse' [*ibidem*: 220; for other examples, see Baland and Platteau, 1996: 210–16].[10]

*Missing the impact of social capital*

It has been remarked that 'An excessive faith in optimality and the omission of psychological and cultural elements from the calculus help economists to neglect the historical path to the present' [Basu, Jones, and Schlicht, 1987: 18; see also Langlois, 1986, North, 1990]. This certainly applies to the line of arguing of the (qualified) property rights school since it overlooks the fact that not only costs and benefits but also cultural and social norms affect the pattern of institutional evolution. More particularly, by stressing the ability of such norms to adjust to changes in the technical and economic environment, Hayami and Kikuchi tend to overlook the fact that evolution, including long-run institutional equilibria and the corresponding trajectories, are themselves dependent on the initial state of prevailing norms and values (on the initial stock of social capital). Thus, when a society is pervaded by distrust, defection, shirking, and exploitation, co-operative arrangements are unlikely to emerge. A fascinating illustration of this possibility is the Teelin Bay's story told by Taylor [Taylor, 1987]. Teeliners have successfully maintained an old rotation system of access to a small estuary of the Glen River in order to make salmon harvesting orderly and equitable. Cooperation under this system is deemed by the local fishermen so 'natural' that no formal sanction system exists to enforce it: norms of co-operative behaviour are well-established and reputation effects are quite sufficient to deter free-riding. One would have expected that, when a priest came to the village in 1973 to convince its inhabitants to extend co-operation to the whole Glen River, he would have met with a positive response. In fact, the opposite reaction was observed and Teeliners even displayed an attitude of resolute resistance to the project.

As a matter of fact, in post-medieval times, landlords claimed important portions of the river adjoining their estates and did not open them to the peasantry: 'locals might be employed to tend the landlord's weir or crew his net-boats, but unauthorised fishing was theft' [Taylor, 1987: 295]. From this time onwards, there developed a tradition of poaching—'there were even a few individuals who would venture out at night and stretch a net across the entire width of the narrowest part of the river' [*ibidem*]—which came to be regarded by local fishermen as a sort of sport run at the expense of the landlord *via-à-vis* whom latent hostile feelings were thereby manifested. When the government took over ownership, this local cultural significance of poaching as an expression of hostility and opposition to outside authority persisted. In Taylor's words:

> Poaching, however, was also a valued tradition. Just as the landlord's role was to police his holdings, the tenant's role was to poach. Old men spoke with undisguised relish about the good old days, when close watch over the waters made poaching a true challenge. Otherwise law-abiding men would wink and smile at their own reminiscences of successful expeditions and even of capture and confinement. Today, small fines and the lack of effective enforcement seem to have made poaching a somewhat less challenging sport, but sport it remains. Evidently the fact that the landlords are gone and the Irish government or Gael-Linn's bailiffs are now the regulators makes little difference in the local perception of the 'sides'; it is still locals versus outside authorities [Taylor, 1987: 300].

Given this tradition, Teelin fishermen are not ready to consider putting an end to poaching practices. 'The problem, as they see it, is that poaching, as long as it does not violate local rights of access as defined in the rotation system, is a "natural" local characteristic. No one could imagine giving it up' [Taylor, 1987: 300–1].

Southern Italy offers an even more striking example of the inability of a society to develop more efficient institutions owing to pervasive lack of trust, exacerbated individualism, and total absence of law-abidingness [Banfield, 1958; Gambetta, 1988a; Putnam, 1993]. These characteristics which are the product of a long history of external domination (see infra, Chapter 7 for further details) are reflected in all aspects of cultural life, and are also found to prevail in small, close-knit, and traditional communities of Sicilia and Calabria.

The above examples refer to extreme cases where societies are trapped in a 'distrust equilibrium' (characterized by zero social capital). Depending on initial social conditions, other evolutionary paths are, of course, possible as attested by the contrasting experience of northern Italy described by Robert Putnam. It can even be hypohesized that, when social capital endowment is very high, a society can largely dispense with collective regulation and rely on the emergence of a decentralized equilibrium of cooperative behaviour. At lower levels of initial social capital, however, a greater measure of collective regulation is necessary under the form of information exchange, organizational structures (which will presumably be more hierarchical), monitoring functions, sanction mechanisms, arbitration procedures, etc.[11]

Moreover, it is not only the initial state which may influence the future institutional evolution of a given society but also the specific history which led to that state. In particular, past experiences of successful cooperation appear to be an important factor determining the ability of a society to rely on decentralized cooperative behaviour while developing regulatory schemes. Fortunately, there is ample evidence to show that positive experiences of cooperation can actually be constructed. Ostrom thus describes an interesting case where cooperation in the management of an irrigation system in Sri Lanka (the Gal Oya project) became possible thanks to an external intervention aimed at building up an history of cooperation among water users. This result was achieved by deliberately creating small groups and trust-enhancing situations in which people were confronted with day-to-day vital problems to solve, before moving to more complex interaction frameworks [Ostrom, 1990: 166–72]. This example is especially interesting as the successful intervention from outside—including the use of 'catalyst' agents working at the grassroots level—took place in a social context characterized by acute distrust and ethnic tensions nourished by continuing cooperation failures. Without the external impulse to reverse the course of history, the Sri Lankan irrigators of Gal Oya would have remained trapped in a distrust equilibrium reminiscent of the South Italian predicament.

*Ignoring the distributive effects of privatization*

The process of devising new institutional arrangements is likely to be divisive because of its distributional implications. Thus, a move towards privatization may be opposed by traditional rights-holders or a fraction of them if the distributive consequences of such a change are unfavourable to them or regarded as unacceptable [see, e.g., Dasgupta and Heal, 1979: 77; Runge, 1986; Bromley, 1989; North, 1990; Eggertsson, 1990; Libecap, 1989a, 1989b; Platteau, 1992]. Note that what is considered distributionally unacceptable will again depend on the prevailing values in the society and also on the political weight of the various subgroups involved. Here is therefore another way through which the culture and social fabric of a community bear upon its institutional trajectory.

In fact, there is no unique way of dividing a common property resource and, assuming away monetary transfers among former users destined to compensate for the loss of traditional access rights, distributive effects must be reckoned to vary according to the particular method adopted. Let us therefore look at a number of alternative forms of division and examine their distributive impact from the point of view of the customary rights-holders. Three such forms readily come to mind:

(i) The common property resource is divided among the customary users in proportion to their respective rates of use in the pre-division situation. Hence the name 'proportional division' given to this first method of partitioning a resource previously held in common.

(ii) The common property resource is divided equally among all the customary users (the equal division).

(iii) The common property resource is divided equally among a restricted number of traditional users (equal division with exclusion), or it is appropriated by a small minority of powerful individuals.

The distributive consequences of these various forms of division are discussed below in a more detailed manner [for a related discussion, see Baland and Platteau, 1998a].

*Proportional division* Division of a resource according to past rates of use is often propounded by theorists as the solution most acceptable by all customary users. This is because nobody's interest will be hurt in the new situation which Pareto-dominates the previous one [Roemer, 1989]. It can however be shown that, under certain conditions, proportional division, in spite of its apparent fairness, produces perverse distributive effects that favour the richest categories of users. This happens when the latter have access to rewarding alternative income opportunities (so that their rate of use of the commons in the first instance was comparatively low). In the post-division situation with a competitive labour market, they tend to lose much less, as wage earners, than the poorer resource users who will end up being employed at much lower wages (for more details, see infra, Weitzman's argument). As asset owners, however, they have a lower share of the resource rents. Baland and Maniquet (1998) describe the conditions under which the former effect dominates the latter.

An example of the principle of proportional division is found in the many Swiss villages which allotted rights to common pasturage on the basis of the number of cows that could be fed during the winter from the hay produced on the private parcels of their owner [Netting, 1981]. It is also encountered in all the cases where rich villagers give up any claim to common lands to the profit of poorer users who have a more intensive use of them. This usually happens when the commons are of so low value that their appropriation by the poor does not represent any serious stake for the rich.

Proportional division does not, however, seem to be frequently applied. There are two main reasons for this. First, to be implemented, it requires reliable information about past production performances on the commons, an information which is liable to be seriously disputed by at least some of the competing claimants. Second, the underlying principle of sharing may run counter to traditional conceptions of community membership according to which access to resources validates membership in a community and inequality in the distribution of access rights would be perceived as reflecting an implicit hierarchy in social status. To put it in another way, even though some members did not actually make use of their rights as much as others in the past, the fact remains that, as full-fledged members of the group, they continue to have the same virtual rights of use of community resources. If such resources are divided, therefore, they should not be discriminated against.

*Equal division* Under equal privatization, as rents are divided equally among all former rightsholders, some of them may be worse off because they were using the resource intensively before division. When the commons are primarily used by the rural poor, for instance, as a partial protection in times of unusual economic stress [Jodha, 1986, 1992; Das Gupta, 1987; Agarwal, 1991; Beck, 1994], equal division may make the vulnerable segments of the society worse off, thereby prompting their resistance to it.[12] Conversely, when the commons (such as grazing lands) are more intensively used by wealthier users, equal division may again be opposed, this time by the richer segments of the community. The redistributive effects of equal division thus depend on the initial wealth of those rightsholders who draw more income from the commons.[13] The main virtue of the uniform allocation formula is its minimal informational requirement, as it does not rely on individual characteristics.

The canonical case of equal division is the process of individualization of land tenure masterly described by Boserup. In this case, division is not opposed owing to the relatively equal standing of all rights-holders. I cannot resist the temptation to quote Boserup at some length:

> Virtually all the systems of land tenure found to exist before the emergence of private property in land seem to have this one feature in common: certain families are recognized as having cultivation rights within a given area of land... As long as a tribe of forest-fallow cultivators has abundant land at its disposal, a family would have no particular interest in returning to precisely that plot which it cultivated on an earlier occasion. Under these conditions a family which needed to shift to a new 5plot would simply find a suitable plot, or have it allocated by the chief of the tribe, with no regard to the question of who had formerly cultivated particular plots. But the situation is apt to change with increasing population, as good plots become somewhat scarce. The cultivators may then wish to begin to recultivate a given plot before the normal period of fallow has elapsed. Under such conditions, a family is likely to become more attached to the plots they have been cultivating on earlier occasions, because it is becoming difficult to find better plots elsewhere which are not already taken up by another family. In other words, the members of the tribe would tend to become more conscious and jealous about their special right to the old plots, and they may hasten to recultivate them lest the cultivation right be forfeited by desuetude...Thus, the attachment of individual families to particular plots becomes more and more important with the gradual shortening of the period of fallow and the reduction of the part of the territory which is not used in the rotation. By the same token, the general right for the members of the tribe to clear a new plot becomes less valuable... As more and more land is subject to specific cultivation rights little land will be available for redistribution by the chief, and valuable land for redistribution will become available mainly when a family dies out or leaves the territory... Redistribution of land thus becomes a less important and less frequently exerted function of the chief, and in the end it disappears altogether...[Boserup, 1965: 79–81; in the same vein, see de Zeeuw, 1997: 585].

Note also that the establishment of a feudal landlord class—usually originating from intruding tribes—as a ruling group with the right to extract tribute from the members of the conquered tribe, does not seem to interfere with the hereditary cultivation rights of the peasants. In the words of Boserup again, 'Usually the position of the cultivator with regard to his rights in land does not change because a feudal government imposes itself and levies taxes and labour services. The cultivator families continue to have their hereditary cultivation rights, both general and specific, and redistribution of land by village chiefs may continue without interference from the feudal landlords' [Boserup, 1965: 83].

*Exclusionary division* A possible form of exclusionary division is by dividing the resource equally, but among a restricted number of previous users only. There is thus much evidence in the literature of processes aimed at excluding some users from access to natural resources. These processes are rarely random.[14] They actually tend to discriminate against well-defined subgroups of users, of typically lower social and political status. Among them are former slaves, holders of secondary rights (particularly, herders and women), minority tribespeople, and immigrants (especially those of recent origin). In most cases, the processes of exclusion of vulnerable categories of claimants and division of resources are not simultaneous. As has been already pointed out, exclusion tends to occur in the first place and, even though it may possibly give rise to a strengthening of collective regulations, it is usually followed by division of the resource among the remaining claimants.

The current evolution of land tenure arrangements in Sub-Saharan Africa typically obeys this pattern where division takes on the form of granting increasingly stable rights to individual users on well-defined parcels of land (see *supra*). In this process, customary rights of access for outsiders and nomadic pastoralists are gradually restricted by the host community [see, e.g., Noronha, 1985; Laurent et al., 1994][15] and, at later stages, exclusionary processes start to affect weaker categories within that community itself. Thus, access to land is, to an increasing extent, denied to divorced women or widows (and to their children), as well as to native villagers who have outmigrated [Moore, 1988; Whitehead, 1990; Seppälä, 1993; Watts, 1993; Mackenzie, 1993; André and Platteau, 1998; Van den berg, 1997]. In so far as it applies only to a certain category of families—those with general cultivation rights in the village lands—, the above description of individualization of land rights by Boserup is, strictly speaking, an illustration of exclusionary division of common property resources.

In the above case, exclusionary division of the village common property is thus carried out through (increasingly) restrictive definition of community membership. It is worth emphasizing, however, that exclusion may also take on the form of more or less forceful private appropriation of local commons by the village elite. Note that in this case scale economies and risk-reduction properties of communal ownership are preserved, yet at the expense of erstwhile claimants who lose their traditional access rights. The best documented historical example of such an exclusionary process is the so-called enclosure of common lands that occurred in England in two main waves during the 16th and the 18th centuries. Through exclusion of customary rights-holders, English landlords succeeded in appropriating for themselves the major part of village commons. Cohen and Weitzman (1975) and Allen (1992) have persuasively argued that this historical appropriation process was essentially driven by the landlords' interest in redistributing income in their favour and not by their desire to introduce technical changes and to benefit from scale economies. The shift to the new property regime has been imposed by the landlord class either in an open fashion or in more indirect and subtle ways involving the poor's apparent consent—the second wave of enclosures was accomplished by some 5,000 acts of Parliament and at least an equal number of voluntary agreements [McCloskey, 1972: 15].[16]

There are numerous contemporary examples of similar privatization processes in the developing world. An interesting illustration is the aforementioned division of common-grazing land in present-day Botswana studied by Peters [1994, mainly chap. 3]. It deserves to be described in some detail.

In the Kgatleng district of the southeastern part of the country, private investment in boreholes has provided a key means for the wealthier cattle owners (foremost among whom were chiefs and elders) to acquire de facto private ownership rights over the surrounding grazing lands that were traditionally under communal control. The institutional change was effected through the operation of borehole syndicates manipulated to the advantage of the cattle owning political elite (the chiefs, the leading royal families and wealthy commoners) but cast as a traditional form of kgotla (the customary assembly and structure of authority for Tswana people). In the words of Peters, 'the choice of the syndicate and its designation as kgotla solved the unstated problem of the legitimacy of private ownership of stock-watering boreholes in the grazing areas. The chiefly elite and leading men of the commoner were the only ones who could afford to undertake borehole development, and they clearly favored a type of organization that gave them more leeway in providing more exclusive rights to valued resources and in separating them from the unprogressive mass. (...) Referring to the new group form of ownership as kgotla meant that a radically new organization was clothed in a well-known and legitimate gown. (...) From their inception, then, the new borehole syndicates had a double face: a traditional organizational form that could include more than the owners, yet a new corporation that guaranteed privileged access to valuable resources to some at the cost of others' [Peters, 1994: 67–70].[17]

The (deluding) appearance of group ownership which the adoption of the syndicate form helped to preserve prevented people chased away from areas where new boreholes were drilled from apparently contesting the new occurring changes. Opposition was all the more dampened as 'many poorer families were incorporated into the syndicates and granted access to water and pastures either informally as dependents (junior kins or clients who paid no fees) or formally as hirers (who paid fees).' [Peters, 1994: 74]. Especially worth noting is the fact that most syndicates were opposed to ranches precisely because they did not want to antagonize common people too much. In the words of Peters:

> In addition to the fact that most of even the big owners considered the financial costs of establishing a ranch to be too high, there were political constraints on their overt embrace of the new policy....the public embrace of the new policy in the late 1970s was a demonstration of exclusionary rights to land that was made difficult by the large number of persons likely to be excluded from a more permanently divided commons, the dangers of sabotage by those excluded, and the persistent power of the ideology of common tribal affiliation and one of its main embodiments, the common range...While most syndicates were not interested and even opposed to ranches, they were all interested in protecting themselves against being forced to absorb nonmembers [Peters, 1994: 177, 187].

An important lesson from the above story is that the transaction costs of resource division may be very high if allowance is made for all the expenditures that may have to be incurred to overcome the resistance and the resentment of customary rights-holders against the new property arrangement. As a matter of fact, the costs of enforcing exclusive property rights depend on the way distribution of wealth is affected and on the perceived legitimacy of the new arrangement by the dispossessed users.[18] Even wealthy Tswana cattle owners appear to be reluctant to enclose their ranches because the costs involved are too high, particularly due to fears of jealous acts of sorcery and sabotage—'if fences were put up, someone would cut them down' [Gulbrandsen, 1990: 171–72; Peters, 1994: 169].

There are many other reported cases in which village elites indulge in greedy acts with a view to appropriating common-property resources for their own profit. Often, customary custodians of local resources grant exploitation licences to outsiders as though they were private owners, implying that they collect underhand dues on their own account. In the Niger river delta, Mali, for example, the expression 'profiteer water master' has recently gained currency in certain areas where there are mounting tensions about rights of access to inland fisheries [Fay, 1990b: 232–3; see also, Verdeaux, 1990: 203; Freudenberger and Mathieu, 1993: 16; Hviding and Baines, 1994: 29–30; Colchester, 1994: 79,82]. In Asia, common-property resources may be appropriated by powerful elite members pulling the strings of pseudo-legal auctioning mechanisms. A vivid illustration of such practices is the allocation of water bodies used for inland fishing in Bangladesh as described in the aforementioned study by Toufique (1997).

In the context of a transition between traditional subsistence-oriented economy and an emerging market economy, undue appropriation of village-level natural resources by unscrupulous local elites may aim at their disposal through illegitimate and secret sales acts. This may happen when they suddenly realize that common property assets command a substantial value on the (sales or rental) market, yet fear that regular illicit transactions (such as underhand rental dealings) will soon be detected and resisted by common people. The temptation to do so is all the stronger as the sale price of the resource is high enough to open up entirely new economic opportunities for the customary custodians. It must also be pointed out that when the transition period is characterized by a high uncertainty about the nature of future rights of use, the elite is in a privileged position to respond to this uncertainty by appropriating the resource and realize its market value [Baland and Platteau, 1996: 281].

Recognizing exclusionary division as an important empirical case of distribution of the commons, it is not clear that, even when a former user is deprived of his customary rights of access, he will necessarily lose in the process. This is because he can be hired as a wage earner to work on the privatized resource. Weitzman (1974) demonstrates, however, that under these circumstances dispossessed resource users are necessarily worse off [see also Samuelson, 1974]. As a matter of fact, the wage earned in the newly created labour market is always lower than the income obtained under communal ownership. In the case of quasi-linear preferences (so that the labour supply curve is unaffected by income changes), it is easy to represent this argument diagrammatically. Assume that the average product, $AP$, is decreasing in the variable factor, $L$ (this is indeed the classical situation where the

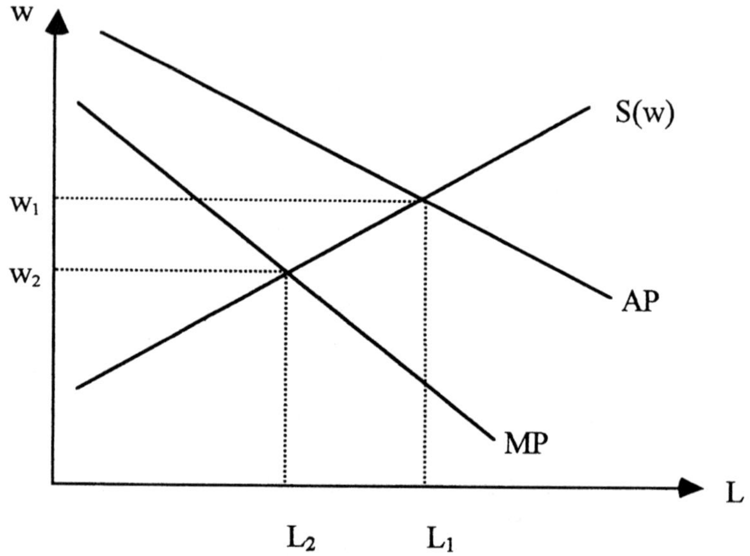


Figure 3.1: The welfare impact of privatization

tragedy of the commons arises). Thus the marginal product of the variable factor, *MP*, is also decreasing and, for each level of *L*, *MP(L)* < *AP(L)*. Let us draw the supply curve of the variable factor, *S(w)*, where $w$ stands for its market price, and assume that $S'(w) > 0$. Then we can draw the diagram depicted in Figure 3.1.

First, consider the open access situation. The variable factor is remunerated at its average product equal to $w_1$. In the new situation, with a competitive labour market, the wage rate will be set at the level $w_2$. Comparing the two, $w_2 < w_1$, $L_2 < L_1$, and $w_2L_2 < w_1L_1$, so that the remuneration of the variable factor falls.

Under common property, with no free entry and a given number of users, all rents from the resource need not be dissipated, and income, *w(CP)* is higher than $w_1$. As a result, it will also be higher than $w_2$. As for the amount of labour spent under common property, it is of course smaller than that obtained under open access (since output is restricted and labour is the only production factor considered), yet larger than that achieved under private property. It is therefore certain that the wage bill is greater under common than under private property.

The practical implication of this analysis is, in the words of Weitzman, that 'there may be a good reason for propertyless variable factor units to be against efficiency improving moves (...) like the introduction of property rights (...) unless they get a specific kickback in one form or another.' [Weitzman, 1974: 234]. It is indeed striking from Weitzman's proof that former resource users lose not only in terms of employment but also on account of reduced individual labour earnings. This is because the rent collected by landlords exceeds the extra output society achieves by shifting from the open-access (or the common property) to the private ownership equilibrium [Samuelson, 1974].

However, when workers are heterogeneous with different skill levels, the above result can be reversed implying that dispossessed rights-holders may possibly benefit from privatization of the commons [Brito et al., 1997]. The Samuelson-Weitzman argument implicitly assumes that labour is homogeneous and that the landowner has sufficient information to monitor worker performance. In these conditions, the same outcome can be achieved by him regardless of the institutional arrangements. When workers are heterogeneous, on the contrary, institutional arrangements associated with ownership as well as the technology that creates the externality become crucial and the outcome of privatization (whether it is Pareto-improving) is highly sensitive to the particular assumptions made. More precisely, the institutional arrangements of a licensor (the private owner charges a fixed fee for the use of the fixed factor) or a two-part tariff on effort or output (a linear tax with a fixed entry fee) can lead to an increase in the income of the variable factor after privatization (since, in hose cases, the owner is not able to appropriate all the gains from privatization).[19]

A final remark is in order. When the division is incomplete or partial, say because privatization affects only the most valuable part of the resource, exclusion of some users may easily lead them to over-exploit any remaining commons. Perverse effects are then likely to develop which may lead to a degradation, rather than to an improvement, in the average state of the resource [Baland and Platteau, 1996: 41–42]. In a Karnataki village analyzed by Karanth, 'the consequences of privatization of common-property resources in land was that there was a gradual depletion of village pasture. Farmers became increasingly dependent upon the forests for grazing, which in turn led to depletion of forest resources too' [Karanth, 1992: 1687]. According to Bromley, 'the marginal ecosystems are asked to take on those slaughed off from the highly commercialized lands, the exclusion rights that run with fee-simple land redirect people to the marginal ecosystems.' [Bromley, 1986: 594].[20]

In addition, the very (big) users who benefit from privatization may be tempted to continue to use their customary rights of access to the remaining commons and to thereby contribute to their degradation. For example, the livestock projects funded by the World Bank to establish cattle and sheep ranches in Botswana turned out to be glaring failures, partly because 'ranchers moved their excess cattle back onto the communal range, although the [new grazing land] policy had proposed that the commercial ranches would be the funnel for removing cattle from the overcrowded communal areas' [Peters, 1994: 149].

*Rotating access to limited indivisible resources* As is evident from the above discussion, division of common property resources may take on different forms but each of them has important redistributive effects which may undermine their acceptability among customary rights-holders. The process of resource division is clearly liable to involve significant reshuffling of individual status and thereby threaten the existing social balance. As a consequence of these potentially disturbing effects, in the absence of a powerful village elite able to either act as enlightened leaders or to impose a self-interested mode of division, community decisions tend to be biased in favour of the status quo even though this institutional inertia may result in resource degradation. Thus, in the area around Yalogo in the northern (sahelian) part of Burkina Faso, local agriculturalists do not dare fence irrigable customary lands for the purpose of intensive vegetable cultivation because they do not want to call into question the herders' traditional rights of access during the dry season (personal observation).

Alternatively, community decisions can lead to institutional innovations within the communal ownership regime when there is a determined resolution to ensure equity and safeguard social peace among resource users. For instance, when following population growth a resource domain becomes too narrow relative to the size of the user population, a frequent solution consists for communities of guaranteeing to all their members a rotating access to the scarce resource sites. In the case of the Alanya fishery (Turkey), local fishermen began in the early seventies to experiment, on a trial-and-error basis, with a mechanism for regulating the use of the available fishing sites in an equitable manner. This institutional innovation was actually motivated by the need to reduce the incidence of conflicts that had become increasingly frequent and violent due to enhanced competition among fishermen for the better sites, as well as by the need to decrease the costs resulting from more difficult search for, and more intense fighting over, a fishing spot.

The guiding principles of the system eventually adopted are the following. First, within the area normally used by Alanya fishermen, all suitable fishing locations are named and listed. Second, a list of all eligible fishermen is laid down and in the beginning of the fishing season the eligible fishermen meet in the coffee house to draw lots and are thus assigned to a given fishing site except those who draw blanks because the number of candidates exceeds that of the available sites. Third, once the season has started, each fisherman makes a daily move eastward to the next site and, after the middle of the season has been reached, each fisherman moves west so as to give all participants equal opportunities at the stocks that migrate from east to west during the first half and from west to east during the second half of the season [Berkes, 1986].

In a lagoon fishery located near Sète in southern France, mussel fishermen use a similar system (personal observation). Here, however, despite the scarcity of fishing sites, rights of use are assigned for a full year. If rotation is thus much lower than in Alanya, it is because mussels are cultivated in the sea and they have a long crop cycle making a fishing site akin to a land plot. As for the losers in the lottery—the lottery decides not only how the best sites are to be allotted but also who is going to be denied access to the lagoon—like in the Alanya fishery they have to fall back on other activities and wait till the next year's registration process to try their chance again [for other examples in various sectors, see Alexander, 1982; Jeay, 1984; Guha, 1985; McKean, 1986; Cordell and McKean, 1986; Messerschmidt, 1986; Mahdi, 1986; Arnold and Campbell, 1986; Taylor, 1987; Lawry, 1989a; Platteau and Seki, forthcoming].

*Overlooking the role of the state*

That the state can influence the outcome of institutional change through its policy choices is suggested by abundant evidence. To begin with, states can have different views about the role of user communities in owning and managing local natural resources. At one extreme, a state can decide to give maximum empowerment to user communities by passing legislation specifically designed to support common-property systems. For example, in Japan the legal sanctioning and the constitutional guaranteeing of the property rights of fishing communities (organized as co-operative associations) over inshore waters has been an important factor underlying the success of a highly original system of decentralized management of coastal fisheries [Ruddle, 1987; Asada et al., 1983; Platteau and Seki, 2000]. In South Korea, Nepal and the Philippines, the law entitles village communities to generate the necessary rules, regulations and operational measures required to enforce local-level collective management of forestry resources. This has implied that the state (and the forest department in particular) relinquishes power and responsibility to manage forests through village forestry programmes [Arnold, forthcoming].

In Indonesia, the government came in support of decentralized management of coastal fisheries by granting fishermen communities exclusive tenure rights over a delimited portion of the sea. In this case, however, the motive behind the legal support of user groups was purely political: to placate mounting Islamist and nationalist opposition forces by earmarking local waters for (Muslim) Indonesian small-scale fishermen at the expense of Chinese-owned industrial vessels [Mathew, 1990; Baland and Platteau, 1996: 258–60]. Given the heavy involvement of Suharto in Chinese business ventures, it is not surprising that enforcement of the exclusive fishing rights of small-scale coastal fishermen has been much less rigorous than in the case of Japan. In other words, the class-orientation of the Indonesian regime has determined a strategy which, despite appearances to the contrary, has not resulted in the devolution of *de facto* property rights to artisanal fishermen communities.

In other, much more frequent instances, state interventions have had the intended or unintended effect of destroying local capacities for collective regulation. In the case of Sahelian forests, for instance, when scarcity became apparent in the late 1960s, state-imposed rules 'emasculating local organization' have hindered resource management efforts at local level. 'As it happened, most villages had lost their power of independent activity as the result of efforts of both the colonial and independent regimes to establish controls over major forms of organization in rural areas. Villages (or quarters within them) had no authority to enforce sanctions against violators of locally devised use rules' [Thomson et al., 1986: 399].

In addition, owing to highly imperfect enforcement of state regulations or to pervasive corruption, nationalization of natural resources or equivalent measures have often transformed regulated common properties into *de facto* open access resources [see, e.g., Kone, 1985: 100; Lawry, 1989a: 5; Baland and Platteau, 1996: 235–62; Noronha, 1997: 54]. In some instances, open access is almost deliberately created by the state, such as when its declared policy is to make natural resources which were formerly owned and managed by local communities (e.g., the inland fisheries in the Niger delta, Mali) accessible to all national citizens [Baland and Platteau, 1996: 247–48].

A similar outcome may ensue when the government heavily subsidizes the intrusion into traditional resource territories of modern business interests with which it often actively colludes. In Brazil, for instance, the exemption from taxation of virtually all agricultural income combined with the rule that logging is regarded as proof of land occupancy has strongly encouraged rich people to acquire forest lands for the purposes of maximum exploitation [Binswanger, 1991; Mahar, 1988]. Not only deforestation but also dispossession or disfranchisement of traditional user communities have resulted from this ill-conceived policy.

In the Philippines, to take another example, the now defunct government agency Panamin (Presidential Assistance to National Minorities), which was officially set up for the purpose of protecting the indigenous people's rights and interests, actually played a disastrous role amouting to sheer betrayal of its mission. In the words of Marcus Colchester, 'far from preventing the pillage of indigenous lands by mining companies, loggers and hydropower projects, Panamin collaborated with the armed forces in depriving the peoples of their ancestral lands' [Colchester, 1994: 74]. The fact of the matter is that the majority of this agency's board members 'came from wealthy industrialist families, many of whom had direct financial interests in companies encroaching on indigenous lands'. This was certainly the case for Manuel Elizalde, a relative of President Marcos, who played the key role in Panamin. His political base and personal wealth, indeed, lay in extractive concerns such as mining, logging and agribusiness. Moreover, he maintained his own private army in Cotobato in Mindanao to fight the insurgent indigenous peoples who, in despair, took up arms against the government by joining the communist insurgency group [*ibidem*: 75].

Degradation of common properties is particularly likely when the state subsidizes destructive techniques to be used or activities to be performed by private individuals or companies. Just think of the considerable public support, mainly in the form of tax concessions and provision of infrastructure (as well as international loans from the World Bank and other donor agencies), given to the expansion of beef-cattle production in the fragile ecological conditions of the Amazon basin [Feder, 1977, 1979; Repetto, 1988; Dasgupta and Mäler, 1995: 2426–28], or in countries like Botswana, Mexico, or Costa-Rica. With particular reference to Botswana, Zufferey went so far as saying that 'if one considers the amount of financial support allocated to the cattle industry in comparison to that allocated to planning and managing land resources it would not be entirely wrong to say that disaster is actually subsidised' [Zufferey, 1986: 89; in the same vein, see Binswanger, 1991]. Subsidization of imported trawler boats in many Asian countries constitutes another striking example of a government-supported thoughtless acceleration of the rate of exploitation of a commons which ended up disfranchising small-scale fishermen and crew labourers [Kurien, 1978, for India].

The situation obtaining in East Kalimantan's forests, Indonesia, vividly illustrates the possibility that customary rights-holders be deprived of access to village commons when licensing rights are awarded to private companies. Thus, in the early 1970s the Indonesian government granted timber concessions to a large number of foreign and national companies, and, according to Jessup and Peluso, this had several detrimental effects on local communities. In particular, 'despite their legal right to collect minor forest products within timber concessions, villagers have at times been denied entry to those areas, and timber company personnel have otherwise infringed on the rights of local residents'. For instance, there is evidence of timber company guards confiscating *rattan* from collectors, of loggers raiding caves and selling the stolen birds' nests to unauthorised buyers, and of timber companies illegally cutting Borneo ironwood, a species reserved for local use, acts which sometimes led to violent confrontations between local inhabitants and company guards or loggers [Jessup and Peluso, 1986: 520–1].

In Sarawak, Malaysia, forest-dwellers feel equally helpless even if, like in the above case of Indonesia, the process of dispossession is less brutal and open than in the Philippines. We are thus told that, in Sarawak, 'the corrupting influence of the timber trade has promoted the domination of the economy by nepotistic, patronage politics', with the consequence that rural peoples 'can no longer rely on their political representatives to defend their interests': as a matter of fact, 'the practice of dealing out logging licences to members of the state legislature to secure their allegiance is so commonplace in Sarawak that it has created a whole class of instant millionaires'. The consequences of this policy bias in Sarawak are particularly catastrophic. As a matter of fact, 'the World Bank has estimated that the country is logging its forests at four times the sustainable rate, while the International Timber Organisation predicts that the primary forests of Sarawak will be logged out by the turn of the century' [Colchester, 1994: 79, 82]. In such circumstances, it is not surprising that most popular protest movements in Asian forest areas have directed their main criticism at the logging licenses generously distributed by too often corrupt governments.

In lending support to rural elites and powerful urban interests (including its own high-ranking personnel) to help them gain access to valuable natural resources, national states may have recourse to various legal subterfuges. An oft-used method, already applied by the colonial powers to redistribute indigenous lands in favour of white settlers, consists of withdrawing lands from village control by labelling them state property and later awarding them to friends of the regime through de-classifying procedures. Such a method, for example, is currently employed by the Senegalese state in the case of the lands of the Senegal river valley, much to the fury of helpless customary rights-holders [for other examples, see Bassett and Crummey, 1993].

Note finally that, in the aforetold story of exclusionary privatization of common grazing lands in Botswana, the state has also given an helping hand to powerful private interests: 'There is no doubt that some of the highly placed members of the government and party who promote the policy [aiming at the fencing of the commons] benefit directly as wealthy cattle and borehole owners. In addition, the government's apparent blindness to criticism in calling for expansion of the policy is partially driven by political considerations. Much of the strongest support for the ruling Botswana Democratic Party comes from the wealthier cattle owners. The resistance of government to consider either increasing taxation of cattle owners (a point of contention with the World Bank) or the abolition of dual rights seems attributable to fear of jeopardizing this support' [Peters, 1994: 22].

What all these examples unambiguously show is that exclusionary division of rural commons (see *supra*) is often actively encouraged and even engineered by the state, with the complicity of big national or international business interests. Clearly, therefore, state interventions have an amazing capacity to disturb the evolutionary sequence sketched by Hayami and Kikuchi. It is all the harder to believe in a naive evolutionary view of institutions according to which they always evolve in efficiency-increasing ways. To have a better grasp of the likely institutional trajectory of a country, we need to gain a better understanding of when and how effectively a given state supports enforcement of private property rights and contracts, or public property of nationalized resources; when and why it views local communities, groups and organizations as a threat to central power or, alternatively, as an effective relay to national policies and as one of the pillars of a democratic polity; and, above all, under which circumstances and through which methods it allies with powerful actors (rural or urban) by helping them to appropriate natural resources at the expense of customary rights-holders (which means that we need to know more about the class nature of the state).

### 3.4 CONCLUSION

The (qualified) property rights doctrine, duly supplemented by the induced institutional innovation hypothesis, and the seminal work of Boserup have undoubtedly laid the basis for a serious discussion of the complex issue of evolution of property arrangements. Regarding land rights, attention has been drawn to the critical role of factor endowments, particularly that of population growth and agricultural commercialization. This said, their analysis of the transformation of property systems is still far from providing us with a complete and satisfactory theory. There is the oft-made critique that, by giving pride of place to efficiency considerations in their explanatory scheme, they have unduly neglected the potentially powerful influence of distributive considerations. It is simplistic to assume that once aggregate benefits from an institutional innovation exceed the costs, this innovation will spontaneously emerge. The way the benefits are distributed among the various actors involved and the respective political weight of the latter are bound to influence outcomes, as the history of institutions amply attests.

Lack of attention to equity aspects is not the only limitation of the property rights approach. The role of social capital and, above all, that of the state are also bypassed. Such neglect has led property rights theorists and their evolutionist followers to overlook evolutionary trajectories different from privatization and collective regulation, including the dreadful prospect of resource degradation under an open-access regime. Moreover, by overlooking the considerable ability of state agents to trigger and support exclusionary processes of commons division, this approach tends to present too benign a view of evolution of property rights.

In the following chapter, I actually pursue the discussion by shifting attention from the question of the division of communal resources to that of individualization of land rights. This will lead us to consider an important component of private property, namely transfer rights, that has so far been left aside. Until now, indeed, attention has been centered on private rights of use the costs and benefits of which determine whether it is profitable or not to privatize (in the sense of dividing or apportioning) common properties.

## APPENDIX: THE ANALYTICS OF COMMON PROPERTY

### I. COMMUNAL OWNERSHIP WITH fiXED MEMBERSHIP VS OPEN ACCESS

Consider an unfenced piece of grazing land on which cattle belonging to various herders can mingle freely [see Baland and Platteau, 1996: 30–31]. Given the limited character of the resource, the average product per cattle head is greater than the marginal product, and the average product is a declining function of the total size of the herd grazing on the land. Denoting by $Y$ the total output generated on the common pasture area, by $N$ the total number of animals put to grazing, and by $n_i$ the number of animals placed by individual $i$, assume that the production technology is described by the following

$$Y = a \cdot N - b \cdot N^2 = a\left[\sum_i n_i\right] - b\left[\sum_i n_i\right]^2$$

profit function of any resource user can be written
Further assume that $p$ is the rental price of an animal unit so that the profit function of any resource user can be written thus

$$P_j = \frac{n_j}{\sum_i n_i}\left[a\left(\sum_i n_i\right) - b\left(\sum_i n_i\right)^2\right] - pn_j$$

To begin with, let us first analyze the question of open access. When a given resource is in open access, the agents have to decide whether or not they should 'enter' and start exploiting the resource. Their choice is based on a comparison between the price to bear for entry and the expected (average) income. At equilibrium, the net expected benefit is zero. Since the agents' private evaluation of expected benefits does not take into account the fall in others' incomes caused by their entry, the resulting situation will be typically inefficient. The open-access equilibrium number of cattle heads placed in the pasture area, denoted by $N^o$, is obtained by setting *Y/N* equal to $p$ and characterizes the Tragedy of the Commons:

$$N^0 = \frac{a-p}{b} \tag{3.1}$$

Let us now consider a situation where an exclusive right of access to the resource is assigned to a well-defined social group: there is communal ownership of the resource to the extent that membership rules exist and are enforced by an authority structure. This regime is analytically distinct from the open access situation in the sense that agents are now expected to interact strategically with each other. In other words, they do not any more think that the final outcome is independent of their own individual decisions (as is the case under open access) but, when they make their decision, they take into account the intensity of harvesting effort decided by the other agents. Since all users behave in this manner, decisions are strategically interdependent. The appropriate framework to analyze such interdependent decision-making is non-cooperative game theory and a suitable equilibrium concept is that of Nash equilibrium (given the strategies followed by all other users, an individual's best response is not to deviate from his chosen harvesting effort).

To keep calculations as simple as possible at this stage, let us assume that there are only two herders in the rights-holding group. The profit function of, say, the first herder is therefore

$$P_1 = \frac{n_1}{n_1+n_2}\left[a(n_1+n_2) - b(n_1+n_2)^2\right] - p \cdot n_1$$

Given $n_2$, the profit-maximizing number of cattle heads for user 1 is:

$$n_1^N = \frac{a-p-b \cdot n_2}{2b} \tag{3.2}$$

*Mutatis mutandis*, the same result obtains for the second herder. Solving this two-equation system yields the Nash-equilibrium values of cattle herd size which are identical for both herders:

$$n_1^N = n_2^N = \frac{a-p}{3b} \tag{3.3.}$$

The aggregate Nash-equilibrium herd size is:

$$N^N = \frac{2(a-p)}{3b} \tag{3.4}$$

Note that, as expected, the pressure on the common pasture is lower under communal property with membership rules than under open access: in this example, the total herd size when agents belong to a well-defined rights-holding group is equal to two-thirds the size obtaining under conditions of free entry. Unlike in the case of open access where competition between many users drives them to dissipate the whole resource rent (since they decide to enter and exploit the resource as long as the net expected benefit from doing so is positive), users operating under communal property with fixed membership stop short of reaching this extremely wasteful result.

It is interesting to generalize the above Nash-equilibrium result and examine how it evolves as the number of rights-holders increases. Denoting by $M$ the total number of members in the rights-holding group, it is easy to show that

$$n_i^N = \frac{a-p}{(M+1)b}$$

The ratio of the Nash-equilibrium total herd size placed in the common pasture to the open-access equilibrium value is then

$$R^{N,0} = \frac{N^N}{N^0} = \frac{\sum_i n_i^N}{N^0} = \frac{M}{M+1} = \frac{1}{1+\dfrac{1}{M}} \tag{3.5}$$

It is then straightforward that, when $M$ becomes great, the total herd size placed in the common pasture under communal property with fixed membership will increase and gradually approach the open access outcome: lim $R^{N,O}$ when $M$ tends to infinity is equal to 1. In words, when the number of members in the rights-holding group is very high, the outcome of their strategic interactions does not differ from that obtained under the free and rent-dissipating competition of the open access regime. This is because the higher the number of rights-holding members the smaller the extent to which they can take into account the negative consequences of their actions on the productivity of the common property [Baland and Platteau, 1996: 31].

### II. PRIVATE PROPERTY, COMMUNAL PROPERTY WITH RULES OF USE, AND OPEN ACCESS

Let us determine the number of cattle heads that would be allowed in the pasture area if the latter resource were the private property of a single owner. Since (economic) externalities would then be perfectly internalized, this number should correspond to the social optimum. In fact, the maximization problem of this private owner can be written in the following manner:

$$\underset{N^p, G}{Max}\; N^p \cdot G \quad subject\ to$$

$$G \leq \frac{Y}{N^p} - p,$$

$$Y = Y(N^p, A),$$

where $A$ is the total grazing land area, and $N^p \cdot G$ is the total rental income of the private owner given that he charges a unit rent of $G$ per animal and that $N^p$ is the number of animals allowed to graze in his pasture. Both $N^p$ and $G$ are decision variables used by the owner. The first constraint is a participation constraint: if it is violated, nobody would be interested in putting his animals to graze in the pasture because the rent charged by the owner is too high to make this operation profitable. At equilibrium, this constraint must obviously hold with equality. As for the second constraint, it is simply the production function describing the way output modifies as the number of animals grazing in the pasture area (of a given size) increases.

Substituting the two constraints in the objective function yields

$$Max\left(\frac{Y(N^p, A)}{N^p} - p\right)N^p \quad with\ respect\ to\ N^p$$

The optimal value of $N^p$ is therefore inferred from the familiar equilibrium equation:

$$\frac{dY(N^{p^*}, A)}{dN^{p^*}} = p \tag{3.6}$$

As for the optimal value of the unit rent, it is obtained by substituting the optimal value of $N^p$ into the participation constraint:

$$G^* = \frac{Y(N^{p^*}, A)}{N^{p^*}} - p \tag{3.7}$$

It is noteworthy that the aforedescribed maximization problem of the private owner is formally identical with the problem facing a collectivity owning the same resource and endowed with the power to define and enforce rules of use so as to reach the optimum social outcome:

$$Max\, Y(N^p, A) - p \cdot N^p$$

This is an expected result since in both cases externalities are perfectly internalized. Also worth noting is the fact that, under constant returns to scale, the same equivalence result obtains when private property, instead of being concentrated in the hands of a monopolist, is parcelled out among several owners. Assume that the land area, $A$, is thus divided among $M$ herders. The production function of each of them is then given by

$$y = y\left(n^p, \frac{A}{M}\right) = y(n^p, a)$$

Considering output per unit of pasture area, we get:

$$z = \frac{y}{a} = z\left(\frac{n^p}{a}\right)$$

The maximizing problem of each herder is therefore

$$\underset{n^p}{Max}\, a\left(z - p\left(\frac{n^p}{a}\right)\right)$$

And the F.O.C. is simply equal to

$$z'\left(\frac{n^{p*}}{a}\right) = p,$$

which implies that $\left(\frac{n^{p*}}{a}\right)$ and $\left(\frac{y}{a}\right)$ are both constant. In other words, whatever the value of $a$, that is, whatever the number $M$ of users among whom the total available pasture area, $A$, is divided, the number of animals put to graze per unit area remains identical. As a consequence, total herd size or aggregate output is clearly identical whether private property is concentrated in the hands of a single owner or shared out among a given number of rights-holders. Moreover, it corresponds to the efficient outcome that would be achieved under a collective property regime.

In the particular case of the function $Y = a \cdot N - b \cdot N^2$, it is easy to see that the efficient solution is

$$N^{p^*} = \frac{a-p}{2b} \tag{3.8}$$

In other words, under private ownership or under the equivalent regime of complete collective ownership when rules of use are added to membership rules, the pasture would contain only half the number of animals that would be grazing under open access conditions. For another thing, comparing equation (3.4) with equation (3.8) shows that when there are only two members in the rights-holding group, the number of grazing animals under communal property with membership rules (but no rules of use) is equal to four-thirds the socially optimum number that obtains under either private ownership or complete collective (communal) ownership.

## NOTES

1. This point is not always well understood by social scientists who often erroneously attribute to economists the view that communal property is 'inherently' less efficient than private property [see, e.g, Firmin-Sellers, 1996: 151].
2. Thus, in early-nineteenth-century Thailand when land was abundant and labour scarce, 'there was a well-developed legal system to govern transactions in labor commitments. In contrast, the system of usufruct land rights was not as extensively developed' [Feder and Feeny, 1991: 138].
3. As should have now become clear, if a regular due is paid to the community's head by some users (typically, strangers adopted into the community) in exchange for access to local resources, it should not be construed as a rent reflecting the scarcity price of these resources (since land is abundant by assumption), but rather as a sort of tribute or gift manifesting acceptance of the local chief's political authority and willingness to abide by the locally prevailing rules [Meek, 1949: 132; Boserup, 1965: 82–83; Weigel, 1982: 64; Gruenais, 1986: 290].
4. In the words of Feder and Feeny: 'If the group holding exclusive communal rights is large enough, the distinction between communal property and open access becomes moot' [Feder and Feeny, 1991: 137].
5. Note that the indivisibility of natural resources needs not always arise from their spatial spreading. Thus, for example, a water source is extremely difficult to apportion to several users even though it is a highly concentrated resource.
6. High yield variance is also one of the five conditions favourable to common property listed by Netting. The four other conditions are a low value of resource productivity (see *supra*), few possibilities of intensification, a large area needed for effective use (see *supra*), and a large labour- and capital-investing group [Netting, 1976: 144].
7. Risks confronting herders do not only arise from climatic variations affecting the fertility of grazing lands but also from the occurrence of epidemics hitting the entire herd at the same time. To reduce the latter risk, the stock must be dispersed over distant areas with uncorrelated risks of animal diseases. Yet, in this case, common property of pastures does not provide a complete solution since the scattering of the herd entails an obvious supervision problem. This

problem is often solved by entrusting various portions of the stock to different herders with whom the owner has previously established trust relationships.

8. With the help of a two-player bargaining model, Peyton Young (1993b) has succeeded in showing that self-interested boundedly rational individuals can establish a convention amounting to de facto property rights in a situation where they compete for the use of an open access resource. Rationality is bounded because the players do not know the preferences of their opponent and can only infer the probability distribution of his harvesting efforts from observation of his actual behaviour in a limited number of random cases (recollections of preceding events are random). In the very long run, Young demonstrates, there could emerge a convention that turns out to be 'generically stable' because it is not easily upset by mistakes. This convention specifies an asymmetric division of output where a higher share accrues to the player who is less risk-averse and has a greater information-collecting capacity. It appears as the self-generated outcome of a stochastic process and, once established, it is self-enforcing in the Nash equilibrium sense even though actors are not aware that such an equilibrium is being played (since they do not have prior knowledge of the other's risk preference and their capacity to collect informaton is limited).

   In other words, the institution of (de facto) property rights evolves in a spontaneous manner because people gradually learn from experience that limiting their level of effort helps increase their income. In this framework, therefore, no prior design or purposeful attempt by any individual or group of individuals is needed to establish such an institution. As stressed by Young, the result 'does not depend on agents' calculations about others' utility functions, their information, or the extent of their rationality. None of these things is common knowledge (or even mutual knowledge). The only thing we assume is that agents respond more or less rationally to concrete information about actions taken by their predecessors... The Nash solution is favored over the long run simply because it is the most *stable* given the agents' preferences and the random forces that constantly buffet the process about' [Young, 1998: 120].

9. This is particularly evident in the account provided by Hayami and Kikuchi of the differential evolution of rural social organizations (as measured by the tightness in community structure) in Thaïland's Central Plain on the one hand and in Japan and the mountainous areas of the Philippines (such as in the Ilocos region), on the other hand. In this account, indeed, the role of population density and topography (mountainous terrain is more congenial to local-level infrastructure) is quite predominant: thus, while in the major part of Thaïland's Central Plain, rice farming depends on the annual flooding of a major river delta, which is beyond the control of peasants either individually or in local cooperative groups, in Japan (and the Ilocos region of the Philippines) it initially developed in fan-shaped terraces in the valley bottoms and intermountain basins, a topography which makes local cooperation effective in controlling a water supply based on small streams [Hayami and Kikuchi, 1981: 22–23]. Note that, when public goods such as irrigation infrastructure require a spatial basis exceeding the rather confined limits of a village community, state intervention is called for. A complete, but daring, induced institutional innovation theory would argue that the right kind of state would emerge in such circumstances to solve the public good problem that conditions people's survival [see Wittfogel, 1957 and Allen, 1997, for attempts in that direction].

10. Careless management of privatized pastures contrasts with traditional mechanisms of collective regulation. Indeed, 'in earlier periods, the Kgatla, like other Tswana groups, had attempted to regulate, to a degree, the use of water sources and pastures. The chief had reminded cattle holders to water their herds from seasonal pans and streams in the rainy season, leaving the major rivers and springs so that the grass could regenerate in time for the return to those more permanent sources during the dry season. But these regulatory practices were disappearing along with the ritual role of the chiefs, which gave way gradually to the various committees designed to make tribal administration more democratic and more efficient.' [Peters, 1994: 82].

11. Note that this relationship between social capital and institutions runs in both ways since a past history of strong regulation tends itself to encourage resentment and resistance to collective regulation.

12. In so far as dividing equally the commons deprives agents of the possibility of falling back on an important source of complementary income in times of distress, equal division may in fact be Pareto-dominated by the inefficient common property regime [Baland and Francois, 1997].
13. Similar effects are also observed under collective regulation with uniform quotas [see Johnson and Libecap, 1982; Baland and Platteau, 1997].
14. For theoretical arguments explaining why random selection processes will generally be opposed by a majority of users, see Baland and Platteau (1996: chap. 8); Fernandez and Rodrik (1991) and Steinherr and Thisse (1979).
15. Examples can also be easily found in Europe in past centuries. Thus, at the end of the 15th century, as a result of rising pressure on the Alpine ecosystem the inhabitants of Törbel village signed a convention establishing an association to achieve collective regulation over the use of the alp, the forests and the waste lands. One important feature of this convention is that access to the latter was strictly limited to local citizens [Netting, 1981].
16. Note that, for an area to be enclosed under a Parliamentary Bill, a petition had to be signed by rights-holders representing 70–75 per cent of the area, not 70–75 per cent of the number of rights-holders [Allen, 1992].
17. Interestingly, the Tsana chiefly elite used modern efficiency arguments to vindicate their strategy of private appropriation. They explained: 'Where anything is used tribally no proper care is taken of that thing because any man can come along and use it, well knowing that any expenditures attaching to it he has not to bear alone.' [Peters, 1994: 64].
18. In fact, the shift to private (corporate or individual) rights over water sources could even be justified in terms of customary law in so far as, in being man-made, boreholes can be claimed as exclusive property by their initiators. This is in contrast to surface waters that were regarded as common property.
19. De Meza and Gould (1987) have shown that with multiple inputs labour may also be better off under private property than under free access provided that, inter alia, the externalities under the free-access regime are severe enough.
20. To take an example from pre-industrial Europe, Gilles and Jamtgaard report that 'the decline of the English commons may have resulted from the exclusion of animals from agricultural lands. In the English open field system, animals grazed on the commons during the summer months and fed on stubble and hay during the rest of the year. As fields became privately owned, animals had to spend longer periods on the commons. The result was over-grazing' [Gilles and Jamtgaard, 1981: 138]. Migration of workers from newly enclosed to unenclosed areas also contributed to the degradation of the commons system. 'The (...) effect was to be seen in the so far unenclosed towns and villages where some of the dispossessed tenants moved. The over-crowded squatter settlements set up on the border of these towns were a direct result of enclosures. Chambers notes that Nottingham, by its decision not to enclose, left itself no choice but to grow within its ancient manorial boundaries, and before the end of the 18th century, there were complaints of severe overcrowding. "By turning its face against enclosures, it had condemned itself to a period of unparallelled overcrowding and squalor..."' [Cohen and Weitzman, 1975: 326].

# Chapter 4

## PROPERTY RIGHTS IN LAND

### PART II: INDIVIDUALIZATION OF LAND TENURE

### 4.1 INTRODUCTION

As we have seen in Chapter 3, common properties can follow different evolutionary trajectories depending upon a host of complex factors, including not only the benefits of internalization of externalities and the (transaction) costs of privatization but also the social capital endowment of the particular society concerned, the character of state interventions and the redistributive impact of privatization. A common property may thus get reinforced through collective regulation, be partitioned into individual parcels of resource, or dissolve under the deleterious influence of the forces of strategic competition when neither private rights of use nor collective rules are established. In the present chapter, I assume that the common property resource has been successfully divided among a certain number of users.

Two questions then arise: to what extent do the private rights over the resource need to be consolidated and deepened, and does the required evolution take place in a more or less endogenous manner? In other words, the issue is both about the degree of individualization of land tenure that population pressure and increasing commercialization make necessary, and about whether the evolving environment is able to produce the new forms of land tenure.

According to one view, the main source of the inadequacy of land tenure systems in economically backward countries such as Africa is a fundamental disequilibrium or misfit between systems embodying a long tradition of extensive farming practices on the one hand, and the requirements of output growth in the context of intensive agriculture on the other hand [Lewis, 1955: 121; Eicher and Baker, 1982: 98–99; Giri, 1983; Falloux, 1987; Ault and Rutman, 1979; Gourou, 1991: 156]. Therefore, if this view is followed, nothing short of a drastic alteration of customary land rights under the aegis of determined public authorities is likely to constitute a viable solution to output losses resulting from the aforementioned misfit.

Another, much more optimistic doctrine—which, incidentally, has been endorsed by the World Bank in its report on the African economic crisis [World Bank, 1989: 104]—denies the empirical validity of such a static interpretation of African land systems. It instead proposes a dynamic picture in which indigenous land rights, under the impulse of market forces, are capable of significant autonomous evolution in the right (efficiency-enhancing) direction. Hence the label 'evolutionary theory of land rights' (ETLR) given to this doctrine [Platteau, 1996c]. Yet, it must be noted that, even in this view, a central role is reserved for public authorities inasmuch as autonomous changes in land rights need to be supported by a governmental intervention designed to formalize and consolidate these newly emerging rights.

This chapter is constructed as follows. In Section 2, answers to the above questions by evolutionary theorists of land rights are presented. In Section 3, the presumed effects of the individualization of land rights (particularly, the development of transfer rights in addition to use rights) and their formalization under the aegis of a central public authority are critically assessed in the light of empirical evidence available for Sub-Saharan Africa. In Section 4, discussion of the evolutionary views is being pursued by assessing the mechanism of induced demand for, and supply of, the institution of land titling. In the concluding section (Section 5), some policy implications from the findings discussed in the previous section are drawn.

## 4.2 THE ETLR: A PRESENTATION

### *The evolutionary sequence of land rights*

*General considerations* The basic contention of the ETLR is that, as land scarcity increases, people demand more land tenure security. As a result, private property rights in land tend to emerge and, once established, to evolve towards greater measures of individualization and formalization. Deepening individualization takes place along two main dimensions, namely the range of the rights held, and the extent of autonomy afforded by the landholder in exercising these rights.

The range refers to the package of rights enjoyed by the landholder, including rights of use and rights of transfer. Typically, rights over a given piece of land begin to be asserted by being able to freely choose which crop to grow, to freely dispose of the harvest output, and to prevent others from exploiting the same parcel (e.g., by grazing their livestock). Individualization makes its way through the gradual extension of use rights (for example, the right to recultivate the same plot of land even before the normal period of fallow has elapsed, or the right to plant trees and to bring other improvements to the land, are increasingly recognized) and, above all, through the addition of transfer rights. In an ascending order of hierarchical importance, the latter comprise the right to lend the land along traditional lines (that is, as part and parcel of a wider relationship of reciprocal exchange between two families and lineages), the right to give it, to bequeath it, to rent it out (against cash payments) to mortgage it and to sell it.

Individualization of land tenure is also reflected in the growing autonomy enjoyed by farmers regarding their decisions of use and, particularly, regarding their decisions to transfer land. Thus, in the initial stages of individualization, the rights to rent out or to sell land parcels are seriously circumscribed by the requirement that land ought to remain within the family or the lineage. It is the responsibility of the lineage heads to see to it that this condition is duly abided by and this is why their permission is explicitly required before any sale of land can take place. Such condition is however gradually relaxed as land becomes more scarce.

Turning now to formalization, the claim of the ETLR is that at advanced stages of the individualization process land transactions become increasingly supported by written evidence. In the ultimate stage of this process when the land becomes extremely scarce and valuable, public sector involvement is called for as there is a pressing demand for legally protected land titles. Maximum security of land tenure can then be achieved.

In other words, the ETLR contends that in most stages of the transformation process, a spontaneous movement towards individualization (and formalization) of land rights unfolds itself under the combined pressure of growing land scarcity and increasing commercialization of land-based activities. Yet, in the final stage, this endogenous evolution must be aided by a public intervention designed to consolidate and legally sanction the rights that have emerged on the field. Regarding the first aspect—the endogenous part of the process—, the following sequence typically comes out of many writings dealing with the situation of SSA specifically.

*Endogenous evolution* The considerable flexibility of indigenous land tenure arrangements in this region is tirelessly emphasized by many scholars.[1] In effect, as attested by the recent experience of many African countries, growing population pressure and increasing market penetration, particularly since colonial times (when commercial crops such as oil palm, cocoa, coffee, cotton, groundnuts, etc. have been introduced), have given rise to gradual but meaningful changes in land tenure practices in the direction of enhanced individualization of tenure, larger incidence of land sale transactions (first disguised, then increasingly in the open), increased use of money in connection with land loans, and a shift from matrilineal to patrilineal inheritance patterns.

During colonial times (and even before their advent in a few localized areas of high population density), increasing emphasis has been put on individual (or family) appropriation of land for exclusive use; rules of inheritance have evolved towards a more and more direct transmission of land between father and sons and, as a result of the increasing individualization of land tenure, the younger members of the village groups or communities have started to emancipate themselves (albeit rather slowly) from the elders' authority. Moreover, customary modes of land transfers through gifts, exchanges, loans, renting, pledges or possessory mortgages have intensified whereas sales of land, though often redeemable to the seller, have begun to take place running counter to one of the most deep-rooted customary limitations on land use. At first, sales were sanctioned only among members of the group (of common descent or residence), later to outsiders with approval of the group or its head, still later without such consent [Bruce, 1986: 38, 40]. In addition, sales may be initially subject to a right of preemption by family members or to a right of repurchase by the seller [Bruce, 1993: 42].

Note that, with greater integration of rural areas into the market economy and accentuating population pressure, the above modifications in African customary land tenure arrangements have tended to accelerate during the postindependence period, often in spite of the formal land laws enacted by the state (particularly so with respect to land transfers). Thus, in a country like Kenya where land hunger was pronounced due to white settlement, land markets had existed in many areas as early as the 1930s, although sales were redeemable to the seller (head or representative of descent group) upon repayment of the original price. Yet, by the end of the colonial period irredeemable land purchases began to emerge entailing a shift from clan rights to individual rights over land [Barrows and Roth, 1989: 5].

A recent study conducted by the World Bank shows that in a sample of ten regions in Ghana, Kenya, and Rwanda, the proportion of operated parcels acquired through purchase varies from less than one per cent to nearly 30 per cent while that which holders think to be freely saleable without requiring any sort of external approval varies from a low 6 per cent to more than 50 per cent. Moreover, these proportions appear to be higher when population pressure is stronger and/or commercialization is more advanced, at least in the case of Ghana and Rwanda [Migot-Adholla et al., 1991: 160–64]. In the highly populated prefecture of Gisenyi in Rwanda, Kanama commune (566 inhabitants per square kilometer and a rate of population growth of 4 per cent p.a.), as many as 39 per cent of the parcels operated in 1993 had been acquired through purchase, compared with only 29 per cent five years earlier [André and Platteau, 1998]! In addition, these frequencies were close to the proportions of operated land area acquired through purchase.

To my knowledge, it is only in certain areas of Uganda that such a high incidence of land purchases has been observed. For example, Baland, et al. (1999) have recently observed, on the basis of a survey of a large sample of 35 villages in the central part of the country, that 47 per cent of the total land area owned by the sample households have been purchased,[2] which is very close to the proportion of 45 per cent found for the areas of Mpigi (central Uganda) and Kabale (southern Uganda) by Swallow et al. (1994). It is interesting to notice that many land purchases in Uganda are the result of rural-rural migration, an important phenomenon in this country.

*Public sector involvement* Let us now turn to the second aspect—public sector involvement—of the hypothesized transformation of land rights in countries where land has become increasingly scarce. According to the ETLR, formal private property rights, far from being imposed *ex abrupto* by public authorities, actually emerge in response to a pressing demand indirectly expressed by increasingly insecure landholders. The story goes on like as follows.

When land acquires a scarcity value, landholders begin to feel uncertain about their (customary) rights and disputes over ownership of land, inheritance and land boundaries tend to multiply. Indeed, landholders assert increasingly individualized use rights to given plots as population continues to rise: the right to resume cultivation of a specific plot after a period of fallow; the right to assign the plot to an heir or to a tenant; the right to prevent holders of group or secondary claims (e.g. the right of pastoral herders to graze their animals on crop stubble) from exercising their traditional prerogatives; and the right to dispose freely of the land. This is bound to give rise to numerous conflicts which become more difficult to resolve and entail rising litigation costs. Yet, with the appreciation of land prices, the expected gain from obtaining specific land rights justifies to an increasing extent the transaction cost of disputation. This rising incidence of land conflicts and the accompanying threats to social order provide clear signals on which the government is called upon to act.

That litigation causes significant efficiency losses in the rural economy is evident since valuable resources are spent in non-productive activities. What must be added is that, even when there is no open dispute, the strategies used by people to claim new lands or to protect customary access are often costly not only from a private but also from a social viewpoint [see Meek, 1949; Berry, 1984: 89–96, 1988: 62–71; Noronha, 1985: 88–89, 208; Le Roy, 1985; Platteau, 1992: 163–175; Roth, 1993: 316–317]. This is particularly obvious when such strategies cause an underutilization of land resources, such as when landholders are reluctant to land or rent out their land for fear of losing their rights to it, or when they erect makeshift structures on the land or cultivate it in a desultory fashion to create the illusion that it is occupied and actually brought under cultivation.[3]

The expected response of national governments to these clear signals is to carry out administrative reforms so as to put an end to the wasteful use of rural resources and to the social tensions arising from land disputes. Sooner or later, such reforms will necessarily include a formal registration of private land rights and full-fledged land titling procedures (requiring the completion of a cadastral survey). As a consequence of formal adjudication, all conflicts will then be solved, leaving nothing to dispute. Social peace and political stability will follow.

A perfect illustration of the aforedescribed process is provided by the experience of Thailand. In the latter part of the 19th century, the agricultural terms of trade appreciated significantly following the expansion of international trading opportunities and a decline in the transportation costs. Land values rose perceptibly even though the area cultivated per person in fact increased owing to the flexibility of the agricultural frontier. Land disputes soon became endemic, which induced the Thai government to respond with a series of procedural and administrative reforms which culminated in the creation of a formal system of land titling in 1901 (cadastral surveys covering most of the commercialized areas in the central plain followed). For the economists who have studied the case of Thailand, the induced character of such institutional innovations leaves no doubt. For example, we are told that:

> ... the appreciation of land prices led to an increase in the demand for more systematic procedures for defining property rights in land. *The government in fact responded to the demands and a new system of property rights gradually evolved.* In part, the new system evolved as a practical solution to the land disputes that became so common as land became more valuable ... the new system of property rights reduced the divergence between the private and social rates of return on land development [Thomson et al., 1986: 415–16—my emphasis; see also Feeny, 1988: 283–87; Feder and Feeny, 1991: 138–39].

It is thus in response to the increased benefits of defining private property rights in land and to the growing need to resolve and reduce the incidence of land disputes through a centralized legal mechanism that the government started to create what was to become the current system of land rights in Thailand. Moreover, 'government officials, as landowners, shared in the gains from titling and were therefore willing to supply the institutional changes being demanded, especially in those areas in which they owned land' [Feder and Feeny, 1991: 139]. Looked at in this way, the task of the government appears essentially non-problematic. It only consists of supporting a change that is desired by everyone (including the officials who own land themselves), that is, of facilitating or hastening 'a transition caused by fundamental economic forces' [Bruce, 1986: 51]. In the words of Barrows and Roth, 'registration is best viewed as a policy to assist in the evolution of land tenure institutions under way ...' [Barrows and Roth, 1989: 24].

This conception of the role of the state in development is evidently close to that underlying Marx's general theory of modes of production in which change is essentially fuelled by the spontaneous unfolding of contradictions between productive forces and relations of production while the state's main function is apparently confined to shortening the transition period between two successive modes of production and to formalizing or consolidating the new mode. This is also a far cry from the voluntarist position of those who believe that, in Africa at least, the state must forcefully intervene to alter a land tenure system deemed incapable of a sufficiently rapid autonomous evolution [Ault and Rutman, 1979; Eicher and Baker, 1982; Giri, 1983; Falloux, 1987; Gourou, 1991].

The supply/demand mechanism behind the ETLR is explicitly grounded in the market analogy. There is some sort of 'political market' in which demand for an institutional innovation (land titling) is expressed and to which supply responds when a pivotal variable (relative factor endowments) reaches a certain threshold level. Thus, writes Runge, 'institutional innovation in property may by understood as similar to innovations in technology'. In the 'market for property institutions', 'demand results from the assurance which certain arrangements of rights provide and the supply is a function of the relative cost of providing particular rights ...' [Runge, 1984: 808, 810].

Now, an essential prerequisite for the market concept to work is that there exists a well-identified price-opportunity cost on whose variations both supply and demand can be shown to depend. Unfortunately, most analyses of the emergence of rules or institutions which rely on a crude market analogy fail to specify the exact nature of such a price: in these instances, reference to the market appears as a pseudo-analytical device to evade the main issue as to how the rules or institutions concerned actually come into existence.

In the case of land titling, however, the problem is less serious because it is possible to construct a consistent, market-like story, which fits the evolutionary account rather well. In such a story, the price regulating demand and supply may be thought of as the cost-price of registration-titling (costs of land surveying, mapping, identifying possessors, recording rights, updating the land record, etc.).

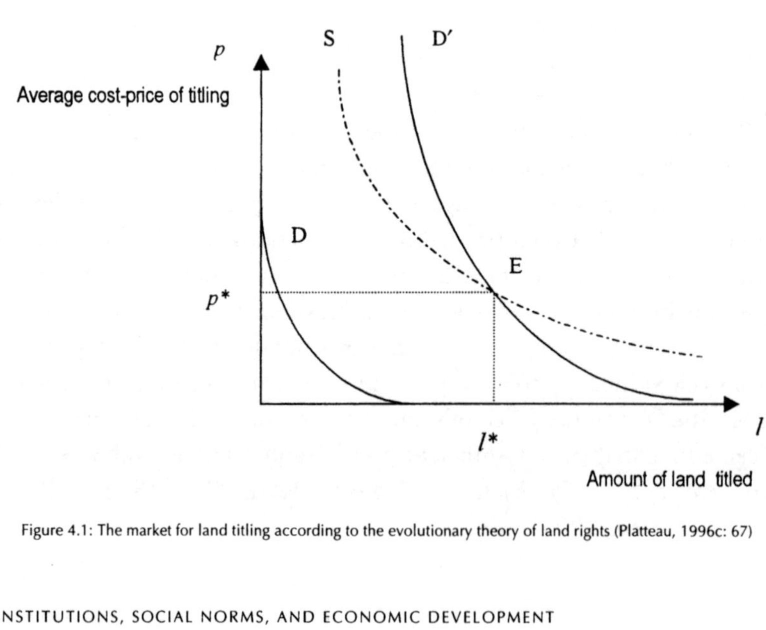


Figure 4.1: The market for land titling according to the evolutionary theory of land rights (Platteau, 1996c: 67)

Assuming that the government, the supplier of this innovation, applies a cost-recovery rule and charges each beneficiary the average cost of land titling, and assuming also that a major part of the expenses involved are of a fixed nature—which explains why land agencies usually wait until a threshold number of requests are made before travelling to the site [Alston et al., 1996: 29]—, we obtain an atypical, negatively-sloped supply curve such as that shown in Fig. 4.1 above. The demand curve has a standard shape.

The evolutionary argument can be simply captured by saying that appreciation of land prices following population growth and/or agricultural commercialization causes the demand curve to shift eastwards from, say, position $D$ to position $D'$. In the initial situation, no titling takes place because, given the importance of fixed costs, the government cannot recover its expenditures at the price which even the most interested farmers are willing to pay to have their land titled. In the new situation, on the contrary, $l^*$ hectares of land are titled for which the owners concerned agree to pay an average price, $p^*$, per hectare. Note incidentally that $l^*$ is smaller than the total land area since only in regions characterized by acute land scarcity are rights-holders ready to pay the necessary price to have their parcels titled. Over time, however, the state gradually enlarges the scope of its titling operations as the demand curve continues to move to the right.

Alternatively, it is possible to assume that the government subsidizes land titling operations instead of charging the full cost on the service users. In this case, governments can be conceived as granting property rights to citizens in the hope of making tangible benefits from increased efficiency and productivity, through growing tax revenues or enhanced political support [Levi, 1988; Riker and Sened, 1991]. In the words of Itai Sened: 'We should expect rule makers to grant rights when the cost of forcing duty-bearers to respect the rights of right-holders is smaller than the benefit they expect to gain from the enriched right-holders who pay taxes and the net value of political support they hope to obtain from the new right-holders *less* the political opposition of duty-bearers' [Sened, 1997: 79]. In this manner, even selfish governments can be trusted to implement adequate institutions of law and order in general, and property institutions in particular [*ibidem*: 85–86].

### *The beneficial effects of land titling*

Two types of beneficial economic effects are expected to follow from the establishment of duly recorded private property rights in land:

allocative effects resulting in more efficient use of the land available, on the one hand, and dynamic effects resulting in land conservation and improvement, on the other hand [Demsetz, 1967; Johnson, 1972; Ault and Rutman, 1979; De Alessi, 1980; Feder, 1987, 1993; Feder et al., 1988; Feder and Feeny, 1991; Barzel, 1989; Libecap, 1989a; Binswanger et al., 1995; Feder and Nishio, 1997].

More efficient use of the land can itself arise from two distinct sources. First, more efficient cropping choices are made possible because decision biases in favour of short-cycle crops that arise from tenure insecurity are removed when land titles are introduced. Second, under the same circumstances, land is transferred from less to more dynamic farmers and consolidated into larger holdings, thereby eliminating the excessive fragmentation and subdivision encouraged by traditional land allocation and inheritance patterns. When property rights are not clearly ascertained and effectively enforced, willing buyers who do not belong to the same community must incur significant search, enforcement and litigation costs as a result of which a wedge is driven between the land's value of marginal product in the owner's use and the value of marginal product if used by the most productive alternative user. The price of land does not then reflect its true social value. Due to the significant transaction costs arising from asymmetric information, land transfers are inhibited among stranger farmers, thus causing the volume of land transactions to be less than optimal. By putting an end to ambiguity in property rights, land titling drastically reduces transaction costs and encourages land acquisition by those able to make the best use of it.

In making its case for the establishment of freehold titles even before the countries concerned became independent, the report of the East Africa Royal Commission (1953–1955) thus expressed the view that: 'the ability of individuals to buy and sell land...opens the door to that mobility and private initiative on which a great sector of economic progress tends to depend...individual tenure should lead to the release and encouragement of new genius and to new experiments in finding the most productive use of land' [cited from Kiamba, 1989: 132]. Lord Swynnerton who played a major role in the initiation of an ambitious land titling programme in Kenya in the mif-fifties expressed his views still more forcefully:

> In the past Government policy has been to maintain the tribal system of tenure so that all the people have had bits of land and to protect the African from borrowing against the security of his land.... In future, if these recom-

> mendations are accepted, former Government policy will be reversed to enable energetic or rich Africans to acquire more land and bad or poor farmers less, creating a landed and a landless class. This is a normal step in the evolution of a country [Swynnerton, 1954: 10—cited from Carter et al., 1994: 146].

Note that the development of the land market is often supposed to induce a switch from subsistence cultivation to commercial agriculture under the impulse of dynamic, market-oriented agricultural entrepreneurs [see, e.g., Falloux, 1987]. Gershon Feder and Raymond Noronha (1987), for example, have illustrated this point by referring to the colonial experience of Uganda where in 1900 the British had granted absolute title to the so-called *mailo* lands to the king, his kinsfolk, and other senior officials. We are told that the introduction of freely transferable private property rights to land so early in the century as compared with the rest of East Africa 'gave to the ambitious peasant opportunities...and it certainly facilitated the purchase and development of the big coffee farms of the fifties which attracted *Ganda* traders, businessmen and others in commercial farming'. As a result, a land market grew up and 'a man with capital was able to buy land and start farming on his own account', thus opening the way for the emergence of a class of commercial farmers.

Full-fledged private property rights do not only improve the allocation of land among different uses and among different users, but they also enhance investment incentives. The dynamic impact of land titling on investment behaviour can be actually decomposed into demand and supply effects. Or, to put it in another way, landowners whose rights are legally protected can be expected to be both more willing and more able to undertake investment.

They are more willing to invest for essentially two reasons. First, there is the point made long ago by John Stuart Mill that, when farmers are better assured of reaping the future benefits of their present efforts and sacrifices thanks to secure rights of use, they have more incentives to invest in soil conservation measures, land improvements and other operations that raise productivity in the long term [Mill, 1848: Book V, chap. VIII]. This 'assurance effect' therefore follows from the fact that when farmers feel more secure in their right or ability to maintain long-term use over their land, the return on long-term land improvements is higher. Conversely, lack of tenure security can be thought of as creating a risk of land loss that causes a decline of expected income from investment or, alternatively, as shortening the farmer's time horizon, thereby discouraging him from performing actions that yield benefits over time. Second, when land can be more easily converted to liquid assets through sale—that is, when superior transfer rights have the effect of lowering the costs of exchange if the land is either rented or sold—, improvements made through investment can be better realised, thereby increasing its expected return. Investment incentives are then again enhanced [Besley, 1995c: 910–12; Platteau, 1996c: 36]. This second effect may be called the 'realisability effect'.

Farmers are not only more willing but also more able to invest because, when freehold titles are established, land acquires collateral value and access to credit is therefore easier. This is especially true regarding formal lending sources which often have imperfect information on the borrower. The 'collateralization effect' nevertheless remains important in so far as informal credit obtainable from informal lenders without using land as collateral is typically less advantageous than formal credit [Feder and Nishio, 1997: 5]. In fact, the emergence of a class of professional moneylenders in the countryside—and the concomitant emergence of a class of landless people—is seen as the natural outcome of both the reduction of the lender's risk and the possibility of foreclosure in case of default [Hicks, 1969: 107].

As pointed out by Besley, the key assumption to make this argument valid is that better land rights lower foreclosure costs. Note also that this 'ability to invest' effect can be framed as an incentive effect as well. As a matter of fact, more individualistic land rights resulting in improved collateral options may be expected to reduce the equilibrium interest rate, and since the interest rate is set equal to the marginal productivity of capital invested in land, investment is stimulated [Besley, 1995c: 909–10]. More importantly, the increase in the farm's collateral value is likely to increase the amount it can borrow (perhaps from zero to some positive value). Either change in the conditions of credit supply will reduce the farmer's shadow price of capital [Carter et al., 1994: 155–56].

If we except gifts (including inheritance), land may thus change hands in two main ways: through foreclosure or through voluntary market transactions. In both cases, greater economic efficiency is the expected outcome, whether in static or dynamic terms. All the above economic arguments, it may be remarked, are easily formalised [see Feder and Feeny, 1991; Besley, 1995c; Zimmerman and Carter, 1997], yet formalization adds little to their understanding.

Beyond the above efficiency effects, land titling has the additional advantage of providing the government with a precious tool for assessing property taxes and thereby increase its revenue. Furthermore, by identifying the possessors of rights over each and every land parcel, the centralised recording of land rights enables public authorities to bring clear and definite solutions to any land dispute or complaint and to thereby lay down the basis of law and order in the countryside. Ultimately, as has already been pointed out, social peace and political stability will also prevail.

From the foregoing presentation of both the predicted evolution of land rights and the expected effects of this evolution on economic efficiency and social order, it is evident that the ETLR assumes that a well-intended mechanism is at work in societies subject to growing land pressure. Land arrangements tend indeed to evolve in an optimal fashion, whether the criterion of optimality is static efficiency, economic growth, or political stability. In particular, these arrangements transform themselves in a way suited to the intensification of agricultural production and the preservation of soil fertility. As land becomes more scarce, it needs to be more intensively cultivated so as to be made more productive. This requires in turn that important investments be undertaken so as to conserve land and to gradually improve its productive capacity. Such investments will be actually forthcoming since, thanks to the largely endogenous transformation of land rights, farmers will be provided with greater investment incentives than before. Also, as it becomes scarcer, land needs to be more efficiently allocated, an effect that will ensue from the same evolution of tenure systems towards formalized individualization.

To say that the evolutionary process is well-intended does not, of course, imply that it must be smooth. The pervasive incidence of land disputes and litigation during the transition period leading to public registration of land rights reflects the conflictual process through which the more efficient land system emerges. Moreover, it is a real possibility that land distribution becomes more unequal as this process unfolds. However, this is considered to be a natural accompaniment to specialization and growth from which everybody will ultimately benefit. Here again, the similarity with Marx's doctrine of historical evolution is striking: contradictions and the ensuing tensions and conflicts are the very means through which institutional innovations take place in response to changes in factor endowments or technology.

## 4.3 THE ETLR PUT TO TEST: THE EFFICIENCY EFFECTS

### *Effects of tenure individualization on investment and land yields: the evidence (with special reference to Sub-Saharan Africa)*

The empirical evidence on the relationship between land rights and investment or land yields in African agriculture is so far largely inconclusive. This holds true whether the incidence of investment is compared between lands protected by a formal title and non-registered lands, or between lands characterized by varying degrees of informal individualization or tenure security.

In empirical studies, Kenya is a reference country because it is one of the few African countries where a programme of individualized titling has been systematically applied to rural lands for several decades (since the fifties). Interestingly, the evidence available so far does not show that agricultural investment and land yields have increased as a result of this programme [Green, 1987: 20–22; Haugerud, 1989: 62–90; Pinckney and Kimuyu, 1994: 11–12; Migot-Adholla et al., 1991: 165–66; Migot-Adholla et al., 1994b: 135–38]. Thus, for example, on the basis of a comparison with the Kilimanjaro region in Tanzania, Thomas Pinckney and Peter Kimuyu concluded that: 'With increased individualization of land rights under the indigenous systems between the 1920s and the 1960s, it is likely that our sample of Kenyan farmers would have invested rapidly in coffee during the 1960s even if the land titling had not taken place' [Pinckney and Kimuyu, 1994: 12].

Technically speaking, the most satisfactory test of the impact of land titling in Kenya is that carried out by Michael Carter, Keith Wiebe and Benoit Blarel (1994) on the basis of a cross-sectional farm-level data set from the highly commercialized Njoro area (in the Rift Valley). This study is particularly reliable because it avoids the causality problem of inferring from the existence of a significant relationship between titling and agricultural investment that causality runs from registration to enhanced investment. When title acquisition and title maintenance involve real expenditures, it is indeed *a priori* possible that farmers tend to register land parcels that benefit from comparatively high levels of investment, or that registered farms are those which have better profitability conditions justifying such expenditures. In this case, registration does not stimulate investment but is positively related to it [Roth et al., 1994a: 194]. In the words of Carter et al.:

> ...when title acquisition is costly, identification and measurement of the effects of tenure reform are complicated because the best-endowed farmers,

> most likely to benefit from enhanced tenure security, are also most likely to seek title to their land. Farmers less favourably endowed, are in turn, less likely to acquire title. Simple comparison of the performance of observed title and untitled farms thus tends to overstate both the realized effects of title on farmers who have obtained it and the potential effects of title on those who have not [Carter et al., 1994: 165].

The study by Carter et al. circumvents the above identification problem by carefully separating the effect of land title *per se* from the characteristics of the farms and farmers observed to have more legally secure tenure arrangements. More precisely, it estimates the impact not only of titles but also of other factors such as the farm's market access (measured by the size of the farm itself negatively associated with the shadow price of capital) that affect the economic value and likelihood of investment. What the authors show is that in Kenya title status is systematically related to farm size and mode of access to land to the point that true title effects vanish once these mediating factors are duly taken into account.[4] Moreover, with the help of an ingenious econometric test, the authors have been able to disentangle security-induced demand effects from credit supply effects of land title. Their analysis provides no confirmation of the existence of the former type of effects (the 'assurance effect').

Let us now consider countries where titling is optional instead of being a gradual but compulsory process as in Kenya. In the Shebelle region of Somalia, the effects of land title on various types of agricultural investment have all been found to be insignificantly different from zero: 'a comparison of smallholder untitled and titled farms showed little difference in investment in equipment, fencing, drainage, bunding, irrigation pumps, or wells, and the overall level of investment was extremely low' [Roth et al., 1994b: 224–25]. Another study on Uganda reached a somewhat more ambiguous conclusion, however: registration here appears as significantly and positively related to investments in fencing, continuous manuring and mulching, and positively but insignificantly related to all remaining long-term investments. Also, effects on investment tend to be more positive when registration is voluntary than when it is imposed by the government [Roth et al., 1994a: 193].

In Zimbabwe, smallholders—without having private title to their land—have achieved rapidly increasing maize yields, and their productive performance is not inferior to that of the biggest commercial farmers [Harrison, 1992: 131]. Another study by Moor (1996) in the same country has however shown that tenure security has had a significant and positive effect on long-term on-farm investments. (The impact on credit could not be assessed given the low incidence of credit use in the sample area). Yet, the sample area was peculiar in so far as it was used for resettlement, implying that no customary tenure system existed before the granting of land titles.

Turning to countries where the incidence of registration is low or practically nil, we basically find the same ambiguous or inconclusive results regarding the impact of more individualized land rights on investment and yields in agriculture. The best-documented country here is Ghana. In this country, we learn from a World Bank study of three different regions using multinomial logit regression analysis that 'improvements made after the parcel was acquired were highly associated with security of tenure in Anloga, but to a lesser extent in Wassa, although not in Ejura'. In Anloga, owned parcels over which operators had complete rights were more likely to have drainage or excavation improvement. The ability to freely transfer land (as opposed to first obtaining lineage or family approval) was also positively related to investment in drainage or excavation improvements. In Wassa, tree crops were more likely to be planted on land with more complete transfer rights while in Ejura 'there was no relationship between category of land rights and investment in tree crop planting or destumping' [Migot-Adholla et al., 1994a: 113–14].

A more sophisticated analysis by Besley (1995c) on the basis of the same World Bank data (on which more will be said below) has led to somewhat different conclusions, however. For the region of Wassa, Besley's findings actually support the idea that better land rights facilitate investment. Yet, for the region of Anloga where the World Bank study found the most significant relationship between security of land tenure and investment, Besley concludes contrariwise that no such significant relationship emerges. Hence the author's warning against viewing the explicit development of private property rights as 'a panacea for problems of low growth and investment' [Besley, 1995c: 936].

The results obtained by Besley are more reliable because his econometric method controls for the endogeneity of land rights, an important possibility in the African context. Land rights are endogenous when they depend in part on past investments, a likely outcome when the latter consist of tree planting: in Africa, indeed, the planting of trees is a well-recognized method of enhancing tenure for holders of temporary or fragile claims to the land [see note 3 and Bruce, 1988; Noronha, 1985; Robertson, 1987; Atwood, 1990; Place and Hazell, 1993; Sjaastad and Bromley, 1997; De Zeeuw, 1997]. To avoid this endogeneity bias, the decision to invest must therefore be explicitly allowed to affect future land rights, thus creating a two-way relationship between land rights and investment.

In a recent paper, Anne-Sophie Brasselle, Frederic Gaspart and Jean-Philippe Platteau (1998) have also controlled for the possible endogeneity of land rights while attempting to assess their impact on investment behaviour in a sample of villages in Western Burkina Faso.[5] The methodology used in this study is even more appropriate than that adopted by Besley both because the land rights variable is constructed in a more meaningful manner and because the econometric technique is more suited to the problem at hand. On the one hand, while Besley simply adds up rights by giving equal weight to each of them, Brasselle et al. have based their definition of the land security variable on a hierarchical ordering of various land rights (if no lexicographic relationship could be detected between use rights, a clear hierarchy was found between transfer rights).[6] Note that by using a single OLS model to estimate a reduced form equation of land rights as the first stage of the investment equation, Besley implicitly assumed that an ordinal variable behaves as though it were a metric variable. On the other hand, Besley uses a linear probability model to estimate the investment equation, which enables him to use the method of instrumental variables to correct the endogeneity bias at the cost of impairing the efficiency of the estimators. The two-stage conditional maximum likelihood model and the simultaneous probability model (with correction of the variance-covariance matrix by means of the bootstrapping technique) used by Brasselle et al. avoid this difficulty.

The results obtained in this latter study show that (1°) land tenure security is, indeed, strongly influenced by investment; and (2°) once this endogeneity bias is properly controlled, increased land rights do not appear to stimulate investment (the exogeneity of land tenure security in the investment equation is not rejected). This conclusion is in the line of other, less sophisticated studies on Burkina Faso which submit that, with the exception of tree planting, investments do not vary significantly between owned and borrowed fields [Saul, 1993; De Zeeuw, 1997: 589–92]. The same methodology as that described above has been applied by Baland, et al. (1999) in their aforementioned study of central Uganda and they have reached exactly the same conclusion: once due allowance is made for the fact that investment may influence tenure security, there is no remaining effect of the latter on the former variable.

Still another study conducted in western Niger by Gavian and Fafchamps (1996) concludes that there is no evidence that laws and customs regarding the transferability of land have an effect on (short-term) investment decisions. There are thus no significant differences in the farmer's investment behaviour when he owns his land individually (which implies that he has the right to freely dispose of it) and when the land farmed is a so-called *hawjou* land which has been borrowed from a pool of community lands entrusted to the village chief. If users of *hawjou* lands have the same use rights as owners, they cannot sell or lend the land directly to each other while, if they die or retire, descendants must confirm with the chief their right to cultivate the same fields. Moreover, the *hawjou* system 'explicitly stipulates that unneeded fields must be returned to the chief for reassignment within the community' [Gavian and Fafchamps, 1996: 463].

A paper that proposes a different conclusion actually confirming the positive impact of (customary) tenure security on investment that is hypothesized by the ETLR is devoted to a peri-urban area of the Gambia [Hayes et al., 1997]. The authors indeed contend that secure tenure tends to stimulate long-term land improvements and tree planting, but to discourage medium-term improvements.[7] To the extent that medium-term improvements (consisting of traditional soil improvement methods, namely, the fallowing and manuring of the plots) appear to behave as substitutes for short-term commercial inputs (particularly, fertilisers) and that the use of such inputs is encouraged by greater tenure security, the latter result may not run counter to the main thrust of the study's findings. More worrying is the fact that the econometric method used does not control for the possible endogeneity of land rights, a surprising choice given that tree planting emerges as an important investment category in the study.

In Rwanda, to take a last example, the ability to bequeath land appears to be an important determinant of investment: in a World Bank study based on the situation encountered in three different prefectures (Gitarama, Ruhengeri, and Butare), 79 per cent of parcels which may be bequeathed were improved as opposed to 27 per cent of those which could not. On the other hand, 'among permanently held parcels, there is no difference in the incidence of land improvements between 'preferential transfer' and 'complete transfer' land, nor does the requirement of prior approval matter'[8] [Migot-Adholla et al., 1991: 166; see also Place and Hazell, 1993: 12–16, 22–27; Barrows and Roth, 1989: 13; LTC, 1990; Bassett, 1993a: 17; Bruce, 1993: 51].

*Effects of tenure individualization on investment: discussion*

(i) Contrary to expectations, the above evidence about Kenya and some other African countries shows that, essentially, the impact of land titling on investment behaviour is not confirmed. At this stage, it is useful to pause for a moment and to look at the evidence available for some Asian and Latin American countries. In their pioneer study of Thailand, where comparison of investment behaviour was effected between farmers possessing legal land titles and squatters with no such document, Feder and associates came to the important conclusion that most of the impact of title ownership 'stemmed from the fact that titles increased farmers' access to formal credit, rather than from the elimination of actual risk to the land rights of the farmers' [Feder and Feeny, 1991: 145]. Where no organised credit sources existed, legal titling did not make much change. In the same vein, a study conducted in the state of Andra-Pradesh (India) by Pender and Kerr (1994) has reached the conclusion that land rights status as measured by its transferability has had little effect on investment and credit, presumably because of the scarcity of formal credit sources in the survey areas.

In another study devoted to rural Paraguay, Carter et al. (1997) have estimated the impact of titling on investment and productivity in a way that differentiates according to the wealth level of farmers. The results obtained by them are much less encouraging than those of Feder and his co-authors. Indeed, what the former authors show is that, due to a wealth bias in the credit market, small farmers below a certain wealth threshold do not improve their effective access to credit following land titling.[9] Unfortunately, this threshold is such that a large majority of households do not actually come close to it. For all these credit-constrained households, titling enhances the demand for investment in capital goods attached to land, yet binding liquidity constraints prevent them from increasing the total level of investment (so that there is substitution of attached for unattached capital).

From the analysis of regions where land titling exist, there is thus converging evidence that the assurance (or the induced-security demand) effect does not operate under ordinary circumstances. As we have seen above, the experience of Kenya actually suggests the same conclusion [see, in particular, the study by Carter et al., 1994]. The point can be made, however, that in the particular case of resettlement or new colonisation areas (and in urban or peri-urban areas), where risk and asymmetric information with respect to land rights are especially high, the granting of titles is likely to increase the assurance that the returns of an investment will accrue to those who make it and thereby to promote land improvement and conservation [see, e.g., Alston et al., 1996, for Brazil; Moor, 1996, for Zimbabwe; Friedman et al., 1988, for the Philippines]. In frontier areas where land was previously ownerless and is being claimed by individuals migrating from other areas, the security afforded by land registration is expected to be especially important [Feder and Feeny, 1991]. Yet, even that more qualified statement must be taken cautiously since the aforementioned study of Thailand by Feder et al., which did not find evidence of an assurance effect, was carried out in a resettlement area.

What must be added now is that the evidence regarding the impact of greater informal tenure security converges with the evidence gathered in land titled areas. More precisely, as is apparent from the above survey of the African situation, there is no solid basis for claiming that increased individualization of land rights generates an assurance effect. As it turns out, in customary land areas basic use rights seem to be sufficient to induce landholders to invest and the adding of transfer rights (with the possible exception of the right to bequeath land) does not appear to significantly improve investment incentives.

Also worth emphasizing is the fact that in agrarian societies in general, and in African rural communities in particular, basic use rights can be held by farmers despite appearances to the contrary. As a matter of fact, what appears to the external observer as precarious rights may actually be rather long-term entitlements in the specific context of these societies.

Just to take a striking example, land borrowals may not necessarily expose the farmer to a high risk of losing access to the land cultivated and the returns to the investments made. This is because land borrowing and lending transactions, at least among native farmers, are often part of a wider relationship between two families or lineages, and the desire to keep such a relationship going ensures that borrowing arrangements are frequently renewed or not easily ended. Use rights over borrowed lands can actually be bequeathed to descendants when the borrower and the lender belong to the same lineage and when land has been lent for an indefinite period. For example, in the case of Burkina Faso, we learn that: 'Because of the strong tradition of transfer of intergenerational use rights, inheritable use rights prevail even for fields on long-term borrowing arrangements (borrowed by ancestors and subsequently passed down to current users through inheritance)...Most farmers consider withdrawal of use rights unthinkable for long-term borrowings that have been within the current user's household for more than one generation' [Matlon, 1994: 52–54; see also De Zeeuw, 1997].

Also worth bearing in mind is the aforementioned *hawjou* system under which farmers are granted stable use rights over lands borrowed from the community. Such observations—which have been confirmed for other African countries as well[10]—imply that land tenure security on lands that appear to be held under a rather precarious arrangement may in fact be much higher than what this arrangement suggests on the face of it. This may explain why, for example, immigrant farmers who have comparatively low levels of tenure security as measured by standard yardsticks may possibly feel entitled to make long-term improvements in view of the stable relationship prevailing between them and the native households from which they have received land. Such improvements, in turn, may actually enhance their tenure security [Brasselle et al., 1998].

Clearly, under normal circumstances, the local informal order embedded in the rural community guarantees basic land rights to all villagers (including migrants) and these are sufficient to induce investment. There is then no need for the state to intervene through centralized procedures aimed at formalizing land rights [Atwood, 1990; Migot-Adholla et al., 1991; Platteau, 1992, 1996c, 1997; Bassett and Crummey, 1993; Bruce and Migot-Adholla, 1994]. If, for one reason or another, the village informal order is absent, has vanished, or is proving unable to regulate access to land, however, the state may be well-advised to substitute for the missing social structure. Resettlement or new colonisation areas, as well as areas subject to acute land pressure (including urban or peri-urban areas) are cases in point.

A last point needs to be considered. When access to land through a rental contract is genuinely temporary, investment operations are discouraged, an effect that is often manifested in the explicit prohibition to plant trees and carry out other types of land improvements [see, e.g., Gavian and Fafchamps, 1996]. The owner thus clearly expresses the fear that rights to his land could be claimed by his tenant. In this case, it must be noted, thanks to insertion of such prohibition clauses in the (implicit) contract and to their effective enforcement, transfers of land through rentals are made possible. The conferring upon landowners of unimpeachable rights to their land through titles is therefore not necessary to allow such land transfers.

This said, land allocation and use would be improved if land investments (including the planting of trees within the framework of agroforestry programmes) by tenants were permitted and their value were realizable by the investor otherwise than by claiming the land for himself, either by internalizing the benefits over the rental period or by getting a rightful compensation from the owner upon the termination of the contract. There is good ground to believe that, by reassuring owners about the definitive character of their ownership right, land titling could encourage types of land rental contracts that promote investment to the best possible extent (e.g., through a lengthening of the contracting period).

Yet, it is also possible that evolution of indigenous tenure systems will gradually lead to appropriate institutional innovations that are less costly than registration and titling. Letters of occupancy granted by local chiefs to rightsholders, such as they are found in Zambia [Sjaastad, 1998: 161], or locally produced documents attesting land rentals in a way similar to that used for land sale transactions in some parts of rural Africa [André and Platteau, 1998: 42], provide a good example of the kind of solution that the indigenous order can produce. Moreover, it is noteworthy that in some regions improvements in farmland are seen as held by the individual who carried them out and, as a result, he might be compensated for them, if needed [Cohen, 1980: 360]. In Zambia, again, when a litigant loses an ownership dispute, he is usually compensated for land improvements [Sjaastad, 1998: 176].

(ii) To the extent that investment enhances tenure security, it is possble that the incentive to invest is higher under an indigenous tenure system than under the freehold regime. This is likely to be so if the investment is expected to lead to a small productivity increase and to a large reduction in the probability of eviction from the land [Sjaastad and Bromley, 1997: 555–57].[11] Such an outcome ought not to be interpreted as an advantage of indigenous tenure over freehold since investments aimed exclusively at enhancing tenure security apparently entail a social waste of resources caused by an acute competition around land in the public domain. Yet, even if the benefits of investments under indigenous tenure are smaller than those that would be generated under freehold, the relevant comparison is between the difference in benefits and the costs of rights specification and enforcement; not between the direct costs and benefits of investment as though freehold rights were costlessly established [*ibidem*: 558]. Note that in many cases the security-enhancing investments undertaken by African farmers are far from being unproductive (think of tree planting, erection of anti-erosion barriers, building of ditches and furrows, etc....).

(iii) It has been pointed out above that, when it exists, the positive influence of land titling on investment behaviour is generally channelled through the credit supply or collateralization effect. Yet, as has also been documented, this effect is far from being systematically present: use of production credit by farmers may remain low in spite of the emergence of mortgageable land. The prediction of the ETLR according to which organized credit sources will spontaneously arise in response to land registration to meet the latent demand of credit-rationed farmers is much too simplistic. Low credit use may actually be caused by two distinct types of factors. On the one hand, it may result from supply failures that have their origin in various imperfections not only in the credit market itself but also in other rural factor markets, particularly the land market. On the other hand, it may be determined by demand failures that prevent farmers from tapping available credit sources. Let us consider these two sets of factors in more detail, starting with demand failures.

*Demand failures* Smallholders may fail to apply for loans because they perceive a high risk of losing their land through foreclosure, as the experience of Kenya testifies [Green, 1987: 8; Shipton, 1988: 106, 120; Barrows and Roth, 1989: 9]. This may be especially true of subsistence-constrained farmers who fear their ability to repay loans taken for investment purposes is very low (unless payoffs are short-term). Perceptions of risk of default and aversion for land mortgage may actually vary depending not only on economic position but also on other characteristics such as age of the landholder. In Kenya, for example, it is mainly elders who reject the idea of land mortgage while younger men may be more attracted by the prospect of ready cash and, as a result, they are more liable to have their lands foreclosed [Shipton, 1988: 106, 120]. Unfortunately, the latter do not necessarily use credit for productive or investment purposes. 'Urgent' consumption needs which elders may well regard as luxury can easily drive young people straight into landlessness, whether inadvertently or not. Interestingly, to reduce intra-family conflicts around land mortgages, public authorities in Kenya have required the agreement of family members prior to any use of land as collateral by the title-holder (see infra).

Another important reason behind the farmers' failure to respond to the availability of loanable funds is the lack of attractive investment opportunities or the absence of conditions critical for their successful exploitation [see *supra*, Chapter 2]. This typically occurs when no technological package suitable for intensive agriculture is on offer, such as is often the case under rainfed farming conditions [Platteau, 1990: 324–335]; or when investments embodying technical progress are highly labour-intensive (e.g., fencing, digging of furrows and ditches, tree planting, building of anti-erosion barriers, etc.) and family labour is sufficient to supply the required effort (so that no capital is needed for the purpose of advancing wages); when the required infrastructure, input-delivery, output-marketing or extension services are not available [Roth, 1993: 316]; when visible wealth is being arbitrarily taxed (a risk to which agricultural investments are particularly vulnerable); or when, as will be amply discussed in the next chapter, dynamic farmers are discouraged from improving their land and accumulating capital because of jealousies of the chief and other villagers [Bruce, 1986: 29, 31, 1993: 39–40].

*Supply failures* Failures to provide credit in spite of titling may arise from different sources. Clearly, they may result from imperfections in the land market that tend to make registration ineffective. This obviously happens if titled land is not considered a reliable collateral by credit-givers because it is difficult to foreclose or because, the market being thin, it is not easy to dispose of in case of default [Okoth-Ogendo, 1976: 175; Collier, 1983: 163–164; Noronha, 1985: 197–198; Bruce, 1986: 40; Barrows and Roth, 1989: 9]. Discussion of the latter possibility is postponed to the next sub-section where the functioning of the land market in rural areas is analyzed. Here, I concentrate on the problem of foreclosure costs remaining high even in the presence of titling.

Difficulties in foreclosing land (or other immovables) may originate in either the official or the civilian sphere, or in both. The first case occurs when the judicial system is ineffective or partial. This is a widespread phenomenon in SSA, particularly in urban and peri-urban areas where official titles are generally granted to private owners of land and buildings. In actual fact, a complaint frequently voiced by institutional credit-givers—not only state finance corporations but also commercial banks and other private credit agencies—is precisely that foreclosure on property belonging to rich and powerful borrowers cannot be legally enforced because the judicial system is under the strong influence of their political allies.

In Senegal, for example, such interferences on the part of powerful private lobbies which are tightly linked up with the political establishment (of the Socialist Party) are considered to be part of the Senegalese public way of life: in everyday parlance, they are actually referred to as *agir à la sénégalaise*. In Kenya where influential people in government and politics bought larger plots (so-called Z-plots) under the land settlement schemes, we learn that: 'By mid-1969 no cases of chronic loan defaulters from Z-plot holders had yet been referred to the Attorney General, although by the end of 1969, 158 recommendations for eviction of other settlers had gone to the Sifting Committee in Parliament with 84 evictions resulting' [Wasserman, 1976: 155–156—quoted from Van de Laar, 1980: 173]. Clearly, perverse equity effects result from the operation of a land market (with free mortgage) when it is combined with a biased legal system.

If anything, the situation has worsened in Kenya. Corruption is so widespread in the legal and judicial systems that registration does not offer serious protection to title-holders and that banks have nowadays stopped accepting land titles as collaterals. Testimonies abound to show that the power of money exceeds that of legality to vindicate claims to land. In other words, to protect access rights against deceitful claimants, the possession of a title is not sufficient: too often, it is the amount of the bribes offered to the judge which will decide which party is going to win the case irrespective of any legal supporting evidence (personal field observations).

Popular expression of anger and active opposition can also 'break the transmission' between registration and credit supply. This happens because, when people do not consider the new system of (land) rights as legitimate and do not accept the reshuffling of wealth it may imply, they may succeed—especially in young nations with 'soft' states as we find them in SSA—in blocking the normal functioning of the legal system. Costs of foreclosure may then remain high. Thus, in Kenya again, lending authorities have had great difficulty foreclosing on land mortgages chiefly because 'the presence of many kin around mortgaged land makes it politically unfeasible to auction the holdings of defaulters' [Shipton, 1988: 120]. In urban peripheries, notes another study, 'although some banks have accepted titled land as collateral and auctioned it off in cases of default, in some cases purchasers were not able to take occupation of the land for fear of reprisals' [Migot-Adholla et al., 1991: 170].

Governments may not want to run counter to popular demonstrations of this kind lest their political basis or the fragile consensus on which their national policies rest should be undermined. In the case of Kenya's White Highlands repeopled with native farmers after the departure and compensation of European colonists (the land settlement schemes referred to above), the government was eventually compelled to restrain the use of land as collateral. The fact of the matter is that: 'The cry of land hunger had fed the nationalist rebellion that had brought the government to power. To turn people off the lands that they had fought to capture would be to risk the wrath of the true believers in the nationalist revolution' [Bates, 1989: 74]. The pressure on the government was all the stronger as the official opposition represented by a radical party (the KADU or Kenya African Democratic Union) lobbied intensively on the land issue [*ibidem*: 67–68].

In the above, it has been assumed that the land registration system itself works properly and that difficulties arise downstream from the central recording process. In fact, ineffective operation of this system resulting in the invalidity of the title documents may well prevent any reduction of uncertainty and lowering of foreclosure costs. As has been emphasized with reference to several Asian countries by Feeny (1988) and to India by Wadhwa (1989), a major problem with cadastral surveys is that they are often incomplete and there is a lack of diligent record keeping of all intervening changes in land ownership. In the words of David Feeny, in virtually all sampled countries 'the legal provisions "exceeded" administrative practice in the degree of sophistication and precision of the land rights ... the transaction cost of establishing and operating the [registration] systems were considerable and much higher than the costs of enacting the enabling legislation' [Feeny, 1988: 295]. The difficulties are obviously compounded when landholdings comprise numerous parcels which are often minuscule.

In SSA, where administrative capabilities are much less developed than in Asia, the problem is bound to be all the more serious, not a minor consideration when it is borne in mind that high costs are associated with registering land (site visits, land surveys, maps, registration proper,...). This is amply confirmed by available evidence. Even in a country like Senegal where land registration has been allowed, on a voluntary basis, only during a limited period of time and demanded by relatively few people, we are told that 'the Senegalese bureaucracy is still processing registration claims that were filed in the two-year grace period granted by the 1964 National Domain Law' [Golan, 1990: 51]. In Kenya and Uganda, successions and other transfers of title have gone largely unregistered, as a result of which land records hardly reflect the present day reality, thus destroying the utility of the record and possibly engendering new uncertainties [Doornbos, 1975: 68; Bruce, 1986: 58; Saul, 1988: 273; LTC, 1990: 4].

In the case of Kenya, Green does not hesitate to say that failure to maintain a valid record of successions and absence of updated records constitute one of the major disappointments of the land titling program [Green, 1987: 11]. As for Shipton, he writes: 'So the emergent land market is largely unregistered. It is likely to remain so. The government does not have the resources to monitor, let alone control, the many kinds of land exchanges that happen every season in the farm neighborhoods. By their very nature, these defy recording and classification: for the most part they are *ad hoc*, unnamed, individually tailored agreements in which land is only one of many mutually interchangeable goods;... the lines blur between loans, rentals, barter, swaps, and sales' [Shipton, 1988: 123].

It would however be wrong to conclude that discrepancies between records and reality arise only from administrative deficiencies and implementation problems. They may also be the outcome of deliberate attempts by villagers to ignore or sabotage the system when it is used by the government to introduce policies that are deemed improper. Thus, in Kenya again, the government's attempt to limit the subdivise impact of indigenous inheritance systems led to an enormous amount of evasions which undermined the registration system as a whole [Bruce, 1986: 68]. More generally, people's failure to register transactions is often to be ascribed to adherence to customary tenure rules in registered areas. Customary law (such as subdivision of land among all the sons) 'in fact continues to govern the way in which most people deal with their land, making tenure rights ambiguous. The land law failed to gain popular understanding or acceptance, individuals continued to convey rights to land according to customary law, and a gap developed between the control of rights as reflected in the land register and control of land rights as recognized by most local communities' [Barrows and Roth, 1989: 7].

To sum up, as a result of glaring failure to build up and update reliable land records, titles shown on the register are increasingly at variance with the facts of possession and use and considerable confusion is created over legal property rights. The impact of land registration is therefore undermined and, since credit agencies are not able to rely on titles as evidence of land ownership, the collateral effect fails to materialize. In Zambia, it is the very process of issuing titles that is disturbed by interventions from customary authorities. Thus, for example, the District Council in Mazabuka upholds traditional norms of prohibition 'by refusing to relay title applications to the Lands Ministry in Lusaka, although they had no authority to withold them; applications would only be accepted for small, fenced-in tree gardens around the dwelling, not for agricultural fields' [Sjaastad, 1998: 250].

Besides difficulties in repossessing land collaterals and realizing them in the market (or in getting titles issued), there are supply constraints arising from the strategy of credit-givers. First, commercial banks and financial institutions are often reluctant to lend for land purchases because they are unwilling to tie up their capital, raised largely through short-term deposits, for long periods of time [Dorner and Saliba, 1981; Stringer, 1989]. Moreover, bankers usually prefer lending against more reliable streams of income than those found in agriculture. Second, considerations of administrative costs may lead banks and other credit agencies to set a minimum size of loans which often exceeds the capital needs of smallholders [Barrows and Roth, 1989: 9], or to refuse to lend to them on the ground that their property is costly to dispose of in the event of foreclosure due to the tiny size of fragmented landholdings. Following titling, distribution of credit is thus likely to become more unequal and this is bound to affect farm income distribution.

Figures 4.2 and 4.3 below are intended to represent the wealth-differentiated impact of titling. Following Carter et al. (1994), market access, a shorthand variable that indicates the terms on which a farm unit can gain access to capital and participate in other commercial relationships, is measured along the horizontal axis in both figures. Market access can be thought to be systematically related to farm size and wealth level. While in Figure 4.2, the expected present value of an investment, $E[PV]$, is measured along the vertical axis, in Figure 4.3 it is the net farm income par unit area which is represented along that axis. The current cost of the investment considered is $C^*$, assumed to be constant and independent of market access. Any farm for which the expected present value of the investment exceeds the cost $C^*$ would therefore be expected to undertake the investment project.

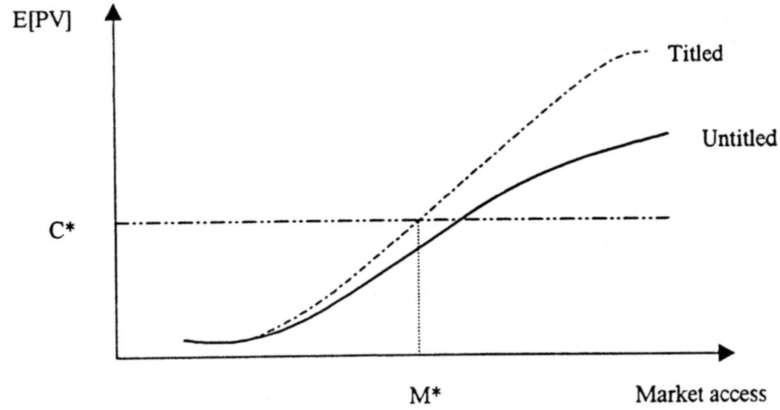


Figure 4.2: Differential returns to investment with and without titling (Carter et al., 1994: 151)

In Figure 4.2, the solid curve, labeled untitled, represents the expected present value of the investment for untitled farms on the field in which the investment would be made, whereas the dashed curve, labeled titled, represents the same value for titled farms. For reasons explained above, the shift in the $E[PV]$ function with titling asymmetrically favours farms with better access. As drawn in the figure, $M^*$ represents the level of market access at which investment in a titled field would become worthwhile.

In Figure 4.3, it is therefore only above $M^*$ that the two curves representing net farm incomes per unit area—one for untitled and the other for titled farms—begin to separate. For farms with weak market access, net farm income would be unaffected by land titling the potential effects of which are overwhelmed by market access problems, particularly by severe capital constraints. As for farms better-situated in terms of market access or other productivity-enhancing characteristics, net farm income would increase as acquisition of title makes heretofore unprofitable investment worth undertaking [Carter et al., 1994: 151–55].

If titling is optional and requires real expenditures, only farmers with market access in excess of $M^*$ would seek title, thus giving rise to an aforementioned statistical identification problem. Note that the gap between the solid curve and the dashed curve which reflects the differential gain that can be obtained from land registration (or, more generally, from an increase in tenure security) grows with market access: the higher the market access (the greater the farm size) the larger the value of land titling.

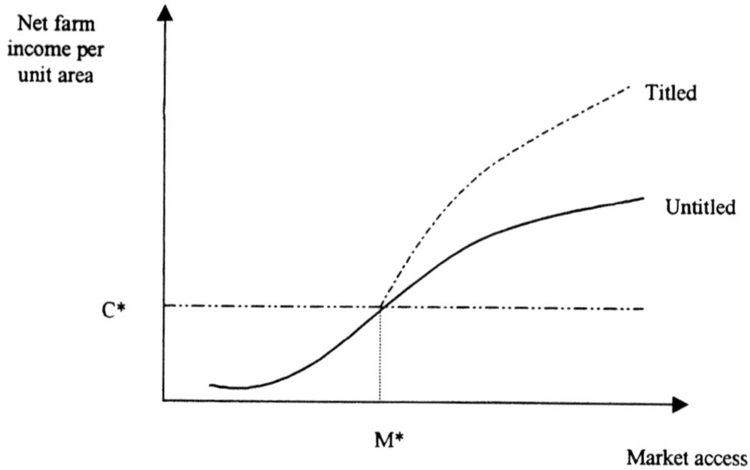


Figure 4.3: Wealth-differentiated effect of titling on farm income
(Carter et al., 1994: 154)

The above analysis, it must be noted, suggests policy implications which widely differ from those usually associated with the ETLR. As a matter of fact, to the extent that land titling affects investment behaviour only through the credit-supply effect, it may be better to address the collateral problem directly (perhaps through the formation of informal co-operative borrowing groups) than to resolve it through expensive titling programs [Carter et al., 1994: 156]. To avoid setting off unequalizing processes, special attention ought to be lent to market access problems, particularly with respect to capital, that tend to hit smallholders who constitute the bulk of the farming population. On the other hand, if lack of credit use in agriculture also comes from the demand side as a result of various market and state failures, the most sensible thing to do for a government is to try to remove non-tenurial constraints with a view to freeing this demand [André and Platteau, 1998].

In the foregoing discussion, only the collateral (credit supply) and the assurance (induced security) effects have been handled. The realisability effect, which now appears to have a supply as well as a demand component (since credit-givers are also interested in the realisability of land assets, including land improvements), has been left aside. This is because it depends on the way the land market is activated as a result of greater tenure security in general, and of land titling in particular. Allocative effects also obviously hinge on the activation of the land market. Before this aspect is being tackled, a last point needs to be made regarding the collateral effect.

*A final remark* It is probably wrong to think that the collateral effect can only occur if the land is duly titled. As is documented in the next subsection, informal land market transactions can be supported by written evidence sufficiently reliable to allow the use of land as collateral by local credit-givers. In Rwanda, for example, credit-cum-savings rotating associations known as tontines are able to seize on the land of a defaulting member [André and Platteau, 1998]. The fact that individualization of land rights does not often appear to encourage investment (see *supra*) may therefore be due not only to the above-referred lack of assurance effect once a minimum set of basic rights (including the right to bequest) are guaranteed but also to the kind of factors that we have just analyzed in connection with titling (e.g., an absence of investment opportunities requiring credit, the fear of losing family land through foreclosure, etc.). In other words, it is not necessarily true that by measuring the impact of informal tenure security on investment incentives only the assurance effect is being tested.

*The functioning of the land market: evidence and discussion*

The present analysis is articulated around two main statements. First, in ordinary circumstances the land market does not appear to be activated by the provision of greater tenure security, including titling. As a result, the realisability effect predicted by the ETLR is generally insignificant. Second, when it is active, most land transfers do not seem to promote efficiency, thus making for weak allocative effects. The empirical facts underlying each of these statements and the explanations accounting for them are examined in succession below.

*Lack of land market activation* Evidence from Kenya is that land sale transactions have *not* increased following land reform except during the earliest stages, that is, before registration had been completed (indeed, in the knowledge of pending registration, the educated elite took advantage of the situation to acquire additional lands). When they are transferred, the majority of parcels continue to follow the path of customary channels (lending, gifts, inheritance or non-registered sales) among which inheritance stands foremost [Haugerud, 1983: 80; Collier, 1983: 156–158; Bruce, 1986: 56; Green, 1987: 13–18; Barrows and Roth, 1989: 10–11; Migot-Adholla et al., 1991: 160–164; Mackenzie, 1993: 200].[12]

Evidence from many other African countries confirms the important role of inheritance as a mode of land acquisition. Thus, from a survey of sixteen different areas belonging to six countries with titling programmes and/or high population densities (Kenya, Rwanda, Burundi, Uganda, Malawi, Zambia), it comes out that, on an average, 63 per cent of the land parcels have been obtained through inheritance and various kinds of gift transfers, 16 per cent have been acquired through market purchases and the rest through other means among which state allocation stands foremost. Median figures are very close to the averages yet the ranges can be quite large, reflecting contrasted situations between Uganda, where the incidence of market purchases is quite important, and other countries in the sample [André and Platteau, 1998: 18–19]. Note moreover that observations made in Asia would seem to confirm that rural land markets are rather inactive despite the existence of titles [see, e.g., Rao, 1972; Bliss and Stern, 1982; Bardhan, 1984: 95; Sarap, 1996: A-108].

Supply considerations largely explain why land sale markets are thin in SSA. As a matter of fact, landholders are typically reluctant to sell their land, even when they get an employment outside the agricultural sector and they reside in town. Land continues to be perceived as a crucial asset for the present and/or future subsistence of the family, all the more so as it is a secure form of holding wealth and a good hedge against inflation ('It is our bank and we will not part with it', said the member of a founding lineage in a village close to Matam, Senegal). That considerations of social insurance determine attitudes of deep attachment to land is understandable in a context of scarce alternative employment opportunities and risky labour markets. For many people working in urban areas, indeed, land serves both as an insurance against uncertain employment and against landlessness in the next generation of the family, and as a pension fund for their old days [Bruce, 1986: 56; Green, 1987: 27; Lawry, 1993: 58].[13]

Such social security considerations often underlie the apparent persistence of indigenous control over land transfers even when they are duly registered: thus, in Kenya, many owners of titled lands do not consider that they are entitled to transfer their lands outside the lineage or to make permanent transfers without having previously obtained the approval of their family or community. This is not always the case, however. It has thus happened (in Kenya) that 'young, unemployed men sold land registered in their name, leaving their parents destitute' [Green, 1987: 7], and that 'poor peasants, given title to their land, promptly sold it, spent the cash and were soon left landless and cashless to' [The Economist, 21–27 January, 1995: 49].

It is precisely to prevent such decisions being made without sufficient consideration for their future consequences (that is, to prevent myopic behaviour on the part of thoughtless rightsholders) or for their immediate consequences for other family members (that is, to force selfish rightsholders to take account of externalities) that rural communities or family units require to be consulted beforehand. Such interference with the free play of market forces is justified in so far as these communities are ultimately responsible for the subsistence of their individual members, and will therefore be called upon to assist any member who has become destitute out of bad luck or wanton behaviour.

In the case of Kenya, this situation of a constrained land market is reinforced by the fact that District Land Control Boards in charge of approving land sales are frequently reluctant to permit transactions which would leave families (and their descendants) landless and destitute. That is why they insist that all adult members of the household (including women) of the title-holder are to be present at the hearing to indicate their agreement with the sale. The government has actually sanctioned this *de facto* situation since a presidential directive aimed at minimizing land disputes requires the agreement of family members in addition to that of the title-holder prior to any sale or use of land as collateral [Haugerud, 1983: 84; Mackenzie, 1993: 200; Pinckney and Kimuyu, 1994: 10].

In Zimbabwe, likewise, a proposal by a land tenure commission appointed by the government (October 1994) provides that individual farmers should be given the right to own their land, but their right to buy and sell it should be subject to the approval of the traditional village council (the *sabuku*) which in pre-colonial days used to be vested with the prerogative of allocating local lands [The Economist, 21–27 January 1995: 49].

There is a remarkable lesson to draw from the above: it is under the pressing need to prevent land disputes and family conflicts from multiplying too rapidly that the state has decided to retreat from the most radical interpretation of freehold tenure and to revert to some customary principles of land allocation. Contrary to predictions, central registration of land has not led to a reduction of land disputes but, if anything, to their exacerbation. Consequently, public authorities are well-advised to rely on decentralized, customary mechanisms of intra-family negotiation and dispute settlement.[14]

Economic considerations are not the only rationale for keeping family land. Other, more symbolic motives that belong to a traditional realm of values also seem to play a role. Thus, as has been already pointed out in Chapter 3, in tribal societies the collective identity of a people is narrowly tied with the ancestral land. Since its value is embedded in the social structure and history of a particular community [Riddell et al., 1987: 82–83], land represents far more than a mere input into an agricultural enterprise and it is impossible to abstract it from all the social, ritual, affective and political meanings associated with it.[15] People continue to strongly adhere to the traditional ethical principle that land ought to belong to the 'sons of the village', to the members of the local community (most commonly defined by descent or adoption) whose families have been living on the land for several generations and have therefore developed ritualistic and strongly emotional identity links with it. This is all the more so as the ancestors' cult is still very much alive (ancestors are actually believed to continuously intervene in present-day human affairs) and is deeply rooted in the (corporate) land of the lineage [Caldwell and Caldwell, 1987: 415–417].

Reluctance to part with ancestral land is especially strong when it threatens to go to outsiders. Already during the colonial period, indigenous people felt it a sacred duty to protect family or clan property and to prevent ancestral land from passing into European hands.[16] Nowadays, the same attitude can still be largely observed and, as expected, the land market is more severely restricted where kinship ties are strongest, for example, more restricted in Kenya's former African reserve (where it operates mainly among members of the same ethnic group) than in the former white settled areas and in urban peripheries [Migot-Adholla et al., 1991: 169; Pinckney and Kimuyu, 1994: 15]. What Zufferey has noted with reference to Botswana (Eastern Central District) still applies to many countries in SSA: 'Owning land thus appears to confer to the local residents a sense of identity and membership in a specific social group in comparison with the *bahaladi* (foreigners) who are, in contrast, expected to apply for land' [Zufferey, 1986: 79].

In SSA, original occupants may not hesitate to use violence to oppose the transfer of traditional family or communal lands to outsiders, committing acts of sabotage, looting, burning and theft on the property and crops of the new landholders. An extreme example of the excesses to which this opposition may lead is the so-called 'Manifesto of the Oppressed Negro-Mauritanian'. Written by an extremist group belonging to the black (haalpulaar) community of

Mauritania, it is an aggressive reaction to the post-1983 introduction of private land rights conferred (by adjudication) upon stranger owners over irrigated lands located on the right bank of the Senegal river.[17] In this manifesto, the Negro-Mauritanians are invited to use any conceivable means to prevent their customary lands from passing into the hands of the *Beydane* elite (of Moorish origin), that is, 'to boycott, ban, kill if needed, all those who encourage the sale of land; destroy, burn the possessions of these strangers who come to develop your lands while the land should belong to our villages' [quoted from Bayart, 1989: 82].

Since cultivators on both sides of the river belong to the same (haalpulaar) community,[18] and since some people residing on the left bank (that is, on the Senegalese side) used to cultivate lands located on the right bank (that is, on the Mauritanian side) over which they had customary access since generations, the transfer of lands on the right bank to Moorish owners was bound to create serious tensions between the two neighbouring countries. These tensions could not be contained and led to a war between Senegal and Mauritania in April 1989 [Leservoisier, 1994: Chap. 10; Maiga, 1995: 54–57].

It is also worth noting that, on the left bank, there is growing resentment and mounting opposition against transfers of land through 'illegal' sales—chiefs or other powerful individuals sell customary land without the consent of the community and unduly appropriate the proceeds (see *supra*, Chap. 3)—to rich purchasers. Opposition is especially directed at capitalists or civil servants from Dakar and at the well-to-do *Moor* elite which acceded to economic prosperity through its leadership role in the export oilseeds boom in the Sine-Saloum. It is easy to multiply examples of this kind.[19]

Land alienation to strangers, whether through sale transactions or state mandatory allocations, is not necessarily opposed by the use of open violence. Milder and more subtle forms of hostility such as malpractices of deceit, manipulations and double deals directed against strangers are frequent occurrences. In Kenya, for example, 'farmers who have pledged their land titles as security for loans are sometimes tempted into selling their land to strangers without informing them of the charges on the land', which leaves them free to default on their loans if they wish [Shipton, 1988: 111]. Also, some farmers sell their land to several (stranger) buyers at once or agree to sell 'in the expectation that after they have collected their money, the sale will be ruled void by the local land control board and district registrar and they will succeed in evading repayment of the money paid by the buyer' [*ibidem*].

Efficiency costs obviously result from determined resistance of local people against drastic reshuffling of land rights, whether through the land market or otherwise. These costs may take three main forms. First, as illustrated above, new uncertainties arise that tend to multiply precisely the kind of transaction costs (search, enforcement and litigation) that the ETLR predicts will be reduced by the creation of freehold tenure. Second, there are all the costs which the new, 'illegitimate' owners must bear to protect the land property they have acquired in violation of local customary norms (perhaps as a result of land sales by a 'corrupt' land master or village chief). Such costs are of both a fixed and recurrent nature: thus, land and related property need to be not only enclosed and fenced but also constantly guarded against malignant interference.[20] Third, social turmoil in the countryside can give rise to serious labour market imperfections that may entail considerable efficiency costs at the level of the whole economy. This will happen if landless villagers, prompted by a desire to take revenge for the loss of their customary rights of access, decide to harm the interests of the new private owners, at least when these owners are strangers.

As wage labourers, they may be incited to indulge in labour-shirking and mismanagement of assets while, as sharecroppers, they will pilfer inputs, underreport output and overreport non-labour factor costs. These moral hazard problems can be controlled only through continuous and tight monitoring, thus increasing the effective cost of labour dramatically. To such problems, landowners may nevertheless respond by adopting capital-using input combinations or labour-augmenting innovations so as to ease the problems of controlling hired labour and to avoid sharecropping their lands.[21] From a social viewpoint, mechanization of the production process, when it is conceived as a means of breaking labour supervision constraints that would not have arisen under another land rights system, appears as unfortunate. It corresponds to input mixes that are ill-suited to the factor endowments of African societies since fixed capital in the form of sophisticated imported machinery will cause a serious drain on their scarce savings and foreign exchange resources. In Kenya, we are thus told that most of the new landless 'do not appear to be moving into tenant or agricultural wage-labor roles, but leaving agriculture generally as the remaining farmers employ more labor-efficient methods' based upon mechanization [Bruce, 1986: 54; 1988: 44].[22]

There is an important implication of the above analysis: incentive problems resulting from lack of legitimacy of the new land arrangements may create serious imperfections in the labour and land rental or sale markets with the effect of impeding the equalization of land-labour ratios across farms that allocative efficiency would dictate. Clearly, the conventional view according to which the creation of formal private land rights encourages efficiency-enhancing transfers of land (and investment) by unambiguously reducing and even eliminating transaction costs must be called into question and duly assessed against the background of specific social contexts. When due allowance is made for subjectively induced transaction costs, it can no more be taken for granted that individualized freehold tenure minimizes total transaction costs.

To sum up, market transactions cannot be expected to be automatically triggered off by the establishment of secure private property rights in land, even when they are legally backed and centrally registered. This is essentially because supply of land to the market is limited owing to social security considerations and symbolic reasons. It must now be added that the aforementioned ineffectiveness of the registration system (reflected, in particular, in a lack of diligent record-keeping of changes in land ownership) is also bound to fetter the development of the land market since the expected reduction of uncertainty of land transactions may not materialize. On the other hand, when land sale transactions (or other types of transfers) take place that run counter to traditional social norms, there is no guarantee that the sum of transaction costs decreases and that efficiency improves.

Clearly, land titling is not a sufficient condition for land market activation. We will see now that it is not a necessary condition either.

*Lack of efficiency-enhancing market transfers* (i) Under conditions of acute land scarcity, unmitigated by a sufficiently rapid development of land-saving technical innovations and new income-earning opportunities outside the agricultural sector, land sale transactions tend to multiply even when they are illegal and the land is not titled. This is all the more likely to happen if the customary order and its social security mechanisms are weak or have eroded under the pressure of individualistic tendencies encouraged by market development (including the individualization of land tenure itself) [Baland and Platteau, 1996: 279–83]. Desperation sales are then the mechanism through which the above-discussed shortage of voluntary supply is overcome and the land market is activated. (As will be pointed out later, a high incidence of migratory flows is another circumstance susceptible of activating land sale transactions). Interestingly, Kaushik Basu (1986c) has shown that, depending on the belief of the agents regarding the easiness with which a land lost can be bought back later, a land market can be in two distinct self-reinforcing equilibrium positions. The market may be rather inactive—in which case 'individuals hesitate to sell land because land turnover is low, and it is their hesitation which, in turn, reinforces the low turnover' [Basu, 1986c: 164]—, or it may be quite active—when individuals do not hesitate to sell land because they believe they will be able to buy land back, if needed. What is proposed here is that one important mechanism susceptible of moving the land market from the low-level to the high-level equilibrium is a succession of forced sales made under duress.

That land sales in SSA tend to be caused by distress conditions has been frequently noted in the literature [Collier, 1983: 157; Bruce, 1986: 36; Green, 1987: 7, 17; see also Sarap, 1996: A-109, for India]. Unfortunately, there is a glaring scarcity of detailed studies on this matter. One of the few such studies is that by Catherine André and Jean-Philippe Platteau (1998) about a hill settlement in Western Rwanda. In their paper, the authors show that, contrary to the general picture apparently prevailing in SSA, there is an active land market in the survey area. Thus, they estimated that in 1993 not less than 40 per cent of land parcels owned by local inhabitants had been acquired through market purchases. Moreover, the incidence of land sale transactions appears to have increased with an amazing speed during recent times since the same proportion was only 29 per cent five years earlier. The closure of the land frontier in Eastern Rwanda and of migration possibilities in both Uganda and Zaïre (causing reverse migration movements) combined with rapid population growth to suddenly cause an enormous amount of land hunger that was not counterbalanced by an expansion of non-agricultural employment opportunities. Increasing activity of the local land market triggered off by rising numbers of distress sales rapidly ensued.

As a matter of fact, the study found that, out of 247 recorded land sales, almost two-thirds have been motivated by the need to finance emergency expenditures (food and medicine), to repay debts or to meet social exigencies. Especially worth singling out is the fact that in more than 30 per cent of the cases it is the sheer need for survival that has forced the household to part with a fraction of its landholding. In addition, almost 17 per cent of land sales have occurred because the household had to incur litigation expenses usually connected with land disputes or to pay various kinds of fees (including bribes paid to judges with a view to influencing court decisions). It is only in about one-third of the cases that land sale transactions can be presumed to have fostered efficiency: parcels were thus sold due to bad location (usually an excessive distance from the owner's house), to the owner's desire to rationalize his property, or to reallocate his wealth (such as when he uses the sale proceeds to construct a new house, to finance a migratory move or schooling expenditures, etc.).

It bears emphasis that the rapidly increasing activity of the land market took place in spite of its largely illegal character. Indeed, below a critical size of two hectares, land property is permitted to be neither alienated nor subdivided or fragmented (decree n° 09/76 of 1976, March 4, art. 3 and art. 82–83). From evidence provided in the paper, it is evident that all sales of land parcels are in violation of the law: local inhabitants are too poorly endowed in land to be allowed to part with some of it.

One important lesson from the above Rwandan story is that spontaneous individualization of land rights, unassisted by any process of titling or registration at the state level, can be extremely effective in activating the land market even when land sales do actually violate the law. In this respect, it is quite revealing that land sale transactions were typically attested by written documents established in the presence of witnesses, thereby ensuring the validity of land transactions. A similar conclusion has been reached in another recent micro-village study devoted to a village situated at about 40 km from Cotonou, the capital city of Benin [J.F. Dubuisson, 1998]. The contrast with neighbouring Kenya is almost complete since in the latter country, as we have seen earlier: 'Most smallholders, even after registration, do not do the things with their land that registration seeks to empower them to do, such as selling or mortgaging their land without consulting family and neighbours' [Bruce et al., 1994: 261].

This demonstrates that what matters are *de facto* rather than *de jure* rights. In Kenya, exercising prerogatives formally attached to full-fledged private property rights guaranteed by legal titles would contravene important community norms that are embedded in the indigenous tenure system. In Rwanda (and in some other parts of Africa), by contrast, relentless population pressure and an history of much more individualized settlement patterns making for the absence of genuine community life have caused the land tenure system to evolve so radically that *de facto* private property rights have emerged even in the absence of state-led registration. The same observation can be made with respect to Uganda.

(ii) In order that land sale transactions can lead to efficiency gains, land must be transferred from less to more dynamic farmers. This would happen (1°) if land transactions were motivated by differences in endowments of human capital across agents or (2°) if agents with heterogeneous land endowments use the land market to realize gains from the exchange of land exploited with different factor intensities. (In this latter case, it must be noted, size-stratified factor intensities and associated agricultural productivity are driven by factor market imperfections) [Zimmerman and Carter, 1997: 7–8]. Such does not appear to be the main case, however.[23] As a matter of fact, the large incidence of distress sales documented above suggests that those who abandon ownership are not relatively inefficient farmers, but smallholders who face a comparatively high level of risk exposure and dispose of their land when stochastic outcomes compel them to do so [*ibidem*].[24] With the help of a dynamic stochastic programming technique and using West African background data to set the parameters of the their simulation model, Fred Zimmerman and Michael Carter (1997) have reached the intuitive conclusion that under certain covariate risk realizations, poorer and marginally more efficient producers can actually sell land to wealthier and marginally less efficient producers.

The presence of multiple rural market failures—arising, in particular, from absent insurance markets, wealth-differentiated credit markets, and declining self-insurance capacities on the part of poor rural dwellers[25]—may determine individual wealth trajectories that are highly dependent upon initial endowments. Thus, a succession of bad shocks may drive poor farmers to sell land parcels while better-endowed farmers are able to insure against such shocks through access to credit, temporary depletion of accumulated non-land assets, diversification of income sources (including access to non-agricultural incomes), etc....

In the Rwandan case study of André and Platteau, almost half of the households belonging to the lowest landownership category did sell land but could never buy any, compared with a proportion of only 4 per cent for the three highest categories (1993 figures). On the other hand, only 10 per cent of the poorest households were able to buy some land without selling any, as against a proportion of 27 per cent for the three highest categories. (Note that almost 40 per cent of the whole sample did simultaneously sell and purchase land at some point of their individual history).

Can it be said that land purchasers tend to be relatively efficient agents? Given the paucity of in-depth case studies, the empirical basis available to answer that question remains too narrrow. One study, however, provides an empirically reliable answer to the above question. It is the study recently carried out by Denis Dubuisson (1998) in irrigation schemes newly developed in North Burkina Faso (Yalogo region) and devoted to rice cultivation. In this work, landowners on the perimeters belonging to several villages are clearly distinguished according to their main occupational status and according to whether they have accumulated plots through (illegal) market purchases. The conclusion reached by Dubuisson is inconclusive: there are no statistically significant differences in land yields between rich purchasers (who have acquired several parcels) and other owners (mainly, original occupants who own just one parcel), nor between agriculturalists on the one hand, and merchants or other owners whose main occupation lies outside the agricultural sector (such as local officials and administrative staff), on the other hand. True, some parcels acquired by investors have been put to efficient use (in particular, those owned by successful Muslim merchants operating in Yalogo city, who have understood the profitability of irrigated rice cultivation and use chemical fertilizers bought in Ouagadougou), yet other parcels, in particular, those acquired by public employees, are ill-exploited or even left fallow.[26]

There are actually many grounds to believe that, at the least, there is no systematic tendency for transacted lands to fall into efficient hands. This is essentially because, in many cases, the motives behind land purchases are not driven by effficiency.

To begin with, demand for land may be guided by non-economic motives such as social prestige and political power. It is thus common practice that not only traditional elite penetrate the modern network of administrative-political power but also, in the other way around, the new urban elite try their best to get elected, co-opted or appointed to traditional chieftaincies after having acquired a significant acreage of local land [Doornbos, 1975: 58, 67; Berry, 1988: 59–60, 67; Bruce, 1988: 42–43; Bayart, 1989: 215–219]. In Uganda, for example, where the land market is relatively active compared to many other African countries, land ownership conditions a political career in so far as 'owners of land have the right to sit on local councils, the first step on the political ladder, and owners are eligible for appointments as chiefs' [Barrows and Roth, 1989: 14—quoting Mukwaya, 1953]. Here is a well-established method, which has antecedents in Europe,[27] that enables a modern elite to root their newly achieved status in a lasting base little vulnerable to the fluctuations and turmoils occurring at the national or regional levels.

In addition, land purchases may arise out of economic considerations that have nothing to do with efficiency. Under conditions characterized by the underdevelopment of capital markets and a lack of sufficiently safe investment opportunities, investment in land is very attractive for people with significant savings, usually people with regular incomes from non-agricultural sources [Haugerud, 1983: 80–83; Bruce, 1986: 56, 1993: 42; Green, 1987: 27; André, 1989; Mackenzie, 1993: 209–210]. Also, the same social security and insurance considerations that motivate landholders to stick to their land (see *supra*) may operate to make them or other people wish to buy (additional) land that is not immediately required for subsistence. The land thus acquired may not be brought into efficient cultivation, at least in the short or medium run, a particularly obvious feature of land parcels that are casually exploited or worked by poorly supervised tenants.

Given the above, it is not surprising that absentee ownership may be widespread in areas where the land market is active, or that holdings acquired by the educated urban elite 'go largely uncultivated' or 'tend to be poorly managed and less productive than smaller farms around them' [Bruce, 1993: 42; see also Collier,1983: 152–153, 159; Green, 1987: 9; Golan, 1990: 15–16; Leservoisier, 1994: 181–82]. In Machakos (Kenya), for example, absentee ownership was found to be as high as 81 per cent of the total holding sampled (most farmers own a single parcel) while in Kericho, around one-third of the holdings fell into this category [Green, 1987: 22; for other estimates of the same order of magnitude, see Collier, 1983: 151–152].

Note finally that, inasmuch as (distress) sellers frequently sell only a portion of their holdings, while most purchasers are not agricultural entrepreneurs seeking to enlarge their farm, holdings which grow by purchase are typically formed in a fragmented state and consolidation does not result from the operation of the land market [Bruce, 1986: 56; Green, 1987: 27; André and Platteau, 1997].

Implicit in the foregoing discussion of the rural land market are distributive effects of land sale transactions. These effects will retain our attention in the next section which is specifically concerned with critically assessing the evolutionary mechanism of induced demand for, and supply of, the institution of land titling.

## 4.4 THE ETLR PUT TO TEST: THE INDUCED DEMAND-AND-SUPPLY MECHANISM

In Chapter 3, it has been emphasized that distributive rather than efficiency considerations are likely to be a core force determining whether given technical or institutional innovations may take place. Moreover, what is considered distributionally acceptable depends on the prevailing social values and on the political weight of the various groups or subgroups concerned by the change. Both types of considerations may, of course, converge if the efficiency-promoting change is supported by the dominant groups(s) or if the losers can be fairly compensated. Yet, there is no guarantee that such happy outcomes will automatically materialize.

In the specific case of land rights, it has been argued above that advanced systems of individual tenure—including its utmost development in the form of titling and centralized registration—do not necessarily enhance efficiency when introduced in societies characterized by living informal orders at village level. In fact, complete transfer rights do not seem to be required for efficiency in present-day Africa—the agriculture of which is still situated at relatively low levels of technology development—and, as a result, deepening individualization of land tenure in the sense of adding these rights to a core set of fundamental use rights and a few important transfer rights (particularly, the right of bequest) is likely to be premature.

This conclusion is actually reinforced when adverse distributive consequences follow from the establishment of freehold tenure. These adverse effects may take place through two distinct mechanisms: the mechanism of adjudication of land rights, on the one hand, and that of the land sale market, on the other hand. Let us consider them in turn before drawing the implications of their operation on the demand for freehold tenure and land titling. This will lead us to a criticism of the induced-demand mechanism postulated by the ETLR. A critical appraisal of the induced-supply mechanism will end Section 4.

### *Equity problems raised by the adjudication of private property rights*

Empirical evidence from several African case studies shows that 'registration can create rather than reduce uncertainty and conflict over land rights' [Atwood, 1990: 663]. This confirms Boserup's diagnosis that 'each new step on the road to private property in land may well create less and not more security of tenure, and a vast amount of litigation is the obvious result' [Boserup, 1965: 92]. Two sources of increased uncertainty accompanying the establishment of full-fledged private property rights in land deserve to be mentioned here: the loss of derived rights at the expense of vulnerable categories, and the unfair assignment of rights to the powerful.

*Loss of derived or secondary rights* The idea that land registration is grounded in an adjudication procedure that does nothing else than recognize and record accurately existing land rights is unacceptable. In effect, if titling may reduce risk and transaction costs for some categories of people, it may simultaneously create new uncertainties for other categories which rely on customary or informal practices and rules to establish and safeguard their land claims [Atwood, 1990: 663–64]. In other words, as the experience of Kenya reveals, sections of local populations face a serious risk of being denied legal recognition of their customary rights to land during the registration process [Green, 1987: 6, 22–23]. This is especially true of women, pastoralists, hunter-gatherers, casted people, former slaves and serfs, people belonging to minority tribes, etc., who have traditionally enjoyed subsidiary or derived (usufruct) rights to land.[28] As noted by Green, increased security for the registered owner—usually the male head of household—'may mean greater insecurity for other users, who may after the reform use the land only at the sufferance of the owner' [*ibidem*: 26; see also Coldham, 1978; Bruce, 1986: 54; Bruce and Fortmann, 1989: 7; Mackenzie, 1993: 208–213].

Ultimately, if an equity problem arises, it is because traditional tenure rules and rights which determine access to land (and water points) in such a way as to assure employment for the able and social security for the poor, the old and the disabled defy recording and classification.[29] Put in another way, it is impossible to bring to the adjudication register all the multiple rights claimable under customary law [Barrows and Roth, 1989: 8]. Given that the complex bundles of rights associated with given parcels are extremely hard to sort out (where one person's bundle of tenurial rights stops and where another's begins is often very difficult to determine) and that a landholding unit (such as the 'compound' in West African societies) is rarely under a single management rule (if only because women manage 'their' fields fairly independently), the cost entailed by a comprehensive registration would be prohibitively high, all the higher as the bureaucratic machinery is confronted by a considerable information gap. Such a machinery has indeed much less information and knowledge of land tenure history of rural communities than these communities themselves [Riddell et al., 1987: 30–31].

In fact, when customary group rights and community control are extinguished by a procedure of registration/titling, there is a transfer of transaction costs from local land authorities to the state and it is the inability of the state to bear them that explains the failure to adjudicate and register all rights existing under the customary system [Barrows and Roth, 1989: 21]. It must also be added that traditional systems of land tenure involve a great deal of flexibility and recording all the adjustments implied would prove extremely difficult.

To sum up, due to high information and other transaction costs, governments in poor countries are typically unable to record accurately all existing land rights. Such a failure is likely (1) to create new uncertainties for vulnerable sections of local populations and (2) to reduce the efficacy of traditional institutions or mitigatory factors that used to provide economic security to all members of village communities and to help hold economic differentiation in check. The latter effect is particularly worth pondering over when economic opportunities in the outside economy are few and no alternative insurance systems exist.

*Unfair assignment of rights to the powerful* In a social context dominated by huge differences in education levels and by differential access to the state administration, there is much to be feared that the adjudication/registration process will be manipulated by the elite in its favour. If the experience of Thailand can serve as any guide, then it indicates that such a fear is well justified: land records have been manipulated by powerful government officials so as to allow elites (individuals, families, or private companies) with a high level of political connections 'to obtain ownership of land that, under the traditional system, would have been controlled by homesteading cultivators'. Original occupants (especially when they belong to non-Thai minorities) found it difficult to protect their customary rights owing to 'differential access of claimants in land disputes to the Thai bureaucracy' [Thomson et al., 1986: 413–414; see also Feeny, 1988: 286–287, 294–296]. The same kind of difficulties, and the consequent fear of land registration on the part of dominated sections of the population, have been documented with respect to other Asian countries [see, e.g., Wadhwa, 1989; Viswanath, 1997, for India], and to Latin America and the Caribbean as well [Stanfield, 1990].

The situation is not different in SSA. During the colonial period already, in countries where lands could be immatriculated (such as those under French colonial rule), numerous malpractices have been observed which allowed powerful people (including bureaucrats, particularly land surveyors who are 'prominent experts in land grabbing') to dominate land allocation procedures, especially inside or near urban areas. As for rural lands, the few people who took advantage of the registration system had often manipulated the law to expropriate collective rights for themselves [Bayart, 1989: 113; Golan, 1990: 19; Haugerud, 1983: 78; Mackenzie, 1993: 212]. The case of Uganda where chiefs used (voluntary) land titling reform to snatch land (including communal grazing areas) away from the poor is well-known [Doornbos, 1975; Noronha, 1985; see also Firmin-Sellers, 1996, for Ghana].

Contemporary evidence points in the same direction, as can be judged from the experience of the few countries where a land titling programme has been implemented; or from that of the numerous countries where registration of rural lands has been allowed during a transitory period accompanying a reform vesting bare ownership of all non-immatriculated lands in the state; or, again, from the experience of countries where public lands form an important category in national land laws. In the first two cases, the experience is similar: clever, well-informed or powerful (and usually educated) individuals often successfully jockey to have parcels not previously theirs registered in their own name while the mass of rural people are generally unaware of the new land provisions or do not grasp the implications of registration.[30] An extreme, almost caricatural illustration is provided by these few well-connected Kenyans who succeeded in having pasture lands registered in their own names on the ground that they would bring them into cultivation. In fact, as the experience soon revealed, their intent was not to exploit the land in question but just to use it as collateral in order to obtain loans from banks in Nairobi. Proceeds of these loans were used to finance children's university studies abroad and the plan was to shun repayment and let the land be foreclosed (personal communication of Okoth-Ogendo).

In Mauritania, to revert to an aforementioned example, good irrigated lands traditionally claimed by local Negro-African communities on the right bank of the Senegal river have been adjudicated to private owners with a view to encouraging their efficient exploitation. Yet, as things turned out, these lands were allotted to people of Moorish origin by an essentially Moorish administration and many of them were not actually brought into cultivation [Leservoisier, 1994: 181–84].

As for allocation of public lands, there are plenty of accounts showing that it is often politically manipulated. In Nigeria, just to take one example, under the cover of national development projects extensive land tracts 'running to hundreds of hectares' have been granted (on a long-term basis) to 'political friends' even though this led to the dispossession of many villagers of their customary lands [Zubair, 1987: 133; see also Mugangu Matabaro, 1997, for Congo ex-Zaïre].

It is often the ability to use both the statutory and the customary law—to the extent that, as the experience of Kenya reveals, customary rights are not extinguished with the introduction of freehold tenure and the registration of individual title—that enables powerful individuals or groups to enhance their interests. Customary law is then manipulated, appearing as a 'continuously evolving code' referred to by those individuals or groups to claim large tracts of land to be registered under the freehold system of tenure [Glazier, 1985: 231; Berry, 1993]. Thus, for example, Coutts, then district commissioner in Fort Hill district, pointed out in 1948 that certain unscrupulous persons are using the custom of redeemable sale of land 'to take back land which has been made fertile by a younger more progressive person' [Mackenzie, 1993: 207]. Under such circumstances, subscription to custom or tradition, while appearing to maintain the status quo, in fact represents the strategy adopted by clever actors to effect the kind of social transformation favourable to their particular interests [*ibidem*: 203].

Nowhere is this more apparent than in the case of colonial Ghana where competing claimants to land referred to different interpretations of land and social customs to assert their rights. Thus, in the Ga state,

> ... given the African's fear that Europeans would purchase all land were it offered for sale,...the Ga elites sought to srenghten their rights over land (and thus further their economic pursuits) by 'reinventing tradition'. First, the members of the Reindorf family defended a version of customary law that vested all land in the extended family, rather than in the divisional or paramount stools. Second, the family members manipulated the family history so as to narrow the boundaries of the extended family and reduce the number of

> claimants to family land. Third, the Reindorfs struggled to enforce their preferred version of custom by reinventing the institutions of the traditional state. They sought to gain control over the Ga Mantse, or paramount chief, because the Mantse had the authority to arbitrate all land disputes brought before the Ga Native Tribunal... In 1921, representatives of this disadvantaged group [a substantial portion of the Ga citizenry and the disinherited Ga chiefs] mobilized to articulate a different, more distributionally favorable definition of customary law... They argued, instead, that all Ga lands were owned by the divisional stools; and that the divisional chiefs managed the land on behalf of the stool subjects [Firmin-Sellers, 1996: 40, 44].

Etienne Balibar and Immanuel Wallerstein have aptly noted that while the real past is unchangeable the 'sense of the past' is a social construct that is subject to constant re-interpretations:

> The sense of the past is something that allows to act in the present otherwise than would have been possible without it. It is an essential element of the socialization of individuals... The sense of the past is above all a moral and therefore political phenomenon.... Since the real world continuously changes, what is relevant for present policies also changes continuously and unavoidably. As a consequence, the content of the sense of the past is also being unceasingly modified. Yet, as it implies by definition the assertion of an immutable past, nobody can never admit that the past has changed or could have changed [Balibar and Wallerstein, 1988: 106—my traduction; see also Berry, 1993].

Thus, in the bloody conflicts which opposed the Moorish and the Negro-Mauritanian (haalpulaar) communities around the problem of access to irrigated lands on the right bank of the Senegal river, the two parties presented radically opposed versions of the history of soil occupation in the disputed area. While territorial claims by Moors are based on an history of military control by warlike tribes (as is typical of a pastoral-nomadic people), the legitimacy claimed by the haalpulaar people refers to an history of erstwhile occupation and exploitation of the land (as can be expected from sedentary agriculturalists) [Leservoisier, 1994: 242].

Given the high level of politicization of wealth allocation in SSA and the highly unequal chances of getting access to strategic information or influencing bureaucratic and judiciary decision-making [see, for example, Sklar, 1979; Hyden, 1983; Berry, 1984; Young, 1986; Bayart, 1989], registration can be said to supply a mechanism for transfer of wealth in favour of the educational, economic and political elite [Barrows and Roth, 1989: 8]. Insofar as it encourages the assertion of greedy interests with powerful backing and is likely, wittingly or not, to reward cunning, titling opens up new possibilities of conflict and insecurity. This evolution can have disastrous consequences for vulnerable sections of the population if loss of land is followed by outright eviction [see, e.g., Doornbos, 1975: 60, 66, 73, for Uganda].

A final remark is in order. If titling is not (fully) subsidized and a price is therefore charged on landholders, the strategies of powerful individuals is all the more threatening as lack of access to credit and low wealth levels prevent smallholders from registering their land. Price of registration thus acting as an important rationing mechanism, smallholders are highly vulnerable to attempts by the elites to grab their (untitled) lands while, on the contrary, the latter can immediately protect their own. In other words, titling increases tenure insecurity of the poor because it places a formidable weapon in the hands of the rich who have both better ability to pay the price of registration and superior knowledge of government bureaucracy and procedures [see, e.g., Roth, 1993: 318–319].

*Adverse distributive effects of the land sale market*

(i) The discussion in the previous section has shown that, in countries subject to growing land scarcity, the land market is likely to be activated by poor smallholders who are driven to distress sales. In the words of Zimmerman and Carter, 'the interplay between land scarcity and risk seems likely to drive the endogenous emergence of the land market and to provide the basis for its operation' [Carter and Zimmerman, 1993: 1–2]. Because relatively minor differences in initial endowments map into different risk-coping capacities, the land market, when it arises, tends to polarize the land ownership distribution and it is quite possible that 'moderately endowed farmers find their asset position unsustainable over time in the face of stochastic shocks' [Carter, 1997: 583].

Traditional systems of social security could, in principle, provide an alternative to land sales as a way to cope with these adverse shocks. However, there are good reasons to believe that such systems are gradually eroding under the combined impact of population pressure and land market development, a process which Carter (1997) describes as the 'individualization of risk exposure' [see also Reardon et al., 1992, for Burkina Faso]. On the one hand, relatively well-endowed households are able to accumulate land and increase their self-insurance capacity, as a result of which they become ever more independent of the reciprocal logic of customary risk-sharing networks. As they pull out, leaving behind those with smaller asset bases, the effectiveness of such networks diminishes to the disadvantage of smallholders. On the other hand, individualization of land tenure tends to threaten informal sharing and risk-pooling arrangements customarily made within extended households. This is especially apparent when family members spend a growing portion of their time on their individual fields while shunning work on compound fields from which collective subsistence was traditionally ensured.

To properly assess the equity effect of land market development in densely populated areas, the role of non-agricultural income-earning opportunities must be brought into the picture. As a matter of fact, the direction of this effect critically hinges upon the access of poor households to emerging rural labour markets. If this access is sufficiently open to them, off-farm incomes may both provide them with a self-insurance mechanism that reduces the need to sell land under distress conditions and enable them to buy up land, thereby enlarging their initially low endowments. If, on the contrary, access to off-farm income opportunities discriminates against poor households, the development of rural labour markets is likely to reinforce the above-described tendency of the land market to increase initial inequality. To the extent that richer households are usually better educated and better connected, the latter scenario will predominate.

The work of André and Platteau (1998) in Rwanda is one of the few available studies that document in detail the distributive effects of emerging land markets in conditions of acute population pressure. Let us consider in some detail the results of this study that are most relevant for the present purpose.

While land distribution in Rwanda was known to be relatively equal even during recent times, the Gini coefficient for owned lands in the survey village was found to be as high as 0.411 in 1988. Five years later, it had continued its upward move to reach 0.436. Likewise, the Gini coefficient for operated lands increased from 0.357 to 0.389 between 1988 and 1993. In addition, by decomposing the Gini coefficient, the authors reached the conclusion that the percentage contribution of market purchases to overall inequality in land distribution increased dramatically, from 24 per cent in 1988 to 47 per cent in 1993.

Clearly, in this area, activation of the land market has had the effect of accentuating inequalities in land endowments. Underlying this disequalizing logic is a positive relation between landownership position and access to regular income opportunities outside the agricultural sector [see also Reardon et al., 1992, for Burkina Faso].[31] Indeed, even though households located at the lowest rungs of the landownership ladder are those most in need to complement their agricultural incomes, they are disadvantaged in their access to non-agricultural employment. First, low wealth and weak access to credit hinder poor households from setting up a non-farm business in contrast to wealthier households who can better rely on their own cash resources and have better access to credit. Second, poor households are excluded from patronage relationships which in Rwanda are critical to obtain wage employment and are usually intertwined with the all-pervasive networks of the political establishment at communal and upper levels.

Table 4.1 below substantiates this disequalizing process in a striking manner. It can indeed be seen that, in both survey years, a large majority of the sample households with either a present (first row) or a past experience (second row) of regular non-agricultural incomes (RNAI)

Table 4.1: Relation Between Position on the Land Market and Access to Regular Non-Agricultural Income Opportunities (1988 and 1993)

| Access to off-farm income opportunities* | Proportion of households which bought land | Proportion of households having sold land without buying any |
|---|---|---|
| 1. Among hholds currently earning RNAI | 1988: 21/27 (77.8%)<br>1993: 30/39 (76.9%) | 1988: 3/27 (11.1%)<br>1993: 6/39 (15.4%) |
| 2. Among hholds with an history of RNAI and currently earning only AI or INAI | 1988: 13/13 (100.0%)<br>1993: 17/17 (100.0%) | 1988: 0/13 (0.0%)<br>1993: 0/17 (0.0%) |
| 3. Among hholds with no present or past experience of RNAI | 1988: 3/16 (18.7%)<br>1993: 4/31 (12.9%) | 1988: 8/16 (50.0%)<br>1993: 20/31 (64.5%) |

* RNAI stands for Regular Non-Agricultural Incomes; INAI for Irregular Non-Agricultural Incomes; and AI for Agricultural Incomes. A past history of RNAI means that the household concerned has earned RNAI for at least five consecutive years in the past.

have been able to purchase land. Moreover, the minority of households presently earning regular non-agricultural incomes and having not yet bought land are all households which have enjoyed access to these opportunities for only a short time. Conversely, less than one-fifth of the households with no past or present experience of RNAI have purchased land some time in their life cycle. The proportions are markedly reversed between the two types of households when one considers the situation of those which have sold land without having ever been able to buy any.

Note that there is a direct relationship between access to regular non-agricultural incomes and access to credit as local rotating saving-and-credit associations (known as 'tontines' in Rwanda) tend to exclude farmers with no regular incomes from which to pay their periodic contributions to the common pot. Since membership in these associations gives access to consumption credit, exclusion from them deprives poor households of an important and flexible insurance device [Platteau, 1997]. Thus, poor households which are outside patronage networks giving access to regular employment opportunities will also suffer from lack of access to credit and insurance facilities. They are trapped in a vicious circle of poverty while those which have access to these opportunities enjoy the cumulative advantages that can be derived from them: a larger land asset base allowing better risk management and improved access to credit through local collective initiatives .

An aforementioned study on irrigated rice schemes in North Burkina Faso confirms that the operation of rural land markets in SSA is likely to lead to a deepening inequality in the land distribution [D. Dubuisson, 1998]. This study indeed shows that, in some villages particularly well located (close to the town of Yalogo), an active land market has developed within rice perimeters even though it is officially forbidden (note that a land market does not exist for drylands devoted to traditional staples). Supply of land comes mainly from distress sales by impoverished farmers or from voluntary sales by inexperienced right-holders who did not perceive in time the profitability of rice cultivation and were possibly persuaded to give up this activity by deceitful potential purchasers. As for (big) purchasers, they are typically merchants or state officials (see *supra*).

In the areas where a land market exists, land concentration has therefore proceeded rapidly within a short span of time: thus, the Gini coefficient for land distribution has increased from 0.033 at the time of allocation of rice parcels by a foreign NGO (in the early nineties) to 0.273 in 1997. The percentage contribution of market transactions to overall inequality in land distribution has perceptibly increased from 29.2 per cent to 38.4 per cent during the same period. The role of non-market mechanisms, albeit diminishing, remains important. Thus, it is mainly through such mechanisms that powerful villagers occupying key positions in the bureau in charge of the perimeter's management try to tilt the allocation of these parcels in favour of their own family (e.g., by using figureheads to vindicate access to more parcels than what the rules allow, or by unfairly confiscating parcels belonging to initial right-holders on the ground that they did not pay their water dues sufficiently rapidly).

This said, a positive relationship between land endowment and access to non-farm income opportunities needs not necessarily obtain since it depends upon the structure of the rural labour markets which may vary from one area to another. In a recent aforementioned study [Baland et al., 1999] devoted to central Uganda, no significant relationship was found between initial land endowment of the households and the fact that they earn regular non-agricultural incomes. A striking result of this study is that villagers with a comparatively low initial land endowment have a stronger propensity to purchase lands: thus, more than 80 per cent of the households which did not inherit any land have acquired land parcels through the market while the corresponding proportion for those which did inherit some land is hardly 36 per cent. For the latter households, any additional acre of inherited land reduces the amount of land purchased by about 0.30 acres.

Another study about a village situated at about 40 km from Cotonou (Benin) has reached a similar conclusion, yet, as is evident from Table 4.2 below, the mitigation of initial inequality of land distribution through market purchases is much less impressive than in the study devoted to Uganda [J.F. Dubuisson, 1998]. Similarly, a study by Place and Migot-Adholla (1998) in Kenya did not find that land markets were used to accumulate land—most purchases formed the only piece of land available to the buyer. Finally, Pinckney and Kimuyu (1994) did not find evidence of households involuntarily losing rights to land in their Kenyan study site, yet they may have failed to capture such households since households that have lost all their rights to land are the most likely to have migrated from the area surveyed.

(ii) Titling, as we have seen earlier, is neither a necessary nor a sufficient condition for land market activation. Yet, superimposed on

Table 4.2: Evolution of inequality in land distribution (as measured by Gini coefficients) under the impact of land market transactions and other transfers (Uganda and Benin)

| | Uganda (36 villages) | Benin (Hayakpa) |
|---|---|---|
| Inherited lands* | 0.74 | 0.49 |
| Inherited + purchased lands | 0.59 | 0.43 |
| Total operational lands | 0.53 | 0.34 |

Source Baland, Gaspart, Place, and Platteau, 1999; J.F. Dubuisson, 1998: 91.

Note Inherited lands also include lands permanently given by parents to children while they are still alive (*inter vivos* transfers).

an active land market, it may reinforce the disequalizing process at work in this market. This is because there is a serious possibility that land titles only enhance formal credit supply for large-scale producers who enjoy a privileged position in terms of market access (see *supra*).

As a result of rural market imperfections, titling has more economic value for privileged farmers owning comparatively large amounts of land and other forms of wealth. Incentive for title acquisition is therefore stronger for them and, as we know, this incentive may be actually compounded by other strategic advantages in terms of access to the government bureaucracy (see *supra*). What must be added now is that, in the same logic of differential market access, titling raises the value not only of the initial land endowment of relatively well-endowed farmers, but also the value to them of the land of less advantaged neighbours. If a free land market exists, therefore, registration of land 'may have the unintended consequence of boosting the relative land acquisition incentives and economic power of the already well-endowed' [Carter et al., 1994: 155].

By addressing the credit supply problem directly, as has been suggested earlier, the adverse distributive consequences (and the considerable costs) of a titling programme would be averted.

### *The faulty mechanism of induced demand and supply*

*The induced demand schedule* The conception of demand depicted in Fig. 4.1 is basically flawed because it simplistically assumes a homogeneous social structure (manifested in an uniform and smooth demand schedule), thereby evading issues of bargaining power and class struggle.[32] In reality, as is evident from the foregoing discussion, there are potential losers from the establishment of freehold tenure. Different groups of socially differentiated people are confronted with distinct cost-benefit configurations and have varying perceptions of the risks of institutional change. Schematically, two such groups can be distinguished. On one side, we actually find well-to-do individuals who seek to increase their private share of the newly emerging economic opportunities while, on the other side, there are less privileged individuals whose main concern is to secure guaranteed access to a resource upon which their livelihood crucially depends. It is actually evident from a large amount of empirical evidence pertaining to various parts of the world and diverse periods of social history that, if the former class of people tend to claim private property rights in land, the latter strongly favour maintenance or re-establishment of collective rights. As Bates has illustrated, such conflicts over collective as opposed to individual forms of tenure or property have also characterized SSA where they still remain a vital issue today:

> In Uganda, for example, it took the form of the militant reassertion of traditional clan rights over the lands that had been alienated to the chiefs under freehold tenure. The dedication to clan rights formed much of the basis of the Bataka Association—a movement of the farmers and the clan heads who opposed the power of chiefs in general and their private rights over the 'mailo' lands in particular. Analogous disputes broke out among the Kikuyu. Prosperous farmers sought to advance their claims to individual tenure, while others sought to emphasize collective rights to 'mbari' lands out of fear of losing their rights to land in the Kikuyu reserves. The assertion of private rights over collective property by the chiefs of the Gold Coast underlay much of the rural politics in that area. And, in the contemporary period, the attempts by the state in Tanzania to promote collective rights to land in the cash-cropping regions of that territory has apparently found favor among the rural poor, who fear the loss of land rights in the countryside, while meeting with resistance on the part of the prosperous farmers, who naturally see such measures as threatening the gains which they seek to secure through cash-crop production [Bates, 1983: 100].

In Kenya, the district commissioner in Fort Hall district remarked in 1944 that 'the protagonists of outright purchase (a minute proportion of the tribe) are entirely self-interested; mainly they are persons who have "purchased" large areas of land which they are now unwilling to allow to be redeemed' (as the customary practice required) [Mackenzie, 1993: 207]. The main concern of the poor is clearly security of tenure in its most fundamental sense, that is, absence of risk of loss of land and the right to bequeath land to children [Land Tenure Center, 1990: 15].

Opposition of weaker sections of population to land titling is fundamentally grounded in the fear that, once land rights are formalized, stronger people will be tempted to refer to modern law and conflict-resolution mechanisms rather than to the customary law and practice that guarantee the rights of access to land and the fundamental rights to daily subsistence of all community members. Also, by encouraging individual emancipation from the collective logic of the village life, reference to the new legal order situated above the local community threatens to undermine all relations of mutual dependence and forms of acting together that are characteristic of the traditional village system. Thus, in Zambia, many of the answers provided by villagers about the question of the desirability of titles reflect the fear that these documents would somehow send a bad signal to the rest of the community, that is, 'a fear of setting oneself apart and becoming isolated' [Sjaastad, 1998: 164].

This said, weak people may possibly demand titling if they consider it as the only effective means of protecting them against outsiders—including the state—who might try to usurp or expropriate their land [Golan, 1990: 17].[33] Yet they may then want collective rather than individual titles (thus ensuring continuance of customary overlapping rights wherever feasible) inasmuch as they feel stronger when they are united around a traditional social structure. At least, this attachment to old forms of security are likely to persist so long as economic opportunities are scarce or perceived as unstable [Bruce, 1986: 32]. By contrast, demand for well-defined individual titles (perhaps not alienable, however) may be expressed by ordinary people when, as was observed in Zimbabwe, they have migrated to new settlement areas lying outside the jurisdiction of the chiefs and their traditional forms of rural social organization [Barrows and Roth, 1989: 18].

Finally, it must be reckoned that, in some important instances, titling may turn into a 'weapon of the weak'. This especially applies to women whose rights of access to land in the event of widowhood, divorce, or separation are increasingly imperilled under the pressure of land scarcity [André and Platteau, 1998; Platteau, 1996c: 40–42]. By acquiring the formal right to inherit titled land or to purchase such land on the market, they become effectively protected against attempts by kinsmen to deprive them of their customary rights (e.g., the right of a widow to stay on the land of her deceased husband, or the right of a divorced woman to subsist on the father's land in her native village). Yet, one should not underestimate the strength of the informal pressures exercised on women in order to prevent them from formalizing their rights. These pressures are typically driven by a fear to see family land passing into stranger hands through land sale transactions engaged in by women.

*The induced supply schedule* The main problem with the induced supply schedule postulated by the ETLR and depicted in Fig. 4.1 is that the state is implicitly posited as a unique and coherent decision-maker which carries out, or responds to, the 'will of the people'. There are at least two serious problems with such a view. First, given the above-stressed heterogeneity of rural actors, what is meant by the 'will of the people' is not clear. The government and/or state administration may side with one class (community) or another depending on power configurations and articulation between state and social classes or groups. In Mauritania, as I have already pointed out, the *Beydane* state supported the interests of the Moorish elite with which it is clearly identified when it embarked on a program of adjudication of private property rights over good irrigable lands on the right bank of the Senegal river. Obviously, the assumption of a benevolent state operating above the arena of class conflicts is abandoned in the political-economy approach of Sened and others (see *supra*, Section 4.2). In their approach, indeed, there are potential opponents to the establishment of private property rights and the government duly takes the ensuing political costs into account when making its decision to grant or not to grant such rights to those who press for them.

Second, it is highly simplistic to assume that the state machinery constitutes a coherent actor. If possible contradictions or conflicts between various departments or ministries concerned are ruled out, it becomes difficult to understand the many hesitations, compromises, or ambivalent, vague and confused laws that have characterized land policy in SSA during the last decades.

Just to give one example, in Senegal, two strands of thought opposed within the interdepartmental committee for the application of the Law on the National Domain (passed in May 1964), that of the Ministry of the Interior and that of the Ministry of Planning and

Development. It is revealing that seven years elapsed before a general statement of the law could be translated into more or less operational decrees of application. When the decree No. 72–1288 of October 1972 was eventually issued, it became clear that the former Ministry had won the battle. Instead of a decentralized conception regarding rural communities as autonomous associations entitled to settle land matters largely in their own way (which they still actually largely do in actual practice), the view prevailed that they should function like urban communes (districts) to be incorporated into the Senegalese politico-administrative system. Rural elections in 1984 demonstrated that the political objective behind the 1972 decree has been attained since 'the dominant party which held a quasi-monopoly power over the lists of candidates triumphed in all the rural communities of the country' [Le Roy, 1979: 74–76, 80; Caveriviere and Debene, 1988: 189; Platteau, 1992: 154, 158–59].

This example actually points to another flaw in the induced supply schedule, namely that, contrary to what is again implicitly assumed, state leadership can have a 'large range of choices in goal formulation, agenda setting, and policy execution' [Bardhan, 1989: 13]. The state is not simply an agent responding rather passively to the demands expressed by its (supposedly rational) citizens—acting as principals—voicing their needs through the political arena or via the abstract signal of rising litigation costs. There is overwhelming evidence that land reform programmes in many Third World countries have largely occurred in response to motivations or objectives specifically pursued by the state itself: breaking a feudal order or containing traditional elites, pacifying masses of impoverished peasants (or small tenants) which represent a threat to political stability, or channelling the rural population into the state apparatus to ensure better political control.

That state leadership is having a policy agenda on its own where political objectives figure prominently is certainly an accurate description of the situation of many African countries. Considerations of political stability are especially important, not a surprising fact given the inherent fragility of national consensus and 'softness' of state establishments in SSA. African states have to navigate carefully through the dangerous waters of different subcultures, regional and ethnic aspirations, and various other centrifugal forces. It is because they are so eager to avoid the social disruptions which may follow from the disequalizing effects of a free land market that they tend to oppose the creation of freehold tenure, particularly when there is a serious risk that lands will thereby pass into the hands of trading minorities of foreign extraction.

To return to the example of Senegal, in preparing the Law on the National Domain, Senegalese lawmakers aimed above all at ensuring a politically and socially viable system. In the current analysis and ideology of the time, this meant that the power of the gerontocratic traditional structure had to be curbed (so that young people be incited to stay in the countryside); that the clout wielded by Islamic brotherhoods had to be contained (so as to stop the rise of a 'bourgeois neo-feudalism'); that local rural organizations had to be given enough margin of manoeuvre (so as to steer clear of a formal, regimented tenure system thought to be inopportune and politically dangerous given the great mosaic of Senegalese subcultures); and that registration had to be avoided (so as to prevent a minority of educated people from manipulating the law to expropriate collective rights for themselves) [Le Roy, 1985: 674–75; Golan, 1990: 19–22]. Evolution of realities on the ground show unfortunately that such hopes have not been fulfilled, partly because the Law was ill-conceived and partly because it has been badly implemented, not necessarily for innocent reasons.

## 4.5 CONCLUSION AND POLICY IMPLICATIONS

### *Where the ETLR fails and why*

The ETLR represents an important attempt at predicting transformation of land rights in countries where land becomes increasingly scarce due to population growth and/or market integration and agricultural commercialization. As is evident from its confrontation with the African experience, it makes two essential valid points, namely that (1°) land arrangements and practices, far from being static, are evolving autonomously under the pressure of growing land scarcity, and that (2°) the significant shifts thus taking place are geared towards increased individualization of tenure rights, including enhanced transferability of land assets.

The ETLR meets serious difficulties, however, when the critical step of formalization of private property rights under the form of land titling and central registration is considered. This is both because demand for, and supply of, freehold land tenure are not 'induced' in the way predicted by the theory, and because the expected effects of formalized land rights on static and dynamic efficiency have not actually materialized.

The first of these failures is to be blamed upon a naïve view of induced demand and supply mechanisms. On the one hand, demand for titling is assumed to be emanating from homogeneous agents who all have an interest in having private land rights consolidated in the most formal manner. In this way, potential interest conflicts are overlooked, which directly follows from the fact that the adverse distributive consequences of titling are largely bypassed, especially those that take place at the adjudication level and that seem generally much more disquieting than those resulting from the operation of a free land market as such. The fact of the matter is that smallholders tend to resist any change which they perceive as jeopardizing customary patterns of economic security through guaranteed access to land. The state, on the other hand, is portrayed as willingly responding to this homogeneous demand, considering only the net aggregate benefits of titling. It has no agenda of its own and it is assumed to act only on the basis of efficiency considerations. The reluctance of most African governments to engage in systematic titling programmes shows that the ETLR lacks a real political-economy perspective.

Regarding the second failure, especially noticeable are the absence of the expected assurance, realizability and collateralization effects of titling (or more individualized forms of informal tenure short of tiltling). To begin with, it seems that basic use rights possibly accompanied by a few fundamental transfer rights (most notably, the right to bequest) provide sufficient security to induce farmers to invest in many parts of SSA. These rights are typically well-guaranteed by village communities. Also, demand for investment may remain rather low because of a variety of non-tenurial constraints that can often be ultimately ascribed to various market and state failures. Many of these constraints have been described in Chapter 2, and we know that at least some of them should be gradually relaxed as population density rises.

What needs to be stressed here is that, to be valid, the ETLR requires that the theory of induced technical change holds true. In other words, evolving factor endowments, while yielding pressure for change in the land rights system, must simultaneously induce technical advances suitable for intensification of agriculture. Attractive new investment opportunities will then be available for private investors who, thanks to enhanced security of property rights in land, would now be more willing and able (through the credit supply effect) to invest in agriculture. Unfortunately, as explained in Chapter 2, the theory of induced technical change cannot be expected to work properly in a context of extremely rapid population growth and severe structural constraints of a physical nature such as they are found in SSA [see, among others, Pingali and Binswanger, 1984; Lele and Stone, 1989; Platteau, 1990; Cleaver and Schreiber, 1992].

Under such circumstances, technical advance is to arise not from the spontaneous forces of the market but from deliberate, intensive and prolonged efforts by specialized public agencies (what Lele and Stone call 'policy-led intensification'). As a result, there is no guarantee that new technical packages become available when farmers are ready to invest. The problem is further compounded by the fact that in SSA the natural environment is very fragile and diverse, population is widely spread, and the functioning of state bureacracies is hampered by organizational, financial, ideological and other complex problems which affect their ability not only to foster technical change but also to provide essential inputs and services to agriculture.

As for the failure of the collateralization effect, it may result from imperfections in the land market that contribute to maintain foreclosure costs at a high level. But it may also reflect the fact that lack of collateral is not the only problem constraining rural credit supply and that other market imperfections stay. It is true that, as explained in Chapter 2, credit and other rural market imperfections are expected to recede as population density increases, that is, precisely when more individualized land rights become justified. However, as is evident from the experience of countries in other continents, including highly densely populated countries (such as India and Bangladesh), rural financial markets remain fragmented even after the collateralization of land. In fact, if the impact of titling on credit is differentiated according to wealth, it appears to manifest itself only for large farms enjoying privileged market access conditions. Registration of their land does not allow smallholders to gain better effective access to credit.

Finally, land titling is neither a necessary nor a sufficient condition for the activation of the land market, as the contrasted experiences of Kenya (where the land market is rather inactive despite titling) and Rwanda (where the market is quite active despite the illegal character of most land transactions) or Uganda reveal. The realizability effect (this also holds true of the static allocative effect) does not require titling, yet, at the same time, the availability of titling does not automatically ensure that land exchange will carry low transaction costs.

*The importance of community-based solutions*

As a rule, comprehensive land titling is not a cost-effective operation in most of SSA today. This is all the more so as landholdings are typically highly fragmented (an important self-insurance device in areas subject to considerable environmental risks) and as African governments face tight budget constraints. Hence the need to explore 'community-based solutions to tenure insecurity and a "state-facilitated" evolution of indigenous land tenure systems' [Bruce, 1993: 50–51].

In other words, since reality shows that in SSA direct state intervention in land matters is better minimized—state intervention is indeed a major source of farmers' insecurity—, and that village systems are frequently able to evolve to meet new needs, one may conclude that indigenous land tenure arrangements still have a dominant role to play. What the region requires is a pragmatic and gradualist approach that reinstitutionalizes indigenous land tenure, promotes the adaptability of its existing arrangements, avoids a regimented tenure model, and relies as much as possible on informal procedures at local level [Bruce, 1986: 64–68; Atwood, 1990: 667; Migot-Adholla et al., 1991: 170–173].[34]

Reliance on local communities offers significant advantages. First, contrary to formal procedures such as land titling which are costly and impose definitive land rights, informal practices at village level are cheap (they economize on information costs) and flexible. Second, even though social differentiation is not to be underestimated, African village communities tend to provide social security to all their members and to ensure that everybody can participate in new opportunities. Such considerations of social security and equity usually dominate pure efficiency concerns, which should be regarded as a positive contribution in a generally insecure economic environment [Lawry, 1993: 73]. Third, still today, enduring customary systems tend to receive remarkable consensus, in particular consensus on the normative order justifying land claims [Saul, 1993].

Emphasizing a crucial role for village communities is not falling into the snare of romanticism. After all, substantial evidence has been provided in this and the previous chapters to show that indigenous communities tend to adopt parochial and even chauvinistic attitudes towards outsiders. Recognizing their role is rather a pragmatic attitude grounded in a realistic assessment of SSA's present predicament. The fact of the matter is that the top-down approach has miserably failed all over SSA,[35] and these communities form living systems which have at their disposal many effective means to preempt or subvert any change ushered in from without which they do not like. Turning them around or opposing them in land matters is all the more difficult as tenure rights are embedded in socio-cultural systems that are not easily bypassed (they embody rules about virtually all aspects of social life, such as marriage, inheritance, homage and power, etc.).

What is therefore needed is an approach based on cooperation rather than confrontation.[36] This implies, whenever feasible, a strengthening of local capacities for management, information, and dispute settlement rather than imposing from above the mechanisms of a formal state legal system [Atwood, 1990: 667]. In most cases, it also implies recognizing the rights of original occupants to 'vacant' land located in their ancestral territories [Bassett, 1993a]. Owing to the persisting influence of traditional concepts of corporate land ownership and identity, it is indeed a more effective strategy for the state to (skilfully) negotiate acceptable compromises with customary native communities if the objective is to open pockets of abundant land to stranger cultivators or to improve village lands that are not optimally exploited. Such compromises can, for example, lead indigenous communities to rent out land to landless people in a peaceful atmosphere where their original rights are not disputed or subverted by the state.

Stories actually abound where areas that had been developed to allow more productive agriculture (usually at the initiative of international development projects) were opened to stranger farmers due to lack of interest on the part of members of the local community. In most cases,—such has happened, for example, in the Zorgho region in Burkina Faso which was developed under the auspices of the PDLG (Projet de Développement Local du Ganzourgou)—, when the land improvement scheme proves successful, indigenous farmers typically react by opportunistically claiming back what they consider as their own 'ancestral' lands and by demanding the expulsion of all stranger farmers. To prevent such extremely tricky situations from arising, the issue of land rights must be squarely addressed and debated with the local community before the development scheme is started.[37]

This being said, when informal institutions and practices are no more reliable methods of adjudicating land rights and ensuring land tenure security, African governments may have to undertake a formal registration procedure. There are special circumstances where titling may thus be worthwhile, such as when indigenous tenure systems are absent or very weak (e.g. in new settlement areas); or when traditional lines of authority have been severed and loyalties to lineage and communal groups eroded [Migot-Adholla et al., 1991: 170].

Yet, even when uncertainties and tensions prevail that cannot be adequately reduced by local communities,—particularly with respect to inter-community relations—, or when local practices involve efficiency or equity costs deemed excessive, the government does not necessarily need to have recourse to the most costly solution. Thus, short of registration, it could lay down a number of basic, well-publicized principles aimed at validating certain kinds of land claims or transactions [Migot-Adholla et al., 1991: 170; 1994a: 114–17].[38] Through appropriate institutions where government representatives sit side by side with customary authorities, it may be possible to negotiate the best ways of implementing these principles (given local conditions) and to verify that they are duly abided by. Interestingly, some African countries have already made significant progress in that direction, as witnessed by the experience of Senegal. There, the Law on the National Domain dispossessed traditional landowning nobilities of any claims such as tithes and rents which they had on farmers in return for access to 'their' land, and authorities succeeded in ensuring access of former slaves to land parcels in the irrigation perimeters developed along the Senegal river [see, e.g., Diemer and Van Der Laan, 1987; Bloch, 1993].

As Martin Weitzman (1993) has pointed out in another context, conventional economic theory that draws on the property rights literature may be inadequate because it misses a critical dimension, namely the ability of groups or communities to solve potential conflicts internally, without having recourse to explicit legalistic rules of behaviour. Since such an ability depends to an important extent on the history or culture of the society concerned (an element of social life that cannot be easily changed), this literature can be blamed for a false pretention to universal applicability. In fact, when communities have a good problem-solving potential, as many experiences in Africa testify, trying to impose formal rules and procedures on them is counter-productive and involves a considerable waste of resources.

## NOTES

1. See, in particular: Meek, 1949; Hill, 1963; Boutillier, 1963; Raynaut, 1976; Cohen, 1980; Berry, 1984; Noronha, 1985; Coquery-Vidrovitch, 1985; Bruce, 1986; Pingali and Binswanger, 1986; Feder and Noronha, 1987; Robertson, 1987; Downs and Reyna, 1988; Bates, 1989;

Atwood, 1990; LTC, 1990; Migot-Adholla, et al., 1991; Platteau, 1992; Mackenzie, 1993; Roth, 1993; Lawry, 1993; Saul, 1993; Bassett, 1993a, 1993b; André and Platteau, 1998.

2. Moreover, half of the households have farms comprising at least one purchased parcel.
3. Thus, for example, in Ghana and Cameroon, tenants cannot plant cash crops while in Zanzibar they are prevented from planting trees. The basis for these restrictions is 'to deny tenants the opportunity of claiming title to land by virtue of their length of possession' [Feder and Noronha, 1987: 154]. In many areas, the most widespread method of exercising control over land consists of planting trees. It is easy to find instances where 'economically valuable trees are grown not primarily to profit from their produce as to affirm title to land'—planting cocoa and coffee trees in Cameroon, of coffee trees in Liberia, of cocoa trees in Ghana, or of clove and kola trees in Zanzibar [*ibidem*: 153]. In some regions of Côte d'Ivoire, the cultivators planted coffee and cocoa trees with very wide spacing 'so that the returns are "inefficient" and the ten hectares planted produce what could have been obtained from three hectares of close-spaced trees' [Noronha, 1985: 208]. To give a final example, it is only for the sake of protecting their customary rights of access to pasture lands located along the Senegal river that Fulani herders have taken to irrigated farming near the town of St Louis in Senegal. In a revealing manner, work on small-scale irrigation schemes has been entrusted to old members of the social group who do not take this occupation very seriously. By contrast, young members continue to devote all their time and efforts to traditional pastoral activities to which they attach overriding importance in spite of low returns [Mathieu, 1987, Vol. 1: 200].
4. In the study area, all land is titled. However, because of the different institutional environments under which subdivision and resettlement have taken place, not all farmers have yet been granted individual title to their land. Sampled farms include some that are held with title, some that are held without title, and some that are composed primarily of land that has been rented or borrowed [Carter et al., 1994: 144].
5. The studies by Moor (1996) and by Alston et al. (1996) about the impact of land titling on investment behaviour in Zimbabwe and Brazil, respectively, also control for the endogeneity of the land rights variable, but in a way that differs from that followed by Besley. In the latter study, investment is measured continuously but, unfortunately, it is defined 'as the portion of the farm placed in improved pasture and permanent crops' [Alston et al., 1996: 45] which is only indirectly related to the notion of investment (which is a flow and not a stock).
6. The discrete land security variable constructed by Brasselle et al. is based on a hierarchized set of five distinct bundles or categories of rights. Households thus belong to:

   *category 1* (the category of minimal tenure security) if, on the one hand, they do not hold any right of transfer and, on the other hand, they have less than two rights of use (whether permanent or transitory) besides the rights to choose the crops to cultivate and to prohibit grazing by others' livestock, or do not even hold the latter two rights (or one of them);

   *category 2* if they do not hold any right of transfer and have at least two permanent or transitory rights of use in addition to the two aforementioned rights;

   *category 3* if they hold the right to bequeath land, with or without approval by another person or group of persons, and at least two permanent rights of use in addition to the two aforementioned rights;

   *category 4* if, besides the right to bequeath, they hold the right to make land loans (with or without approval by another person or group of persons) and at least two permanent rights of use in addition to the two aforementioned rights;

   *category 5* if, besides the rights to bequeath and to lend, they hold the rights to give or to rent out land (with or or without approval by another person or group of persons) and at least two permanent rights of use in addition to the two aforementioned rights. This last category corresponds to the highest possible degree of land tenure security, given that the right to sell land is not recognized in the sample area.
7. Following Migot-Adholla et al. (1991), or Place and Hazell (1993), tenure security is defined on the basis of a three-type categorization, distinguishing between complete, individualized rights, including the right to rent or sell the land ('complete transfer' rights); preferential rights, including the right to bequeath ('preferential transfer' rights); or limited, use rights ('limited transfer'

rights). In other words, fall in the latter, minimal category all the parcels for which the farmer has no permanent transfer or alienation rights, but may have some temporary transfer privileges. The intermediate category describes parcels that may be permanently transferred but only within the family or lineage (that is, through gift or bequest), while the upper category regroups parcels that may be alienated outside the lineage through the right to sell. Hierarchy exists among these three rights' categories since complete rights include preferential and use rights, while preferential rights include use rights.

8. See the previous footnote for the definition of these three land rights' categories.
9. As a result of titling, small farmers have a higher probability of getting credit as measured from a notional credit supply curve, yet they are too poor for an effective supply to take place
10. Thus, in Kenya, we are told that, before land registration was initiated, land borrowals did not prevent tenants from investing because they could hope to have their improvements compensated in the event of losing access to the land borrowed: 'Both the Chagga and Kikuyu allowed "tenants" on land belonging to one lineage; those tenants paid a fee up front for use of the land. The lineage could redeem the land at any time by repaying the original amount, but the redeemer had to reimburse the tenant for any improvements made to the land' [Pinckney and Kimuyu, 1994: 12].
11. To be more precise, if the initial probability of eviction is low, even a small reduction will be sufficient to make investment incentives stronger under indigenous tenure than under freehold. On the contrary, if initial insecurity is high, a large reduction will be required for that purpose. Also noteworthy is the fact that the likelihood of indigenous tenure providing the higher investment incentive increases with the discount rate. Indeed, when the discount rate is high, distant incomes are penalized. Since they matter more under a freehold system which gives maximum assurance that future rewards will accrue to the investor, high discount rates tend to reduce the relative attractiveness of investments carried out under freehold.
12. In Paraguay, to take a country out of the African continent, the evidence does not lend support to the 'titling induces an active land market' hypothesis either [Carter et al., 1997].
13. In this respect, an interesting informal contract is that whereby a widow who is without family and lacks the minimal resources for farming leases out her land and designates the lessor as heir to it provided that the latter provides her with all basic subsistence requirements, including food and clothing [Lawry, 1993: 70].
14. I therefore find it hard to agree with Johnson that the right to alter one's asset composition by selling land is a 'valuable right' that any government should respect for the sake of efficiency; or that 'shielding individuals from mistakes, regrets and their consequences, may serve to stifle initiative and destroy the incentive to acquire information for oneself' [Johnson, 1972: 270]. To view any land sale as a perfectly rational decision to alter one's composition of wealth is simplistic since it basically assumes that all individuals are able to behave rationally in the sense of economic theory. In the real world, smallholders' irrational behaviour may arise from a variety of factors such as myopia and imperfect knowledge or foresight about their long-term income prospects or the long-term consequences of their present decisions in conditions of rapidly changing ecological and socioeconomic environment; or it may result from the fact that they continue to obey traditional social norms—in particular those prescribing certain consumption patterns—in the same conditions.
15. Lewis once wrote that 'there is probably no country in the world where land is bought and sold solely for its value as a factor of production, and no country where non-economic factors do not frustrate schemes which would otherwise increase output' [Lewis, 1955: 91]. This certainly applies *a fortiori* to SSA inasmuch as kinship ties remain strong and ethnic, local or regional feelings remain central considerations in social and political life.
16. Thus in Nigeria, 1922–23, the Egba asked through their chief that they be allowed by the British to mortgage their *urban* lands to foreign companies so as to be able to raise money from local European banks. Yet they were keen that such principle is not extended to *rural* lands because they felt it a sacred duty not to take any risk that their ancestral property will be lost to foreigners [Meek, 1949: 266–267].
17. For a short description of this reform, see Crousse, 1986 and Grayzel, 1988.

18. The haalpulaar ('Toucouleur') community is a mix of Fulani and Serere ethnies.
19. In Ghana, as the frontier land became gradually exhausted, indigenous (*Akan*) ideology began to reassert with vigour 'the inalienable rights of the native custodians of the land, and the inalienable rights of individual usufruct' [Robertson, 1987: 77]. In Senegal (Peanut Basin) where freehold titling and land market do not exist, we learn that every year villagers 'meet to trace the borders of the land and set the rules so that everyone bands together to keep the land in the village' [Golan, 1990: 15; see also Riddell et al., 1987: 31 for Zaïre]. In Western Burkina Faso (a country where indigenous land tenure systems are still very much alive), local residents fear a flood of migrant settlers (mainly Mossi) into their ancestral lands, but, so far, thanks to the strength of their traditional social structure (based on agnatic lineages), they have succeeded in effectively blocking further settlement on their territory [Saul, 1993: 81–82].
20. In Lesotho, for example, commercial farmers seem to be reluctant to farm land outside of their village area 'for fear of increased supervisory costs and losses due to crop damage and theft' [Lawry, 1993: 70].
21. Note that mechanization of agricultural activities has not only the effect of replacing labour (except when it allows multiple cropping) but also that of disciplining the efforts of the workers. Indeed, it is often the case that 'the pace and quality of output are primarily determined by machine specifications rather than by the quality of the operator's effort, thus reducing the importance of labour supervision' [Eswaran and Kotwal, 1985: 362].
22. Along the Senegal river in Mauritania, the new *Beydane* owners bring their good *waalo* (irrigable) lands under intensive (rice) cultivation through a system of owner cultivation assisted by labour-saving mechanical devices. Such a choice has been motivated by the desire to overcome difficult supervisory problems in a social context dominated by tense inter-community relations.
23. For Paraguay also, a recent study concluded that there is little indication that land markets shift land to the more efficient [Carter et al., 1997].
24. From a study of two agro-ecological zones in Burkina Faso, Carter has shown that even the relatively narrow range of asset inequality that obtains in this country 'maps steeply into the full range of risk exposure', from near zero (for households in the top quartile) to near 100 per cent (for those in the land-poorest quartile) [Carter, 1997: 583].
25. Self-insurance has always played a significant role as risk-coping device in SSA, either at the individual or the (extended) household level. During the last decades, however, it has been dangerously impaired for the poorer strata. Owing to rapid population growth, increased monetary expenditures, and natural or man-made calamities such as repeated droughts, animal epidemics or armed conflicts, many small peasants in SSA have gradually lost assets which have traditionally performed an important insurance function by serving as a sort of contingency fund [see, e.g., Dercon, 1998]. For example, in not a few regions, agriculturalists used to own a number of cattle heads partly as a way to insure themselves against various contingencies and to cope with downswings in their consumption levels. Animals could thus be sold (or killed) under duress while the stock was normally replenished in good years [for a more guarded conclusion about the risk-hedging role of cattle in SSA, see Fafchamps et al., 1998]. Yet, due to the parcelling out of the family herd through inheritance, the increasing scarcity of pasture lands (resulting from population pressure on land resources), and/or the need to dissave so as to make ends meet during several consecutive years of crop failure, it is not rare to see peasants without any animal left. Therefore, when a new emergency occurs, they may be obliged to sell land assets if they cannot rely any more on traditional kin networks, mutual help groupings, or other risk-pooling mechanisms. Unfortunately, although widespread in SSA, the latter are highly imperfect due to natural risks (such as drought or pest attacks on crops) which are strongly covariant, at least within the confines of groups sufficiently small to overcome incentive problems [Wiessner, 1982; Cashdan, 1985; Gersovitz, 1987; Ellsworth, 1988; Udry, 1989, 1990, 1991; Von Braun and Webb, 1989; Platteau, 1991; Carter, 1991; Von Braun, 1991; Fafchamps, 1991; Webb et al., 1991; Deaton, 1992a, 1992b; Alderman and Paxson, 1992; Carter, 1997].
26. Note that, in most cases, investors are actually people native of the area where the land is located and who were therefore entitled to one parcel at the time of initial allocation.

27. Thus, land also served as a privileged avenue to political power (and social prestige) in eighteenth-century England. According to Ashton, indeed: 'Throughout the eighteenth century the number of estates owned by men who had recently come to fortune by way of some trade or profession increased. City men and manufacturers moved to the country, sometimes for the amenities it offered, sometimes as a step to Parliament, but often because they cherished the ambition of ending their days on at least level terms with the squires' [Ashton, 1955: 34].
28. For an elaboration on the risk of women's marginalization as a result of land titling programmes, see Haugerud, 1983; Shipton, 1988; Fleuret, 1988; Whitehead, 1990; Watts, 1993; Mackenzie, 1993. It goes without saying that women are especially vulnerable in cases of divorce from or death of the male head of the household [Barrows and Roth, 1989: 8].
29. In Senegal and in Gambia, for example, women, older relatives, poor relations, and other 'marginal' compound members all have rights to compound land under the stewardship of the head of the 'compound' [Von Braun and Webb, 1989; Golan, 1990: 53–54].
30. See, for example, Coldham, 1978: 99; Le Roy, 1979: 72–73; Gastellu, 1982: 275; Wolf, 1982: 247–249; Koehn, 1983, 1984; Noronha, 1985: 145; Engelhard and Ben Abdallah, 1986: 61; Feder and Noronha, 1987: 156–157; Green, 1987: 7; Hoben, 1988: 216; Berry, 1988: 68; Goheen, 1988: 301–305; Shipton, 1988: 106–107; Kerner, 1988: 179; Bruce, 1988: 44; Atwood, 1990: 662–663; Roth, 1993: 317; Firmin-Sellers, 1996.
31. In Asia and in Latin America, on the contrary, it seems that access to such opportunities helps correct land endowment inequalities [see, e.g., Ho, 1978, 1979, for Taiwan; Walker and Ryan, 1990, Sarap, 1996, for India; Lopez and Valdes, 1997, for Latin America].
32. Note that a well-known alternative to the naive supply-demand model, the interest-group theory of property rights (which seeks to explain the structure of property rights in terms of interaction between interest groups in the political market), leads to the conclusion that economic efficiency, however it is defined, is not the natural outcome of free interactions in the imperfectly competitive market for political influence [see Olson, 1965, 1982; Denzau and Munger, 1986; Mueller, 1989].
33. Research conducted by the Land Tenure Center (university of Wisconsin) actually indicates that, nowadays, in a number of African countries, 'farmer demand for individual title comes less from a desire to change agricultural practices and increase production than from their sense that a title conferred by the state may be the best way to defend against reallocations of land by the state and its local representatives, whom they see as the major threat to their security of tenure' [Bruce, 1993: 50–51].
34. Interestingly, the same conclusion was reached in a careful survey of the land situation in Latin America and the Caribbean [Stanfield, 1990].
35. For a useful survey documenting many failures in state attempts at agrarian reform, see Okoth-Ogendo, 1993. For a more general critique of the top-down approach in SSA, see Hyden, 1983; Rondinelli, 1993.
36. See the fascinating study by Bassett on Northern Ivory Coast where examples of the two attitudes can actually be found in the explosive context of Fulani sedentarization [Bassett, 1993b: 143–149].
37. See Saul, 1993 and Bloch, 1993, for other illustrations with respect to Burkina Faso and Senegal.
38. That the government can, in such cases, avoid the high costs of land registration is illustrated by the experience of Lesotho where a comparatively cheap system of occupation permits, possibly convertible into formal lease-rights, has been instituted. According to one study, all commercial farmers felt that this system 'provided them with sufficient security to farm commercially' and 'none of them perceived a customary allocation as inadequate or a disincentive to investment'. At the same time, they could easily recognize 'the social security role of the customary tenure system' [Lawry, 1993: 71].

# Chapter 5

## EGALITARIAN NORMS AND ECONOMIC GROWTH

### 5.1 INTRODUCTION

In this chapter, attention is focused on a particular kind of traditional agrarian societies, namely tribal societies in which classes are absent and the only existing social differentiation is along sex and age lines. They are especially numerous in Sub-Saharan Africa and in the mountainous areas of Asia and Latin America. The analysis offered in the following pages pursues a double objective. The first objective is to achieve a better understanding of the motives and values that cause tribal societies to opt for radical measures of redistributive taxation which are potentially hostile to economic change. As for the second objective, it consists of identifying the ways possibly used to surmount or evade the barriers to growth that result from the pervasive presence of egalitarian norms.

The idea is indeed that tribal societies cannot be blocked forever in self-sustaining stationary equilibria when confronted with drastic changes in the external environment confronting them and, particularly, in the range of economic opportunities available. Even though traditional institutions and values can undeniably slow down economic expansion by discouraging capital accumulation and the self-seeking pursuit of wealth, interstices must exist in the social fabric through which progressive individuals can bring the seeds of change. In other words, I essentially agree with Kaushik Basu, Eric Jones and Ekkehart Schlicht (1987: 5–6) that a cultural explanation may be valid in the short or medium run, but not in the long run because customs, values and norms are often bound to ultimately adjust as a result of economic changes.

The first query is attempted in the first four sections below. Section 2 tries not only to explicitly relate distributive practices or egalitarian rules to underlying social norms and principles of equity, but also to explain the emergence of egalitarian norms and principles in the specific material conditions prevailing in erswhile tribal societies. In Section 3, it is further argued that witchcraft plays an important role for the enforcement of egalitarian norms in tribal societies, thus pointing to the repressive side of societies which are too often romanticized. As for Section 4, it highlights the adverse consequences of egalitarian norms or redistributive taxation from the viewpoint of economic growth. In the spirit of Chapter 1, Section 5 attempts to depict such norms as a selection procedure or set of beliefs leading to a particular equilibrium outcome of a social game comprising multiple equilibria. It is in Section 6 that the second aforementioned issue is eventually addressed. In this penultimate section, various mechanisms available to overcome traditional social restraints on the individualistic pursuit of wealth are systematically discussed. This theme is actually pursued in Section 7 which also provides concluding comments and a comparative perspective to contrast the experiences of Sub-Saharan Africa and Asia in the light of the analysis presented in the previous sections.

## 5.2 EGALITARIAN NORMS IN A CONTEXT OF RESOURCE ABUNDANCE AND PERVASIVE UNCERTAINTIES

Three essential features of tribal, lineage-based societies will retain our attention in the first part of this section as they will help us understand in the second part why egalitarian tendencies are strong in these societies and how resistance against deviant behaviour can be vindicated.

### *Three important characteristics of tribal societies*

(i) Tribal societies are typically found in land-abundant economies based on production activities characterized by spatial mobility such as shifting cultivation and nomadic grazing. They contrast with strongly immobile village communities based on settled agriculture as they are found in much of Asia and Europe. Since land commands little value in the former type of economies, private property rights on land have not become well established (corporate forms of ownership however prevail as explained in Chapter 3) and, therefore, social stratification in rural communities based on land ownership has not much progressed unlike in land-scarce regions. As has been pointed out in Chapter 2, easy access to land-use rights in a context of low population density and the prevalence of rather rudimentary technologies determine a high degree of self-sufficiency of family units. The market for labour is therefore not much developed and, except in slave-based hierarchical societies that have typically gone through profound Islamization prior to the nineteenth century,[1] class differentiation and landlessness are not perceptible phenomena.

That class polarization is not expected to take place in land-abundant societies is actually the direct implication of Domar's analysis of slavery or serfdom. His point is indeed that in a two-factor economy based on land and labour alone, it is impossible to have (more or less) free land (which implies a high land/labour ratio), free peasants, and non-working landowners simultaneously. Any two elements of this triad can nevertheless co-exist [Domar, 1970: 21; see also Boserup, 1965: 73; Mathur, 1991: 47–49; Binswanger et al., 1995: 2670–73]. Tribal societies are thus characterized by the simultaneous presence of free peasants and free land (and by the conspicuous absence of a class of non-working landowners),[2] while the cases of slavery, serfdom, debt peonage or indentured labour correspond to situations where there is free land and non-working landowners, yet no free peasants. Note that such forms of unfree labour are profitable only if the quality of labour effort does not matter much and its supervision is therefore easy, or if unfree labourers have been adopted into the owner's family in a way that promotes their emotional identification with the latter.

In SSA, like in other land-abundant areas (or densely populated areas with acute labour shortage) in other continents (such as Thailand), ruling families, lineages, or larger social groups did try hard to 'capture peasantries' or develop systems of property rights in man. Yet, the very fact that strongly hierarchical societies stratified along caste lines—and not only along the usual age-sex lines—were limited to certain parts of the region (well-known examples are the *Hausa* and the *Songhaï-Zarma* in Niger and Mali, the *Bambara* in Mali, the *Wolof, Toucouleur* and *Soninké* in Senegal, the *Maures* in Mauritania, the *Tutsi-Hutu* in Rwanda-Burundi, the *Peul* aristocracy in Guinea, northern Nigeria, and northern Cameroon) is evidence that their attempts were far from being always successful [see, e.g., Robertson, 1987: 24; Diop, 1981; Bray, 1983: 13–15; Feeny, 1989: 285–96; Kumar, 1992; Platteau, 1995c]. As pointed out in Chapter 3, the possibility of acquiring membership in stranger communities (migration was a common phenomenon) combined with the rudimentary character of cultivation techniques opened many 'exit options' to the hunted-down cultivators who wished to escape the grip of oppressive rulers or chiefs, particularly so in the dense forest areas of humid central Africa.

By contrast, settled village societies of Asia typically combine non-working landowners with free peasants: land being a scarce factor subject to market exchanges, it tends to become concentrated in the hands of a class of landowners. At the least, there is a continuum of landholding sizes running from rather large farms to minute parcels of land.

(ii) It is a well-known feature of all traditional agrarian societies that they are highly vulnerable to violent fluctuations in their climatic and environmental conditions. Exposure to risk (including periodic outbreaks of disease) is especially important in land-abundant economies in so far as land-intensive techniques and activities usually involve a high degree of dependence on natural factors. Thus, it is evident that extensive modes of harvesting natural resources are more nature-dependent than relatively intensive forms of agriculture or cattle breeding that enable men to better control the effects of environmental hazards (e.g., through irrigation and terracing, or through in-house feeding and tending of animals). It is therefore not surprising that protection against the vagaries of nature is a constant concern for members of such societies and that a wide range of self-insurance strategies and risk-egalitarian or risk-pooling arrangements assume decisive importance in their everyday life [see, e.g., Scott, 1976; Platteau, 1991; Cashdan, 1990].

It is when incomes are subject to rather short-term variations and these variations are poorly correlated across individual households that the prospects for mutual insurance or risk-pooling are the most promising. These conditions are more likely to be met in activities like fishing and hunting-gathering which are characterized by almost continuous harvesting operations subject to highly variable micro-climatic conditions. Non-covariate, relatively frequent hazards also exist in agricultural societies, yet they tend to be found in a more limited range of activities as illustrated by localized fires or animal and human illnesses. In such situations, as recent economic theory has shown, self-interest alone may lead people who have constant interactions to redistribute incomes through voluntary transfers or state-contingent loans.

This is because if one individual is lucky enough to have an excess of food this day or this week, then it makes sense for him to share with another individual who is in deficit in the expectation that the latter will be similarly generous when he is lucky in the future. In the words of the anthropologist Evans-Pritchard, 'it is scarcity and not sufficiency that make people generous, since everybody is thereby insured against hunger (...) in a community where everyone is likely to find himself in difficulties from time to time .... he who is in need today receives help from him who may be in like need tomorrow' [Evans-Pritchard, 1940: 85]. It has been proved that mutual insurance arrangements of this type can be self-enforcing if the framework of people's interactions allows reputation effects to come into play: free riding on assistance in a multilateral mechanism will be punished at later stages and, given these punishments, people find it in their long-run interests to meet their informal obligations so as to remain entitled to assistance in case they in turn fall into distress. This is why it is important that actors together play a repeated game of infinite or indeterminate duration [Sugden, 1986: chap. 7; Kimball, 1988; Fafchamps, 1992, 1994; Coate and Ravallion, 1993; Thomas and Worrall, 1994; Kocherlakota, 1994; Besley, 1995a, 1995b; Wijaya, 1996].

For mutual insurance mechanisms to be self-enforcing (which they need to be in so far as agents are unable to make binding committments in a world where legally enforceable contracts do not exist), an important condition is that the rate of discount of future incomes must be low enough. There are several possible interpretations of this condition: people must not be too impatient (they must not have too strong a preference for current incomes), they must be confident enough that interactions between them will continue (so that reputation effects can come into play), or the expected length of time elapsing between successive realizations of random shocks (for example, the length of time between income draws) must be short enough so that agents with a given time preference may expect to fall into distress and to need the others' assistance within a reasonable span of time [Coate and Ravaillon, 1993: 14]. When a wide variety of production and consumption random shocks are being pooled, the prospects for successful risk-egalitarian schemes are considerably improved since, given the repetitive nature of these shocks, everyone can expect to have his contributions reciprocated within a reasonably short span of time. In such circumstances, reciprocal transfer payments will asymptotically approach balanced reciprocity (as the number of draws goes to infinity, a tangible return to voluntary contributions will occur with probability one), which is an all-pervasive normative principle in these societies [Platteau, 1997].[3]

(iii) There is a third feature of tribal societies that needs to be stressed in the context of the present discussion. Exposed to brutal changes in an environment on which they exert so little control, people from these societies eagerly look for ways to placate the deep anxieties that the apparently blind play of natural forces arouses in them. Lacking scientific knowledge, they have no other choice than to explain natural phenomena in non-rational, magical terms.

Nature is thus anthropomorphized and the relationship between man and nature is conceived in the personal mode. People look at their natural environment and behave towards it as though it were a human being, admittedly of an exceptional type: nature actually takes on the form of supernatural agencies (deities or cosmic forces) that are often seen as the spirits of dead ancestors. This conception has two important implications. First, far from considering themselves as agents able to act externally on an objectified nature, primitive people feel immersed in it. They have no ambition to transform their environment since this would imply that they can detach themselves from it in order to manipulate it in a deliberate manner. In their minds, nature is inviolable in the sense that it is not an object upon which man can exert his shrewd and violence; it is conceived of as an order and never as a raw material awaiting to be exploited [Bourdieu, 1977: chap. 1; 1980: chap. 7].[4] Second, nature is viewed as an active partner that continuously intervenes in human affairs. It is both a Providence that looks after the survival of the tribe conceived as a collective entity and a cruel stepmother who can severely punish human beings when they violate natural laws.

The above aspects deserve to be further explained and illustrated. Human beings, precisely because they are only human beings, are unable to provide for their own subsistence needs. They require the *active* assistance of supernatural agencies that are ultimately responsible for the provision of human necessities. In fact, these agencies deliberately choose whether to meet human needs or not since food cannot reach humans unless it is purposefully directed to them. Thus, for instance, describing the worldview of the Mbuti pygmies in Central Africa, Maurice Godelier noted that, in their minds, 'it is not the hunters who catch the game but it is the Forest [meaning all the animate and inanimate beings that inhabit it] which makes a gift to them of a certain quantity of game so that they can catch it and subsist on it...' [Godelier, 1974: 340–1]. The Bakusu in Zaire are convinced that animals and certain types of food are released and supplied to them by ancestors who act as custodians of the food resources upon which man's livelihood crucially depends [Baland and Platteau, 1996: 211–2]. Recent observation of the life of the Mende farmers in Sierra Leone reveals that, although living from the forest, they 'do not see themselves as standing over it, either to exploit or to conserve it. In local eyes the relationship is the other way round—the community is under the protection of the forest' [Richards, 1995: 139].

In the same vein, the Boreal forest Algonquian Indians would never have admitted final responsibility for variations in resource availability: if the beaver disappears, it is ultimately because the creator and the trickster-transformer intended to destroy it [Brightman, 1987: 133]. This interpretation is confirmed by Berkes who insists that, among many North American Indian groups, 'it is the animals who are considered to be making the decisions; hunters are passive' [Berkes, 1987: 86]. In West African fisheries, local water spirits are thought to be the sources which activate or withdraw fish [Fay, 1990a]. And, finally, from an account of ecological practices and beliefs of the Ponams fishermen of Papua New Guinea, the point comes out that fish themselves, associated with supernatural powers, are construed as the agents of ecological change: 'Contrary to the materialist view of a self-ordering and self-sustaining natural environment, Ponams held that the ordering and operation of the world was dictated by God. God and the fish themselves were the critical agents of change in natural resources' [Carrier, 1987: 153].[5]

If supernatural agencies are ultimately responsible for the suppy of food and other necessities, their benevolent attention to human needs is not unconditional. In the words of Pierre Bourdieu, 'Nature, obeying the logic of gift exchange, shows its kindness only to those who pay a tribute in the form of toil'. In fact, 'The relationship between toil and work is the same as that between gift and trade (...) The discovery of work or labour implies the disenchantment of the natural world, that is, its reduction to its economic dimension only' [Bourdieu, 1980: 198, 200—my translation]. This is precisely what is perceived to be unacceptable in societies that narrowly depend on natural forces and whose members feel themselves to be part of nature. In the words of Bourdieu:

> However low its efficacy may be, the action of the farmer has the effect of transforming nature because it is violent, yet it cannot appear as such to the farmer. Indeed, to admit that human effort is able to transform nature would involve a radical conversion of the relationship between man and the world: persuaded that he has at his disposal no means to effectively influence his own destiny and the future of his production, the farmer feels responsible only for his own actions, not for their failure or success which depend on natural and supernatural powers [Bourdieu, 1977: 39—my translation].

In tribal societies producers do not have the same notion of work or labour as that found in societies based on more intensive use of natural resources and on the association of human efforts with fixed capital. In the worldview of the former societies, the effort applied to natural resources and the outcome achieved are two separate things that cannot be causally related. The only link between effort and outcome is that of a 'diffuse exchange with nature': in return for human toil or effort (conceived as the price to be paid to a necessary order), nature provides bounties that are necessary for human survival [Bourdieu, 1980: 198–200; Van den Breemer et al., 1995: 103–4, 108]. And because individual producers are not rewarded from their own labour efforts, the logic of exchange or the tacit contract between man and nature is seen to operate at a collective level. Thus, if the members of a well-defined group accomplish their work (and other social or ritual) duties, land which is held under corporate ownership is expected to yield in normal circumstances the produce required to sustain them all.

*Distributive implications: egalitarian norms*

The aforedescribed structural characteristics of tribal societies exert a significant influence on the way distribution-related values are shaped. More precisely, they are responsible for the emergence of strongly egalitarian norms that form another (derived) striking feature of these societies. Let us now examine from such a standpoint the respective implications of each of these three basic characteristics in turn.

(i) First, in small communities with no material basis for class differentiation but pervaded by highly personalized relationships, everybody tends to constantly look at each other and to care much more about relative than absolute position. In this context, the effort of any individual to improve his own lot generates positional externalities and is going to trigger off similar efforts by others who do not want to lag behind in the race for status. Assuming that laggards have the ability to catch up with the leaders, the problem is, of course, that such efforts are mutually offsetting and that inefficient equilibria arise precisely because investment in status enhancement is more attractive individually than collectively. To produce the desired realignment of incentives, a society may use prescriptive regulation (such as social norms enforcing consumption limits) or taxation [Congleton, 1980; Frank, 1995, 1996]. Redistributive norms that enjoin economically rising individuals to share their surplus with fellow members of their own community may be interpreted as a form of taxation designed to curb positional race for status, that is, as a device that compels them to take positional externalities into account in their choices.

Tribal communities therefore appear as societies prone to resist any differentiation process whereby individuals strive to enrich themselves. Behind such a resistance is also the fear that the assertion of wealthy individuals will introduce a competitive spirit within the community that will sooner or later undermine its social cohesiveness. In other words, the very dynamic of modification of relative status positions is perceived as a dangerous force susceptible of jeopardizing the fragile social equilibria typical of small-group societies based on highly personalized relationships. Note that, contrary to the arguments to be presented below, the justification of egalitarianism in terms of a so-called positional arms race does not require uncertainty, nor does it presuppose that individuals are unequally endowed in skills or motivations suited for economic success (even purely transient disequalizing moves randomly initiated by one individual or the other are deemed to be socially undesirable and wasteful).

(ii) There is another fear that easily prompts members of tribal societies to oppose any individual attempt at rising above the rest of the group economically. This is the fear that, if left free to choose, individuals with a high realized income will be tempted to evade their solidarity obligations and to defect altogether from mutual insurance mechanisms (since, by accumulating their surplus income, they can self-insure effectively). Those left behind may then easily end up being worse off in so far as the insurance ability of a group diminishes when its size is reduced if it is small to start with: indeed, when one member is lost from a small solidarity pool, that pool is less able to spread risk.

In addition, because wealth accumulation affords protection against collective risks (something that mutual insurance can never provide), the departure of a wealthy member means forsaking the possibility of using the mutual insurance system as a mechanism of intertemporal consumption smoothing [Fafchamps, 1992: 160, 163]. Here, private wealth accumulation is perceived as an anti-social behaviour because it is an attempt to break away from traditional solidarity networks. Paraphrasing Guy Hunter, tribal communities are 'levelling societies, in which attempts by equals to gain individual advantage are constantly suspected and bitterly resented. No doubt this springs from fear that the fundamental security of the village will slowly be lost if one individual after another can reach a platform of prosperity from which he might not need the help of the community and could therefore excuse himself from helping them' [Hunter, 1969: 40].

The rationale of egalitarian norms that can be strongly enforced upon all community members follows from the following fact: individuals who have willingly entered into local networks of reciprocal transfers with a view to insuring themselves against various contingencies may choose to opt out whenever they have accumulated enough wealth after a series of good shocks to self-insure adequately. This will be done to the sorrow of those who experienced successive bad shocks or sufficiently unfavourable circumstances to prevent them from building up stocks of stored wealth. To put it in another way, in a world pervaded by production and other types of risks, if participation in an informal risk-pooling mechanism operating as a mutual aid network or a social egalitarian scheme is purely voluntary and if members can freely withdraw when the expected payoff from participation becomes smaller than the payoff from non-participation, there is a serious risk that the scheme gradually unravels, thereby jeopardizing the subsistence prospects of the other members.

Coercing the lucky individuals to remain within the social egalitarian scheme will obviously avoid that outcome. The interesting point is that, assuming that idiosyncratic shocks are sufficiently severe or frequent and randomly distributed (and their effects are possibly amplified by collective shocks) and also assuming that community members are equally (or not too unequally) endowed in the initial situation, they will not only decide to join the scheme but they may also support the laying down of social norms and vote in favour of rigidly enforced rules aimed at preventing members from quitting when favourable circumstances make it worthwhile for them to do so. This is because, *ex ante,* they ignore what their income trajectory will be and they therefore fear the breaking down of the risk-pooling mechanism over time.[6]

(iii) The third motive behind the strong egalitarian tendencies operating in tribal societies arises from a cultural value or standard of fairness that is itself derived from the above-described worldview typical of these societies. More precisely, inasmuch as 'work, in the sense of persistent individual effort, is never recognized as the reason of success' and success is attributed entirely to 'luck' and 'is never believed to be brought about or furthered by personal effort and initiative' [Rogers, 1969: 118–9], private appropriation of persistent surpluses is deemed to be unfair. In other words, a worldview that tends to consider any income as essentially 'unearned'—naturally leads to a progressive concept of justice according to which rich people ought to share their income with others.

As has been pointed out earlier, when 'luck' is a transient phenomenon caused by uncorrelated income variations, members of tribal societies are willing to enter into decentralized arrangements of reciprocal transfer payments. They can indeed entertain the hope that net payments within the risk-pooling scheme will more or less balance out over time as situations of the participants are easily inverted. Yet, when 'luck' appears to be sustained over time or when it is transient but takes on the form of an extraordinary surplus, the allegedly lucky individuals may no more be expected to spontaneously share their income with other group members since the principle of balanced reciprocity is unlikely to be satisfied in such circumstances. Only social pressure or sheer coercion can then make prosperous individuals share their luck (apparent or real) with fellow group members. Thus, the scorn and moral sanction associated with greed in tribal societies have the intended effect of deflecting wealthy individuals from the temptation to follow their own interests and, for instance, to leave local social security arrangements. Marcel Fafchamps pushes this point very far when he writes that 'It is not so much private accumulation of wealth that preindustrial societies combat but the fact that some of its members may accumulate wealth while others are in need' [Fafchamps, 1992: 153].

Social pressure is thus exercised in the name of a principle of justice that is known in social choice theory as the resource-monotonicity principle: everyone should benefit from growth (see *supra*, chap. 1). In Gambia, for instance, the concept of *badingya* represents harmony, cooperation, and shared progress (or shared decline). By contrast, the concept of *fadingya* refers to selfish ambitions and competitiveness: these individualistic proclivities are considered both negatively—inasmuch as they can lead to the breakdown of structures of mutual support and to the collapse of community spirit—and positively—inasmuch as they are also recognized 'as being driving forces necessary for the advancement of the group as a whole' [von Braun and Webb, 1989: 515–16; see also Sylla, 1994: 170–76, for the Wolof in Senegal]. Egalitarian norms may be even more requiring than the monotonicity principle in so far as they typically demand that an individual does not benefit more from his own success than other members of his social group (economic growth should not disturb the existing distribution of income), not just that the latter share in the former's rising prosperity.

In the Mandara mountains in the extreme north of Cameroon, we are thus told that jealousy is a major problem impeding the work of the so-called Village Development Committees: when several quarters are gathered in a committee the main worry of every quarter seems to be that 'the others should not benefit more than them' [Drijver and Van Zorge, 1995: 155].

Likewise, in the southern part of Congo (ex-Zaïre), an anthropological study about the social and economic impact of a fishery development project located in Bukavu (lake Kivu) has revealed that the economic success of the inhabitants of Kalengera village, who had received priority access to the new gill net technology introduced by the project on account of their relative poverty, is deeply resented by the inhabitants of neighbouring villages. To express their frustration and anger, the latter do not hesitate to steal gill nets from their lucky owners as well as other equipment goods from the project premises. Even more tragically, some of them go so far as systematically catching juveniles with the apparent purpose of sabotaging the (future) productive performance of gill net operators, regardless of the cost entailed for themselves. By acting thus, 'they (the inhabitants of Mulambula village) believe that they will one day succeed in emptying the lake of its entire fish stock and thereby block the progress of the gill net owners'. As a result of these vengeful actions, it is expected, the project's beneficiaries will be compelled to abandon their contemptuous attitude *vis-à-vis* their brethern and to restore their old cooperative relationships with them. In addition, the project staff will be led to correct the injustice they had committed by favouring a special stratum of the local fishing population [Melard et al., 1998].

Within Kalengera village itself, equally strong redistributive pressures have led the new owners to give up working their newly acquired nets so as to enable other fellow villagers to earn the labour incomes generated by the gill net technology. It is noteworthy that, by thus ceding to local pressures for a more equal distribution of the benefits produced by this technical innovation, the new owners lose on a double count. In addition to the loss of labour income, they must accept the fall in their profits that is caused by the various moral hazard problems arising from absentee ownership, in particular, the understatement of output following illicit disposal of a portion of the catches through secret marketing channels. These problems, so characteristic of fishing activities [see Platteau and Nugent, 1992], seem to largely account for the considerable productivity differences observed between autonomous fishermen, on the one hand, and trainee fishermen operating within the framework of the fishery project responsible for the introduction and diffusion of the new technology, on the other hand [Melard et al., 1998].

## 5.3 THE ROLE OF WITCHCRAFT AS A DETERRENT TO PRIVATE ACCUMULATION OF WEALTH

Compliance with egalitarian norms is not left to the goodwill of the individuals concerned. As has been suggested in the previous section, it is actually backed by powerful sanctions that comprise social pressures, constant harassment, and the use of effective mechanisms of ideological intimidation. It bears particular emphasis that feelings of envy and jealousy are actually instrumental in bringing about a redistribution of income between presumably lucky and presumably unlucky individuals in so far as they can easily degenerate into active hatred if they are not assuaged by corrective gifts. Hatred is indeed something which people are keen to avoid because it is liable to cause psychological oppression and physical harm. Harming the successful individual is achieved through subtle mechanisms involving witchcraft practices [see, e.g., Jewsiewicki, 1993 for vivid illustrations from ex-Zaïre]. In tribal societies, while transient or ordinary luck is believed to result from the normal course of natural events, persisting or exceptional luck is attributed to the obscure and treacherous manipulation of supernatural forces. This is a very serious misgiving inasmuch as such manipulation is perceived to be thwarting others' projects and even jeopardizing the survival of the entire social group. In the words of Keith Thomas,

> A man who gets ahead in a tribal society is likely to awaken the suspicion of his neighbours. Among the Bemba of Northern Rhodesia, for example, it is said that to find a beehive with honey in the woods is good luck; to find two beehives is very good luck; to find three is witchcraft. In such an environment, witch-beliefs help to sustain a rough egalitarianism. They are a conservative force, acting as a check on undue individual effort. Similarly, in twelfth-century England the chronicler William Malmesbury could complain that the common people disparaged excellence in any sphere by attributing it to demonic aid [Thomas, 1973: 643–4—cited from Elster, 1989a: 261].

The same mechanism has been observed by Clyde Kluckhohn among the Navaho Indians:

> Credence in witchcraft...tends, along with other social mechanisms, to prevent undue accumulation of wealth and tempers too ready a rise in

> social mobility. A rich man knows that if he is stingy with his relatives or fails to dispense generous hospitality to all and sundry he is likely to be spoken of as a witch. Individuals know also that if they accumulate wealth too rapidly the whisper will arise that they got their start by robbing the dead of their jewelry [Kluckhohn, 1944: 63—cited from Elster, 1989a: 260].

More recent studies show that witchcraft accusations and practices continue to play an important role in repressing individual acquisitiveness and mobility in contemporary African rural societies. Some authors even contend that such accusations and practices are on the rise. Thus, René Bureau does not hesitate to speak about 'a massive resumption of witchcraft accusations' in the coastal area of Cameroon where 'the immense majority of those accused of being *balemba* [sorcerers] have an enviable place, function, fortune, or influence' [Bureau, 1996: 123–24—my translation].[7] In rural communities of Rwanda (prefecture of Kibuye in the western part), to take another example, Danielle de Lame observes that only gifts can appease jealous feelings (*ishari*) and dismiss accusations of misplaced pride (*ishema*) which cause a lot of fear and apprehension in the mind of prosperous individuals. Such fear is actually reflected in the all-pervasive belief in poisonings (*uburozi*) which designate the many forms of baleful spells [de Lame, 1996: 182].

A traditional healer from a neighbouring prefecture in the same country (Gitarama prefecture) admitted to being increasingly approached in order to solve problems related to poisoning. According to him, the increasing incidence of poisoning threats is due to 'recent changes in economic conditions that arouse people's spite since nobody accepts that someone else surpasses him in wealth' [Migeotte, 1995: 159–60—my translation]. Among the Venda, Sotho, Shangaan and other people of South Africa, we are told that those named and killed as witches were often doing nicely: they had large numbers of cattle, or had worked in the cities and earned a pension for their old age. Jealousy seems the most common motivation for the killing of witches [Minnaar, Offringa, and Payze, 1992—cited from *The Economist*, December 9, 1995: 95].

Note that poisoning and other forms of killing are not necessarily applied to the successful or dreaded persons themselves. What happens in most cases is that living animals belonging to them are the first to be harmed on the ground that 'Who hits a dog aims at its master' (Rwandan saying reported by Migeotte, 1995: 157). This is all the more likely to happen if the animals constitute the element of wealth that is actually coveted, like the cattle heads threatened with poisoning in the numerous examples reported in Migeotte's study [*ibidem*: 155–8]. Such threats or actual killings obviously serve as warnings that a more serious punishment (like the dead of close relatives) could be meted out to the deviant if he does not comply with the implicit request contained in those threats.

What needs to be stressed is therefore that evil spirits are conceived as being ultimately activated by human actors when they are angered by the behaviour or situation of fellow villagers. Edward Evans-Pritchard has thus insisted in his pioneering work on the Nuer tribe of Sudan that the evil 'soul' of witchcraft is set to work by anti-social feelings like envy, spite, jealousy, anger and hatred. If these feelings are absent, the witchcraft remains 'cool' and harms no one [Evans-Pritchard, 1937]. Likewise, among the Mossi of Burkina Faso, a lazy individual is called a *suurri soba,* and it is commonly feared that such an individual will become a *sukiri,* meaning a jealous, envious and mean person who poses a threat to other people because he can use the baleful powers of magic to harm a successful comrade [Badini, 1994: 141].

Among the Maka people (Eastern Cameroon), as we learn from Peter Geschiere, everyone is believed to possess a double (an evil spirit called *djambe*) which he develops depending upon his individualistic proclivities and personal ambition. A *djambe* can be activated (it can be 'taken out' of the person's body), yet this is a daring and dangerous step which gives access to unknown powers and at the same time exposes the person to frightening threats, such as falling into a lethal ambush. In the popular understanding, an owner can make his *djambe* work during the night for secret purposes and its actions will not be remembered during daytime (hence the deep fear of night and obscurity among the Maka) [Geschiere, 1995: chap. 1]. Whereas before sorcerers were reputed to 'eat' their victims—that is, to kill them with the help of a magic trick—, now that so many opportunities for economic differentiation have arisen, they are said to transform them into kinds of zombies whom they force to work exploitatively in their invisible plantations in order to enrich themselves. This evolution is also perceptible among other people in Cameroon, such as the Beti, the Bakossi, the Douala, the Batanga, the Bamileké and the Bamenda [*ibidem*: 175, 192–8; see also Fisiy and Geschiere, 1991; Geschiere, 1994; de Rosny, 1981, 1992; Ardener, 1970; Bureau, 1996].[8]

A few remarks are in order at this stage. First, witchcraft is effective as soon as the vulnerable person believes in it. Indeed, he will then interpret all the misfortunes which befall him as having been caused by malevolent acts of personal enemies, even if no direct evidence is available to substantiate those suspicions. In all African village societies, 'illness as "irregular" death are considered as punishments for a committed misdeed' [Badini, 1994: 145; Jewsiewicki, 1993: 91; Bureau, 1996: 116–17]. A climate of fear is thus created that may prove an awfully effective way of ending deviance. Second, there seems to be a particularly strong relation between sorcery and kinship. As pointed out by Geschiere, in Cameroon sorcers are supposed mainly to attack their relatives and the gravest accusation against a successful individual is that he is ready to sell parents in order to accumulate riches for his own profit [Geschiere, 1995]. It is within the lineage that ideological intimidation is mostly resorted to. This is not a surprising observation in so far as jealous feelings tend to be all the more intense as relations between people are closer.[9]

Third, repressive measures against successful individuals are also observed in tribal societies built on a ranked hierarchy of constituent groups and possessing a strongly centralized structure focused on the chief. Thus, in many African villages, the chief or the elders do not easily accept that rank and file people rise above them by acquiring new or ancient symbols of wealth and status (like cocoa plantations and roofs made of corrugated iron). All efforts to accumulate such symbols are unavoidably viewed as conscious attempts to overturn the existing social order (in which chiefs and elders are richer but also stand as the main agents of redistribution) and they immediately arouse insinuations or open accusations of sorcery [Geschiere, 1995: 210, note].[10] For example, we learn that in Botswana someone considered by a Tswana chief to be a dangerous competitor was accused of witchcraft and stripped of his property. 'In such cases, the chief was able to justifiably "eat" the miscreant' [Peters, 1994: 32]. Typically in Africa, the emergent farmer tends to be seen 'as a new focus of power and influence in competition with traditional leaders'. As a result, 'he may be badgered to use his tractor to plow the chief's or community land' and, 'if he refuses when such requests become too burdensome, he may be criticized for lack of respect, a failure of community spirit. Jealousy can give rise to accusations of witchcraft, which can result in banishment' [Bruce, 1993: 39–40]. Of course, as pointed out by Evans-Pritchard, witchcraft accusations against social superiors are excluded [Evans-Pritchard, 1964: 243].

Fourth, as forms of land utilization become more intensive and the role of labour and human ingenuity becomes more evident, there is bound to be an erosion of the old belief according to which economic success is not the outcome of individual effort or other factors subject to voluntary human control. Yet, as the aforementioned observations about Cameroon testify, people may still find it convenient to blame prosperous individuals on the alleged ground that they resort to witchcraft practices. To be effective, indeed, the accusation of witchcraft needs not necessarily refer to the tricky production of 'luck' through vicious manipulation of supernatural forces. It may also be based on the allegation that the economic success of some individuals is the result of some hidden and treacherous exploitation of fellow villagers. In the example concerned, exploitation is invisible as it is supposed to secretly occur during the night [see also Rowlands and Warnier, 1988]. In Rwanda, likewise, 'a rich individual is supposed to possess obscure powers which enable him to appropriate wealth belonging to persons with whom he interacts' [de Lame, 1996: 183]. In tribal societies people who strive to improve their situation are thus represented as malignant agents who do not hesitate to enrich themselves at the expense of others, which is of course considered as a deeply reprehensible behaviour on ethical grounds [Peters, 1994: 200–201]. The underlying ideology is clearly based on the image of the zero-sum game or the 'limited good', a popular representation that, interestingly enough, was to pervade even European societies till modern times.[11] (It is no doubt revealing that one had to wait until the eighteenth century to see major thinkers such as Bernard de Mandeville and Adam Smith undertake to disprove such a deep-rooted idea).[12]

Fifth, the well-known fact that witchcraft is often summoned to explain disturbances of the natural order is to some extent related to its function of deviance repression. As a matter of fact, in adverse circumstances when collective risks occur, the whole society falls under duress and people tend to view their predicament as the outcome of a natural disturbance which is itself caused by a social disorder among themselves. In other words, they see an analogy between what happens in the universe of cosmological forces and what happens in the sphere of human relations. In actuality, the perceived precariousness of any equilibrium of natural forces (given their lack of scientific knowledge, they are unable to conceive that the natural world possesses a built-in equilibrium and obeys systematic laws that contribute to its automatic reproduction) is believed to be a reflection of the profound instability of any social balance among humans [Godelier, 1974: 340–3; Bourdieu, 1980: 225–6].

An important strategy used to bring back favourable natural conditions therefore consists of identifying and then removing the causes of social tensions and conflicts so as to placate the disturbed supernatural powers and to restore harmony between the natural and the social spheres of the cosmos. Such moments of intense social crisis triggered by environmental disturbances usually provide privileged occasions to suppress deviant behaviour, mitigate inequalities and sanction breaches of respect of customary status positions. For example, during a drought that occurred in the Rwandan village studied by Migeotte, a woman seen as materially advantaged was accused of preventing the rain from falling (since it was sufficient for her to look at the sky to make it release the rain and she refused to do it out of malevolence) and of being thereby responsible for the hardship caused to the local villagers [Migeotte, 1995; 168].

Sixth, it would be misleading to think that the use of witchcraft is a peculiarity of Third World societies in general, and of African societies in particular. In actual fact, the same practices have apparently played a similar role in traditional European societies and, according to some authors, they have become particularly widespread during the phase of transition from the egalitarian mutually dependent village community of preindustrial times to the more individualistic and socially differentiated structure of market-based societies. Thus, for example, Alan Macfarlane writes that 'one of the major reasons for the rise of witchcraft accusations in the sixteenth century was the tension caused by a conflict between a traditional ethic of mutual responsibility and charity, the norms of self-contained and subsistence villagers, and the new acquisitive and individualistic spirit of capitalism and protestantism' [Macfarlane, 1978: 59]. It is also noteworthy that even in countries with a comparatively long history of industrialization, remnants of witchcraft have lingered till recent times in some remote parts of the countryside.[13]

## 5.4 THE ADVERSE CONSEQUENCES OF TRADITIONAL EGALITARIAN NORMS FOR ECONOMIC GROWTH

### *General considerations*

Economic modelling of voluntary reciprocity as an informal social insurance mechanism is typically based on the assumption that effort does not affect the probability to obtain a particular income (when decision-making is state-contingent) or to leave a particular income state (when decision is made only after the state of nature is revealed). If the conclusion of these models about the possibility of self-enforcing reciprocal transfer payments is therefore relevant for hazards that are largely beyond man's control, this ceases to be true when the level of effort has an important influence on the income achieved: because a hard worker may expect low probabilities to leave high income states and high probabilities to leave low income states, the latter states are less severe and the need to insure against them is less pressing. In other words, economic theory suggests *a contrario* that redistribution will not spontaneously take place when human effort impinges upon economic achievements in a significant manner. This explains why in such circumstances transfers have to be socially imposed on the richer, supposedly more 'lucky' individuals (see *supra*, Section 2). Obviously, direct or indirect coercion in regard of the use of income comes at a high efficiency price since the perverse incentive effects that it tends to generate are ignored.

That development economists were sensitive, during the fifties, to the incentive costs of traditional egalitarian practices is particularly evident from the following extensive excerpts from two pioneer books of development economics which I shall elaborate on in the subsequent discussion:

> At the same time the [family] system, which is largely indiscriminate in its operation, minimises the inducement for people to improve their own position because they can count on being provided with the means of subsistence at a level not very different from that of the majority of their kinsmen, including the more energetic, thrifty and able. The system has other adverse effects which are less obvious. It obstructs the spreading of the banking habit since people are unwilling to have banking accounts the contents of which are likely to be divulged to kinsmen. Generally, it weights the scales against investment in forms which are particularly conspicuous in a largely agricultural society. It also adds to the reluctance of foreign firms to employ members of the local population in positions of trust and responsibility. Indeed, it often discourages men from accepting such posts or similar posts in government service, because increased responsibilities do not necessarily bring with them the personal enjoyment of a proportionately increased reward if the larger income, or part of it, has to go into the family pool [Bauer and Yamey, 1957: 66].
>
> Where the extended family exists, any member of the family whose income increases may be besieged by correspondingly increased demands for support from a large number of distant relations. This is at any time a deterrent to making superior effort, (...) There are many reports from Asia

> and Africa of able men who have refused promotion because the material benefit would accrue mostly to relatives whose moral claims they do not recognize. A strong sense of family obligation (...) may cause a man to appoint relatives to jobs for which they are unsuited (...) In primitive societies men fear the effects of witchcraft if they offend their families, and it may be fear, rather than affection, which drives them to nepotism [Lewis, 1955: 114].

As pointed out in Chapter 1, recent economic theory actually bears out the view that egalitarian norms such as those found in tribal societies are inimical to growth. According to a well-known result of social choice theory, indeed, when combined with some other axioms which are highly plausible intuitively the monotonicity principle does not turn out to be compatible with (static) economic efficiency. This result holds a fortiori true when efficiency is defined in dynamic terms. It is useful at this stage to offer a few comments on the kind of incentive problems mentioned in the above excerpts and to then proceed by describing a game in which egalitarian norms result in an inefficient equilibrium.

*Efficiency costs: an illustrative discussion*

It may happen that the cost of redistribution is not borne by the successful individual himself and in this case, of course, he is not personally affected by incentive problems. This typically occurs when success takes on the form of acceding to a valuable position in the state bureaucracy or even in private companies and this position is used to give jobs (or other favours) to fellow kinsmen regardless of whether they have the required qualifications (or whether they meet standard eligibility criteria). In many instances, however, the successful individual is called to use his own income as the source from which transfers are made to the benefit of other villagers and to kith and kin in particular. Inasmuch as he conceives of these transfers as legitimate contributions,—say, because he wants to pay back relatives for past expenditures and efforts devoted to his own promotion or because he wants to help other members of his family out of sheer altruism or norm obedience—, they can be considered to be voluntary and no adverse incentive effect needs to take place.

This being said, it is often the case that the economic success of an individual breeds parasitic behaviour, which is especially vicious when it does not stop until the rich individual is ruined and brought back to the fold. It bears emphasis that the negative effects of traditional norms of generosity and redistribution in terms of incentives to savings and innovation are not confined to the countryside but may also affect modern cities where many proprietors are unable to resist kinship demands to any great extent, especially so in Sub-Saharan Africa. In the words of Paul Kennedy:

> Most [African] proprietors also anticipate a number of adverse consequences should kinsmen be permitted a direct involvement in business affairs. Family members, it is said, are unwilling to respond to the same discipline as other employees. They tend to demand special treatment and this provokes discontent among the workforce. Jealous of the owner's success and resentful of his authority, they are also prone to dishonest as well as unreliable behaviour (...) [Moreover], demand to provide jobs for a wide range of kin, irrespective of their qualifications, and requests for cash donations or gifts of varying amounts from a stream of 'visitors' are probably the most frequent claims. Financial contributions to funerals constitute another source of difficulty, although the time spent away from management may be more damaging than the cash demands. Businessmen are often expected to finance the education of nephews, nieces and younger siblings... [Kennedy, 1988: 169; see also Marris and Somerset, 1971: 131–45; Beveridge and Oberschall, 1979: 57–59; Ellis and Fauré, 1995].

These difficulties are so important that in many instances they probably outstrip the benefits obtained through kinship connections, especially during the early stages of business growth (particularly in the form of capital advances and business partnership).

To reduce demands on their income and wealth, local entrepreneurs may resort to a number of strategies that involve various kinds of transaction costs. Transaction costs may thus arise because, owing to pervasive egalitarian norms, progressive individuals opt for non-optimal forms of wealth-holding. In other words, particular forms may be selected for their ability to circumvent obstacles caused by such norms rather than for considerations of economic efficiency. The possibility of holding wealth in cash, for example, is only a mixed blessing. On the one hand, cash holdings are much easier to conceal than grain harvests—as a Burkinabe farmer put it, 'cash money is not like millet since it can be saved without anybody's knowledge' [Dubuisson, 1998]—, yet, on the other hand, they are far from being a perfectly secure asset in so far as they take on a material form which curious or envious people can spot more or less easily. To the extent that the latter is true, cash holdings remain susceptible to social pressures for redistribution. If he therefore chooses to shun away from this form of wealth-holding, a progressive individual is likely to find himself with less cash than he would have wished to keep, thus creating liquidity constraints that he might have averted in the absence of such pressures.

In the same line, to reduce undesirable external demands on his income and wealth, a dynamic individual may choose to disperse his cattle (e.g., by entrusting animals to caretakers living outside his native village) so that it is made less visible. Or else, as was reported to me from Burkina Faso (Yalogo area), he may take his wife and children outside the home to have their meals so that the moral duty of egalitarian meals with kinsfolk is escaped. If the above sort of strategies prove too costly, he may have no other choice than to give up his plan to accumulate capital unless he is ready to summon the police of the modern state to defend his income and assets (a blatantly anti-social behaviour that has its own costs and carries a lot of risk in the traditional society).[14] Such surrender, clearly inimical to economic growth, does not bother other villagers in so far as they do not believe they could benefit from growth: they would in any event earn only low incomes (or so is their belief) and they are therefore eager to keep more dynamic individuals into the insurance pool and to prevent them from improving their relative status position.

That growth-promoting efforts by dynamic individuals can be effectively thwarted under the pressure of egalitarian norms is well illustrated by the existence of specific impediments to the development of informal credit markets in tribal societies. It is thus noteworthy that in Sub-Saharan Africa many informal loans are small, of short duration and used mainly for consumption purposes [Aryeetey, 1997]. There are few long-term credit transactions in the sphere of personalized relations, especially if these relations correspond to horizontal ties. The point is that, while short-term loans of a reciprocal type are likely to be given and repaid because they perform an insurance function (see *supra*), the same cannot be said of long-term loans which carry a high risk largely caused by the ruling standards of fairness. As a matter of fact, borrowers do not feel morally obliged to repay debts incurred from richer villagers since they consider that non compliance with repayment obligations is a legitimate way to effect redistribution of income between rich (lucky) and poor (unlucky) people. The effect of this behaviour is of course to discourage prosperous people who succeeded in accumulating wealth on their own to extend credit to fellow villagers or kinsmen who are economically weaker. In other words, egalitarian norms hamper the diffusion of economic progress.

The same phenomenon can also be observed in non-African countries where kin-based relations are important, such as certain areas of the Philippines and Vietnam [Szanton, 1998: 254–260; Malarney, 1998: 282].

Recently, Mick Moore (1997) has expressed the opinion that the balance of advantages and disadvantages of family/kin ties works in the way opposite to what has been suggested above. Essentially, Moore's argument is that no business can be thriving unless it can be supported by a close network of social interaction and personal links: isolated incipient businessmen are bound to face insuperable constraints on their way to prosperity. The importance of social connections for setting up and developing a business is hard to deny, yet the crucial question is the nature of the required connections. As the examples quoted by Moore himself testify, the ties established and used by African businessmen often lie outside the sphere of immediate kith and kin relations, that is, outside the purview of connections within which egalitarian norms are operating. He thus refers to the fact that in West Africa many successful indigenous entrepreneurs began as salaried employees of European companies and that personal connections developed at that stage proved very useful when they decided to set up their own business. In Nigeria, Zambia, and Kenya, too, indigenous businessmen rely on Western contact established locally or when they studied abroad [Moore, 1997: 303–4].

There is clearly a fatal flaw in Moore's argument: to refute what he calls the 'family/kin drag' thesis defended by modernization theorists, he stresses 'the centrality of social links to business success' but continuously confuses kith and kin relationships with non-family social connections. When I shall later discuss (in sub-section 5.4) the various ways out of the efficiency/equity dilemma in tribal societies, particularly the role of religious conversion, more will be said on the importance of tight networks of intra-community social interaction, yet of a type that radically differs from genuine kinship relationships. On the other hand, in the final section of this chapter, I will say a few words about the possibility of collective economic emancipation of kinship groups: in principle, indeed, traditional egalitarian norms can not constitute an obstacle to growth if all members of the group are simultaneously upgraded.

## 5.5 A GAME-THEORETICAL PERSPECTIVE

The reason why redistributive mechanisms that are costly in efficiency terms can persist in tribal societies should now have become evident. Incentive problems are a subject of concern only for those community members who feel confident in their income-improving abilities. The others do not perceive these problems or attach any importance to them because they do not want to try to accumulate wealth. That the behaviour of the latter type of agents can effectively block economic progress is evident from a simple game-theoretical analysis. To begin with, let us consider a reduced game form opposing two player types that yields a unique, growth-inhibiting Nash equilibrium.

Assume that there are two players of distinct types, one called e (standing for efficient) and the other one called i (standing for inefficient): while the former player can benefit from growth because he is capable of accumulating capital and increasing his income, the latter is unable to emulate him. There are two strategies available to the players: the first strategy (labeled P for Pressure) consists of exercising a neutralizing pressure on any effort of capital accumulation (refusing to improve one's economic position and bringing pressure to bear on the other player to the same effect) and the second strategy (labeled E for Enrichment) consists of adopting the opposite behaviour (taking steps towards economic improvement and refusing to exercise negative pressures on the other player). The payoff structure of the game is given in Figure 1 below. The first number in each cell corresponds to the payoff accruing to the row-player (e) while the second number is the payoff of the column player (i).

By the very assumption of different types of players, the payoffs are not symmetrical. Owing to differential abilities, the payoff of e (6 units) is much higher than that of i (0 unit) when both players choose the enrichment strategy E. Moreover, i suffers more than e when there is a mismatch of strategies: i makes a loss of 2 units when trying to get richer in the face of e's opposition while the correspond-

| | | Imefficient player (i) | |
|---|---|---|---|
| | | Pressure | Enrichment |
| Efficient player (e) | Pressure | 2,2 | 0,-2 |
| | Enrichment | 0,1 | 6,0 |

Figure 5.1: A two-player growth-inhibiting game

ing payoff of e is only zero. More importantly, the two following characteristics of the payoff structure need to be emphasized as they strongly determine the equilibrium outcome of the game. On the one hand, when e plays strategy E, i gets a higher payoff by playing P (1 unit) than by playing E (0 unit). To recall, this is because, by preventing e from becoming richer, i obtains a positive payoff derived from the fact that e stays within the mutual insurance pool and does not enjoy a rise in relative status. (Note that, for easily understandable reasons, i's payoff is smaller when he exercises obstructing pressures against e's accumulation efforts than when both players have chosen to shun away from such efforts).

On the other hand, if i adopts strategy P, e prefers to go along with him instead of striving to accumulate capital: indeed, if e breaks the conservative norm through his economic dynamism, he is punished in a way that makes him worse off than if he had stood still (2 units are better than zero unit). This actually reflects the fact that the pressures exercised by i are effective. Finally, it may be pointed out that the aggregate payoff is higher when the players simultaneously adopt the progressive strategy (6 units) than when they both cling to the conservative strategy P (4 units).

From figure 1, it is evident that player i has a dominant strategy which is to play the obstructing strategy P. Knowing that the other player will thus play this strategy in all circumstances, player e has an incentive to follow suit so that the Nash equilibrium of the game is the (P,P) outcome. This outcome is not growth-maximizing but at the same time there is no other outcome of the game that Pareto-dominates it. Both players would be worse off if they played mismatched strategies while e would improve his utility payoff at the expense of i if they simultaneously followed the enrichment strategy.

In the above reduced game form, therefore, strategic interactions among the two types of players prevent economic growth from occurring in conditions where players have differential capacities for material advance and where economic individualism entails costs by eroding mutual insurance potential and encouraging positional externalities.

Let us now consider the generalized game corresponding to the above reduced form. This is the simple $N$-player assurance game described in Figure 2 below.

If player $j$ accumulates capital privately, he can make a gross profit of $b$ units (corresponding to the present value of the flow of his future expected profits). If all the other members of his community opt for private accumulation, such behaviour does not entail any social cost and the private net gain of player $j$ is $b$ units. If, however, only $n$-2 other members behave in a self-seeking way, player $j$ has to confront the opposition and envy of one community member and the cost of this strained relation is posited to be $c$ units. His net private gain therefore becomes $b$-$c$ units. It is moreover assumed that when the number of other community members behaving according to customary rules increases (that is, when the number of other deviants decreases), the social cost of disapproval rises exponentially, reflecting the fact that the difficulty of isolation increases more than proportionately with the number of opponents. In the extreme case where player $j$ is the only deviant member, the social cost of disapproval is $c^{n-1}$ and the net private gain from capital accumulation is $b\text{-}c^{n-1}$ units. The general form of the cost function of social disapproval is therefore (assuming that $c$ is larger than one):

$$c(x) = 0 \quad \text{if} \quad x = n-1$$
$$c(x) = c^{n-x-1} \quad \text{if} \quad 0 \le x < n-1,$$

where $x$ stands for the number of other members of the community who have engaged in individualistic forms of capital accumulation. On the other hand, if player $j$ does not try to tread the path of entrepreneurship and private capital accumulation, his net gain will be nil whatever the other members of his community choose to do: he foregoes the gain of $b$ and at the same time avoids the cost of social disapproval. It is also assumed that there exists some critical number of other members accumulating, say $x^*$, such that $b - c^{n-x^*-1} \geqslant 0$ and, given the assumption of increasing cost of social disapproval, we have $b - c^{n-x-1} > 0, \forall x > x^*$.

| | | *n-1* | *n-2* | *n-3* | ..... | *0* |
|---|---|---|---|---|---|---|
| Player $j$ | accumulates | $b$ | $b-c$ | $b-c^2$ | | $b-c^{n-1}$ |
| | does not accumulate | *0* | *0* | *0* | .... | *0* |

Figure 5.2: Overcoming cultural resistance to entrepreneurship: an N-player assurance game

In the above game, the number of Nash equilibria in pure strategies depends on the number of willing entrepreneurs, z. Indeed, if $z < x^*$, there exists only one Nash equilibrium which is characterized by universal conformity: nobody ventures to embark upon private accumulation of capital. Yet, if $z > x^*$, there is another Nash equilibrium in which all the willing entrepreneurs attempt to eschew customary rules of income redistribution. Whether the former or the latter equilibrium will be achieved obviously depends upon the members' expectations regarding how the others will behave.

In traditional African village communities, the prevailing situation corresponds to the Nash equilibrium characterized by the absence of any deviance. Everyone is convinced that there are not enough people around to dare go out of the customary path and, based on this expectation, nobody finds it worthwhile to privately accumulate capital because this would entail costs larger than the expected benefits. Along the line suggested in Chapter 1, the norm of egalitarianism thus determines a set of beliefs that supports a particular equilibrium in the social game. This equilibrium is inefficient since economic growth is blocked.[15]

Are we entitled to conclude from the above analysis that it is generally impossible to overcome traditional social restraints on individual wealth pursuit? If it is true, as hinted at earlier, that social pressures against individual acquisitiveness also existed in European societies before modern economic growth took roots, the answer to that question must be negative. In point of fact, even observation of contemporary African societies suggests that social changes do in fact occur which have the purpose and effect of rendering traditional values of egalitarianism and aversion to deviance at least partly inoperative, thus allowing dynamic agents to follow an individualistic path of capitalist accumulation. Three mechanisms that lie at the root of such changes—entrepreneurial coordination and the emergence of patron-client ties, migration, and religious conversion—are discussed in Section 6 below. Yet, there also exists another avenue to growth and development that presents the advantage of avoiding the dichotomous choice between the egalitarian *status quo,* on the one hand, and individualistic forms of capital accumulation based on a refusal to obey traditional egalitarian norms, on the other hand. This way is depicted and critically assessed in the final section (Section 7) that follows.

## 5.6 OVERCOMING OR EVADING SOCIAL RESTRAINTS ON INDIVIDUAL WEALTH PURSUIT

### *Entrepreneurial coordination and the emergence of patron-client relationships*

The generalized game presented in the previous section actually suggests a straigthforward solution to the stagnation problem of African villlage societies. As a matter of fact, since traditional principles of equity are so adverse to change, a single individual, even when endowed with special qualities and powerful psychological resources, cannot successfully defy the conventions of the society. He will unavoidably meet with social disapproval and be eventually squashed by varied forms of opposition, especially when his economic success depends on his behaving as a hard-nose businessman in dealings with fellow tribesmen. To break through, he needs the protection afforded by the deviant actions of a sufficient number of other innovators in his locality. Rising economic opportunities alone will not usually suffice to generate dynamic entrepreneurs in the absence of a critical mass of cultural energies harnessed towards countering social resistance to self-seeking accumulation behaviour. In other words, there is a coordination problem involving threshold effects.

In game-theoretical terms, the presence of at least $x^*$ willing innovators in the village population ensures that the growth equilibrium becomes possible. It is only a possibility, however, since willing innovators must have the right kind of expectations to establish such an equilibrium. More precisely, for the old equilibrium to get broken, willing innovators must be convinced that there are enough other innovators in their community who are ready to adopt the deviant behaviour. Others will no doubt ostracize them, yet this social opposition will not entail costs large enough to deflect them from their accumulation strategies.

Here lies an important rationale for leadership: the leader' role is indeed to mobilize a subgroup of at least $x^*$ players and to induce them to act in concert so as to overcome social resistance against private accumulation. Experience shows that a critical mass of return migrants who have been exposed to outside opportunities for a sufficiently long time are likely to form a core dissident group able to call customary norms and values into question. They may then act as role models dragging other villagers into opposition, thereby causing a virtuous 'bandwagon effect' [Kuran, 1995: chap. 15].

So far, it has been assumed that agents are identical and carry the same 'social weight'. This is obviously an oversimplification of reality.

Even in tribal societies, strong differentiation of social status may exist and it is usually male elders, particularly if they come from dominant lineages, who wield most power and influence. In the above theoretical framework, heterogeneity of agents means that $x$ is a function not only of the number but also of the size of individuals, implying that, if a few individuals of sufficient size adopt a deviant behaviour, the stagnation equilibrium can be broken. A typical way in which such a disruption of the old equilibrium can occur is through the rise of patrons from the womb of the traditional elite. This point is elaborated below.

As pointed out by Fafchamps, patron-client relationships are a formal way of organizing the compensation of wealthy individuals for their continued participation in traditional local insurance systems [Fafchamps, 1992: 160–162]. This solution actually consists of granting them preferential treatment so that they remain incited to help poorer people in their community while continuing to accumulate wealth on a private basis. The basic principle underlying such relationships is that, since the rich have little to gain from a risk-pooling arrangement with the poor, the latter should reciprocate the assistance promised by the former in cases of hardship by providing a variety of services such as labour, labour insurance (answering at short notice to the patron's need for labour services), political canvassing, transmission of useful information (including that about machinations of the patron's enemies), contributions to the patron's social image and prestige, physical support in showdown events, etc. [Wolf, 1955; Alexander, 1982; Platteau, 1991: 129–135; 1995b].

The question arises as to how patron-client relationships can actually emerge within societies possessing a tribal social structure. Considerations of social status and power are bound to play an important role here. As a matter of fact, it is not difficult to conceive that a traditional chief or head of lineage can gradually transform himself into a patron [Hunter, 1969: 40]. Thus, for example, the way Mouride marabouts of central Senegal used their religious leadership to spearhead the expansion of groundnut exports with the full support of the French colonial administration attests that traditional leaders (in this case religious leaders who emerged with the Islamization of Wolof people) can turn into self-seeking capitalist entrepreneurs behaving as genuine patrons with their subjects (in this case disciples in the Mouride order) [Cruise O'Brien, 1971]. Also illustrative of the patronage-based path to capitalist accumulation is the ascent of trader-chiefs of Tahiti studied by Finney (1972), or in SSA more specifically, that of a few Nande elders in Butembo (North Kivu, Congo) who embarked upon large-scale trading of agricultural products and behaved as patrons *vis-à-vis* the most promising local youth whom they employed in their business activities [MacGaffey, 1987]. It is not at all evident that persons with weaker status positions in their native village would succeed in establishing clientelistic ties since they would thereby antagonize existing leaders and provoke a reshuffle of the social and political structure.

When traditional leaders transform themselves into dynamic patrons, they tend to devote a growing part of their energies to the pursuit of private wealth accumulation and, in the process, they evade their erstwhile mission of assuming first responsibility for keeping the forces of individualism in check and thereby preserving stability of the social order. Privileges attached to chieftainship thus become an instrument of economic exploitation rather than a means to redistribute wealth: surplus is extracted from ordinary villagers who accept the situation because they attach considerable importance to the social security element of patron-client relationships. To pursue the above example, members of the Mouride villages of the Sine-Saloum 'paid tithes to their marabout in cash (earned through the sale of groundnuts), in groundnuts, by devoting a share of their time to working the marabout's fields, and/or by providing food crops to feed the disciples devoted to full-time work on the marabout's groundnut estate. Ties that bound followers to their marabouts remained intact over time, for in addition to providing an assured route to salvation, the religious leaders often provided their disciples with credit, seeds, and emergency relief in times of need' [Boone, 1992: 41].

It is also important to note that by guaranteeing the day-to-day survival of his clients, a patron somewhat exculpates himself in the eyes of other villagers. In other words, regular transfers to a personalized set of poor people are not only a service which patrons provide in order to win the effective support of these people in many walks of life, particularly in promising economic activities and in political enterprises. By evoking tradition, they are also part of a strategy that allows patrons to pursue their private wealth accumulation objectives without arousing too much hostility from common people (including non-clients) [de Lame, 1996: 180–81]. In the words of David Szanton referring to the case of a small town in the central Philippines, 'the fact of differential wealth and power, although readily visible, was frequently phased (disguised? glossed over?) by participants in a "we are all in this together" rhetoric that was at once egalitarian and communal'. This traditional discourse of patronage, 'cast in moral terms of reciprocity, mutuality, sharing, generosity, and redistribution', is precisely what allows the emergent businessmen to prosper wiithout arousing too much anger from their own community [Szanton, 1998: 259]. It is also useful to bear in mind the aforementioned behaviour of rich cattle owners in Botswana (see *supra*, Chapter 3).

In the same line, to make their private enrichment look more acceptable in the eyes of common people, patrons may indulge in gestures of not only private generosity but also public devotion and commitment. Whereas before stress has been laid on the role of religious conversion and shift in group loyalties as a way to escape the hold of traditional egalitarian values, it is the opposite tactic of using existing religious institutions that bears emphasis here. Two strategies readily come to mind. The first one consists for successful individuals of making visible donations to church or temples in order to persuade kith and kin that their success has a manifest pay-off for the whole community. Through the second strategy, an effort is made to reach upper positions in the local religious establishment so as to become more or less immune to criticism. In Gafunzo hill (Rwanda), for example, we learn that the local teacher who had enriched himself to the point of owning as many as eight houses acceded to the position of communion-giver during Sunday (catholic) masses [Migeotte, 1995: 166]. Note that the two strategies may be narrowly linked to the extent that making donations is often the best way to achieve the kind of recognition needed to reach positions that are prestigious in religious terms.

Can witchcraft or sorcery practices block the ascent of patrons? In fact, as shall be now argued, such practices do not necessarily work against economic progress. Their influence depends upon the balance of forces prevailing within the community. In Rwanda, for example, it has been observed that the rich individual is supposed to have obscure powers that protect him against the malevolent acts of envious people and place him beyond the reach of their magical interventions [de Lame, 1996: 182]. Likewise, in his discussion of the role of sorcery in African economics and politics, Peter Geschiere tells a number of stories that can be construed thus: once sufficiently 'sizeable' people dare to break free from customary egalitarian norms, witchcraft seems to operate in favour, rather than at the expense, of self-seeking individuals. The fact of the matter is that community members who take up the deviant route may succeed in protecting themselves against the evil spirits (of jealousy) by appealing to rival spirits bent on defeating them. To succeed, however, this movement of 'counter-sorcery' must apparently be mobilized by a critical mass of powerful individuals [Geschiere, 1995: chap. 4].

The examples described by Geschiere suggest that traditional 'egalitarian spirits' are more likely to be subdued when the counter-spirits are called upon by elders acting as a subgroup. Things turn out as though the more powerful always eventually win and beliefs in supernatural forces are adjusted to vindicate the actual outcome of the struggle between 'traditionalists' and 'progressives'. When the powerful (the elders) stand for the forces of tradition, deviant members (say, young people) unwilling to let others share in their prosperity are effectively represented as a-social beings moved by evil spirits threatening the survival of the community. On the contrary, when the powerful favour individualistic forms of capital accumulation and are the first to get enriched without regard for the community's well-being, ordinary members become resigned to accepting that the new spirits called upon by the powerful to protect themselves are stronger than the erstwhile spirits of equality and solidarity.

In other words, mystical forces are successfully harnessed to resist change when deviants are comparatively weak or relatively few while they support individualistic moves when these are initiated by sufficiently powerful or numerous people, say, when deviants were already powerful in the traditional sociopolitical system or form together a critical mass of mavericks.[16] In the latter case, economically rising persons are looked with fear and respect by ordinary people. Envious feelings are well alive, but they are held in check lest their expression, even if effectuated in a vicarious manner through operation of evil spirits, should cause damaging retaliation. The implication can also be drawn that social values, norms and beliefs are susceptible of evolving and that they tend to evolve when dominant people or categories of people have an interest to make them change so as to justify new types of behaviour which they have chosen to adopt. In the opposite case, values and norms are likely to endure under the influence of the same category of people.

What the foregoing discussion shows is that the end-result of the social and cultural confrontation arising from the availability of new economic opportunities can be analyzed as the outcome of the selection of one among several possible equilibria which will depend on the members' expectations regarding others' behaviour, on the collective action ability of a subset of the community, or on the strategy pursued by a few key persons in the traditional social order. A move by a critical mass of deviant actors is not the only way through which the stagnation equilibrium can be defeated. A physical or a symbolic departure from the native community represent other mechanisms whereby an individual can succeed in overcoming social resistance against private capital accumulation. Let us now consider in turn these two forms of escape from the shackles of the traditional order.

*Migration and the role of stranger entrepreneurs*

Outmigration is a step of last resort that a entrepreneurial individual or a group of them can always take to completely escape the constraints on private wealth accumulation which result from the operation of egalitarian norms in tribal societies: to a non-negligible extent, 'exodus to cities is due to the incriminatory and jealousy-ridden atmosphere' that pervades many African villages [Bureau, 1996: 125—my translation]. The migration required is of a radical kind since it implies that ties with the native area are being sufficiently severed to make family and other social pressures ineffectual. This often implies that the emigrant goes far away from his village (possibly in a foreign country) so that kith and kin cannot easily catch up with him and settle in his new home so as to draw on his income [see, e.g., Poewe, 1989: 99; Kohnert, 1996: 1350]. Only venturesome and autonomous individuals ready and able to go through such a painful emotional experience can actually follow this path towards economic emancipation and entrepreneurship. In fact, it may be the case that dynamic individuals do not really choose but are actually forced to opt for distant emigration owing to continuous harassment and threats provoked by their deviant behaviour [see, e.g., Jewsiewicki, 1993: 63–104].

The question then arises as to how a dynamics of change can be introduced in the countryside if the individuals most likely to start it are leaving in search of more freedom and better economic opportunities. To the extent that family- and clan-based networks pervade urban settlements, the same question may be raised for towns and cities. Part of the answer directly follows from the foregoing analysis: in-migration of stranger entrepreneurs can precisely surmount the obstacles that discourage local deviance and entrepreneurship. For many societies, there is indeed plenty of evidence that entrepreneurs have been members of an alien group. Chinese in Southeast Asia,

Marwaris in various parts of India, Marwaris and other Indian people in Southeast Asia and East Africa, Lebanese, Syrians and other people from the Mediterranean basin (Greeks, Portuguese) in West and Central Africa, Ibos in Benin, Huguenots in England, Germany and Switzerland, Jews in many countries of Western and Eastern Europe as well as in South Africa and Latin American countries provide well-known examples.

To the question as to how one can explain the remarkable contribution of stranger entrepreneurs to the economic development of so many countries, Bauer and Yamey propose the three following explanations, the latter two of which are directly relevant to our discussion. First, as pointed out above, those who emigrate tend to be the most enterprising and ambitious section of the population. This is the positive self-selection effect of migration. Second, there is 'the stimulating effect of a new environment which so often results in a revision of existing habits, methods and attitudes, and in the removal of the social restraints inhibiting economic change in their country of origin'. And, third, emigrants as strangers are usually not subject 'to the institutions and customs inhibiting the more enterprising natives of their adopted country' [Bauer and Yamey, 1957: 108–9].

The interdependence between the above three points needs to be strongly emphasized so as to better understand the convergence of the forces that annihilate the impact of growth-inhibiting customs and values in the case of stranger entrepreneurs. On the one hand, these entrepreneurs are exempt from the obligation to obey egalitarian norms as they apply to the host society. And, on the other hand, being confronted with a new, challenging and potentially hostile environment (see infra), they tend to cooperate along community lines in order to solve the many difficult problems besetting the way of strangers, yet this is done with an attitude of shared progress instead of shared stagnation [see, e.g., Hodder, 1996]. As a matter of fact, this attitude is all the easier to adopt as ethnic entrepreneurs are typically able and enterprising people who left their native place precisely because they wanted to improve their lot and to put their latent skills into more effective use.

For the sake of illustration, just consider the fact that in parts of West Africa many shopkeepers turn out to be Levantines. The explanation of such a phenomenon is straightforward: while local shopkeepers are all the more exposed to requests of relatives as their wealth is there for everyone to see, foreign shopkeepers can easily resist pressures from their customers. This is because, being strangers, they stand outside of the complex web of social obligations that surround other economic transactions in a village or in a town neighbourhood [see, e.g., Barth, 1967]. This advantage is especially important given the strong propensity of local customers to cry for credit and to escape repayment whenever they have succeeded in obtaining consumption loans from the harassed seller. As a result, whereas for strangers shopkeeping may lead to prosperity, it is regarded as a sure avenue to bankruptcy by local inhabitants [see, e.g., Ensminger, 1992: 53].

A striking case which actually resembles a laboratory experiment in social psychology is the fate of small-scale shopkeeping in the city of Dakar (and other Senegalese cities or towns) when a major political conflict broke out in April 1989 between Senegal and Mauritania as a result of tensions around the Senegal river valley (which serves as a border between the two countries). With a vengeful mood typical of these circumstances, Senegalese people were quick to seize on that opportunity to expel all the small Moorish shopkeepers from Dakar and take possession of their assets. Revealingly, however, their efforts at running these shops soon turned out to be a glaring failure, and when the political situation eased previous Moorish owners returned to resume their activities and the shopkeeping business came back to normal. The failure of the new Senegalese shopkeepers was due partly to their unwillingness to work as hard as the Moors (who use to keep their shop open well into the night when supermarkets and modern shops are closed), and partly to the social pressures for redistribution which were exercised on them after the seizure of Moorish assets.

To shift to another continent, the Chinese businessmen residing in the town of Estancia in the Central Philippines are considered as strangers by the local Filipino population. Concretely, this means that Chinese people are not held to or expected to follow local norms of reciprocity or to engage in the larger social and political life of the community. Typically, they expect and obtain immediate payment for purchases in their shops, limiting 'their relationships to local Filipinos to a fairly tight cash nexus'. Interestingly, local Filipinos justify this stingy behaviour on the grounds that as Chinese their primary and legitimate concern is doing business and making money. In effect, they are 'exempted from engaging in the moral obligations, the general social life, and certainly the personal needs of the local Filipino residents' [Szanton, 1998: 256–57].

By contrast, the moral power of sharing obligations 'prevented patronally entrepreneurial Filipinos from going into commerce. A Chinese merchant could have a shop full of goods and insist on cash payments. No one would expect otherwise. A Filipino with the same shop could hardly deny requests from needy kinsmen, friends, and townmates for goods on credit. Not only might debts thus generated never be repaid, thus edging him toward bankruptcy, but he could not even request repayment without fear of insulting his debtor with the implied suggestion that he might not be willing or able to meet his obligation' [*ibidem*: 260]. Likewise, in Singapore, while Malay merchants and businessmen are entangled in personal and social obligations to customers and are thus 'forced to overextend themselves in credit', Chinese traders are impervious to such kinds of local customs [Nagata, 1979: 113; Li, 1998: 159].

In terms of our previous conceptual framework, ethnic entrepreneurs do not cause loss to the host community by pulling out of the local mutual insurance system since they never participated in it. Nor do they directly threaten the cohesiveness of that community since they are themselves excluded from the local system of status ranking. They may of course be perceived as lucky and arouse envy and jealousy, yet by virtue of their belonging to an alien group, their success will not give rise to ideological intimidation and magical repression. This is not only because magical repression may not work against strangers (since they do not believe in the same spirits which are usually related to local ancestors and lineages) but also because, under normal circumstances, members of the host community typically find that there are more advantages than shortcomings arising from the presence of stranger entrepreneurs (after all, they provide valuable services to them). However, as soon as a crisis situation develops in which the advantages become less obvious and the shortcomings more apparent, members from the host community may suddenly turn against the strangers, using them as convenient scapegoats: if hosts are poorer, this can only be as a result of the strangers having become richer (the zero-sum game prejudice).

Therefore, if ethnic entrepreneurs may be quite effective in bringing about economic change in tribal societies, relations between them and the dominant sections of the population are typically tense so that the new situation created by their presence tends to be highly unstable. Unfortunately, there is plenty of historical evidence to show that such a tense atmosphere may easily degenerate into traumatic events, as witnessed by anti-semitic pogroms in Europe in the nineteenth and twentieth centuries and, more recently, by the outright expulsion of Indians from Uganda under President Idi Amin Dada or of all Moorish traders and shopkeepers from Senegal in the eighties (see *supra*).

It is noticeable that, being aware of their vulnerability to such recriminations and displays of violence, ethnic entrepreneurs usually try their best to persuade members of the host community that their profit-making accords with local values and generates a manifest pay-off for local people [Kennedy, 1988: 146]. Thus, Jewish entrepreneurs in Hungary did not hesitate to magyarize their names to appear as patriotic as native Hungarians [Janos, 1982] and, in many instances, ethnic entrepreneurs (and, sometimes, even local ones) ostensibly fund local charitable activities and support sports, educational and cultural events. The story of the *Popo* migrants from Benin in Pointe-Noire (Congo-Brazzaville) is instructive in this respect [see also Chapter 6]. After a communal flare-up which led to the expulsion of quite a number of them from the host country, the *Popo* seized upon any opportunity to demonstrate their loyalty toward the host society and government, for example by supporting a series of fund-raising campaigns launched by the Congolese government to finance projects of national interest. The *Popo* thereby succeeded in improving their image in the local eyes and officials developed good relations with them on account of their co-operative spirit and goodwill [Jul-Larsen, 1993].

There is yet another consequence resulting from the fact that stranger entrepreneurs are generally flouted and hated by local rural (and urban) communities, partly because they refuse to give in to local solicitations for help: they form derogated groups which are not accepted into traditional occupations and ways of earning livelihood (for instance, they cannot accede to land) and, above all, they are barred from access to positions associated with social prestige and political power. Yet, such discriminations and prejudices have precisely the effect of leaving them no other choice than to concentrate their energies on money making and to thrive on opportunities from which local people exclude themselves [Lewis, 1955: 89–90, 104–5; see also Janos, 1982]. In the words of Everett Hagen: 'In one of two ways—nonacceptance into traditional channels, or refusal of the recognition accorded others in those channels—social blockage of traditional channels must be present if the availability of other less highly regarded channels is to be attractive [Hagen, 1975: 287–8].

*Religious conversion*

One source of economic dynamism thus lies in strangers whose outsider position enables them to disregard the rules and codes of conduct of the host community without too much fear of hostility. Another source springs from insiders themselves, or from what Everett Hagen has called 'native outsiders' [Hagen, 1975: 279] that is, people who, although they continue to reside within their community, are rather free from its moral and social proscriptions against self-enrichment. Insider individuals make their own contribution to economic and social progress when, as members of the local community, they 'symbolically adopt a kind of "stranger" status by virtue of their conversion to a different religion'. As a matter of fact, 'this places them effectively under an alternative set of obligations and links them to a spiritual community whose members encourage private accumulation and economic experimentation whilst providing resources such as technical knowledge, credit or labour' [Kennedy, 1988: 141–2]. In these new spiritual communities, emphasis is placed on virtues of self-restraint and consumption moderation (such as abstaining from drinking alcohol and gambling) and on the need to concomitantly do away with traditional feasts where lavish expenditures on food, drinks, and other goods are typically incurred.

In most cases, it is conversion to Islam or Christianity that provides the necessary escape from community loyalty with all its attendant social obligations. Thus, for example, Norman Long observed that, 'Although somewhat younger and with less urban experience than their economic rivals, Jehovah's Witnesses were disproportionately represented in the commercial farmer and shopkeeper categories in the Serenje District of Zambia. They also tended to live outside the traditional matrilineal village in their own independent settlements, and in their spare time practised such trades as bricklaying, carpentry or tailoring from which they earned extra cash '[Long, 1970: 146]. Revealingly, these entrepreneurs systematically avoid hiring kinsmen-workers who do not share in the ownership of the farm or its equipment because their employment 'is likely over time to lead to difficult farmer/worker relations which centre around the problem of reconciling the rights and obligations of matrilineal kinsmen with their role as workers on the farm' [Long, 1977: 138]. Indeed, as the experience of non-Christian entrepreneurs show, underlying tensions may easily explode in accusations of sorcery that seriously disrupt the running of the farm.

The important point is that Jehovah's Witnesses 'have little interest in traditional status criteria and espouse an ethic which emphasizes the spiritual and moral dangers of associating too freely with non-believers, even if kin,...' [*ibidem*: 139]. In short, by adhering to this church, the converts are provided with religious justification, spiritual protection and practical assistance in their struggles to disentangle themselves from the demands of their matri-kin; they are therefore better able to concentrate on building up their business and cater for their nuclear family interests [Kennedy, 1988: 142]. Likewise, in the Philippines, Protestants or members of the Philippine Independent Church, 'small in number and socially separated from the bulk of the community', could distance themselves from local kinship and friendship networks and obligations [Szanton, 1998: 259]. In Singapore, we learn that Malay entrepreneurs frequently cite Islam 'as legitimation for business activities that fly in face of social pressures' [Li, 1998: 163].

Another vivid illustration of the possibility for insiders to shun involvement in customary kinship networks through religious conversion and to thereby break free from the fear of group hostility towards those who are perceived to be self-seeking comes from Parkin's study of the Giriama people of coastal Kenya [Parkin, 1972: chaps 2–5]. Paul Kennedy has aptly summarized some of the most perceptive insights from this fascinating study which shows, *inter alia*, how witchcraft beliefs can sometimes be made to work in favour of, rather than against, dynamic individuals:

> ...the conversion of some young entrepreneurs to the Islamic faith might follow a long period of psychological tension and physical illness induced by the possibility of conflict with the elders whose status and power were threatened by the younger men's activities. Such "illness" could be diagnosed as caused by powerful Islamic spirits whose appeasement required nothing less than the religious conversion of those unfortunate enough to become possessed. Once this had occurred, the Islamic ban on the consumption of alcohol and certain foods, as well as the need to follow a partly separate ritual and social life, all provided the opportunity for entrepreneurs to reduce their level of involvement in traditional society. Yet this behaviour no longer incurred community displeasure since it was now judged to be religiously determined rather than the result of selfish individualism. At the same time, the converts were still reasonably close to community affairs and so could use their social connections with the elders in order to gain access to land, reliable information, business contracts and so on [Kennedy, 1988: 142].

In Burkina Faso, likewise, the spirit of protestantism is thought to be stronger than the local spirits and this belief helps people cling to traditional beliefs and customs to accept the presence of Christian converts (personal communication of Pierre-Joseph Laurent). The story told by Jean Ensminger about the Orma pastoralists living near the Tana River in Kenya is also instructive. It shows that the first shopkeepers and traders in traditional Orma regions were Islamic converts who could share the institutions of Islam that are particularly conducive to sound business relations, including codes of law [Ensminger, 1992: 48–62]. It moreover seems that it was young men who converted first to the new religion and there is good ground to believe that 'they did so in part as a challenge to the authority of their elders' [*ibidem*: 59, note].

The prominent role played by certain religious minorities in the world's modern history of entrepreneurship hardly needs to be recalled in this context. Examples abound: Huguenots in France, Dissenters in England, Old Believers in Russia, Parsis in India, Marwaris in Bangladesh and Nepal, Chettiars in Burma, Chinese in most of Southeast Asia, Levantines in West Africa, Gujaratis and Yemenis in East Africa, etc. As remarked by Hagen, 'There appears to be nothing unique and common in the substance of these religions, but only in the relationship of their adherents to the dominant religion: dissent' [Hagen, 1975: 280]. What has been precisely highlighted in the foregoing analysis is one important cause for such dissent, namely the difficulty for dynamic individuals to remain within the shackles of a traditional social order based on erstwhile notions of generosity/hospitality and on rank-based hierarchy that actually impede private capital accumulation through forced dissipation or redistribution of all surpluses. Of course, to be able to convert to a dissenting religious movement, the alternative must be available (such as is the case in Sub-Saharan Africa owing to the importation of foreign ideologies from Europe and the Arab world) or, else, a sufficient number of insiders must get together to create a dissenting movement within the dominant society (such as the Calvinist doctrine in modern Europe or the Old Believers' orthodoxy in Imperial Russia). In the latter case, a coordinating effort is required (see infra).

Note finally that conversion needs not be of a religious type. In this respect, the study of the Paez Indians (Columbia) by Sutti Ortiz (1967, 1973) is revealing. We are indeed told that dynamic peasants who want to reserve the surplus earned in their coffee plantation for private capital accumulation rather than egalitarian it generously with fellow villagers and sponsoring religious fiestas (a source of social prestige and power in traditional Paez society) try to enter into relation with rich white farmers who live close by (and to improve their standing in the church through direct money contributions).[17] This has the effect of estranging them from their native community, which makes their strategy highly risky since in case of failure the social security afforded by the traditional society will no more be available while integration with the white milieu may still be far from complete.

## 5.7 CONCLUSION AND VARIATIONS ON THE THEME

### *Concluding comments*

The idea that everyone should benefit from economic growth is actually quite widespread and, in advanced societies, it has eventually given rise to the welfare state and the principle of progressive taxation. The problem in traditional agrarian societies of the tribal type lies in the fact that this idea is taken to the extreme: since anyone's material success is attributed to good luck, it is considered to be the duty of a successful individual to let others share in his prosperity even to the extent of eroding it completely. The explanation of individual success in terms of luck and of individual decay in terms of ill-luck follows from the pervasiveness of environmental uncertainties coupled with absence of scientific knowledge in societies totally dependent on natural resources for their livelihood. In the sphere of material relations, resistance against private capital accumulation is motivated by the desire to prevent dynamic individuals from leaving the insurance pool and from threatening social cohesiveness by modifying relative status rankings.

Can we expect that market penetration will undermine beliefs in the constant action of supernatural powers in human affairs? According to Eric de Rosny (1981), the market economy is not more transparent than the subsistence economy: price fluctuations and the vagaries of the labour market, which has become essential for people's survival, appear to be unpredictable and beyond all control. Access to critical government posts may equally appear so hazardous (there are so few posts for so many candidates) that only some sort of lottery manipulated by *supra*-human forces can assign them. In Rwanda, likewise, rural people perceive that access to wage employment is normally obtained by chance, as a result of deliberate manipulation of supernatural powers [de Lame, 1996: 157–61, 181]. It is therefore not surprising that traditional beliefs in the role of luck and witchcraft continue to serve as current explanations for wealth differentials.

On the other hand, however, people who benefitted from exposure to modern education and experience of wage employment (particularly in non-agricultural activities) are likely to realize and spread the view that rewards, rather than being arbitrary, are related to effort and skills [Bourdieu and Sayad, 1964: chap. 4]. Moreover, the gradual intensification of agriculture and cattle-rearing as land becomes scarcer as well as the use of more and more capital-intensive methods in marine fishing tend to make the role of labour and capital as genuine production factors increasingly conspicuous in erstwhile tribal societies. This being said, successful individuals are still susceptible of being harassed on the ground that they owe their prosperity to vicious manipulation of supernatural forces. Instead of being accused of tricky production of 'luck', they are now suspected of being involved in systematic and treacherous exploitation of fellow villagers or kinsmen. It is also possible that they just do not dare express their new views about the critical role of labour and risk-taking for economic success because the social milieu in which they live is fundamentally hostile to an interpretation of reality that may vindicate changes deemed to be dangerous. In fact, a (deluding) equilibrium situation can thus arise in which everybody has become convinced that income is at least partly determined by effort, yet nobody publicly professes such a view, the conservative elements of the society because such an admission would run against their interests and the progressive elements because they fear being accused of individualism.

Villagers eager to follow the individualistic mode of living diffused by the modernization ideology are obviously willing to break away from customary egalitarian rules and social obligations. They are usually young people who find it more and more difficult to put up with the domination of elders over the village life. In many cases, they are forced to emigrate in order to escape the wrath of vengeful spirits thrown at them by angry parents, chiefs, and lineage heads. Not infrequently, elders themselves opt for self-seeking types of behaviour which they are however in a better position to conceal from sight: thus, they use their authority position to engage in obscure dealings whereby they sell collective goods (such as community lands) underhand for their own private profit while they try to save appearances by distributing gifts and favours (thereby posturing themselves as patrons) and by continuing to use the old community-focused language to describe new practices that actually depart from community values (so as to mystify the commoners).[18] Suspicious younger members may react bitterly against such duplicity and sometimes go as far as mobilizing supernatural forces against their elders [see, e.g., Verdeaux, 1990: 203; Fay, 1990b: 232–3; Hviding and Baines, 1994: 29–30; Geschiere, 1995: 204–8].

On the face of it, progressive members of the community will win if their spirits are stronger than the old spirits which protect social cohesion by attacking all forms of selfish accumulation; otherwise they will be defeated. In reality, what takes place is a vicarious struggle between those who want to break through traditional barriers against private accumulation and those who are keen to maintain the old order of things based on egalitarianism and the respect of status differentials (defined around age, sex and lineage criteria). As has been argued in the previous section, the old order is more likely to collapse if the elders cease to set an example of other-regarding behaviour and come to form a critical mass of self-seeking capital accumulators.

*Another way?*

The analysis presented in this chapter suggests that confronting tribal societies is a dichotomous choice between a conservative approach aimed at protecting the customary *status quo* centered on social security, on the one hand, and a dynamic path involving individualistic forms of capital accumulation based on a refusal to follow traditional egalitarian norms, on the other hand. Fortunately, things need not be so clear-cut in reality. There may indeed exist a way out of this dilemma if dynamic individuals eager to improve their lot succeed in creating a co-operative framework within which individual capital accumulation can proceed. This is precisely why rotating savings and credit associations (ROSCAS) organized at local level are never opposed by villagers: they provide a socially accepted alibi to protect people's savings against all sorts of social pressures, thereby demonstrating that traditional obligations can be reinterpreted to allow for modern economic exigencies [Henry et al., 1991: 130].

ROSCAS are arrangements whereby participants make regular payments to a common pool (the 'pot') which is periodically allotted to each one of them in turn, so that all savings collected are immediately disposed of. The order of the sequence according to which the fund is received may be determined at the beginning of the period, or it may be purely random with the beneficiary being chosen through a lottery system at the time of the distribution, or again it may be a function of the relative intensity of the participants' needs at that time. In the latter case, decision about who receives the pot may be possibly made through auction with the members bidding for it [see, e.g., Lelart, 1990; Henry et al., 1991]. Whatever the exact sequence followed for the assignment of the common fund, the basic principle underlying all ROSCAS is that every participant will have his series of periodical contributions returned to him (her) in one shot at some (determinate or indeterminate) date within an agreed time period.

The subtlety about these associations lies in the fact that they enable all participants to individually save and possibly invest part of their incomes (they actually provide a coordinating mechanism that systematizes and disciplines the members' savings efforts) while at the same time creating a sense of solidarity and togetherness well in tune with the old spirit of village life. The latter effect obtains not only because all participants equally contribute and benefit from the scheme, but also because many of such associations buid up an insurance fund to help their members in difficulty (usually through special loans). Moreover, the extremely tight discipline self-imposed by the members (regarding the times of payment of the periodic contributions and the amounts to be contributed) within a clearly democratic setup creates special bonds among them. Owing to this dual characteristic of both pursuing customary modes of interpersonal relations and allowing private accumulation of income surpluses (through a co-operative mechanism), rotating savings and credit associations can be considered as new collective forms of organization that permit the emergence of individualistic economic pursuits. In the words of Daniele de Lame: 'The multiplication of tontines in Rwanda is remarkably anchored in people's collective representations: savings, accumulated within the framework of a tontine, ceases to be an individual evil to become a positive activity that benefits a group of people among whom money is encouraged to circulate... It is perceived by farmers as an effective method of mutual assistance' [de Lame, 1996: 171—my own free translation].

The creation of informal savings associations such as the ROSCAS thus often takes place in the name of development, a symbolic operator that refers to collective endeavours aimed at improving the situation of the masses. Because of this symbolic association, elders inclined to oppose changes that are liable to undermine their traditional status and authority find themselves in a difficult position. Their position is still more uncomfortable if the mavericks are not content to set up coordinating mechanisms within which private accumulation is made possible but also join together to build up local public goods, such as schools, roads, anti-erosive barriers, or irrigation schemes. [Laurent, 1995, 1998].

Three decades ago, Albert Hirschman actually laid stress on the fact that most community development projects from malaria control to seed improvement 'are perfectly compatible with, and indeed are based on, the idea that the benefits from them must accrue equally to all. Where this idea prevails, such "grassroots" projects and activities have therefore a good chance of success...[while] the belief or suspicion, however mistaken, that a project will lead to individual enrichment rather than to collective benefits may easily spell its failure' [Hirschman, 1958: 12].

When successful in the above-indicated way, innovators are particularly hard to oppose. They may use their improved position to question negative aspects of tradition (such as redistributive mechanisms that involve socially wasteful expenditures through which mutual control is exercised and family alliances are sealed) whilst maintaining and strengthening the positive ones. Clearly, this requires that they accept to perform as new leaders in their own community, a path that is obviously dangerous to tread, especially if they do not achieve some form of *modus vivendi* with the traditional leadership [Johnston, 1981; Baland and Platteau, 1996: 337–43].

Such an approach to development, it must be noted, runs squarely counter to the aforementioned prescription of Gerald Meier and Robert Baldwin (1957) according to which projects should be encouraged that break up village life by drawing people away from their native area and thereby foster the emergence of impersonal relations (see chap. 1). Paul Kennedy inclines towards the same view since he insists that kinship-based relations must eventually give way to new, more anonymous relations as market integration proceeds, an important theme which constitutes the focus of the next chapter:

> But until such time as the process of socio-economic differentiation taking place in African societies reaches a point where kinship relationships no longer extend so firmly across the growing cultural, income, educational and residential divides between classes (so that each emergent class, or incipient class, possesses its own sub-culture and the means of providing viable intra-class support for fellow members), then serious attempts to at

> least neutralise the worst effects of kinship interference represent a considerable advance even if they do not offer a perfect solution (...) Indeed, the ability of capitalist entrepreneurs to distance themselves socially from the pressures of community life is simply an aspect of a far wider, more complex process whereby much larger, impersonal, national markets gradually evolve along with a system for mobilising loanable funds and a supply of free wage labourers who (temporarily at least) are also separated from their community of origin [Kennedy, 1988: 146–47, 170].

*Redistributive norms in settled agricultural communities*

This chapter must end with a note of caution. As stressed in the beginning, the foregoing analysis is not purported to apply to all traditional agrarian societies, only to those possessing a tribal structure. It is therefore of little relevance for many parts of the Asian and Latin American continents [see Platteau and Hayami, 1999]. In particular, Asian agrarian societies markedly differ from African rural societies according to the three dimensions described in subsection 5.2. Thus, the former societies have a strong tradition of settled agriculture (where the relationship between some critical investments such as irrigation, terracing, or manuring and agricultural yields is undeniably clear and visible) and in these societies property rights on arable lands have long been established with significant class differentiation or stratification in terms of ownership of land and other assets. Contrary to African societies which are centered on the lineage and are therefore permeated by values of rather extended solidarity, Asian societies, like all peasant societies (including European societies), have evolved over centuries social and family patterns based on the conjugal family.

This evolution probably took place under the increasing pressure of population on land resources which led to intensification of agriculture and progressive individualisation of land tenure rights. Intensification of agriculture is a form of land exploitation that requires conscientious labour and is therefore liable to substantial management diseconomies: hence the emergence of the family farm as the most appropriate production unit to overcome the incentive problems caused by intensive agriculture [see Hayami and Kikuchi, 1982; Binswanger and Rosenzweig, 1986; Hayami and Otsuka, 1993; Hayami, 1997].

Moreover, paralleling the spread of settled agriculture came the development and diffusion of the great religions that invariably assume the existence of universal laws which are independent from human wishes and cannot be manipulated by witchcraft and the development and diffusion of scientific knowledge that can be discovered through systematic procedures by the human mind. Although the traditions of animism and witchcraft are still alive in Asia, their grip on people's minds is much weaker than in the societies not yet converted into the great religions. Finally, uncertainty is reduced in settled agrarian communities, especially when they are based on irrigated cultivation which has yield-stabilizing effects. Hence the reduced need for risk-pooling arrangements and the increased recourse to self-insurance mechanisms [Platteau and Hayami, 1999].

To be sure, redistributive norms do also operate in Asian village communities. In seeking neighbourers' goodwill or in fearing their envy, incentives operate for the rich to redistribute income and wealth to the poor. Such transfers take place within a logic of patronage well described by James Scott:

> The prosaic, even banal character of these social controls belies their importance. Well-to-do villagers avoid malicious gossip only at the price of an exaggerated generosity. They are expected to sponsor more conspicuously lavish celebrations at weddings, to show greater charity to kin and neighbours, to sponsor local religious activity, and to take on more dependents and employees than the average household. The generosity enjoined on the rich is not without its compensations. It redounds to their growing prestige and serves to surround them with a grateful clientele which helps validate their position in the community. In addition, it represents a set of social debts which can be converted into goods and services if need be [Scott, 1976, pp. 41–42].

Clearly, egalitarian norms in Asia are not loaded with egalitarian beliefs as strong as in Sub-Saharan Africa. Rather, they are based on the claim 'that all should have a place, a living, not that all should be equal' [Scott, 1976, p. 40]. This principle explains that such norms often take on the form of 'work egalitarian' whereby a relatively rich farmer abstains from working the land by himself in order to employ poor neighbours and thereby guarantee their subsistence [Geertz, 1970; Hayami and Kikuchi, 1981; Platteau, 1991, 1995b; Fafchamps, 1992]. The employees reciprocate to the employer by putting in conscientious work efforts. If expectations regarding this reciprocity mechanism become firmly established through a long-term personal relationship, transaction costs on labour employment can be greatly reduced.

In this way, reciprocity norms in Asian village communities have contributed significantly to reducing transaction costs for the exchange of outputs and inputs, and they have thereby facilitated the rapid intensification of agricultural production (the so-called green revolution) based on increased use of labour and capital inputs. Reciprocity norms have also underlain successful development of contractual mechanisms in support of commerce and industry in East Asia, as illustrated by the history of Japan and current developments in Southeast Asia [Smith, 1959; Hayami and Kawagoe, 1993]. The contrast between the growth-retarding effect of egalitarian norms in African tribal communities and growth-enhancing effect of reciprocity norms in Asian village communities suggests the existence of multiple equilibria in social systems that have evolved on the basis of different resource endowments and histories but under the same general principle of guaranteeing subsistence of all community members [Platteau and Hayami, 1999].

This said, as has been argued in Section 5 of this chapter, the differentiation of African agrarian societies through the progressive development of patronage relationships out of traditional kith and kin networks may represent a significant evolutionary path that may get these societies gradually nearer to their Asian counterparts. Increasing mobility and the spreading of universal religions emphasizing the virtues of self-restraint are two other important processes susceptible of creating suitable conditions for capital accumulation and economic growth in SSA: the first process encourages the emergence of stranger entrepreneurs while the second one promotes the rise of dynamic 'native outsiders' from the womb of traditional rural society.

*A final remark*

To close this chapter, it is interesting to mention a recent empirical study conducted in the United States (Fong, 1998) that indirectly confirms one of the central theses propounded here. The study indeed shows that people who believe that income earned is largely a function of personal effort tend to oppose welfare transfers (they think that the welfare state is already doing 'too much') while those who believe contrariwise that income is largely a matter of chance tend to support welfare transfers (they think that the welfare state is doing 'too little'). This result is confirmed by experimental studies that show that 'the same people who are altruistic toward deserving people are often indifferent to the plight of undeserving people, and motivated to hurt those whom they believe to have misbehaved' [Rabin, 1998: 21]. In other words, redistribution can still be valued in modern market societies, yet it is mainly vindicated on the ground that people ought not to bear the (full) consequences of bad luck. From this, it follows that, in societies where many people think that the role of bad luck is much less important than that of personal effort and risk-taking in determining individual economic performances, a lot of resistance will be put up against welfare state institutions. Conversely, in societies where the opposite belief prevails, the predicament of the poor will arouse much more sympathy and welfare transfers will be considered as necessary to mitigate inequalities.

## NOTES

1. Geographically, such societies live at the northern edge of the Sahel, from Mauritania to Lake Chad and further towards the Red Sea or along the Northern Pacific coast (e.g. Zanzibar). Many of them are pastoralists (such as the Tuareg, the Borroro Fulani, or the Ogaden Somali) their neighbours (such as the Wolof and the Soninké along the Senegal river valley), or mixtures with Arab traders [Lesthaeghe et al., 1994: 32–33; Platteau, 1992: 84–95].
2. As explained by Purushottam Mathur with reference to Guyana, people in tribal societies could not be enslaved because 'they knew too well the byways of the forest and hills in the country; whenever any attempt was made to use them, they would in a few days escape into the jungle and could not be brought back'. This solution was not available to indentured labourers brought from outside since they could be 'kept out of the forests by the local tribes who would not hesitate in murdering such intruders' [Mathur, 1991: 48–49].
3. It also bears emphasis that, since agents cannot make binding commitments, full sharing of risks does not occur and only second-best solutions are possible. There is empirical evidence available that confirms both the possibility of viable mutual insurance schemes when the above conditions are satisfied, and the deviation from full insurance predicted by the theory [Platteau and Abraham, 1987; Platteau, 1991, 1997; Alderman and Paxson, 1992; Udry, 1994; Townsend, 1994, 1995; Morduch, 1995; Foster and Rosenzweig, 1995, 1996; Platteau, 1997].
4. In common parlance, there is a perfect analogy between the way we use the words 'exploit' or 'exploitation' in relation to human beings and in relation to natural resources. As a matter of fact, to exploit a natural resource implies that violence is used towards it so as to increase the well-being of the acting agents in the same way that to exploit a fellow human being means that he is being taken advantage of through the use of force and deception.
5. It would be wrong to believe that the above kind of belief has entirely disappeared from industrialized countries or that it has done so a long time ago. Thus, a rather recent study conducted in the Gulf of Mexico (United States) has revealed interesting mutual stereotypes among neighbouring communities: while fishermen are regarded as lazy by farmers because 'they live from resources which are "free for the taking"', 'in their turn, fishermen consider the farmers' success as resulting from their land, not from their own efforts' [White, 1977: 39]. Similar beliefs were held till very recent times in the European peasantry. For example, we are told that in the French countryside land was viewed as an active agent that 'carries the crops much in the same way that it serves as a basis for all sorts of buildings' [Badouin, 1971: 25—our translation]. The French peasant traditionally perceives himself as a collaborator or a partner of nature and the isomorphism between man and land can be taken very far since, like man, land must be fed to be capable of producing [Barthez, 1982: 32–5].

   It is worth noting that economic thinking has actually reflected the prevailing beliefs about the role of natural factors. Indeed, in the French agrarian society of the eighteenth-century, the Physiocrats developed an economic theory based on the idea that land is the only source of value and, therefore, agriculture is the only productive sector in the economy (all transforming activities are 'sterile'). It is not coincidental that an alternative theory that reversed the perspective by placing human effort or labour at the heart of the process of value creation (the so-called theory of labour value) emerged in England at a time when this country was starting to emancipate from the natural economy through comprehensive industrialization [Platteau, 1978: Vol.2, 400–406].

6. Michael Carter and Frederic Zimmerman (1993) have shown that the unravelling of a village-level social sharing scheme and the consequent polarization of the agrarian class structure are the expected outcomes of the interplay between risk and factor scarcity when no coercion is resorted to. They have nevertheless assumed that agents are heterogeneously endowed to start with, yet initial wealth of most members is not sufficiently large to make them shun mutual risk-sharing in the beginning of the game. Using a dynamic stochastic programming model simulated on the basis of West African data, they assume intertemporally rational decisions about consumption and investment in assets (such as stocks of grain, livestock and land) susceptible of being liquidated when adverse shocks severely reduce present consumption.

   Simulation results show that the most numerous class of agents is comprised of those who are threatened by the prospect of a possible consumption shortfall, but for whom such a shortfall is not inevitable. These agents accumulate grain as a consumption buffer against the vagaries of risky production. They, in particular, stand to gain from a risk-pooling scheme, which protects their consumption and asset endowments at least for a short time by taking up the risk-buffering role that would otherwise be played by their land and other endowments. Yet, in the long run, as some agents want to become ever more independent of the reciprocal logic of customary risk-sharing, the force of structural evolution drives the moderately risk-sensitive agents to fall back upon the less attractive risk-coping potential of stored grain. From then on, some of them will face successive or especially severe adverse shocks that will impugn their stocks of stored grain, and reduce them to selling land to meet subsistence.
7. Elsewhere, the author writes that 'belief in the *ekong* [the most effective power in the hands of a sorcer] has never been as strong and as generalized as it is today' [Bureau, 1996: 115].
8. Among the Douala, people believe that witchcraft powers are acquired in an ultra-secret society admittance to which is conditioned upon the killing of a person, preferably a close relative such as a mother or a son. The most common way to harm people consists of removing their 'soul of life' and to reduce them to slavery after their funeral. The victims then work for the sorcerer on the Coupé and Manenguba mountains. The sorcerer uses his flying powers to go to his secret plantation and collect the fruits of his slaves' labour [Bureau, 1996: 107–108].
9. The feelings of jealousy, rivalry and covetousness which give rise to witchcraft can nevertheless be considerably extended. For instance, they can affect the competition among tribes, clans and villages for getting development projects. The belief is then that the tribe, clan or village which wins a project does so because its spirits won a decisive battle against the spirits of rival tribes, clans or villages [Geschiere, 1995: 197–98, footnote].
10. Thus, in a village studied by Geschiere in Cameroon, a man who accumulated wealth and used part of it to buy a new local suit (a beautiful *boubou*) was severely rebuked by the local chief to whom he was forced to hand over his new garment. This was done without any compensation, just on the ground that 'he should not have displayed such a luxury while the chief had to go without it' [Geschiere, 1995]. Anyone familiar with rural life in Sub-Saharan Africa could tell numerous stories of this kind.
11. It is worth noting that the historian David Landes contends that, in its rigid original form at least, the guild system prevailing in Medieval cities of Europe was actually influenced by the zero-sum game ideology of immigrants from the countryside. The emancipation from this traditional logic came from outsiders settling down in outlying urban zones, an interesting feature to be borne in mind when reaching Section 6 of this chapter. In the words of Landes:

   > 'To be sure, the towns and cities were themselves shaped by the countryside: immigrants from the fields brought with them values, habits, and attitudes that made more sense on the land and then set them as a straitjacket on urban activity. Thus the organization of tradesmen and craftsmen in corporate guilds assumed a zero-sum game—one man's increase was another's diminution—like pieces in a bounded field... So,...no price competition; no trade-

off of quality and solidity for cheapness; no buying low ("jewing down", in popular parlance—bad habits always belong to someone else) to sell high; in short, no market competition. Everyone who did his job was entitled to a living. Laudable but static. The aim was an egalitarian social justice, but it entailed serious constraint on enterprise and growth—a safety net at the expense of income. That was the principle... But attempts to sustain local monopoly were thwarted by the growth of suburbs (*faubourgs)*, where urban rules did not apply. There outsiders and Jews settled in, and journeymen worked for masters who had outgrown their shop. There market restrictions did not hold... Here was the beginning of putting-out and division of labour, with substantial gains in productivity' [Landes, 1998: 42–43].

12. One of the biggest achievements of economic theory since Adam Smith's times has indeed been to argue persuasively that the zero-sum game only occurs on the efficiency frontier. When allocation of resources is inefficient, an income-increasing move by one agent does not necessarily cause a fall in the incomes of the other agents. Still more relevant to the context of our discussion, the same holds true when the action of the dynamic agent has the effect of increasing the resources available. In societies where, due to low population pressure, both land and labour are underutilized the latter point is particularly apposite.
13. See, e.g., Des Ombiaux, 1986, for a literary account of the witchcraft that prevailed not so long ago in the Tournaisis area, Belgium.
14. Thus, in the Senegalese coastal village of Joal (on the *Petite Côte*), a prosperous fishmerchant who gradually rose from a fisherman condition would not hesitate to summon the local police to arrest children of poor families who seized a few fishes from his stock piled up on the beach (personal observation). Such a reaction is considered as shameful by other villagers who typically condone open acts of fish theft by poor children. According to custom, indeed, letting these things go is a way to help poor families and what appears as a theft is actually a transfer agreed upon by income-earners provided that the value of the fish taken away remains low. By violating this custom, the prosperous fishmerchant openly reveals his selfish propensities and arouses the scorn and hatred of the other villagers. This is, of course, an extreme attitude, since it would seem that private accumulation is not endangered by small transfers of income towards needy families. Yet, as I was told, the intolerance shown by the greedy fishmerchant serves as a signal that he will not abide any more by customary income-sharing practices whichever they are.
15. In a recent paper, Stefan Ambec (1998) has made an elaborate effort to model an income-sharing norm mutually enforced by social status. Agents have an utility function where reputation explicitly enters as an argument. They are heterogeneous not only because some may be rich while some others may be poor (income is drawn randomly), but also they may have different tastes for reputation. If an individual who turns out *ex post* to be rich follows the social norm of sharing his income with the poor, he does not suffer from a loss of social status. On the contrary, if he refuses to comply, he suffers from a punishment which is directly proportional to the number of poor people and the number of rich people who are norm-followers and therefore willing to sanction violators. What the author shows is that, if the enforcement capacity is high enough (if the punishment inflicted by each sanctioner on norm violators is important enough), there exists an equilibrium where all the rich conform to the sharing norm. Otherwise, some rich agents will disobey the norm in equilibrium, a result that is explained by the agents' heterogeneous taste for reputation. Another equilibrium exists where nobody abide by the norm.

    In a second stage, Ambec attempts to endogenize the sharing norm, i.e., he endogenously determines the transfer parameters (bearing in mind that the transfer objective is to share risk *ex ante* by redistributing the revenue *ex post*). This is done within the framework of an overlapping generation economy where agents live two periods. Each generation interacts with the preceding generation at the first period and with the following generation at the second period. The income-sharing norm is designed by the preceding generation and then taught to the next generation. Moreover, when designing a norm, each old generation member's objective is to maximize the expected utility of the next generation (or, more precisely, that of the conformists). However, each generation defines a new norm and this decision is not affected by the current norm or its conformity. Under these assumptions, it is shown that full income sharing is implemented if and only if there is full obedience to the full income-sharing norm, which implies that the mutual enforcement capacity is high enough to induce all agents to share their income. In other words, full income-sharing cannot be observed with some non-conformity. If some agents disobey the norm, a conformist's expected utility is maximized with a partial income-sharing norm. In the case where there is full obedience to the norm but full risk-sharing is not implementable owing to insufficient enforcement capacity, the transfer made will be the higher transfer accepted by the agent which is least sensitive to reputation.

Regarding the former part, it must be noted that the assumption of heterogeneous tastes for reputation determines by itself the possibility that some agents will disobey the sharing norm in equilibrium while others will be norm-followers. In this case, the model only serves to confirm an expected result. Regarding the latter part (endogenization of the sharing norm), the findings hinge on two ideas that are hard nuts to crack: on the one hand, norms are explicitly designed by elders with a view to maximizing the expected utility of the next generation (in other words, norms are purely instrumental devices manipulated by rational calculating human beings) and, on the other hand, the elders' influence is bounded to the next generation (the norm they design is not affected by the current norm).

16. This hypothesis may offer a clue as to why egalitarian forces have triumphed among the Beti and the Maka while they have given way to individualistic forms of entrepreneurship among the Bamileke and the Bakweri in Cameroon (the reference country in Geschiere's study).
17. Typically, villagers who want to stay within the purview of traditional social relations and to achieve prestige within the ranks of their own reference group grow sugar cane, which is fermented as an alcoholic drink to be offered to friends, neighbours and kin as a sign of generous hospitality. The 'progressive' farmers, on the contrary, stop this practice and prefer to grow and sell cash crops with a view to increasing their private wealth.
18. See *supra*, chap. 3, the vivid illustration of this mechanism in the case of cattle-herders of Botswana studied by Pauline Peters

# Chapter 6

## ENDOGENEITY IN THE RISE OF MARKET ORDER

### 6.1 INTRODUCTION

Increasing division of labour, expanding trade, and enlarging markets are related processes that create profitable opportunities for investment and form an essential component of modern economic growth. Yet, for the potential gains from expanded trade to materialize, it is essential that the trust problem inherent in economic exchanges can be solved in a satisfactory manner. This is especially true when development of specialization entails the multiplication of agreements across space and time which are difficult and costly to enforce [Basu, 1986b: 1894]. Thus, when there exists a time-lag, however brief, between each agent performing his side of the deal, in so far as agents have opportunistic proclivities to use for their own benefit any private information in their possession, real world economic exchanges offer considerable scope for cheating and malevolence. Promises to deliver goods and services or to pay for them may not be honoured, promises to return loans may be evaded, low-quality products may be supplied when quality is not easily or immediately verifiable by the buyer, the money used for payment may not be accepted by others as a means of payment, etc.

Max Weber duly stressed the impossibility for capitalism to take firm roots under conditions of 'absolute unscrupulousness':

> the universal reign of absolute unscrupulousness in the pursuit of selfish interests by the making of money has been a specific characteristic of precisely those countries whose bourgeois-capitalistic development, measured according to Occidental standards, has remained backward. As every employer knows, the lack of *coscienziosita* of the labourers of such countries, for instance Italy as compared with Germany, has been, and to a certain extent still is, one of the principal obstacles to their capitalistic development. Capitalism cannot make use of the labour of those who practice the doctrine of undisciplined *liberum arbitrium*, any more than it can make use of the business man who seems absolutely unscrupulous in his dealings with others ... [Weber, 1981: 57].

How can the market order be made to function in a world of costly exchanges arising from pervasive informational asymmetries and how can it evolve in countries that have been accustomed to a traditional pattern of economic exchanges embedded in wider social relations are among the most lasting, challenging and deeper questions confronting economists and other social scientists. Such questions emerge as soon as one views human beings as prone to opportunism and no more as candidly selfish individuals who do not use fraud and deceit to achieve their self-regarding ends.

In Chapter 5, we have seen that sharing norms as they prevail in Sub-Saharan Africa are liable to discourage the expansion of market exchange relationships unless some mechanism operates to circumvent them. In the next chapter (Chapter 7), the point will be made that not only sharing norms but also the honesty-related norms and values that govern the life of tribal societies tend to have such an adverse impact on market development, particularly with respect to more complex transactions. Before discussing this issue proper, however, the present chapter will highlight the trust problem and draw considerable attention to endogenous decentralized mechanisms capable of surmounting it. At the same time, it will point to the limitations of such mechanisms and of any spontaneous order of anonymous exchange.

In Section 2, the attempts by general equilibrium theorists to resolve the market order problem are summarized and the main lessons from their efforts are drawn. In Sections 3 and 4, the possibility that trust emerges spontaneously from the agents' decentralized actions is examined and assessed critically. In Section 3, the focus is on trust-enforcement mechanisms that use reputation effects. Repeated game theory is the analytical tool used by economists to uncover the properties of these mechanisms. In Section 4, the question of whether honesty is sustainable in economic dealings is raised within an interactive framework characterized by anonymous relationships among transactors. Here, evolutionary rather than classical games are used to examine the issue. Once all this is done, the ground will be laid for a more thorough discussion of the nature and operation of social norms of honesty in market-based societies, particularly in Western countries, a task that is carried out in Chapter 7. Chapter 8 will continue the reflection on moral norms by focusing on the issue of their evolution and by stressing the importance of path dependence phenomena. It will then close the book by offering some concluding remarks.

## 6.2 THE PROBLEM OF THE MARKET ORDER: LESSONS FROM GENERAL EQUILIBRIUM THEORY

In standard General Equilibrium (GE) theory in the Walras-Arrow-Debreu tradition, the 'social order' problem of the market is actually eschewed by assuming that competition makes force or fraud unavailing insofar as it determines the terms of trade in a way that individual traders cannot manipulate [Granovetter, 1985: 484]. In other words, economic theorists in the above tradition have succeeded in demonstrating the logical possibility of the market as a self-ordering system (social order can spontaneously emerge from the pursuit of selfish interests even in the absence of any a priori coordination of such interests), but only at the price of assuming 'a total transparency of the whole economic system for each agent' [Boyer and Orlean, 1991: 1], that is, by eliminating the coordination problem altogether.

In such a world of parametric rationality where no room is left for strategic and conflictual behaviour calling for negotiated or co-operative solutions, 'perfect competition turns out, paradoxically, to be the absence of all interaction among individuals' [De Villé, 1990: 16]. The exchange process is the unique socialization process and there is no macro-social structure linking the actors. Clearly, as pointed out by Frank Hahn, the invisible hand can only operate benevolently under conditions that are impossible to meet in the real world [Hahn, 1982].

During the last decades, awareness of this fundamental difficulty has prompted GE theorists to try to depict the market order on the basis of more realistic assumptions. This involves reckoning that in virtually all real world economic exchanges agents adopt strategic behaviour and can bargain to reach acceptable outcomes.

The most important conclusion from recent theoretical attempts conducted within a general equilibrium framework is that the market system cannot be produced and reproduced in a totally decentralized way from the free interaction of rational selfish agents. At some point of the logical argument, some (unexplained) rule, institution or supra-individual mechanism must be posited in order to show that a coherent economic disposition of resources can be effectively attained [Field, 1981: 188–96]. Stable order can be produced in the markets only by assuming the existence of social rules or norms constraining individual behaviour.

Efforts by GE theorists to uncover the foundations of perfect (or imperfect) competition through game modelling are worth mentioning here. Thus, the most salient contribution of the theory of cooperative games (in which agents are actively bargaining and able to make binding agreements with each other) is to have shown that, when the number of agents becomes very high in a finite economy, the core converges towards competitive equilibrium [Debreu and Scarf, 1963]. This result, known as the Equivalence Theorem, has also been arrived at by assuming an economy with a continuum of agents [Aumann, 1964]. Therefore, whether we view a market with a large number of participants as a collection of active, bargaining, and haggling individuals or as a collection of passive price-takers coordinated by some price adjustment mechanism makes no difference in terms of the equilibrium outcome [Gravelle and Rees, 1992: 461]. To put the equivalence result in a still starker manner, in atomless economies where, by definition, each individual participant has a negligible influence competitive equilibria are the sole possible outcomes of the group decision mechanism underlying the concept of core [Gabszewicz and Shitovitz, 1992: 460].

What bears special emphasis in the context of the present discussion is that a considerable amount of information is required if cooperative games are to be played. Thus, for example, in the fixed threat bargaining model of Edgeworth, transaction costs—in the sense of 'the costs of measuring the valuable attributes of what is being exchanged and the costs of protecting rights and policing and enforcing agreements' [North, 1990: 27]—are assumed to be nil, the negotiation process is completely transparent, and agents trust each other. Since such stringent informational conditions cannot be satisfied in real world conditions, one has to conclude that the market order cannot spontaneously emerge from the decentralized actions of free agents.

On the other hand, by handling noncooperative games of a certain kind, GE theorists have succeeded in reproducing the equivalence result obtained in a cooperative game framework [for a survey of major results, see Mas-Colell, 1992]. As a matter of fact, in almost all the models belonging to that family of so-called 'strategic market games' where agents make strategic decisions about quantities given a price-formation rule that is common knowledge,[1] it has been proven that (1°) equilibrium (of the Cournot-Nash type) exists, and (2°) the set of noncooperative equilibrium allocations coincide with the set of (Walrasian) competitive allocations when the number of agents becomes very high (or when there is a continuum of agents in a nonfinite economy) [the basic reference here is Shapley and Kubik, 1977].

Another way of stating this important result is to say that, instead of assuming perfect competition and being content with working out its effects, economists have been able to produce it analytically (through the use of game theory), that is, they have shown that perfect competition can be understood as the logical outcome of the strategic behaviours of the individual participants to the market (assuming these participants to be relatively small). Yet, like in the case of co-operative game-theoretical efforts at modelling perfect competition, the informational requirements are tremendous: the extension of the Equivalence Theorem is obtained by using (one-shot) games with perfect information (about the price-formation rule and the payoffs accruing to all other participants depending on the prevailing price).

The analytical framework of strategic market games has also been recently used to construct a theory of money and financial institutions, two central pillars that provide the command and control system of a modern market society. The need for these key institutions arises from the existence of significant transaction costs generated by the technology of exchange (decisions and contracts utilize time and other economic resources) or by strategic considerations of trust and enforcement (there is a need to write the rules of the game to enforce contract in a world with less than perfect trust).[1] Given such constraints, financial institutions and the minimal conditions required to make them work appear 'as a logical necessity in any attempt to well define the rules of a strategic market game' [Shubik. 1986: 12].[3]

The considerable research efforts deployed by GE theorists during the last decades to dispense with the standard assumption of parametric rationality seem to lead to the following conclusion: it is impossible to bring out the coherence of the market system without positing fundamental or constitutive rules that constrain the agents' behaviour [De Villé, 1990: 32; Field, 1984]. Whatever the analytical path followed to solve the Hobbesian dilemma (and to simultaneously avoid the solution of the Leviathan advocated by Hobbes himself), the problem of institutions or social norms cannot be evaded. Their major role in a society, as North has stressed, is 'to reduce uncertainty by establishing a stable (but not necessarily efficient) structure to human interaction' [North, 1990: 6]. What these institutions or norms can be will become clearer in the next sections (especially Sections 3 and 5).

## 6.3 THE PROBLEM OF THE MARKET ORDER: TRUST-ENFORCING MECHANISMS BASED ON REPUTATION EFFECTS

### *Bilateral reputation mechanisms in village societies*

Traditional village societies are characterized by their restricted size and by the highly personalized and continuous character of the economic (and other) relationships between their members. In this setting, there is solid theoretical ground to believe that social order can be established and maintained in a spontaneous way. Members of small-scale societies, even if they are potential opportunists, have indeed an incentive to refrain from committing dishonest actions because this would run against their long term interests given the operation of strong reputation effects.

Suppose that the problem of social order is represented as a non-cooperative game (binding agreements are not allowed), more specifically as a two-person Prisoner's Dilemma (PD) game where defection corresponds to cheating while cooperation means acting honestly. As long as this game is a one-shot or single-period game, we know that the unfortunate result of mutual war (both players cheat) happens with the predictability of an iron law: given the payoff structure of the game, cheating is a dominant strategy with the result that both players are worse off than they would have been had they instead chosen to behave honestly. It is noteworthy that even if the players could communicate and reach an agreement to cooperate (that is, if preplay negotiations are permitted), they would still have an incentive to break the agreement and to defect. This is a consequence of the fact that the equilibrium is a dominant strategy equilibrium implying that the information structure of the game (played once) does not matter.

Fortunately, the 'iron law' ceases to apply as soon as the game is repeated, thereby creating what is called a supergame. In this case, indeed, honest behaviour may be a (Nash) equilibrium outcome because each player is in a position to punish the dishonest partner for a noncooperative act in the past.

The fundamental reason why cooperation may be consistent with self-interested behaviour is that the repetition of the game opens the door to the possibility of conditional cooperation and punishment, a possibility which is precluded as long as the PD is considered to operate within a single-period framework. More precisely, to show that cooperation is possible, the assumption must be made that the game is repeated infinitely or that information is incomplete—there is some uncertainty about the others' strategies (either because their payoffs or the degree of their rationality are imperfectly known) or about the length of the game (the game horizon is finite but indefinite).

The simple strategy known as 'tit-for-tat' illustrates how a punishment mechanism can be embodied in the strategy itself and thereby allow cooperation to emerge. It is based on the following principles: (i) start by choosing to cooperate; (ii) thereafter, in period *n* choose the action that the other player chose in period $n - 1$. It can be easily shown that, if the expectation that the game will continue to be played is sufficiently high and if future incomes are not too heavily discounted, tit-for-tat is a (Nash) equilibrium strategy (yet not a dominant strategy):[1] if the first player knows that the second player follows the tit-for-tat strategy, a rational response is to use the same strategy [Sugden, 1986: 109–111; Baland and Platteau, 1996: 59–6l].[5]

This being said, it is important to emphasize that the tit-for-tat strategy suffers from a fundamental drawback inasmuch as, being myopic and mechanical, it cannot 'absorb' mistakes understood as unintended deviations from the chosen strategy. In other words, whenever a mistake occurs, blind adoption of this strategy inescapably leads to the considerable social losses that result from repeated display of dishonesty. An endless chain of retaliation and counter-retaliation is initiated which really looks absurd given the fact that the triggering factor was a simple mistake.

Such an absurd outcome is to do with the fact that such a blind strategy is not subgame-perfect because it relies on an out-of-equilibrium threat that is not credible. Indeed, how can a player believe that, if he deviates, the other player will be ready to carry out a punishment threat that everybody knows unmistakably leads to definitive partial defection? Given that, after a mistake has occurred, a player is known to defect at a particular stage, clearly, the other player should also defect at that stage, instead of cooperating. In game-theoretical terms, this idea is captured by the concept of subgame-perfectness. A Nash equilibrium is *subgame-perfect* if the players' strategies constitute a Nash equilibrium in every subgame.[1] In equilibrium, of course, punishment strategies are devised in such a way that they are never actually implemented. But, to be effective, those punishments must be credible in the sense that each player must find it optimal to carry them out if needed, that is in all the possible subgames whether or not on the equilibrium path.

It is important to lay stress on the fact that cooperation in the infinitely repeated PD game is only a possibility. There are in fact many possible Nash equilibria in this extended game, a result known as the Folk Theorem. The theorem states that almost any outcome that on average yields at least the mutual defection payoff (i.e. the minimax outcome) to each player can be sustained as a Nash equilibrium. Still, the fact that mutual defection does not any more appear as the unique equilibrium outcome in the PD game and that cooperation becomes feasible is no mean achievement of economic theorists. In the words of Kreps, 'a good way to interpret the folk theorem, when the players can engage in explicit preplay negotiation, is that it shows how repetition can greatly expand the set of self-enforcing agreements to which the players might come' [Kreps, 1990: 512].[1] As Abreu (1988) has shown, such strategies need not be particularly complex. More precisely, any subgame perfect outcome of an infinitely repeated game can be supported by a 'simple' strategy profile which are history-independent, that is they specify the *same* punishment for *any* deviation, after any previous history, by a particular player.

Now, for cooperative behaviour to be sustained, players must be especially induced to punish those who deviate, even if it is costly to them. This is achieved by resorting to what Axelrod (1986) has called 'metanorms' that is, strategies that punish players who fail to play their part in punishing free riders [Myerson, 1991: 335–37; Seabright, 1993: 120]. Interestingly, Axelrod has shown with the help of a computer-based simulation, that cooperation can be sustained provided that the players start with a sufficiently high level of 'vengefulness', vengefulness being defined as the probability that a player will punish someone who is seen nonpunishing [Axelrod, 1986; see also Elster, 1989a: 132–133 and Dasgupta and Mäler, 1990: 16].

It is now time to connect the above results with the situation obtaining in traditional societies. To the extent that individuals in these societies are in *continuous* interaction, the situation confronting them may be thought of as approximating that of a repeated PD game with infinite or indefinite horizon. Furthermore, insofar as they have *close* contacts within dense social networks, they are rather well informed about each other's acts and payoffs. Clearly, the framework of their interactions closely resembles a game structure: common knowledge prevails (each player knows the payoff functions and strategy spaces of all players) and rule-breaking behaviour is easy to monitor. Under these circumstances, cooperation (mutual display of honesty) becomes possible. People may refrain from behaving dishonestly because they have a strong incentive not to pay exclusive attention to immediate costs and benefits: insofar as long-term benefits (duly discounted) exceed the short-term ones, they can credibly commit themselves to honesty.

Several centuries ago, David Hume (and Adam Smith as well, who spoke about the 'discipline of continuous dealings') had already well understood that, in small-scale social settings, considerations of what is sometimes called reciprocal altruism but really amounts to selfishness with foresight, should lead people to cooperate. The same considerations help explain why they are quite reliable about keeping promises when no legal sanction requires them to do so and when keeping them is inconvenient or costly:[8]

> We can better satisfy our appetites in an oblique and artificial manner, than by their headlong and impetuous motion. Hence I learn to do a service to another, without bearing him any real kindness; because I forsee, that he will return my service, in expectation of another of the same kind, and in order to maintain the same correspondence of good offices with me or with others. And accordingly, after I have serv'd him, and he is in possession of the advantage arising from my action, he is induc'd to perform his part, as foreseeing the consequences of his refusal ... After these signs [i.e., promises] are instituted, whoever uses them is immediately bound by his interest to execute his engagements, and must never expect to be trusted any more, if he refuse to perform what he promis'd [Hume, 1740: Book III, Part II, Sect. V, 521–2].

*Multilateral reputation mechanisms in village societies*

When, as assumed above, there are frequent, long-term bilateral exchanges, the value of the relationship itself may serve 'as an adequate bond to ensure honest behaviour and promote trust between the parties' [Milgrom, North and Weingast, 1990: 3]. Trust arises, as it were, naturally from the repetition of interactions with the same person. The limitations of this bilateral reputation (or sanctioning) mechanism are evident since misbehaviour of a community member in his dealings with another member only affects their mutual relationship without yielding any influence on other, potential partners in the same community. The multilateral reputation mechanism to be discussed below precisely remedies this shortcoming and is, in fact, widely used in traditional village and proto-capitalist societies.

For the mechanism of multilateral reputation to operate effectively within a given social group, what is essential is that mutual information circulates about each other's behaviours in past dealings. In the words of Milgrom, North and Weingast, 'even if no pair of traders come together frequently, if each individual trades frequently enough within the community of traders, then transferable reputations for honesty can serve as an adequate bond for honest behaviour if members of the trading community can be kept informed about each other's past behaviour' [Milgrom, North, and Weingast, 1990: 3]. Within the dense network of small communities, this informational condition is easily satisfied with the result that transactors can use a set of credible strategies whereby they refuse to deal with someone who has cheated any other member of the community in the past. As pointed out by Hayami and Kawagoe:[1]

> In the village community everyone is watching everyone. Gossip about one's misconduct is circulated by word of mouth faster than any modern means of communication. In such an environment a significant cost would be incurred to a person who would violate a contract with his fellow villager, since not only would he lose benefits from the present contract but the resulting bad reputation would deprive him of future opportunities to enter into contracts with other villagers as well [Hayami and Kawagoe, 1993: 167].

In game-theoretical terms, if everyone follows a strategy whereby he acts honestly and moreover punishes (say, by cheating or boycotting) any agent who has cheated some member of the group in the past, this strategy of multilateral punishment (according to Greif's appellation) is an equilibrium strategy and expectations are self-enforcing: believing that all other participants have this strategy, any given individual has an incentive to follow the same and at equilibrium nobody cheats. Greif calls 'collectivist' or 'segregated' these societies where everyone expects everyone else to respond to any act of dishonesty committed in any pairwise encounter within the community space [Greif, 1994a]. (This is in contrast to 'individualist' societies where anyone only reacts when his or her own interest has been hurt). The observed honesty equilibrium is thus the spontaneous outcome of common cultural beliefs of the 'collectivist' type. It reflects a reputation mechanism among self-interested individuals whereby an agent can establish *ex ante* that his most profitable course *ex post* is to be honest: in other words, the transactor can credibly commit to honesty [Greif, 1989: 858, 866–67].

A noteworthy feature of the above social system is that participants are incited to follow the multilateral punishment despite the fact that the agent's strategy does not call for punishing agents who violated the collective punishment procedure [Greif, 1993: 535]. The self-enforcing character of collective punishment obtains insofar as a cheater stands to lose nothing (he expects anyway to be ostracized in the future) and is therefore inclined to cheat again in new interactions. Others thus do better by avoiding new deals with that individual and, in this way, the second-order public-good problem of sanctioning is solved.

In reality, however, the mechanism of collective punishment or ostracization is not infrequently supported or reinforced by the existence of metanorms (see supra). A good illustration of this possibility is provided by the caste system of India where anyone who refuses to punish defectors is sanctioned by other members of the community [Akerlof, 1976; Basu, 1986a]. Furthermore, material sanctions imposed on defectors are reinforced by shame feelings that are triggered by the emotion of contempt in other group members, itself a function of these sanctions. In the words of Jon Elster: when a person refuses to deal with someone who has violated a social norm, the latter may suffer a material loss but, more important, 'he will see the sanction as a vehicle for the emotions of contempt or disgust, and suffer shame as a result'. In fact, the costs to the sanctioner rather than the costs to the violator are what makes the sanction really painful to the latter: 'It tells him that others see him as so bad that they are willing to forego valuable opportunities rather than have to deal with him' [Elster, 1998: 67].

This said, it would be wrong to believe that sanctioning mechanisms in traditional village societies are always completely decentralized. As a matter of fact, these societies frequently resort to explicit and deliberately designed sanction systems that have at least the two following advantages: they may compensate lapses or absorb 'mistakes' (in the sense of deviations from preferred strategy by individual members in the group); and, by incorporating graduated sanctions, they allow deviant members to mend their ways before ostracization is brought to bear its whole effect.

A last point deserves to be made regarding multilateral reputation mechanisms at work in traditional surroundings: networks or groups within which such mechanisms operate are generally based on kinship ties. This has at least three advantages. First, because parenthood relationships are relatively permanent and stable, they ensure that interactions have the required continuity for cooperation to be worthwhile.

Second, thanks to the common cultural patrimony shared by its members, communication tends to be easier and, as a result, individuals are better able to reveal and signal their intended plans of actions and to learn about others' intentions. Such preplay communication may thus allow them to choose strategies favourable to honesty among the many equilibrium strategies available. To put it in another way, the existence of kinship ties helps to establish trust in the sense of fostering beliefs that other agents are also willing to follow a strategy conducive to honesty in a multi-period framework of interactions. The class of strategies called by Sugden (1986) strategies of 'brave reciprocity'—in a two-player game, I start by being honest and, thereafter, I behave like the other player did in the previous round(s)—typically represent strategies favourable to cooperation in repeated games.

Third, the common identity feelings linking members of a same family, lineage, or ethny together have the effect of transforming the payoff structure of the game from a PD to an Assurance Game (AG) at the heart of which is a simple coordination problem. As shall be illustrated in the next section, agents with an AG preference profile are not bent towards free riding on others' honesty (yet, they are repugnant to the idea of being exploited) because they would like mutual honesty to be established.

It is worth noting that, when the (repeated) game is an AG instead of a PD, an important theorem of game theory applies which has been proved by Benoit and Krishna (1985). According to this theorem, if a strategic-form game has multiple equilibria (when it is not repeated) that give two or more different payoffs to each player, then, under general conditions, the average payoffs in subgame-perfect equilibria of long finitely repeated versions of this game are very close to *any* average payoffs attainable in the *infinitely* repeated versions of the game [Myerson, 1991: 338]. (Bear in mind that the Folk Theorem applies in the latter case). This theorem therefore implies that, in an AG, cooperation is a possible equilibrium outcome even though the duration of the game is finite. It thus points up the essential difference that exists between PDs and other game forms: while in PD games, the results obtained under infinitely repeated versions radically differ from those obtained in finite versions (as pointed out above, cooperation is a possible equilibrium outcome only under the infinitely repeated form of this game), this is not true of other game forms.

*Bilateral reputation mechanisms in proto-capitalist societies*

If only for reasons of sheer survival, traditional societies often need to develop exchange links outside the boundaries of the village. This may be because insurance against hunger requires that transactions in food extend to distant areas where risks of crop failure are not correlated with those in the residential agroclimatic zone [Wiessner, 1982; Cashdan, 1985; Platteau, 1991]; or simply because some essential items (e.g., salt or dairy products) cannot be produced locally. In order to solve the problem of trust in external trade relationships, village societies naturally resort to spreading kith and kin across the required space (marriage alliances may, of course, have an important role to play here), or to creating kin-like relations with indispensable partners.

In the latter case, trust is genuinely manufactured through strategies specifically aimed at cementing close personalized relationships between the transactors. A widespread strategy, well-documented in the anthropological literature, is that of gift exchange [see, e.g., Polanyi, 1957: chap. 5; Posner, 1981: 147–8; Bourdieu, 1980: 168–82, 216; Etzioni, 1988: 75; and Platteau, 1991]. Thus, Belshaw's interpretation of the kula system of gift exchange discovered by Malinowsky (1920, 1922) in the Trobriand islands is that reciprocal gifts between candidate (so-called) 'partners' served to open 'channels of substantial trade and social intercourse'. As a matter of fact, 'persons visiting their partners took advantage of the opportunity to engage in trade' since, after exchanging ceremonial gifts, 'partners would exchange gifts of a trade character'. Moreover, 'the security afforded by the partnership would make it possible for the visitor to make contact with other persons in the village and trade with them'. Under these latter circumstances, however, trade included 'a greater element of bargaining' since the cushion of direct gift-giving was no more present [Belshaw, 1965: 16, 19].

What is actually manufactured through periodical exchanges of gifts is often a genuine bond of identification involving sentimental attachment or what Coleman calls an 'expansion of the object self' [Coleman, 1990: 517–8]. If successful, this identification process-which is often sustained by family-like symbolic relations such as godparenthood ties with a partner's child[11]—leads to 'the dressing of one man in the reputation of another', and the occurrence of something good or bad to one of the partners will induce in the other the same feelings he would have experienced if the thing had happened to himself [Geertz, 1979: 137; Coleman, 1990: 519].

Among the Kung San of the Kalahari desert, a person is said to *hai* the partner in his heart, meaning literally to hold and figuratively to be responsible for that person: from then on, each partner can call on the other in times of need [Wiessner, 1982: 66–7]. In the Berber societies of the High and Middle Atlas (Morocco), where caravan trade requires personal protection from a powerful person living in the locality crossed and where strong codes of honour exist, we are told that 'the essential transaction is that a man who counts "stands up and says" to those to whom he counts: "this man is mine; harm him and you insult me; insult me and you will answer for it"' [Geertz, 1979: 137].

As aptly pointed out by C.A. Gregory in the spirit of Mauss's analysis of gift systems, 'gift exchange establishes a relationship between the subjects': it is 'an exchange of inalienable things between persons who are in a state of reciprocal dependence'. (This is in stark contrast to commodity exchange which is 'an exchange of alienable things between transactors who are in a state of reciprocal independence', something presupposing that a neat distinction exists between things and persons) [Gregory, 1982: 12, 18–19]. The exchange of blood among partners is perhaps the strongest form of gift exchange as conceived by Gregory, since blood is an inseparable element of the giver's physical makeup and a vivid symbol of his integrity. This radical form of reciprocal exchange is often practiced in mafia societies whenever members are not bound by natural blood ties: 'Like the Chinese *tongs*, an Italian criminal gang is family-like but not literally a family. In a society where bonds of trust outside the family are weak, the blood oaths taken by members of La Costra Nostra serve as surrogate kinship bonds that allow criminals to trust one another in situations in which betrayal is very tempting' [Fukuyama, 1995: 101]. Finally, it is worth noting that in traditional economies gift exchange is often surrounded by elaborate rituals in which local authorities may play a role, particularly when different tribes are involved [Polanyi et al., 1957; Polanyi, 1968; MeEvoy, 1986: 31].

On the theoretical plane, Masahiko Aoki (forthcoming, Chap. 4) has recently shown that the mechanism of gift-exchange can emerge in an economy as a set of permanent bilateral relationships between pairs of players who initially exchange the same signals and gifts. Assume that some players adopt the following strategy: if the messages they send (e.g., the language used) coincide with those signaled by a randomly matched trading partner, they exchange gifts, play honestly with that partner and continue to deal with him as long as he also acts honestly. Otherwise, they separate and look for new partners to whom they will also have to make gifts. Under some conditions, this strategy is incentive-compatible and cooperation in trade can be sustained to the mutual advantage of traders. These conditions are rather straightforward: (1°) the present value of gains derived from continued cooperation exceeds the cost of one-time gift-giving; and (2°) the same present value realized by performing a gift this year is greater than the value obtainable through renewed gift exchange every year following cheating.[12]

Note carefully that such long-term personalized relationships, because they make any change of partner costly, constitute an obstacle to efficient exchange when the economic environment is unstable. As will be seen below, however, information sharing or pooling within networks of people is susceptible of surmounting that problem, at least to some extent.

*Multilateral reputation mechanisms in proto-capitalist societies*

Historical evidence tends to suggest that reputation mechanisms at work in agrarian societies may also operate in more urbanized societies where protocapitalist forms of development are observable. Yet, as shall be argued below, such mechanisms have important limitations that render them incapable of sustaining alone the process of modem economic growth. Such a conclusion, it may be noted, runs counter to the belief held by a number of sociologists for whom bilateral and multilateral reputation mechanisms are all what a market system needs to solve the trust problem and capture all the available trade opportunities. We are thus told by Granovetter (1985) that 'Actors do not behave or decide as atoms outside a social context ... Their attempts at purposive action are instead embedded in concrete, ongoing systems of social relations ... the anonymous market of neoclassical models is virtually nonexistent in economic life and transactions of *all* kinds are rife with the social connections described' (pp. 487, 495—added emphasis). Moore has taken this argument to its logical conclusion when he writes that 'markets are to a very high degree self-regulating' and it is wrong to believe that effective commercial law is essential to (fast) economic growth [Moore, 1993: 45–46; see also Moore, 1994; Murshid, 1997].

As we know, bilateral and multilateral reputation mechanisms are feasible devices to govern agency relations only insofar as agents can easily acquire information about each other. This tends to hold true in small communities with dense networks of continuous relationships. It is not surprising that, as new trade opportunities open up and more or less peaceful conditions prevail—such as was the case during the period spanning the 11th–14th centuries in Europe and the Mediterranean—, business-inclined people attempted to rely on these solutions to capture them. Thus, it was a natural practice among such people to use kin as agents in long-distance trade. That is, 'a sedentary merchant would send a relative with the cargo to negotiate sale and to obtain a return cargo' [North, 1990: 120]. Provided that the shipping of goods could be properly insured, a merchant could reduce the cost of trade by sending goods to an overseas agent who would look after his business in a foreign trading centre. The system was particularly profitable when merchants could rely on a multilateral reputation mechanism since such a mechanism ensures honest behaviour on the part of agents even when the relations between a specific merchant and agent pair are not expected to recur (an advantage that cannot be obtained under bilateral punishment).

For example, it was used by the Maghribi traders who operated in the Muslim Mediterranean during the 11th century after having migrated from the insecure surroundings of Bagdad to North Africa in the course of the previous century [Greif, 1989, 1992a, 1992b, 1993, 1994a, 1994b, forthcoming]. In effect, thanks to their emigration experience, these Jewish traders came to acquire a strong social identity and to form a highly cohesive group whose members employed each other as agents (without usually resorting to any legal contract), and all retaliated against any agent who had cheated a group's member by refusing to hire him. For reasons that have already been made clear, the system was self-enforcing: 'each merchant was induced to hire only agents who were expected to be hired by others' [1992a: 130] since, given the prevailing expectations, a cheater would have to be paid more to be kept honest.[13]

An important feature of the Maghribi group is that it operated as an effective information-transmission network since traders operating abroad passed on to other members information about trade circumstances their agent(s) faced, thus helping the former evaluate their agents' conduct [Greif, 1989: 880]. The additional gains from cooperation, the value of the information flows, and the expectations concerning future hiring ensured that the Maghribis were motivated to hire and to be hired only by other Maghribis, while non-Maghribis were discouraged from hiring Maghribis [1992a: 130]. By solving the principal-agent problem pertaining to relations between merchants and overseas agents, the Maghribi traders' closed grouping (a non-market institution) therefore promoted the integration of interregional markets in a context where there was no legal framework within which these relations could be organized [1989: 865–66; 1993: 544–45].

Among Italian traders, by contrast, 'a different political and social history led to the emergence of institutions based on political control and bilateral reputation'. After the political faction that controlled Genoa lost its monopoly over the city's lucrative overseas trade by the end of the 12th century, the city grew rapidly and unstable social networks prevented the emergence of any multilateral reputation mechanism while favouring instead the growth of a patron system based on bilateral reputation [Greif, 1992a: 130]. Also, the need was felt to make up for the lack of multilateral reputation mechanisms by developing legal and political enforcement organizations (as well as a legal code to coordinate expectations and enhance the deterrence effect of such organizations): in the absence of such institutions, exchange is indeed more costly when cultural beliefs are 'individualistic' than when they are 'collectivist' [Greif, 1994a].

What needs to be emphasized is that neither the multilateral reputation mechanism nor the bilateral mechanism coupled with a political enforcement organization can be considered to have been efficient. This is not surprising in so far as, while the new institutions were a precondition for trade expansion, their rise in various places were not caused by the appearance of new gains from trade. Rather, the timing of their emergence and hence of trade expansion was determined by social and political factors [Greif, 1992a: 129]. Among the Maghribis, the volume of trade was limited by the size of the group which has itself been determined by historical circumstances and could not grow as trade opportunities expanded.[14] Moreover, 'although this deficiency could have been remedied by an appropriate coordinating organization, such an organization did not emerge' [*ibidem*: 131].

As for the Italian situation, trade magnitude was politically determined under the political coalition system while, under the patron system, agency relations could be governed only at a high cost till a new organization, the family firm, was established during the 13th century. The family firm (a permanent partnership with unlimited and joint liability) is helpful to overcome incentive problems because its lifespan is 'infinite' and it is less likely to go bankrupt than an individual merchant. As a consequence, the price (wage) to be paid to keep agents honest is lower. Interestingly, the family firm did not emerge within the 'collectivist' culture of the Maghribis where it was not perceived as necessary since they had solid reputation mechanisms at their disposal [Greif, 1989: 874–77; 1992a: 131; 1994a; see also Aoki, forthcoming: Chap. 4, for an elegant presentation of Greifs argument].

In fact, Greif's analysis points to the existence of a close and two-way relation between levels of trust and extent of personalization of exchange interactions, on the one hand, and contractual incompleteness, on the other hand: the more incomplete the contracts the higher the level of trust built into long-lasting personalized relationships. These two elements can be seen as mutually determining so that one may define an equilibrium set of norms and contracts [Bowles, 1998a]. Indeed, it is not only that trust and personal commitment are developed when contracts are difficult to specify and to enforce, say, because the quality of the product is highly variable and is costly to measure (this is an important point that will be addressed more fully in the next chapter) but also that, instead of being exogenous, the degree of contractual incompleteness may respond to the levels of trust and reciprocity exhibited by the traders concerned. Thus, the individualism of the Genovese traders prevented them from adopting the kind of multilateral reputation mechanisms evolved by the Maghribis, yet at the same time 'provided an impetus for the development and perfection of ultimately more successful third party enforcement of claims by the Genovese' [*ibidem*: 95].

As shall be emphasized again in Chapter 7, the same individualism apparently led to a rather early development of legal and political enforcement organizations [Greif, 1989, 1994a]. The possibility of different institutional trajectories is clearly suggested by Greif's approach. This is because path dependence is at work in all human societies: once a specific arrangement emerges, perhaps as a result of a historical accident, 'it may become a part of a self-enforcing stable system which is not prone to change in response to welfare-enhancing opportunities. Hence, economic growth in different economies may be diverse due to distinct institutional frameworks of historical origin' [Greif, 1993: 545].[15] An identical view is implicitly held by Paul Kennedy who deals with the situation in Africa. He indeed stresses the ability of traditional groups (such as the Hausa of northern Nigeria) to generate merchant entrepreneurs active in local and even in long-distance trade.

Such an ability, he reckons, 'was largely based on the mutual trust and active cooperation' existing within the original community now organized as a wide network of fellow migrants resident in distant towns and acting as commission agents, informants and sources of accommodation, ... Yet, having said so, he cautions that 'these very systems of customary support which have underpinned contractual relations so successfully may increasingly inhibit the emergence of more advanced types of business behaviour in the future' [Kennedy, 1988: 143–44, 146].

*Variations on the theme*

Before turning to another issue of institutional development, several points need to be made.

(i) First, in the above illustration of the Maghribis, multilateral reputation mechanisms are called forth to govern agency relationships through self-enforcing employment contracts. Such mechanisms can also be useful in many other circumstances, such as when informational asymmetries must be overcome to permit trade to develop between stranger persons or communities. Just imagine, following Aoki (forthcoming: Chap. 4), that an urban merchant wants to do business with agricultural producers who reside in a remote village and have no kinship ties with him whatsoever. A mechanism is needed to reduce moral hazard problems on the sides of both the merchant and the villagers. It can work as follows: the merchant visits the village headman and makes a gift indicating his willingness to trade honestly. If this gesture is reciprocated, an agreement may be drawn up between the two parties and, to the extent that the headman acts as a true representative of his village community and that multilateral reputation and sanctioning mechanisms exist within this community to punish free riders, honest trade can be established as an equilibrium.

For instance, the village headman agrees to check the quality of the goods delivered by local farmers and, in the event of defects, to stand as a guarantor that the damage will be borne by the community. The identified defector will be sanctioned in one way or another (say, through ostracization in internal exchanges or social events). On the other hand, if the merchant cheats, say on the payment made to the producers or on the quality of the goods provided to them, he will be prevented from continuing to trade with any member of the community. Any such member who would free ride on this sanctioning obligation is liable to be punished by his fellow villagers (say, again through ostracization in internal exchanges or social events). The mechanism whereby the threat of collective punishment by the village community thus deters possible cheating by the merchant as well as by individual families, is called a 'community norm' by Aoki. Note that it can work not only between a merchant and a village community but also between two communities (say, a group of merchants and an agricultural community, or two such communities) acting through their respective representatives. In this case, what allows honest trading to take place is the linking of two multilateral reputation and sanctioning mechanisms operating on both sides of the trading process. In so far as the representative of a community acts on behalf of its members whom the merchant or the representative of another community does not need to know, an impersonal mechanism is put into operation.

Such a mechanism may, of course, fail to be established since the corresponding equilibrium is only one among many other possibilities. Thus, for example, it is vulnerable to outsiders mischievously pretending to be part of the community with a view to free riding on the obligations prescribed *vis-à-vis* an external merchant or community. Or, village producers may not hesitate to renege on their promise because internal sanction mechanisms are not effectively applied in a context where an acute competition among merchants provides villagers with many alternative opportunities of getting contracts. To the extent that merchants do not have effective information transmission mechanisms among them, they are highly vulnerable to all sorts of opportunistic behaviour on the part of the rural producers.

A remarkable and well-known illustration of this possibility is the ultimate failure of the system of cottage industries in western Europe. This system was widely adopted in the textile sector, at least in England where the resistance from urban workers to this 'unfair' competition could be overcome:[16] the peasants (mostly women) did the spinning on a putting-out basis after having received the raw material (the raw wool and flax, and, later, cotton) from a merchant who collected the finished yarn after the work was over. Yet, moral hazard problems were pervasive as cottagers quickly learned to cheat the putters-out: they 'would take materials from one merchant and then sell the finished article to a competitor, stalling now one, now another, and juggling their obligations to a fare-thee-well'. They would set some of the raw material aside for their own use and, to conceal the embezzlement, they 'made thinner, poorer fabrics and filled them out by artifice or additive' [Landes, 1998: 208]. The result was 'a costly war between employer and employed', where the former tried his best to enforce constant quality standards at each step in the manufacturing process [*ibidem*; North, 1981: 168; see also Crouzet, 1985].

The manufacturers' spontaneous reaction was to ask help from the civil authorities, calling for the rights to inflict corporal punishment on rural producers responsible for late deliveries and low quality work, to enter the weavers' cottages without warrant and to search for embezzled materials, yet 'these demands got nowhere' [Landes, 1998: 208]. The ultimate solution lay in the rise of the factory conceived as a hierarchical organization allowing for the direct supervision of the rhythm and quality of work: 'the impetus for the factory system was monitoring of the production process by a supervisor' [North, 1981: 168–69]. In the words of David Landes: 'frustrated manufacturers turned their thoughts to large workshops where spinners and weavers would have to turn up on time and work the full day under supervision'.

To gather workers under one roof, there to labour under constant surveillance, was not an easy solution to implement, though: manufacturers found that it was costly to persuade people out of cottages, where they enjoyed the freedom from discipline and 'the privilege of stopping and going as they pleased', and into mills. According to this economic historian, it took power machinery and the huge scale economies generated by it to make the factory able to undersell the cottage products, hence the success of this new organizational system in sectors employing heat-using technologies (fulling, brewing, glassmaking, ironmaking, etc) [Landes, 1998: 209–210].

(ii) Second, kinship or ethnic ties are not the only way to build up a 'collectivist' culture among traders. Adherence to a common religion can achieve the same end by welding non-relatives into a well-knit entity. Indeed, religious conversion ensures that members abide by the same codes of behaviour, share the same rituals and use the same language with the result that they acquire a common identity grounded in the same symbolic universe. If groups are sufficiently small for information transmission to be effective, religion serves not only to encourage cooperation (honesty) but also to signal or identify members.

In West Africa, for example, long-distance trading communities or 'trading diasporas' [Cohen, 1969, 1971] have traditionally shown considerable openness to new entrants on the (obviously restrictive) condition that 'they shared or accepted the essential cultural requirements for participation in the moral community which distinguished the members from the host society: Islam and the appropriate trading language' [Austin, 1993: 115; see also Ensminger, 1992: 51, providing evidence in the case of the Orma of southern Ethiopia and northern Kenya]. The non-fulfilment of this condition explains why European (French) merchants failed to make inroads in cattle trade within what is now the republic of Niger: they were unable to participate as equals in indigenous systems of guaranteeing credit and enforcing contracts that emphasize a common religion (Islam) and language (Hausa) [Austin, 1993: 117]. The connection between long-distance traders or large-scale trading diasporas, on the one hand, and conversion to a universal religion, on the other hand, has been observed in other parts of the world as well [Cohen, 1971: 277; Ensminger, 1992: 169].

(iii) Third, it would be wrong to believe that kin-based relationships are always conducive to effective transmission of information and effective operation of multilateral sanction mechanisms. The opposite may actually hold true. For example, in the fishing and marketing town of Estancia in the Central Philippines, we are told that local Filipinos do not convey to each other information about customers who did not pay their debts, 'for fear of exposing to others that they themselves had been successfully taken advantage of', and also for fear of insulting their debtors by suggesting that they might not be willing or able to meet their obligations. In contrast, Chinese merchants willingly exchange among themselves credit information about Filipino customers, thereby reducing the frequency of bad debts [Szanton, 1998: 256, 260]. The same sense of honour which prevents Estancia's indigenous people from transmitting information about loan delinquents has also been observed among the Mossi communities of the Yalogo region in northeast Burkina Faso. There, a lot of secrecy surrounds all loan transactions because local people are extremely wary of not bringing shame on resident families with whom they are in continuous interaction. When a credit-giver is not being repaid, he punishes the defaulter by refusing to lend him any more in the future, yet does not act to destroy his reputation[17]. In other words, the prevailing code of honour allows for bilateral but not for multilateral sanction mechanisms as is typical of 'individualistic' cultures.

Sanctioning processes are sometimes deemed to be problematic when applied to kin relations. Thus, in Singapore, some entrepreneurs prefer to abstain from trading with close personal relationships to avoid the strains and tensions arising from intra-kin dealings [Li, 1998: 161]. In Ghana, selling on credit to relatives and neighbours seems to be carefully avoided by manufacturing and trading firms because it is considered as amounting 'to the death warrant of the firm'. Payment problems would be frequent 'as friendship and family ties get in the way of pressurizing clients' [Fafchamps, 1996: 441]. In a survey of fifty-eight firms in Accra and Kumasi, no credit sales to relatives and family members were actually recorded [*ibidem*; see also Ledeneva, 1998: 195–200, for evidence on present-day Russia]. In Vietnam, on the other hand, local entrepreneurs apparently regard kin as more difficult to manage than non-kin because criticizing or giving orders to kin is generally difficult and unpleasant [Malarney, 1998: 282–83]. This is not necessarily the case, however, as attested by the observation that, in the Philippines, Chinese entrepreneurs experience many difficulties in disciplining Filipino labour and therefore opt for labourers recruited within the extended family. According to this account, the problem comes from the fact that Filipino workers consider it 'an affront to their dignity' to be ordered about by a Chinese boss, especially in front of their companions [Szanton, 1998: 257].

*Disciplining foreign rulers in proto-capitalisit societies: the need to supplement multilateral reputation mechanisms*

The governance of agency relations is only one of the problems that beset trade expansion in Medieval times. Another critical issue was that of ensuring proper behaviour on the part of rulers of foreign trading centres or even of territories crossed over to reach foreign marketplaces. A bilateral reputation mechanism was obviously unable to prevent such rulers from abusing the rights of alien merchants (e.g., by confiscating their property or arbitrarily increasing tolls) since the volume of trade and, therefore, of revenue which a particular merchant represented was necessarily low (that is, the value of the future trade of the 'marginal' traders to the ruler was zero). Contrary to what one might think, a multilateral reputation mechanism under which a group of merchants would threaten a ruler to cease trading in his realm if he abused one (or several) of them, does not provide a reliable solution either.

The reason is simply that, if individual traders have an interest in joining an embargo decision by a group of sufficiently large size, once such a decision is taken, they will be incited to break the embargo and free ride on others' self-restraint: during a boycott, indeed, trade shrinks to below the point at which, say, bilateral punishment is effective. It must therefore be concluded that, to support the efficient level of trade, a multilateral reputation mechanism must be supplemented by an organization able both to coordinate responses of individual merchants and to enforce embargo decisions upon them. In other words, as repeated play is not sufficient to discipline the foreign ruler at economically efficient volumes of trade, not only is collective action needed but it must also be supported by some mechanism that can ensure 'solidarity of incentives' among the merchants concerned [Greif, Milgrom, and Weingast, 1992: 5–7, 26; Greif, 1992a: 129; 1992b: 4]. It is only then that a ruler is likely to commit himself to non-arbitrariness, because the merchants' threat of retaliation is credible.[18]

Thanks to their social cohesion, Maghribi traders could ensure members' compliance to boycott decisions in a purely decentralized way, yet in the more 'individualistic' culture of western Europe, as no such group cohesion existed, a specific organization had to be in place to surmount the alien ruler's commitment problem. In Italy, each city actually functioned as a merchant guild while it is only after a long process of institutional evolution that the small towns (too small to pose a real threat to foreign rulers) around the Baltic Sea could be incorporated into an intercity guild, the German Hansa [Greif, Milgrom, and Weingast, 1992: 13–17]. This is where the political factor—strangely neglected by Granovetter but strongly emphasized by Hicks [1969: 37–38]—comes into play. As a matter of fact, it is because Italian cities had 'a solid internal political and commercial organization' even before trade expansion demanded it (they were true city-states and the merchant guild was a sub-division of a city administration) that they were able to perform the coordination and enforcement functions required for thriving trade [Greif, Milgrom, and Weingast, 1992: 17, 26].[19] Enforcement was actually based on various inducements or sanctions some of which offered member merchants with a stream of rents in their own city—since the guilds were usually able to exert powerful controls in their home territories—while others relied mainly on the organization's coercive power [*ibidem*; Greif, forthcoming].[20]

Interestingly, there are instructive present-day examples of effective 'collectivist', kin-based organizations designed to discipline foreign rulers. It is certainly not coincidental that most of these organizations seem to exist in countries where political authorities are unable or unwilling to make reliable long-term commitments *vis-à-vis* alien trading communities, such as is still commonly the case in Sub-

Saharan Africa [see the pioneering work of Cohen, 1969, 1971]. To my knowledge, one of the best documented examples is provided by a recent study [Jul-Larsen, 1993] of the organization adopted by the migrant Popo fishermen from Benin in the town of Pointe Noire in Congo-Brazzaville. (Similar organizations actually exist among the Popo staying in Gabon, Cameroun, and Ivory Coast).

The main motive behind the creation of the Association des Ressortissants du Bénin (ARB), an organization webbed into the extended family system of the Popo fishermen on the beaches, was clearly to minimize conflicts with the Congolese society in general and with the state in particular so as to secure continuous and safe access to local fish resources. It is noteworthy that the initiative to create the association actually came from Beninese fish traders (of Yoruba origin) who, for obvious reasons, insisted that Popo fishermen on whose catches their business depends be included into it. To achieve their objective, ARB leaders quickly developed links with key actors within the Congolese society, in the civil society as well as in the state apparatus. Yet, in September 1977, these links did not suffice to prevent the Congolese government, without any forward notification, from repatriating all Popo fishermen who did not possess formal stay permits and from confiscating their outboard engines on the grounds that proper import authorizations were lacking.

However, most of the ARB leadership, possessing legal stay permits thanks to their contacts with high-ranking Congolese officials, remained in Pointe Noire and immediately reacted by deciding that all remaining Popo should refrain from fishing for other purpose than for pure subsistence. Because of the high level of internal authority of the association over all the Popo fishermen operating in the area ('As member of the Popo fishing community, you are under ARB jurisdiction whether you wish it or not and the only way of escaping ARB control is to leave Pointe Noire'), there quickly ensued a severe lack of fish in the markets in town. The government could not remain indifferent to this state of affairs and, after all sorts of incidents, the situation was gradually reversed: the expelled Popo slowly returned and, around 1982, the Popo population in Pointe Noire eventually reached back its 1977 level.

Since this effective demonstration of corporate power by the ARB, the rights of access of Popo fishermen to the local waters have not been any more threatened, and the relationship between their association and the Congolese authorities has significantly improved. Instead of trying to abuse them, army colonels, party officials, police officers or town mayors have accepted the establishment of more or less reciprocal relations with Popo leaders, and these relations have been increasingly characterized by a certain mutual understanding. Interestingly, the ARB has been skillful enough to contribute positively (and not only through the threat of withdrawal) to this improvement by seizing upon any opportunity to demonstrate its loyalty toward the host society and government (like when it supported a series of fund-raising campaigns launched by the Congolese government to finance projects of national interest). In other words, the Congolese government, without losing face, can maintain good official relations with the ARB on account of the latter's cooperative spirit and its usefulness in solving a series of practical problems resulting from the presence of the Popo fishermen in the country. The ARB's effective power of retaliation, which is no doubt the crucial factor disciplining the government's behaviour, remains more or less concealed behind this screen of mutual goodwill.

*Overcoming imperfect information through a private third party*

Let us now assume that the above problem is somehow surmounted: in alien trading centres the ruler exercises forebearance and restraint in using coercive force. There then remains the crucial question as to how merchants coming from different localities can be induced to respect contracts requiring enforcement through time when information is imperfect (past actions of merchants are not known and merchants could renege on their promise and leave the place before being detected). This question cannot be evaded even in the face of evidence that 'merchants could and did communicate extensively, writing letters, engaging in trial relations, and checking the credentials of their trading partners'; indeed, with geographical specialization in production, merchants increasingly needed 'to rely on the promises of individuals with whom they were not well acquainted' [Milgrom, North, and Weingast, 1990: 19].

The difficulty obviously arises from the fact that in a large community 'it would be too costly to keep everyone informed about what transpires in all trading relationships, as a simple reputation system might require'. Clearly, it is the costliness of generating and communicating information—rather than the infrequency of trade in any particular bilateral relationship—'that comes out as the main problem to solve' [Milgrom, North, and Weingast, 1990: 3]. In the aforementioned paper, the authors have shown formally that an institutional solution exists to such a problem: if merchants are able to coordinate their efforts to establish private judges who would centralize information and act as third-party adjudicators of disputes, they could be induced 'to behave honestly, to boycott those who have behaved dishonestly, to keep informed about who has been dishonest, to provide evidence against those who have cheated, and to honour the decisions of the judges' [*ibidem*].

The interesting feature of the system is that private judges are able to promote honest exchanges even though they have actually no binding authority to enforce obligations. In other words, once the third party is established thanks to the merchants' collective action (assuming that this collective action is feasible), the system is self-enforcing and does not call for the use of any coercive power: in the authors' own words, the main function of the private judge consists of transmitting 'just enough information to the right people in the right circumstances to enable the reputation mechanism to function effectively for enforcement' [*ibidem*].

The self-enforcing character of the private judge system hinges critically on the provision that unless a trader makes appropriate queries with the judge about the quality of his current partner, he cannot use the system to resolve disputes and to obtain compensation for damages inflicted on him. In effect, it is the judge's ability to activate a multilateral reputation mechanism by controlling information (if the judge lacks the ability to enforce judgments once a trader left the trading centre, he is capable of verifying past actions and keeping records of traders who cheated in the past) that provides the appropriate incentives prompting merchants to participate in punishing cheaters [Greif, 1992a: 132; Milgrom, North, and Weingast, 1990: 10]. Further, only the names of those merchants who did not pay the compensation required of them when they were found guilty of cheating become part of the judge's permanent record. Finally, it must be borne in mind that acquiring information and appealing to the judge is costly for each merchant. Nonetheless, despite these costs, there exists a (symmetric sequential) equilibrium in which cheating does not occur and merchants are induced to provide the court with the information needed to support honest exchanges [Greif, 1992a: 132].

The above private order institution was apparently used at the Champagne fairs, an important nexus of trade between northern and southern Europe during the 12th and the 13th centuries. The private judge was then known as the Law Merchant, an appellation which refers to the fact that he was chosen from among the merchant community [Milgrom, North, and Weingast, 1990]. It is worth stressing that, if this system has features which tend to make it relatively cheap compared to available alternatives, it can work only under certain institutional conditions. It will thus not lead to a honesty equilibrium (that is, merchants will not use the information-pooling mechanism and, as a result, cheating will not be deterred) if (1°) the merchants live at great distances from one another and their principal assets are illiquid thereby making wealth transfer particularly difficult; (2°) the cost of information query is so high as to exceed the gain of having a honest deal; (3°) the cost of appeal is too high; (4°) the advantage of cheating is too large; (5°) trade is not very frequent; (6°) the Law Merchant is corrupt (this risk may nevertheless be averted under certain conditions). Above all, it must be reckoned that the Law Merchant system does not fully account for trade outside a single trading centre since we do not know how information about a trader's dishonesty in one location could be transmitted to another [*ibidem*: 13–8, 20].

These various constraints, especially the latter, probably explain why the Law Merchant system was eventually replaced by a system of state enforcement, typically in the late middle ages or the early modern era in western Europe.[21] Rather than depend for punishment upon the decentralized behaviour of merchants, recourse to the state authority when nations exercised extensive geographic control enabled the seizure of the property, or the imprisonment, of individuals who resisted paying judgments. Given the enlargement of the trade space, it is likely that the intervention of the state resulted in a reduction of the transaction costs of policing exchange [Milgrom, North, and Weingast, 1990: 21].

## 6.4 THE PROBLEM OF THE MARKET ORDER: LESSONS FROM EVOLUTIONARY GAME THEORY

When anonymity is posited so that all kinds of reputation effects are ruled out, cheating is the inevitable outcome if agents are selfish: this pessimistic conclusion is immediately derived from the fact that cheating is a dominant strategy in the one-shot PD game. In order to demonstrate the possibility of honesty in economic dealings within the framework of anonymous interactions, the payoff structure of the game being played must therefore be modified so as to create more room for cooperation (honesty). Also, the analytical approach is different: evolutionary game theory is used instead of classical game theory with the result that agents have only a limited rationality and that the problem considered is the convergence towards, and stability of, a honesty equilibrium rather than a problem of coordination on that particular equilibrium.

The Assurance Game has a payoff structure indicating that, unlike what obtains in the PD game, agents have a predisposition towards cooperation (honesty) in the sense that they derive a positive utility from cooperating together. In other words, they suffer a welfare penalty if they cheat against a partner who behaves honestly. Moreover, they do not like to be exploited by others, implying that, when their partner is cheating, they feel better by retaliating than by playing honestly [Sen. 1967].

In such a game, there is no dominant (free rider) strategy because the particular outcome 'depends crucially both on prior expectations and on a preference for coordinating one's own actions with the actions of others' [Runge, 1984: 158]. To the extent that the structure of mutual expectations plays a crucial role, multiple equilibria become possible and the Pareto-optimal outcome is one of them. The AG is thus particularly interesting because it provides an escape from the counter-intuitive result that free riding is the unique possible equilibrium in a single-period framework, as the PD game implies. The following symmetric, two-person one-shot game illustrates the above payoff structure and the existence of two Nash equilibria in pure strategies (underlined):[22]

| Players 1/2 | Honest (H) | Cheat (C) |
|---|---|---|
| Honest (H) | 30,30 | 0,20 |
| Cheat (C) | 20,0 | 10,10 |

Figure 6.1: The Assurance Game

It is immediately apparent that, for each agent, the best policy depends on what he thinks the other will do. In fact, optimal choice of one player is Honesty if the probability that the other player will choose the same strategy is assessed by him to be in excess of 1/2, and his optimal choice is Cheat if this probability is less than 1/2.[23] Thus, while there is no certainty that the game will equilibrate at the more favourable of the two (Nash) equilibrium points, HH and CC, this can happen if the transactors have enough confidence in each other, the degree of trust being measured by the probability that the other chooses H instead of C. It may be noted that the degree of trust needed to yield cooperation is inversely related to the intensity of the agents' inclination towards honest dealing. If, for example, it is assumed that each player gets a payoff of 40 instead of 30 when both behave honestly, a player will be induced to so behave if his expectation that the other will follow suit is greater than or equal to only 1/3 (instead of 1/2).

Also worth emphasizing is the fact that the trust problem is reciprocal since it is basically a problem of mutual expectations: the first player, say A, may fear that the other player, say B, will abstain from cooperating not because he prefers to free ride but because B's expectations about his own (A's) behaviour may be pessimistic, and vice-versa for B *vis-à-vis* A. Now, if some form of rudimentary coordination such as preplay communication (in the form of 'cheap talk') is allowed and if the signals sent by the players are interpretable in an unambiguous way, cooperation by both players is much more likely to arise because the players then have the opportunity to reassure one another and to form optimistic expectations about their mutual behaviours [Baland and Platteau, 1996: 92]. What bears noticing is that the nature of interactions in small groups is highly conducive to preplay communication and, therefore, if both players' profile is that of an AG player, the Pareto-superior outcome is very likely to be established even in this one-shot game. (Remember that we have reached the same conclusion, but for repeated games, when we analysed situations structured as PD).

For another thing, if the two AG agents could play sequentially rather than simultaneously, the Pareto-superior outcome would obtain with certainty: one of the two agents would take the initiative of honest behaviour since he would be assured that the other agent will do likewise after having observed his benevolent move.

In order to reflect the reality of an anonymous market, we now assume that there are numerous agents who meet pairwise at random in every period to transact and that they cannot tell if they have met before. The latter assumption, it must be stressed, precludes any reputation effect: anonymity prevails and reputation cannot be lost (a person's past record of choices is not known by anyone). Each agent can choose between the two aforementioned strategies, to be honest or to cheat, and choice strategies are determined simultaneously. We are interested in knowing not only whether honesty in economic transactions can be established but also whether it can be sustained over time.

Since the framework is that of evolutionary games (see Chapter 1, section 5), agents maximize reproductive success and patterns of behaviour that have proven relatively successful in the past are more likely to survive and reproduce. In the human world, where genetic transmission is not available, the mechanism ensuring the survival and reproduction of successful behaviours is that of repetition and imitation [Sugden, 1989: 92]. Here, it is assumed that reproductive success is dependent upon the (cumulative) payoff earned through successive pairwise transactions. Note that, by thus linking payoffs and reproductive success, the most unfavourable assumption to cooperation is adopted since cooperators are penalized in terms of payoffs when they cheat at the expense of cooperative partners. In other words, while selecting a preference profile that is favourable to cooperation, a reproductive mechanism is chosen that makes cooperation as difficult as possible.

Furthermore, it must be borne in mind that behavioural patterns in evolutionary games do not correspond to genuine strategies since they result from myopic choices of agents who do not clearly anticipate the long-term consequences of their present decisions including all the possible reactions of other players.

To make the game more realistic, the presence in the population of a group of inveterate opportunists (acting as dangerous mutants) is allowed. By inveterate opportunists, are meant people eager to exploit any situation to their own profit, whichever the cost they thereby impose on their partners: in other words, these players have a PD preference profile. In the following table, we give an example of what could be the payoffs accruing to two types of agents when they deal with one another, type A players who have an AG preference structure, and type B players who are opportunists. Three payoff matrices obtain depending on whether type A players meet together (first payoff matrix), whether they meet with type B players (second matrix), or whether the latter transact with each other (third matrix). These payoffs are described in Figure 6.2 from where it can be seen that a player B free riding on a player A's honest behaviour earns a larger utility reward than what a player A would earn by free riding on a player B.

Opportunists (type B players) have a dominant strategy, which is to cheat. As for agents predisposed towards honesty and cooperation

| A1/A2 | Honest | Cheat | | B1/A1 | Honest | Cheat | | B1/B2 | Honest | Cheat |
|---|---|---|---|---|---|---|---|---|---|---|
| Honest | 30,30 | 0,20 | | Honest | 30,30 | 0,20 | | Honest | 30,30 | 0,40 |
| Cheat | 20,0 | 10,10 | | Cheat | 40,0 | 10,10 | | Cheat | 40,0 | 10,10 |

Figure 6.2: A game with both opportunists and agents predisposed towards honesty

(type A players), their behaviour can be precised only after having further spelt out the information conditions prevailing in the society considered. To begin with, under the (unrealistic) assumption that types can be perfectly (and costlessly) detected in each and every pairwise encounter, the conclusion is inescapable that opportunists will entirely vanish from the population and honesty will be the only observed behaviour. This is because the optimal strategy of a A player is to act honestly only if he is matched with another player of the same type, otherwise to cheat. As a result, the payoffs of these players dominate those of the opportunists who are doomed [Frank, 1988: 56–60].

If types are undetectable (would-be cooperators and opportunists look alike) but their distribution is common knowledge—everyone knows the proportion P of opportunists in the population—an invasion of the cheating behaviour can be predicted to occur with certainty. In these circumstances, indeed, a type A player will act honestly if and only if the expected payoff of honesty is larger than the one of cheating, which implies that the frequency $P$ is smaller than a certain threshold value, $P^*$ (equal to 1/2 in the above example). Yet, the expected payoff of type B players (when they follow their dominant strategy) is higher than the expected payoffs for type A players (when they act honestly or dishonestly) with the consequence that the proportion $P$ will increase until type A players decide to cheat. It then stabilizes at that level corresponding to the threshold value, $P^*$, meaning that a certain proportion of type A players are able to survive, yet only at the cost of shifting their strategy from honest to dishonest behaviour [Gaspart, 1998].

If identification of types is possible but costly—a technology of detection is available at a fixed cost per use—, a mixing of honesty and fraud may obtain. As a matter of fact, type A players will use this technology if $P$ is large enough (not smaller than $P°$) to justify the cost of protecting against opportunists. If $P°$ is lower than $P^*$ (the threshold value from which type A players turn cheaters), then $P$ will converge towards $P°$ and a stable mix of cooperation and defection will be established: once the population settles at this stable mix, players predisposed towards honesty (who pay the cost of scrutiny) and opportunists have the same average payoff, so that both behaviours, honest and dishonest, can persist [Frank, 1988: 61–63; see also Guth and Kliemt, 1994].

The assumption of common knowledge of *P* is obviously too strong (as pointed out by Gaspart, it is a way to establish a spontaneous coordination among players of the same type) and it is now time to relax it. When the proportion of opportunists in the population is not known to them, agents predisposed towards honesty make their strategic choice on the basis of a continual re-evaluation of the probability that their partners in economic transactions will behave honestly based on concrete experiences in past rounds. Note carefully, therefore, that the expectations which are formed and revised at the end of each period concern not the proportion of opportunists in the population but the frequency of people who cheat (since type A players may strategically choose to adopt the opportunists' behaviour). Because procedures of expectation formation are difficult to model in a way that allows for analytical solutions, games where common knowledge is absent are better simulated. Furthermore, while the analytical model postulates a continuum of agents, simulations are run with a finite number of them.

A first point deserves to be made. In the absence of knowledge about the frequency of cheaters, there is no guarantee that honest behaviour will be generalized even in the extremely favourable case where only agents with an AG preference profile are found in the population. Worse, if a sufficiently large number of agents have pessimistic expectations regarding others' intentions, it might well happen that dishonest behaviour will invade the whole population. Indeed, agents who are initially pessimistic or prudent will be inclined to behave dishonestly for fear of being exploited by malevolent partners. Moreover, those of them who made bad encounters with other pessimists will have their pessimistic beliefs reinforced and therefore continue to behave dishonestly. On the other hand, optimistic agents who started by acting honestly may become discouraged following a series of disappointing experiences with prudent or pessimistic transactors. Given a sufficiently large incidence of pessimistic expectations in the population, trust may thus gradually unravel and leave room for generalized pessimism resulting in pervasive fraud and deceit.

When opportunists are present in the population and their detection is impossible, invasion of cheating behaviour is the expected outcome of the evolutionary game, even though type A players form a large proportion of the population and are very optimistic to start with. As a matter of fact, during the first periods, these players have much chance to be matched together, as a result of which their optimistic expectations are reinforced: they therefore continue to act honestly. It is nevertheless inevitable that a few of them meet opportunists who exploit them. Those of them who have had a series of such bitter experiences revise their expectations in a pessimistic direction and eventually turn cheaters. In the words of David Hume: 'Your example both pushes me forward in this [defection] way by imitation, and also affords me a new reason for any breach of equity, by shewing me, that I should be the cully of my integrity, if I alone should impose on myself a severe restraint amidst the licentiousness of others' [Hume, 1740: Book III, Part II, Sect. VII, 535]. Finally, opportunistic players remain cheaters whatever happens.

As a consequence, the frequency of cheating in the population rises, thereby increasing the probability that honestly behaving agents meet agents who act fraudulently. In turn, this implies that more type A players will shift their strategy towards cheating following the disappointment of their current expectations. The process will continue unabatedly till cheating behaviour has invaded the whole population [Dasgupta, 1988]. The unravelling of trust that underlies this erosion of honest behaviour is proceeding all the more slowly as, among other things, opportunists are more frequently matched together during the first periods. There are two reasons explaining this result. On the one hand, the opportunists' average payoff is relatively low, which reduces their reproductive power compared to the players with an AG preference profile who frequently meet together to their greatest benefit. And, on the other hand, since there are correspondingly few encounters between the two types of players, little revision of optimistic expectations takes place in the minds of type A players so that they rarely change their action.

Assume now that the detection of type B players is possible yet costly. The simulation experiments carried out by Frederic Gaspart (1996) lead to the following conclusion:[24] if type A players are very sensitive to recent experiences and if the cost of detection is high but not prohibitive, starting with optimistic players of type A and a proportion of opportunists lower than $P^{\circ}$, the society does not converge to the 'mixing equilibrium' at $P^{\circ}$ (as predicted by Frank) but to the invasion of the cheating behaviour. In addition, even when more favourable initial conditions are posited (lower sensitivity to recent experience, a higher proportion of type A players in the initial population, a higher initial expectation of meeting someone who behaves honestly), the invasion of cheating behaviour remains a serious possibility if it happens that very few type B players are matched together during the first periods of the game. In the opposite case, convergence towards the mixing equilibrium is observed. When the initial setting is made very favourable to honesty (optimism of type A players is initially very high, their proportion in the population is initially very large, sensitivity to good experiences is extremely high while that to bad experiences is extremely low), the latter result is guaranteed.

To sum up, it is only under special conditions highly conducive to cooperation that honesty may be shown to survive and, even in these circumstances, fraudulent behaviour is not eliminated. The question then arises as to whether ways exist to escape this discouraging conclusion. In a more recent paper (1998), Gaspart treads two different routes. First, he assumes that agents willing to have honest dealings have available to them a 'revenge strategy' (*R*) that they may use to punish cheaters (say, by closely watching them). Thus, when a type A agent plays the *R* strategy against a type B player who cheats, he obtains a payoff that is greater than the payoff earned by the latter (the opportunist is thus penalized) which is itself greater than what they would both have earned had he also cheated. On the other hand, when the *R* strategy is played against an agent of the same type who acts honestly, because that strategy is costly, the payoff earned falls short of the amount obtainable in the case where both players behave in a honest manner.

The analytical version of the game leads to the rather depressing prediction of a mixing equilibrium in which all type A players would play the revenge strategy. In other words, no agent acts honestly at equilibrium and agents with an AG preference profile survive only at the price of playing a costly strategy. The results of the simulations nevertheless show that such a prediction is still too optimistic. In many simulations, indeed, the species of type A players just vanishes from the population. This is due to the fact that their strategies are not homogeneous: a number of them, positively encouraged by honest dealings with players of the same type, decide to behave honestly, which renders them vulnerable to ill-treatment by opportunists when they happen to meet with them. In the analytical model, on the contrary, common knowledge about type distribution allow players predisposed towards honesty to coordinate on the 'revenge' strategy, which enables them to resist a complete invasion by opportunists.

The second route trodden by Gaspart, which introduces a 'territoriality' effect (endogenous change towards local matching), leads to more optimistic conclusions. The idea here is that, following a sort of 'territorial instinct', agents have a higher probability of meeting someone with whom they had a fruitful cooperation in the past, but they will not recognize their former partner (reputation effects continue to be precluded). As a result, the matching process is altered as time goes by. Note that, since opportunists never cooperate with their partners, they are not directly involved in the local matching process. Yet, they will be increasingly matched together as a result of the 'territorial instinct' of type A players.

The analytical treatment of territoriality leads to the conclusion that no mixing equilibrium is possible. What we observe is either the invasion of the cheating behaviour or the triumph of honesty, the latter being likely for low initial proportions of opportunists in the population. The intuition behind this favourable result is simple. The process of weaving a web of neighbourhood relationships is always in progress: if type A players can stabilize their proportion by letting a sufficient number of opportunists cheat other opportunists, then more of the latter agents will be matched together in the future and type A players will have a strictly higher reproductive success on average.

Simulation of the game allows the web-weaving process to be explicitly modelled. It is striking that the results of the simulation massively confirm the analytical probing. No mixing equilibrium is ever observed and the crucial factors causing the occurrence of the invasion of the cheating behaviour or the triumph of honesty are the initial proportion of opportunists in the population and the increment of the probability of meeting someone with whom one has had a honest dealing in the past. What is basically needed to see honest behaviour invade the whole population is that players predisposed towards honesty wait, before starting to cheat, until the networks are sufficiently widespread to give them a higher reproductive success and to restore their trust to a high level [Gaspart, 1998].

Note that the territoriality effect modelled by Gaspart is different from the 'games among relatives' well-known to biologists and recently used by Frank (1988), Bowles (1996) and Bowles and Gintis (1998) in economics. In these games, indeed, it is assumed that, because of some sort of cultural or geographical segmentation—

'because they share a common ancestry and parents have privileged roles as cultural models, or because of a sorting process based on some characteristic correlated with the cultural traits under study' [Bowles and Gintis, 1998: 17]—, individuals of a given type tend, from the very beginning of the game, to interact disproportionately with one another. Under these conditions, as expected, the equilibrium level of the 'nice trait' (cooperativeness) will exceed the equilibrium distribution of types in a population under random pairing. The reason is simply that the effect of segmentation is to partially internalize the externality associated with the 'nice trait': the non-random pairing means that the benefits of honesty are disproportionately likely to be conferred on other individuals willing to deal honestly, thereby favouring the replication of honest behaviour [Bowles, 1998a: 93].

In Gaspart's modelling, instead of a fixed and predetermined bias in the pairing process, there is only a dynamic, progressively evolving tendency towards local matching that is itself the upshot of the way the game unfolds. It is therefore not surprising that cooperation or honest behaviour is more difficult to obtain on the basis of Gaspart's procedure than under the assumption chosen by Bowles and Gintis. In fact, the latter precisely wanted to argue that, to the extent that the impersonality (and hence anonymity) of markets erodes the bases of segmentation, markets inhibit this trust-building mechanism, hence the necessity that they be complemented by community-based governance structures [Bowles, 1998a: 93; Bowles and Gintis, 1998: 22–23].

Gaspart's strategy is different: he wants to show that trust in exchanges can evolve in market economies and he therefore retains the anonymity framework, yet at the price of the questionable assumption that people are attracted to those with whom they had nice encounters in the past even though they do not remember them personally. To give an empirical content to the concept of 'territorial instinct', just think of a process whereby an agent who has been cheated in an encounter reacts by leaving the marketplace where the cheating took place. He then goes to another marketplace where he will remain as long as he is not being cheated. As for opportunists, they tend to stay on where they started to operate. The question which springs to mind is, of course, why opportunists do not change marketplace to infiltrate those where honest agents tend to congregate, which would undermine the prospects of honest trade. Clearly, we need another setting to be convinced that it is possible to build up and maintain trust in market economies. This setting, which calls for the operation of moral norms, is elucidated in the following chapter.

## NOTES

1. Each participant in the exchange economy makes an offer (in terms of quantity) and a price ensues according to the aggregation (price-formation) rule adopted. To each price is associated a final allocation that enters the utility function of each individual and plays the role of a payoff function. Individual behaviour is strategic because each player maximizes his payoff given the actions of all other players.
2. Note that if there were no transaction costs then complete markets could be costlessly constructed and, consequently, exogenous uncertainty could be wiped out by completing markets in contingent trades. The presence of transaction costs creates endogenous uncertainty so that, even in the absence of exogenous uncertainty, money and financial institutions are needed to offset incomplete markets endogenously [Shubik, 1986: 4–5, 58].
3. Thus, in an economy with cash but no credit, there is the theoretical requirement that an individual's buying commitment never be larger than his cash on hand. Yet, *ex ante*, there is no way to enforce this budget constraint unless an inspection procedure is instituted [Shubik, 1986: 18]. If, on the other hand, credit is introduced into the game, default conditions must be part of the rules of this game unless credit is limited in such a way as to enable the debtor to pay back fully even under the worst scenario [*ibidem*: 30]. In a next step in the process of further complicating the model, (thereby making it closer to reality), the existence of a money market can be considered. A theoretical possibility is for everyone to be a banker (every individual is able to issue I.O.U. notes which are accepted as a means of payment by all others). However, for this game to be playable, rules are needed concerning the redemption of I.O.U. notes and what happens if there is a failure to redeem. As pointed out by Shubik, 'if there were no punishment for default the incentive to issue I.O.U. notes would be unbounded and would destroy any proposed active equilibrium' [*ibidem*: 35]. This said, it has to be admitted that the institutional arrangement required to make this 'everyone a banker' game playable—there is clearly a need for a clearinghouse as well as a device or referee to report failure to redeem and to enforce a penalty on defaulters—is too costly to be viable [*ibidem*: 37–38; see also Starr, 1986: 107].

   Another, more realistic model is that in which we find a bank (or a banking system), that is, an agent that buys personal debt and specie, issuing its own notes in payment. If there is no limit to the real value of this note issue, implying in particular that each agent can be issued (in exchange for his personal debt) sufficient notes to finance all of his desired purchases, it is essential that a rule exists to prevent any agent from making purchases in excess of his net worth [Starr, 1986]. Finally, when a Central Bank is introduced (to use fiat money with a view to enabling the traders to achieve optimal trade in the markets) and there is no limit to the volume of government credit that is issued, there must be a rule that each agent, at the end of the game, must repay to the government any debt outstanding [Shubik, 1986: 46–47].
4. In other words, tit-for-tat is a best reply to itself but not necessarily to any other strategy. In particular, tit-for-tat is not the best reply when the other agent plays a 'nasty' strategy consisting of defecting (acting dishonestly) in every round of the game.
5. This needs not be the only rational response available, though. One can indeed use variants of tit-for-tat in which one plays differently at unreached nodes.
6. Bear in mind that a subgame is the piece of a game 'that remains to be played beginning at any point at which the complete history of the game thus far is common knowledge among the players' [Gibbons, 1992: 94–95].
7. A stronger version of the *Folk Theorem* is couched in terms of subgame-perfect Nash equilibrium strategies: it shows that it is possible to find a pair of subgame-perfect equilibrium strategies to support any possible sequence of outcomes (provided it yields on average at least the minimax outcome to each player). In other words, in the infinite version of the Prisoner's Dilemma, any (finite) succession of actions can be shown to belong to a subgame-perfect equi-

librium strategy. As Abreu (1988) has shown, such strategies need not be particularly complex. More precisely, any subgame perfect outcome of an infinitely repeated game can be supported by a 'simple' strategy profile which are history-independent, that is they specify the *same* punishment for *any* deviation, after any previous history, by a particular player.

The result obtained by Abreu is especially powerful since it allows to overcome the potential complexities of plans of actions outside the equilibrium path:

> For instance a player who is being punished for a deviation may have 'myopic' incentives to cheat (i.e., the action stipulated by the equilibrium may not be a single period best response, in one or more stages of the punishment (path)). If so, perfection requires that he be deterred from cheating by the threat of a *further* punishment. This problem reappears at the next level and one is led into a *hierarchy* of punishments. Reflecting this complexity, an arbitrary strategy profile may be contingent on history in essential and elaborate ways. It may involve an infinity of punishments and a complicated rule specifying which punishment is imposed for any particular deviation from the initial path or from an ongoing punishment. Much of this potential complexity is in fact redundant [Abreu, 1988: 384].

8. Uncertainty about the type of the other player, and not only about the duration of the game, may produce cooperation. The most well-known result here is that of Kreps and his associates according to which, in a game of finite duration, a suspicion by one party that the other may practice a tit-for-tat strategy induces the other to adopt the same and both have then an incentive to cooperate till near the end of the game [Kreps and Wilson, 1982; Kreps et al., 1982; Kreps, 1990: 536–43; see also Friedman, 1990: 190–94]. This indicates that the set of Nash equilibria is not robust to slight perturbations. Thus, 'A one-in-one-thousand chance that one's opponent is generous, or that one's opponent assesses a substantial probability that oneself is benevolent, isn't much of a "change" in the game. Yet it completely changes the theoretical prediction', implying that we must be very wary of the theoretical prediction [Kreps, 1990: 542]. This agnostic conclusion can be actually tied back to reputation in the following sense:

> In the finitely repeated prisoners' dilemma, suppose one player assesses a small probability that the second will 'irrationally' play the strategy of tit-for-tat ... In a long-enough (but still finite) repetition of the game, if you think your opponent plays tit-for-tat, you will want to give cooperation a try. And even if your opponent isn't irrational in this fashion, the 'rational' thing for her to do is to mimic this sort of behavior to keep cooperation alive ... We can think of these effects as 'reputation' in the sense that a player will act 'irrationally' to keep alive the possibility that she is irrational, if being thought of as irrational will later be to that player's benefit through its influence on how others play. That is, in this sort of situation, players must weigh against the short-run benefits of certain actions the long-run consequences of their actions [Kreps, 1990: 542–43].

9. In the same vein, see Evans-Pritchard (1940), Colson (1974), Bates (1983), North (1990).

11 See, for example, Cordell and McKean [1986: 89, 91–96]; Levieil [1987: 74–85].

12 Of course, for the cooperative strategy to be sustainable, it is important that the gift should be costly to the giver while not being susceptible of recycling by 'parasites' intending to cheat (e.g., the gift is of no value to others or should be consumed quickly by the receiver). The latter condition is particularly adequate for the reason highlighted by Gregory: a gift is something inalienable that never really ceases to belong to its owner, it is like a betrothal ring that symbolizes a two-person alliance and will have to be returned to the donor should the relationship be broken.

13 The assumption is indeed that 'since the optimal wage decreases in the probability of future hiring, a cheater's optimal wage is higher than an honest agent's wage, and hence each merchant strictly prefers to hire an honest agent' [Greif, 1993: 534].

14 In actual fact the Maghribi traders retained their separate identity as long as they were active in long-distance trade. There is scant evidence of business associations between them and non-Maghribi traders whether of Jewish or Muslim origin [Greif, 1989: 877].

15 Path dependence means that 'the process by which we arrive at today's institutions is relevant and constrains future choices', with the result that one can observe persistent poor economic performance and long-run divergent patterns of development [North, 1990: 93; see also Matthews, 1986: 915; Basu, Jones, and Schlicht, 1987: 13]. Rather than being 'a story of inevitability in which the past neatly predicts the future', it is 'a way to narrow conceptually the choice set and link decision making through time' [North, 1990: 98–9]. The source from which path dependence stems lies in increasing returns which comprise several self-reinforcing mechanisms: large initial setup costs at the time of institutional innovation; learning effects; coordination effects (via contracts with other institutions or with the polity in complementary activities); and adaptive expectations which occur because increased prevalence of contracting based on a specific institution enhances beliefs of further prevalence [*ibidem*: 94–95; see also Bardhan, 1989].

16 In Italy, indeed, the autonomous cities, which held political control over the surrounding countryside, managed to destroy much of the nascent cottage sector while in the Low Countries, the other great medieval center of cloth manufacture, 'urban weavers marched into the villages to break cottage looms; and although the country weavers fought back, the putting out system was held in check for centuries'. In England, by contrast, 'local political autonomies made it hard for the monarchy to sustain corporate (guild) claims to monopoly' and, as a consequence, putting-out quickly developed (by the 15th century, more than half the nation's woolen cloth was being made in rural cottages) while guilds were gradually reduced to ceremonial fraternities [Landes, 1998: 43; see also Jones, 1981: 98–100].

17 I am indebted to Denis Dubuisson who made this field observation.

18. For a formal proof, see Greif, Milgrom, and Weingast (1992).

19. The fascinating question as to why rulers of important European city-states came to look favourably upon trade and tried to promote it rather than stifle it through unwise fiscal policies is clearly beyond the scope of this chapter. Among plausible answers, one may mention favourable geographical conditions [Hicks, 1969], and the acute degree of political competition prevailing among city-states in Europe—itself the end-result of the fragmentation of the Roman Empire and the ensuing division of power between the center (the crown) and local seigneurial authority [Landes, 1998: 36–38]. As a matter of fact, this unremitting competition encouraged continuous advances in military technology, which in turn compelled the rulers to have substantial resources at their command on a more or less continuous basis [Tilly, 1992].

20. As observed by Hicks, religious or ethnic connections among merchants can be helpful in providing the natural leaders and arbitrators needed to ensure effective collective action at local level [Hicks, 1969: 36–37; see also North, 1990: 127]. Yet, Hicks has probably a point when he observed that: 'The fact that European civilization has passed through a city-state phase is the principal key to the divergence between the history of Europe and the history of Asia' where progressive communities (like the Parsees of India) could not rely on the active support of their states [Hicks, 1969: 38]. Note that, as centuries passed and larger political units emerged in Europe, merchant guilds declined since their functions were gradually taken over by the state system [Greif, Milgrom, and Weingast, 1992: 27].

21. Except for the Champagne fairs, there seems to be little empirical (historical) support for the otherwise ingenious private judge system (personal communication of Avner Greif).

22. We do not therefore consider the mixed strategy equilibrium where players mix the two strategies with probability 1/2 of playing each pure strategy.

23. Suppose that this probability is denoted by $(1 - P)$. Then, for each player to be indifferent between H and C, P must satisfy the equation $30(1 - P) + 0P = 20(1 - P) + 10P$, yielding $P = 1/2$.

24. In the evolutionary model of Gaspart, a reproduction rule ensures that players with higher payoffs multiply: whenever a player gets a cumulative payoff of a certain amount, he gives birth to another player possessing the same features as himself. Moreover, expectations about others' predispositions to honesty are adjusted upwards after a good experience and downwards after a bad experience. Matching is decided randomly and moves are simultaneous.

# Chapter 7

## MARKET ORDER, THE RULE OF LAW AND MORAL NORMS

Before turning to the role of moral norms in supporting market exchanges and examining the motivations of norm-following which form the core object of this chapter (Section 3), there is need to re-emphasize the limitations of spontaneous market order institutions conceived as self-enforcing equilibria of repeated games (Section 1), and to point to the limitations of the rule of law and central enforcing agencies to regulate market behaviour (Section 2). The discussion of moral norms will lead us to draw a fundamental distinction between generalized and limited morality. While the latter inhibits the expansion of anonymous market exchanges, the former helps support trust in such exchanges. Norms of generalized morality will receive considerable attention in the course of Section 3 whereas those of limited morality will be commented on and illustrated in Section 4. The final chapter of this book, Chapter 8, is conceived as a direct continuation of the present chapter: it will be devoted to more dynamic considerations specially focusing on the question of the evolution of moral norms and the pervasive presence of path dependence phenomena.

### 7.1 THE LIMITATIONS OF SELF-ENFORCING EQUILIBRIA

As we have learned from the previous chapter, anonymous pairwise interactions among agents are generally not conducive to the sustained presence of 'nice traits' in the population. The difficulty actually arises from the fact that behaviours determined by 'nice traits' affect others in non-contractible ways, and that 'the regulation of non-contractible behaviours through market-like interactions generates analogues to familiar market failures' [Bowles, 1998a: 92–93]. Biased pairing of individuals following some cultural or geographical segmentation could, of course, solve the problem by internalizing part of the externality associated with nice behaviour, yet at the price of giving up the kind of conceptual framework that most closely resembles market conditions. Retaining anonymity but at the same time assuming that probability is higher to meet someone with whom one had a nice encounter in the past leads to the conclusion that honest behaviour can be established but that this is far from a certain result. The problem with this rather strange combination of assumptions, however, is that it is not easy to substantiate empirically: usually, we return to nice people because, in some way or other, we can recognize them, or be informed about them, which amounts to saying that a reputation effect is at work.

Regarding enforcement mechanisms based on reputation effects, we know that there exist a wide variety of situations in which such mechanisms can prove useful to discourage cheating and thereby make market exchanges possible. For example, Chinese businessmen residing in Southeast Asian towns tend to exchange among themselves credit information about indigenous customers, thereby reducing the frequency of their bad debts [Szanton, 1998: 256; see also Hayami and Kawagoe, 1993; Hayami, 1998]. In the more complex situations in which the domain of exchange is so wide, agents are so mobile, or economic transactions are so discontinous, that information cannot easily flow among potential traders, private third party mechanisms are needed to supplement communication networks. Yet, as has been illustrated in the case of the Law Merchant institution, there can be a number of rather stringent conditions to be fulfilled for a decentralized mechanism of information-pooling to be workable. In particular, if the benefits of honest behaviour are small compared with the one-time gain from cheating, or if would-be opportunists heavily discount future incomes, the decentralized punishment mechanism allowed by information-pooling may not be enough to discourage them from cheating. Moreover, agents' mistakes are susceptible of jeopardizing the kind of self-enforcing equilibria that may be produced in repeated games.

More importantly, nothing ensures that the right market governance institutions will be established. In point of fact, repeated game theory only shows that, in various situations, outcomes corresponding to these institutions are a possible equilibrium: it does not say that they will necessarily materialize.[1] Evidently, if distrust is pervasive, nasty strategies (and these include cautious strategies that prescribe non-cooperation in the initial stages of the game) are likely to be followed by a significant number of agents, with the consequence that honesty-enforcing mechanisms are precluded. Thus, Diego Gambetta has insisted that the promising tit-for-tat strategy is inconceivable without at least some predisposition to trust:

> ... when the game has no history a cooperative first move is essential to set it on the right track, and unconditional distrust could never be conceived as

> conducive to this.... This problem may be circumvented by assuming the presence of uncertain beliefs and a random distribution which accommodates the probability of the right initial move being made and being 'correctly' interpreted. Yet there is no reason why the appropriate conditional beliefs should typically be the case, and the optimal move may be hard to come upon by accident (while we may not want to have to wait for it to come upon us). If it is true that humans are characterized by a lack of fine-tuning and a tendency to go to extremes, the assumption that trust will emerge naturally is singularly unjustified... tit-for-tat can be an equilibrium only if both players believe the other will abide by it, otherwise other equilibria are just as possible and self-confirming [Gambetta, 1988b: 227–228; see also Binmore, 1992: 434].

There is undoubtedly a trust problem in the sense that a basic predisposition to trust must be present and be perceived for a cooperative equilibrium to prevail.[2] It is revealing that, in Ghana, contrary to what was observed above in the case of Chinese businessmen, 'there seems to be no mechanism whereby information about clients' trustworthiness is shared among firms other than direct recommendation by common acquaintances'. Apparently, firms relish 'the idea that their competitors have to deal with the same deadbeats by whom they had been burnt' [Fafchamps, 1996: 441].

Unfortunately, the trust problem is especially difficult to solve in modern economies because market-like situations involving competition among many anonymous buyers and sellers (and complete contracts) tend to induce self-regarding behaviour while more personalized exchange settings tend to yield choices consistent with other-regarding or relational preferences [Lane, 1991; Schotter et al., 1996; Bowles, 1998a: 87–90; 1998b; Ledeneva, 1998: 194–200].[3] The evidence pointing to this tendency, whether from historical materials or from experimental psychology (see infra), should not be construed as meaning that the market makes people intrinsically selfish, but rather that it evokes the self-regarding behaviours in their preference repertoires: individuals tend to behave selfishly in the market, altruistically in the family, and reciprocally in the workplace [Bowles, 1998a: 89]. I shall soon return to this important point.

## 7.2 THE RULE OF LAW AS A NECESSARY COMPLEMENT TO SPONTANENOUS ORDER

The most obvious way to get out of the above problem is the emergence of the third party enforcement of legal provisions by the modern, centralized nation-state. Although recognizing that 'quite complex exchange can be realized by creating third-party enforcement via voluntary institutions that lower information costs about the other party', Douglass North has thus laid considerable stress on the fact that 'historically the growth of economies has occurred within the institutional framework of well-developed coercive polities': the state was thus 'a major player' or a 'crucial actor in the process of economic specialization' that took place in Europe during modern times [North, 1990: 14; 1991: 107]. Ultimately, indeed, institutions that can enforce agreements by the threat of coercion are required to sustain complex exchange because the transaction costs of a purely voluntary system of third-party enforcement would be prohibitive [North, 1990: 58; see also 35, 47, 59, 109].[4]

For example, the aforementioned potential obstacles to information-pooling mechanisms probably explain why the Law Merchant system was eventually replaced by a system of state enforcement, typically in the late middle ages or the early modern era in western Europe.[5] Rather than depend for punishment upon the decentralized behaviour of merchants, recourse to the state authority when nations exercised extensive geographic control enabled the seizure of the property, or the imprisonment, of individuals who resisted paying judgments. Given the enlargement of the trade space, it is likely that the intervention of the state resulted in a reduction of the transaction costs of policing exchange [*ibidem*: 21].

In economically advanced countries of present times, it is actually not difficult to find illustrations of the fact that information-pooling mechanisms may need a legal support to work satisfactorily. In Belgium, for example, all credit institutions are now requested by the law to signal to a central agency (located in the Central Bank) all cases of default regarding personal consumption loans and credit to private firms. This is with a view to making such information available to all financial intermediaries. With respect to the first type of credit, when debts are repaid (if they ever are), credit institutions are again required to transmit the information so that the names of amended debtors can be erased from the official 'black list' (one year after the repayment). Moreover, since the 1st of April 1987, financial institutions are obliged by the law to consult the data file before granting a loan to a particular customer (subject to the ultimate sanction of withdrawal of registration certificate). Of course, they remain completely free to decide whether to accede or not to their customer's demand after the file's consultation [ABB, 1989]. Clearly, as the recent amendment of the system testifies, the mechanism did not previously work according to expectations: too many credit institutions did not apparently want to incur the cost of information query. In other words, the system was not self-enforcing [Platteau, 1994a: 565–66].

The development of the rule of law is unmistakably a central characteristic of the modern growth process of all the pioneer countries, as attested by the rising importance of laws for contract enforcement and respect of property rights, notaries for the recording of agreements, state courts for the resolution of disputes, and so on. In the Italian city-states, it is as early as the 12–13$^{th}$ centuries that covenants and contracts became central to all aspects of life, 'and the ranks of notaries, lawyers, and judges burgeoned to record, interpret, and enforce these agreements'. In Bologna, for example, a town of roughly 50,000 inhabitants, as many as 2,000 professional notaries were estimated to operate. Furthermore, an itinerant, professionally trained jurist-administrator elected for a limited term (known as the *podestà)*, came to play a key role in communal affairs [Putnam, 1993: 126; Greif, forthcoming: Chap. 5].

Note that, for North, it is the gradual and unusually successful blending of the voluntaristic structure of contract enforcement via merchant organizations with enforcement by the state, and the progressive encoding into formal laws of behavioural patterns determined by private order institutions that constituted the main factor behind the rise into prominence of the western world during the last centuries [North, 1990: 41, 43; 1991: 107; Kriegel, 1995: 72–78; Landes, 1998: 44].

It has been recently argued that the commercial legal system that is found in advanced market economies may be considered as a substitute to business networks. When the former develops, possibly out of informal contract enforcement mechanisms as suggested above, the latter become less necessary. Raja Kali (1998) has thus shown that business networks,—understood as groups of people trading with each other and obeying the norm of expelling anyone of them who has cheated once—, are endogenous to the reliability of the legal system. If this reliability is high, the anonymous market is likely to set itself at a low-dishonesty equilibrium because opportunists choose to behave honestly. In these conditions, a business network which functions as a self-selection device for individuals of different types,[6] is unenforceable. If, on the other hand, the legal system is largely unreliable, the opportunists behave dishonestly and a high-dishonesty regime comes to prevail. A business network becomes enforceable,[7] yet, in accordance with what has been said above about the existence of multiple equilibria, it must be stressed that nothing guarantees that individuals will actually succeed in organizing themselves into such a personalized network. Thus, if communities do not exist or are too big or too heterogeneous, informal community-based trust mechanisms may be unenforceable and, consequently, there may be no other way to the market order than a system of individual legal responsibility backed by the state.

It is precisely at this point that the possibility must be considered that the relationship brought into light by Kali actually works in the other way around: thus, if we follow Greif's analysis, we would expect legal codes to evolve more quickly in 'individualistic' than in 'collectivist' cultures because cultures based on 'individualistic' beliefs cannot rely on effective multilateral reputation mechanisms and business networks. In other words, 'collectivist' societies are more effective than 'individualistic' societies when division of labour and trade opportunities are relatively limited. Yet, when division of labour becomes more developed and exchange more complex, 'collectivist' beliefs become an obstacle to further development while 'individualistic' beliefs can then lead to an 'integrated' society in which intereconomy agency relations are established. This is apparently because the need for legal and political enforcement organizations without which such relations cannot be sustained at reasonable costs is more clearly felt and acted upon in 'individualistic' societies [Greif, 1994a].

Taiwan provides a good contemporary example of a developing country where the existence of pervasive business networks (known as *guanxi*) rooted in a deep tradition of personalized relations and reciprocal committments has given rise to a dense web of extremely dynamic small- and medium-scale enterprises that do not need to rely on formal legal contracts such as they are used in most advanced Western countries. In the words of Cheng-shu Kao, 'In order to obtain trust, persons have to demonstrate certain qualities according to intersubjective rules. These rules are not objectified, but are usually well recognized by the people involved. Because such informal, rather than formal, rules are used predominantly to regulate business activities, Western contractual relationships do not prevail' [Kao, 1991: 269]. Interestingly, *guanxi* relationships, which are not confined to the family circle, are built up through gift exchanges typical of traditional village societies (see *supra*, Chapter 6). Thus, when a person meets a potential partner with whom he has the right 'feeling', he does not use a contract to seal the deal; rather, he and his business partner reach an understanding that is sealed by reciprocating small gifts, drinks and banquets [Hamilton, 1998: 66].

In the aforementioned work of Kali, the implications of business networks for economic efficiency have been explored by comparing social welfare in two situations: when the anonymous market is the only exchange institution in the economy and when business networks coexist with the anonymous market. He then demonstrates that the existence of a business network may produce a negative externality on the functioning of the anonymous market. This is because it absorbs honest agents, thereby increasing the density of dishonest individuals involved in anonymous market exchange. It is only when a business group is relatively large that economic efficiency is achieved.[8] The lesson is that informal contract enforcement institutions may be inefficient in general equilibrium even though they enhance efficiency in partial equilibrium.[9] Moreover, as the behaviour of many mafias attests, personalized networks, once formed, may have a vested interest in preventing any improvement of the legal system of codes and courts, thereby precluding the achievement of efficiency gains in the economy.

We have seen earlier that informal governance systems may be problematic because they succeed only very imperfectly in discouraging cheating or because, even when they have that potential ability, the suitable self-enforcing mechanism may fail to be established. It must now be added that the partial equilibrium result that informal contract enforcement institutions enhance economic efficiency is not robust to a general equilibrium extension. In particular, the existence of personalized business networks [see, e.g., Woolsey-Biggart and Hamilton, 1992; Hayami and Kawagoe, 1993; Fukuyama, 1995; Hodder, 1996; Hefner, 1998; Hayami, 1998] does not constitute prima facie evidence that the market economy functions efficiently either in a static or in a dynamic sense. Hence the above-stressed need for the development of the rule of law.

That informal norms or mechanisms can be substitutes to formal laws and institutions, and vive-versa, is only one possibility that ought not to be overplayed, however. In many situations, indeed, it is more likely that social norms and laws are mutually supporting, [Axelrod, 1986: 61], thereby vindicating the coexistence of the market, the state and the community. There are actually two sets of reasons why the fundamental problem of the market order cannot be solved satisfactorily by creating highly evolved political and juridical institutions [Elster, 1989a: 276]. First, for small transactions, legal costs are typically too high to justify having recourse to legal procedures and court action [Fafchamps, 1996: 428]. While laws often function best to prevent rare but large defections because substantial resources are available for enforcement (and while legal codification is often useful to clarify rights and obligations as well as to avoid mistakes), social norms are usually best at preventing numerous small defections where the cost of enforcement is low [Axelrod, 1986: 61]. Second, two incentive problems tend to plague legal institutions. For one thing, as underlined by Kenneth Arrow: 'It is not adequate to argue that there are enforcement mechanisms, such as police and the courts; these are themselves services bought and sold, and it has to be asked why they will in fact do what they have contracted to do' [Arrow, 1973: 24—cited from Williamson, 1985: 405; see also Arrow, 1971: 22; Phelps, 1975]. For another thing, it is not because the law exists, even at the request of the people themselves, that it will be abided by them. The fact of the matter is that they have an incentive unilaterally to violate rules which they otherwise support.

In situations where fraud and deceit are widespread, people may be led to demand strong sanction systems so as to prevent rule-breaking and thereby reassure everybody that the rules are followed by others. Under their active or passive support, an authoritarian state bent on establishing or restoring 'law and order' may thus be called into being. As pointed out by Edward Banfield (1958), it is in societies pervaded by distrust and 'amoral familism' (such as those of southern Italy) that people believe most in the need for a strong state to control their untrustworthy fellow citizens [see also Putnam, 1993: 112; Fukuyama, 1995: 99]. The obvious difficulty with this solution is that it involves high administrative costs, creates a repressive climate around economic dealings, and risks entailing a generalized loss of freedom that people may later regret.

True, in order to economize on the costs of policing 'good behaviour', the state can decide to shift part of these costs to the citizens themselves. The easiest way of doing this is through denunciation of deviant behaviour by the people themselves (possibly against some attractive rewards, material or symbolic) when the authorities define what is deviant behaviour. In so far as not joining in this form of punishment is itself taken as an act of rebellion against the authorities, a metanorm (Axelrod) is involved (see infra). Such a metanorm is especially perverse, not least because the vesting of prosecutorial powers in the public tends to be self-defeating. As a matter of fact, it ultimately creates distrust rather than trust and is bound to unleash a witch-hunt by playing upon the worst human proclivities, those born of envious feelings, jealousy and professional rivalry. In the end, one does not know whether someone accused of being a 'speculator' is not just a fair competitor (in the economic, political, or private life domains) whom the denouncer wants to get rid of. As attested by the experience of Stalinist USSR or of the Cultural Revolution in China, distrust may thus not be confined to economic dealings but spill over into all spheres of human interaction. As a result, fear and suspicion infiltrate the whole society and individuals tend to withdraw from as many social intercourses as possible, to shun away from all risky ventures, and to take refuge in private life.[10] It is not surprising that, in such a climate, 'the word 'conscience' had gone out of ordinary use to be replaced by so-called 'class feelings' and later 'the good of the state' implanted in people's minds by 'propagandist brainwashing' [MacDonald, 1991: 123; see also Lane, 1991: 217].

Clearly, the 'Russian way' does not constitute an attractive solution to the trust problem. It is actually the product of a long history of strong central rule and state patrimonialism dating back to the Muscovy state born in the middle of the 15th century [see, e.g., Anderson, 1974: Chap. 6; Raeff, 1984; Platonov, 1985; Riasanovsky, 1993; Pipes, 1995, 1999: Chap. 4; Hosking, 1997]. Western European countries, thanks to their having been placed on a different institutional trajectory, were able to evolve more cost-effective solutions to allow for the expansion of trade relationships and the rise of economic specialization. Two characteristics of these countries's experience deserve attention. First, the domain of public power is restricted, implying that many aspects of social intercourse which create opportunities for conflict could be organized by the individuals themselves, according to certain informal standards or fundamental rules for mutual tolerance. This is an essential feature because 'life in society, as we know it, would probably be intolerable if formal rules should be required for each and every area where interpersonal conflict might arise' [Buchanan, 1975: 118–19]. And, second, to the extent that formal rules are needed to resolve conflicts, the costs of operating law-enforcing agencies is not too high [*ibidem*, and Shott, 1979: 1329].

These two achievements—the thriving of civil society and dynamic associative movements, on the one hand, and a good measure of law abidingness, on the other hand—would not have been possible without the continuous operation of moral norms conducive to the building up of trust. In fact, moral norms act as a substitute for, or a reinforcement of, state-engineered rules or control mechanisms, with the result that enforcement and punishment institutions become of secondary importance. The first effect (substitution) derives from the fact that individuals internalize public good considerations while the second one (reinforcement) arises from their conviction that the law represents the public good. In this perspective, civic consciousness appears as this attitude of respect for the law which tends to prevail among citizens who have such a conviction. When individuals thus place a high value on obedience to law, the announcement and enactment of the rules that constrain behaviour suffice to cause compliance. As reminded by Daniel Hausman and Michael McPherson (1996: 57), Adam Smith did not fail to see that no legal system 'could rely purely on criminal sanctions for its enforcement. A widespread conviction that people ought to obey the law is essential to the maintenance of social order'.

From recent empirical studies conducted mainly in the United States, there is evidence that normative concerns, rather than purely instrumental considerations based on cost-benefit calculus, are an important determinant of law-abiding behaviour. In fact, voluntary compliance with the law depends on the extent to which people assess its legitimacy and assessment of the law's legitimacy is strongly influenced by their assessment of the fairness of procedures used by the police and the courts. Procedural fairness, rather than distributive fairness (fairness of the outcomes themselves) or other aspects of procedures unrelated to fairness, such as expediency and predictability, that seems to be the key to personal judgments of legitimacy understood as the perceived right of public authority to dictate people's behaviour [Tyler, 1990: Chap. 5–6]. In the words of Tom Tyler, 'Recent studies cast doubt on whether an instrumental perspective is adequate for explaining people's reactions to their experiences [with police officers and judges]. Issues of justice are uniformly found to have an important role in shaping such reactions. In particular, issues of procedural justice dominate generalizations from experiences to views about law and authority' [*ibidem*: 84].

Clearly, the fact that laws provide external validation of underlying social norms appears to be an important factor of effective implementation of the former. It also testifies that, in most situations, the law can only work as a supplement (and not a replacement) for informal enforcement of norms [Axelrod, 1986: 61].

## 7.3 THE ROLE OF MORAL NORMS

### *The function of moral norms and the motivations of norm-following*

The sharing norms studied in Chapter 5 as well as the various governance mechanisms or self-enforcing institutions discussed in Chapter 6 have been conceptualized as Nash equilibria of particular games (situations where the agents' preferences or payoffs as well as the information structure of their interactions have been specified). Such equilibria can be conceived as social norms (or community, or club norms) in the sense of behavioural patterns which agents want to follow given their expectations regarding others' behaviours including the punishments meted out to players guilty of non-cooperative moves. In other words, a social norm corresponds to a certain profile of strategies that are self-enforceable and sustainable once established [Aoki, forthcoming: Chap. 1; see also Kandori, 1992; Greif, forthcoming].[11]

Moral norms as they are understood in the remainder of this chapter are a different concept. They are not endogenous outcomes of interactions among individuals acting strategically within a given framework. After all, the behaviour of most people who refrain from running away, without paying their bill, from an oil station or a restaurant which they do not expect to visit again, or from taking free taxi rides, can obviously not be conceptualized as a game equilibrium. Neither does such type of conceptualization square with the results from designed experiments that show relatively high rates of cooperation in PD-structured games that are played only once or where defection cannot be detected, or that show significant levels of generosity even towards strangers.[12]

Rather than self-enforcing equilibria on which people coordinate, moral norms are viewed here as cultural beliefs that have the effect of truncating the players' strategy space or of modifying their preferences or payoffs.

In the former case, by ruling out some strategies because there are things that 'are not done', they may favour the selection of the cooperation equilibrium. Moral norms then provide the kind of 'friction' required to make the 'good' equilibrium more likely [Dasgupta, 1988: 70–71]. For example, in the initial stages of a repeated game, it is not considered ethical to cheat partners who belong to one's community because trust ought to be tried when one deals with people sharing common identity feelings. Subsequently, if partners have behaved honestly in the initial rounds, honest behaviour should be pursued. In other words, the tit-for-tat strategy is a sort of focal strategy suggested by the moral code inherent in community ties and, as we know, if everyone adheres to this strategy, the honesty equilibrium will be established. Some authors actually believe that such a moral code tends to evolve spontaneously when individuals interact frequently [Homans, 1950, 1958; Greif, 1994a]. In the latter case, what makes the honesty equilibrium more likely is a change of payoffs induced by the inculcation of moral norms. Here, one can think of the transformation of a PD into an AG that may occur if such norms penalize any behaviour that exploits the benevolence or goodwill of a partner. A moral norm therefore appears as a social norm that forces or leads people to take others' interests into account.[13]

What is it that motivates people to follow a moral norm? One possibility is that 'people's desire to act on principles that no rational agent could reasonably reject, or their desire not to free-ride, but to do their part in practices of which they approve, can motivate them to follow norms, even when doing so will not benefit them materially' [Hausman and McPherson, 1996: 58]. Thus, the Kantian generalization principle according to which an action is morally possible only if it can be universalized without self-contradiction provides a good ground for moral behaviour: 'one ought to abstain from any action that would threaten to disrupt social order were everybody to undertake it or that one would not be prepared to see everyone else adopt'. The idea is therefore that the good consequences of a moral norm can motivate people to abide by it. Yet, such an explanation suffers from the functionalist bias and remains incomplete as long as a proper account is not offered of the mechanisms by which the favourable consequences help produce or sustain the moral practice [Elster, 1989a, 1989b].

Reading David Hume, one thus gains the impression that, for him, the (presumably long-term) individual interests of economic agents coincide with the 'common benefit', and these agents are able to understand such a congruence. When they do, moral norms can be established. In his own words:

> ... and when each individual perceives the same sense of interest in all his fellows, he immediately performs his part of any contract, as being assured that they will not be wanting in theirs. All of them, by concert, enter into a scheme of actions, calculated for common benefit, and agree to be true to their words; nor is there anything requisite to form this concert or convention, but that every one have a sense of interest in the faithful fulfilling of engagements, and express that sense to other members of the society. This immediately causes that interest to operate upon them; and interest is the *first* obligation to the performance of promises. Afterwards a sentiment of morals concurs with interest, and becomes a new obligation upon mankind [Hume, 1740: Book III, Part II, Sect. V, 522–23; see also Book II, Part II, Sect. VII and Part III, Sect. VI].

A few decades later, Adam Smith came up with his notion of the 'impartial spectator' which allows for the workings of 'sympathy' feelings among individuals and thereby permits the establishment of common moral standards in the population. In his view, saying that all individuals have a capacity for sympathy with others means that they are all able, by an act of imagination, to adopt the others' viewpoint and to understand their reactions [see, in particular, Smith, 1759: Part III, chap. I]. This capacity of sympathetic identification which enables actors to adopt the standpoint of an impartial spectator who observes situations of human interactions dispassionately is the fundamental basis of society: it supplies a system of cultural restraints in which moral checks upon the passion of self-love can be embedded [McNally, 1988: 182; Brown, 1988: 61–62, 67; Young, 1992: 73–77]. In Smith's own words:

> We endeavour to examine our own conduct as we imagine any other fair and impartial spectator would examine it. If, upon placing ourselves in his situation, we thoroughly enter into all the passions and motives which influenced it, we approve of it, by sympathy with the approbation of this supposed equitable judge. If otherwise, we enter into his disapprobation and condemn it...Before we can make any proper comparison of opposing interests, we must change our position. We must view them from neither our own place nor yet from his, neither with our own eyes nor yet with his, but from the place and with the eyes of a third person, who has no particular connection with either, and who judges impartially between us [Smith, 1759: 110, 135].

An important point to make while dealing with moral norms is the following: moral norms are never completely compelling and decision outcomes cannot be considered to be mechanically determined. As has been aptly remarked by Elster, moral beings are usually outcome-insensitive with respect to benefits but not with respect to costs: the costs of cooperation (honesty) may be so high as to offset the call of duty. Furthermore, they are somewhat sensitive to benefits in the following sense: if they do not consider the likely impact of their own cooperation (honesty), they pay attention to the impact of universal cooperation (honesty). It is plausible that the strength of their feelings of duty depends on the difference between universal cooperation (honesty) and universal noncooperation (dishonesty): 'The smaller the difference, the lower the voice of conscience and the more likely it is to be offset by considerations of cost' [Elster, 1989a: 193]. The predilection of economists and some sociologists is therefore to analyze norm-following as a problem of individual choice. In other words, the concept of norm suggests a standard of conduct which people believe they ought to follow lest they should expose themselves to some way of sanctioning or unpleasant experience. Obedience of the norm will occur when the sanctions or discomfort are sufficiently great and sufficiently certain to make disobedience less immediately attractive than obedience [Coleman, 1987: 135, 141–42; 1990: 242–43].

Because people are always somehow sensitive to the costs of honesty, morality does not usually mean unconditional commitment—'each individual behaves the way he would wish others to behave, regardless of which way they actually behave'. This ethical principle indeed appears as too strong a tenet to form the basis of practical morality: honesty is too costly when people who behave honestly are constantly cheated. A more realistic code of moral behaviour is the principle of reciprocity or 'reciprocal fairness' that underlies the payoff structure of the aforementioned assurance game and that has been already mentioned earlier (see Chapter 1): according to this code, 'you behave the way which you would like the others to behave, but only if they actually meet this expectation' [Sugden, 1984: 774–75; Elster, 1989a: 214]. In other words, people want to be kind to those who have been kind to them (the positive reciprocity aspect) and to hurt those who hurt them (the negative reciprocity aspect) [Fehr and Tyran, 1996: 134; see also Rabin, 1993].[14]

If we believe in experimental evidence, reciprocity appears as an empirically important motivational drive [see, e.g., Eiser, 1978; Roth, 1988, 1995; Roth et al., 1991; Dawes and Thaler, 1988; Frank, 1988: 213–16; Camerer and Thaler, 1995; Fehr and Tyran, 1996; Fehr et al., 1997, 1998, forthcoming; Rabin, 1998: 21–24], a finding confirmed by questionnaire studies [see, e.g., Kahnemann, Knetsch, and Thaler, 1986; Agell and Lundberg, 1995] and by some anthropological works as well [e.g., Bromley and Chapagain, 1984; Bagchi, 1992; Boehm, 1993]. Thus, splits obtained in ultimatum games indicate (i) that responders punish proposers if they perceive that the latter make unfairly asymmetrical proposals of sharing the available bargaining pie,[15] and (ii) that proposers seem to anticipate this willingness of responders to punish unfair proposals (they will prefer to take nothing rather than accept a small amount). Also, experiments with 'gift exchange games', such as have been conducted by Ernst Fehr and his colleagues, show that firms tend to rely on their workers' drives of positive reciprocity and to make generous wage offers in order to elicit nonminimal effort levels from them. Such results, it is worth noting, continue to hold under high stake conditions and under double anonymity conditions.

Moreover, reciprocity is more likely in long-term relationships, not a surprising result since there are more opportunities for reciprocation of both the positive and negative kinds when parties interact longer. In addition, people seem to 'determine their dispositions towards others according to motives attributed to these others, not solely according to actions taken'. In particular, volition is central to the propensity to retaliate against negative actions [Rabin, 1998: 22–23].[16]

Another crucial finding is that, as already pointed out earlier in this chapter, the institutional context seems to affect human behaviour. Thus, the impact of reciprocity is negligible if contracts are completely specified. In other words, competitive markets with completely specified contracts quickly converge to the competitive equilibrium even if the resulting allocation is unfair by almost any conceivable definition of fairness (except, of course, the notion of fairness based on market-clearing as a means to prevent waste). By contrast, reciprocity plays an important role when contracts are incompletely specified, even in the cases where incomplete contract situations are embedded in a competitive market. In other words, 'the existence of opportunities for reciprocation may significantly alter market outcomes' [Fehr et al., 1998: 19]. For example, wages offered by firms in conditions of a large excess supply of workers never come close to the market clearing level when firms do not know the effort they would get from the workers who accept their contract. Again, this is because firms try to induce workers' positive reciprocity.[17]

A plausible explanation for this contrast can be framed in terms of a kind of strategic stability of the equilibrium: indeed, whereas in competitive situations a lone selfish (rational) individual becomes the marginal agent and therefore determines the price outcome, the converse is true in settings resembling an ultimatum game or a gift exchange game. Thus, in a Bertrand game, if there is a very small fraction, $\varepsilon$, of individuals who behave rationally (selfishly), the equilibrium achieved will be the same as that which would obtain if all individuals were of the rational type: the equilibrium is strategically stable in that sense. In the ultimatum or the gift exchange game, by contrast, it is the 'irrational' (reciprocally fair) individuals who, through their reciprocating behaviour, exert an impact on the behaviour of the rational (selfish) agents. In the ultimatum game, if the proposer (assumed to be a rational selfish agent) expects the responder to be driven by reciprocal fairness considerations, he knows that unfair proposals will be rejected and are therefore better avoided. In the gift exchange game with incomplete labour contracts, if the rational firm knows that workers are reciprocators, it has no incentive to offer market-clearing wages (in conditions of excess supply of labour). Thus, if there is only a fraction $\varepsilon$ of reciprocators in the population, this is sufficient to force the selfish individuals to adjust their behaviour. To put it in another way, even as high a proportion of selfish individuals as $(1 - \varepsilon)$ is not sufficient to establish the same equilibrium as that which would obtain if there were 100 per cent egoists in the population: the equilibrium is strategically unstable.

### *The role of emotions*

When transactions are one-shot deals that take place between strangers, the principle of reciprocal fairness can be taken to mean that the utility from abiding by a norm, or the disutility from violating it, rises with the level of adherence in the general population [Lindbeck et al., 1996; Ambec, 1998]. Or, in the former kind of situations more specifically, someone who benefitted from a favour becomes the others' benefactor, whereas a harmed person becomes non-cooperative [Fehr and Tyran, 1996: 134]. From the last section of Chapter 6, however, we know that, as soon as we posit the presence of a certain proportion of inveterate opportunists in the population, it is only under special conditions that honest behaviour may be expected to get established and survive under the influence of reciprocal fairness motivations (without being able to eliminate fraudulent behaviour altogether). The sustainability of honesty becomes a more realistic prospect if, instead of simply following the principle of negative reciprocity which implies the giving up of honest behaviour as a result of bad experiences, agents are prone to punish dishonest people in a more straightforward manner, that is, if they adopt what Trivers (1971) has called 'moralistic reciprocity'.

The second-order public good problem of the nature of the incentives to punish non-cooperators then immediately arises. As a matter of fact, if punishment is costly while the benefits of honesty accrue to the population as a whole, why should selfish individuals chose to punish? This problem may be solved if a metanorm suggests the treatment of non-punishment as if it were another form of defection [Axelrod, 1986], that is, if moralistic reciprocators punish not only people who behave dishonestly but also those who fail to punish dishonest agents or who fail to punish non-punishers. When such strategies are common, it can pay to punish, even though the resulting spreading of honesty is not sufficient to compensate some individual punishers for the cost of punishing. If moralistic reciprocators are sufficiently numerous, the cost of punishing dishonest behaviour may be small, and the cost of being punished large [Fehr and Tyran, 1996: 142–43].

Using computer simulation techniques to analyze the impact of metanorms in an evolutionary framework, Robert Axelrod (1986) has also reached striking conclusions. In his models, the agents' payoff structure is that of a PD (and not that of an AG), and a strategy has two dimensions: boldness (the largest probability of being detected that will lead to a choice of defection) and vengefulness (the probability of punishing someone observed defecting). Punishing a defector involves a positive enforcement cost.[18] The dynamics of the simple norms game reveals that the norm of cooperation is not sustainable because after some time players are very bold but not very vengeful, and this outcome is stable.[19] Things turn out much better when the possibility of punishing non-punishers is allowed for. Indeed, in the so-called metanorms game, cooperation can be promoted and sustained in a population provided that initial levels of vengefulness are sufficiently high and that players have correlated degrees of vengefulness against a defector and against someone who tolerates such a violation of the norm. In other words, 'the metanorm provides a mechanism by which the norm against defection becomes self-policing' if the initial conditions are favourable enough [*ibidem*, 1986: 55].[20]

Metanorms may obviously exist and are an interesting mechanism to establish and sustain cooperation or honesty. The difficulty with the metanorms equilibrium, however, is that it represents only one among an infinity of possible equilibria and that nothing therefore guarantees that it will be spontaneously established [for other limitations of higher-order sanction mechanisms, see Elster, 1989a, 1989b].

Another possibility exists that has not escaped the attention of Axelrod (1986: 57–58): a cooperation norm can be promoted and sustained if, instead of incurring a cost for the punishment of defectors, agents are rewarded for such an act, implying that they feel some sort of a gain from punishing (what he calls the 'internalization' mechanism).[21] Honest people can thus be motivated to sanction fraudulent practices because they feel morally shocked or outraged by the behaviour of transactors who cynically exploit the benevolence of other honest agents. To relieve their feelings of indignation and anger (or what Axelrod calls their vengefulness), they are then apparently willing to incur personal costs: emotions drive these moral or self-righteous individuals to behave 'irrationally' (i.e., in a reciprocally fair manner), but in a way that is ultimately beneficial to society. Or, to put it in another way, when a person is motivated by indignation, his act of punishment (e.g., his rejection of a bad offer in an ultimatum game) will give him the 'pleasure of revenge' [Elster, 1998: 69], so that the cost of punishment is only apparent or is compensated for by a pleasurable emotion. In such conditions, reciprocity appears as a propensity to behave honestly with other people sharing the same disposition, and a willingness to punish those who violate the ethical code of honesty, even at a personal cost.

The fact of the matter is that often operating in individuals are internal rewards and sanctions which are manifested in the form of self-satisfaction feelings aroused by abidance of the honesty code[22] and in the form of guilt feelings aroused by violation of this code. The other side of the guilt-feeling process is precisely the aforementioned reaction of indignation and moral outrage sparked by observations of cheating on the part of other individuals. Internal rewards and sanctions are generated by moral norms which have been internalized by the individuals (in Freudian terms, they form their *superego*) and provide society with a self-policing mechanism that exempts its members (or the state authorities) from the need to resort to external monitoring and punishment devices.

Internalization of standards may be said to arise when an individual actually conforms because of a personal attitude about the act itself, that is, when conformity becomes a motive of its own because it is intrinsically rewarding or because deviation is intrinsically costly [Weber, 1971: 22–23; Opp, 1979: 777, 792; 1982: 146; Jones, 1984: 89; Taylor, 1987: 13]. Hence 'internalization refers to the aspect of the process of socialization through which attitudes, values, and behaviour patterns come to be maintained even in the absence of external rewards or punishments' [Jones, 1984: 89–90; see also Aronfreed, 1968, 1969, 1970: 104; Bergsten, 1985: 115; Coleman, 1990: 245, 293]. As a result, moral norms are followed even when violation would be undetected, and therefore unsanctioned, because the moral act, which appears to be in conflict with the immediate or direct interests of the actor himself, is valued for its own sake [Griffith and Goldfarb, 1991; Elster, 1989a: 131, 1989b: 104].[23]

Now, an important lesson from developmental psychology is that moral behaviour and the ability to empathize emerge hand-in-hand with the maturation of specific emotional competencies.[24] In this maturation process, identification obviously plays a crucial role since a failure to follow the standards set (consciously or not) by reference persons is bound to generate the painful feeling that one is unable to meet their expectations and, thereby, to deserve their love or respect. Thus, the principal claim of Kagan (1984) is that moral norms are actually supported by a limited number of simple, highly uniform emotional capacities.[25] According to him, the main motivating force behind moral behaviour is the desire to avoid feelings of guilt and shame[26] which are themselves the combined outcome of unpleasant emotions such as anxiety.

'Bad' or unpleasant feelings stirred by violations of the prevailing moral norms are the ingredients of a 'tortured conscience' which tend to deter many people from breaking these norms. Such deterrence would not occur if violating norms was just felt as a mistake or a lapse from rationality [Elster, 1989a: 188]. Moreover, as found in numerous experiments, subjects induced to commit some transgression (or to believe that they have transgressed) are more likely than nontransgressors to engage in altruistic or compensatory behaviour. This is apparently because they are eager to repair their self-conception or self-presentation so as to convince themselves as well as others of their moral worthiness [Shott, 1979: 1327; Darley and Latané, 1970: 100–101].[27] Also, the fact that guilt feelings may reasonably be thought to increase with the incidence of norm obedience (with the proportion of honestly behaving agents) in the population is to be related to the aforementioned point that the disutility from violating the honesty norm rises with the level of general adherence.

To sum up, the effect of moral upbringing is (1°) to inculcate in people preferences of the reciprocity type by leading them to adopt the others' viewpoint in situations where their own acts are susceptible of causing harm to others; (2°) to instill an optimistic rather than a cynical perception of other individuals, thereby contributing to establish trust in the others' predisposition to abide by the same ethical code,[28] (3°) to make external monitoring and punishment of dishonest behaviour less necessary owing to the desire to avoid guilt feelings and enjoy the pleasure of self-satisfaction; (4°) to drive people to resist the temptation to give in too easily to dishonest behaviour after they had unpleasant experiences in which they were the victims of fraud and malpractices; and (5°) to arouse feelings of moral outrage so that they are willing to detect and punish dishonest behaviour even at a personal cost and when they have not been themselves harmed by this behaviour.

Through these five effects, the inculcation of moral norms helps establish an equilibrium dominated by honest behaviour. If we again refer back to Gaspart's evolutionary model with anonymous pairwise interactions, it is thus evident that the above effects make a honesty equilibrium more likely and more lasting. The first effect modifies individual preferences in such a way that the PD game, where universal cheating is the only (Nash) equilibrium, becomes transformed into an AG where honesty is a possible equilibrium outcome. By establishing trust, the second effect increases the likelihood that honest behaviour will be actually chosen by individuals with a reciprocity-type payoff structure. As for the last three effects, they help establish the dynamic sustainability of the honesty equilibrium.

Note that, in Gaspart's evolutionary game, information is asymmetric (agents ignore the type of the partner with whom they are going to deal) so that complete contracting is impossible. Moral norms based on reciprocal behaviour are therefore liable to create conditions conducive to honesty, all the more so if their internalization ensures a strong variety of reciprocity where guilt feelings govern behaviour and agents agree to punish cheaters at a positive cost to themselves. In competitive situations with complete contracting,—which are not frequent in the real world—, moral norms are of little avail since, as has been explained above, the presence of even a small fraction of opportunistic agents in the population is sufficient to defeat other agents whose motivations are driven by reciprocity considerations.[29]

Finally, it deserves to be emphasized that market economies cannot function effectively if property rights (whether private or public) are not respected by a considerable majority of citizens. A situation in which individuals have the possibility to steal goods or assets belonging to other agents (or to the state) without incurring too high a risk of being detected is not akin to a game (there is no strategic interaction) but to a single-person choice problem. It is straightforward that, in such situations, inculcation of moral norms helps prevent thefts. Yet, since moral beings are reciprocators, they are not ready to endlessly refrain from stealing if they somehow come to learn that many other individuals violate property rights. In other words, a game-like situation is created by the fact that individuals are sensitive to how other people behave, and the game actually resembles the one used to study anonymous exchange between strategic transactors. Through the five above effects, moral norms thus increase the chances that an equilibrium comes into being where respect of property rights is pervasive.

*Generalized morality and the market order*

From the above discussion, it is evident that inculcation of moral norms involves much more than purely cognitive learning. This is particularly true of primary socialization which an individual undergoes in childhood since it takes place under circumstances that are highly charged emotionally [Berger and Luckmann, 1967: 149–57]. What needs to be emphasized now is that primary socialization creates in the child's consciousness a progressive abstraction from the roles and attitudes of concrete significant others (usually the parents) to roles and attitudes in general, implying that the child becomes able to identify 'with a generality of others, that is, with a society' [*ibidem*: 152–3; Lane, 1991: 82].[30] This is an important aspect since any moral rule includes an element of conceptual generality that involves the capacity to recognize the claims of others and to impose such rules both on oneself and on others similarly situated [Griffith and Goldfarb, 1991].

If generalized morality is to be capable of sustaining order in a wide market domain, it is essential that concern for others or ability to see things from another's viewpoint be based on identity or loyalty feelings towards a large reference group. This is precisely the condition which Mark Granovetter finds problematic. He indeed contends that norms of limited-group rather than generalized morality can tame fraud and deceit: in his own words, networks of relations, rather than institutional arrangements or generalized morality, 'are the structure that fulfills the function of sustaining order' [Granovetter, 1985: 491].

Nonetheless, the ability to recognize the claim of a large generality of others is clearly present in the Christian ethical principle according to which we ought not to do to other people what we would not like them to do to us. And Max Weber, as is well-known, has contrasted the achievement of generalized morality (what he called 'universally binding morality') in western Europe in modern times with the limited domain of trust in traditional societies.

Weber's point is indeed that the universal diffusion of unscrupulousness in the pursuit of self-interest was far more common in precapitalist societies than in their more competitive capitalist counterparts [Weber, 1970—quoted from Gambetta, 1988b: 215–16]. While normative behaviour based on the principle of reciprocity ('I cannot expect others to deal honestly with me unless I am honest with them') was restricted to real kith and kin in the former societies, security of expectation or assurance has been provided by the pervasive influence of a code of generalized morality in the latter. Such a code can be considered as 'the great achievement of the ethical religions' which succeeded in destroying 'the fetters of the kin', an outcome which could not materialize in China where 'the fetters of the kinship group were never shattered' owing to the absence of a similar ideology [Weber, 1951: 237—quoted from Pagden, 1988: 139]. Note that reference to the case of China is probably unfortunate since, if this country had no established faith (it was indeed characterized by an extraordinary religious tolerance), it could rely on a rather perfect lay morality (Confucianism) which the mandarinate and imperial court helped maintain and enforce over the centuries [Landes, 1998: 38].

In a similar line to Weber, Adam Seligman has recently emphasized the crucial role of Protestantism in 'privatizing morality', that is, in placing an ever-increasing stress 'on the individual, the individual conscience, and the realm of the private as *the* arena of religious activity'. This revolution implied the rejection of the authority of ecclesiastical institutions and the grounding of religious life in the individual believer's inner ability to know religious truth. Most relevant to the present discussion, it led to the construction of new social identities stretching beyond the confines of traditional ties of the neighbourhood, the village, or the parish [Seligman, 1997: 138–141]. Seligman thus points to a decisive shift from limited to generalized morality when he speaks about the recasting of the bonds of 'community' as a shared tradition into new bonds of 'communality': 'Integrating all communal members in one collective definition, the boundaries between insider and outsider no longer ran through the community, but rather through each individual member', as a result of which 'the crossing of a boundary in the move from profane to sacred and from outsider to insider...became less a public ceremony and more a private rite' [*ibidem*: 136, 141].

Other authors have highlighted the role of political doctrines in the diffusion of generalized morality. The ability to put others on a similar footing with oneself would thus lie at the heart of classical republicanism, a political doctrine (initially formulated by Nicolo Machiavelli and several of his contemporaries and later taken over by Alexis de Tocqueville) centered around the notions of a well-ordered republic and public-spirited commitment to the common good. The emphasis on virtues of civic humanism or consciousness and on the need to withstand the dictates of private interest whenever they undermine the public good were expected to enable men from different kin groups to trust each other, thus making possible the operation of a 'commercial society' [Pagden, 1988: 139; McNally, 1988: 40–43]. The communal republics of Northern Italy during late medieval times served as a reference case for many founders of this political doctrine: thanks to a first and fervent allegiance to their own city-state, members of these mini-republics are supposed to have shown an unparalleled degree of civic engagement, as a result of which trust could be extended beyond the limits of kinship further than anywhere else in Europe in this era [Putnam, 1993: 127–131; Fukuyama, 1995: 108].[31] According to Skinner, the social ethos of Calvinism can be actually seen to constitute a special case of classical republicanism [Skinner, 1974]. In other words, 'it was not a specifically Calvinist or Puritan work ethic which encouraged economic take-off in the Protestant cities of the seventeenth century, or Christianity itself in the medieval cities of north and central Italy, but the secular ethic of classical republicanism' [Pagden, 1988: 139].

The fact of the matter is that it is extremely difficult to disentangle the respective influences of political and religious doctrines as well as their mutual cross-fertilization, even when they appear strongly antagonistic. Just to take one example, free masonry developed in many western European countries as a reaction against church establishments and the pervasive influence of religious tenets. Yet, in some significant respects, it retained ritualistic forms evoking those prevailing among the despised believers and, although dressed in a different gown, it continued to spread moral precepts of the generalized variety. More generally, as pointed out by Blandine Kriegel:

> ...the link between morality and law was being forged ever more strongly and would culminate in Kant's *Critique of Practical Reason*. The tendency was toward the elaboration of a public morality decisively influenced by theological debates. This explains the paramount political importance of the theological discourse of the Renaissance and early modern period. Protestants and Catholics, Lutherans and Calvinists, Arminians and Socinians, Jansenists and quietists: the disputes among these sects did not concern only the path to salvation, the sex of angels, and the nature of the city of God, but also the definition of justice, of the 'human condition', and of the 'new Jerusalem'. We ought perhaps be more attentive to, and willing to recognize, the links between religion and politics... But the impact is by no means univocal or direct.... Just as the word of God enters the human world only by the intermediary of a prophet, and just as grace must be mediated by the elect, so religion in general only passes into politics by means of a human go-between, namely morality... In the matter of morals, as Nietzsche rightly held, the Greco-Roman heritage lost its early appeal, and it was Judeo-Christianity that became the moral tutor of the West. Rome remained its law professor, and Greece its science instructor [Kriegel, 1995: 52–53].[32]

A major lesson to draw from the above discussion is that it is inappropriate to account for 'the rise of the western world' in modern times only in terms of a powerful 'cult of individuality'. Equally important is the fact that in western Europe since the middle ages the emancipation of the individual (within the framework of national spaces) from feudal interference and from erstwhile networks of social and political allegiance[33] went hand in hand with the development of generalized morality in which abstract principles or rules of conduct are considered equally applicable to a vast range of social relations beyond the narrow circle of personal acquaintances.[34] Thus, if attention is turned to the Protestant Reformation, it is essential to enlarge the conventional wisdom according to which it gave a big boost to personal autonomy, education, scientific inquiry, entrepreneurship, and the thrifty use of money and time—all of which values foster capital accumulation and growth [see, e.g., Landes, 1998: 175–181]—, to underline the transformation of social bonds that went with it.

Countries that have a generalized morality but where individual emancipation is held under severe control by the custodians of the ruling doctrine, whether religious (like in Islamic countries where holy men govern society and religion reigns supreme) or lay (like in Ancient China where the mandarinate and imperial court, in their capacity to define the official doctrine, could judge individual thought and behaviour), are not in ideal conditions to develop: private initiative, innovation and dissent are strongly repressed as the whim takes the ruler.[35] On the other hand, countries whose citizens have a large margin of freedom but where no public morality exists to place restraint on the harm which individuals can inflict upon each other (in particular, there is no ethics preaching the respect of private property rights), are not in a more enviable position to seize growth opportunities.

A final word of caution: it must be reckoned that the borderline between limited-group and generalized morality is somewhat blurred because morality is rarely applied indiscriminately to all human beings. It is thus obvious that western societies have typically ceased to apply their moral-ethical principles once they came into contact with non-European peoples on the periphery of 'their' world. The history of slavery and of colonial exploitation is there to remind us of this basic fact: for example, it was considered morally legitimate by Europeans to cheat American Indians on the grounds that they were lazy, irrational, and unwilling to repay their debts [Ortiz, 1967: 203].[36] This being said, if limited-group morality is understood as morality restricted to concrete people with whom one shares common identity feelings while generalized morality is morals applicable to abstract people (to whom one is not necessarily tied through personal, family, or ethnic links), one is on better grounds to argue that the western world has a somewhat unique history rooted in a culture of individualism pervaded by norms of generalized morality.

*The need for reinforcement mechanisms*

We have seen above that primary socialization plays a crucial role in the norm generation process. Nevertheless, moral norms are subject to erosion: they form a 'social capital' [Coleman, 1987] and, as such, they are liable to depreciation, especially so if norm-abiding individuals come to realize that many people around them behave opportunistically. They therefore need more or less continuous reinforcement to be maintained. An important kind of reinforcement consists of what Berger and Luckmann have called secondary socialization. Secondary socialization is 'the acquisition of role-specific knowledge, the roles being directly or indirectly rooted in the division of labour' [Berger and Luckmann, 1967: 158]. Contrary to primary socialization which cannot take place without an emotionally charged identification of the child with his significant others, most secondary socialization 'can dispense with this kind of identification and proceed effectively with only the amount of mutual identification that enters into any communication between human beings' (it is necessary to love one's mother, but not one's teacher).

In primary socialization, the child does not apprehend his significant others as institutional functionaries, but as mediators of the only conceivable reality: in other words, he internalizes the world of his parents not as one of many possible worlds, not as the world appertaining to a specific institutional context, but as *the* world *tout court*. This explains why the world internalized in primary socialization is 'so much more firmly entrenched in consciousness than worlds internalized in secondary socializations'. As a matter of fact, since the main function of secondary socialization is to transmit specific knowledge (in schools, in factories, etc.), the social interaction between teachers and learners can be formalized and the former are in principle interchangeable [Berger and Luckmann, 1967: 154, 161–62].

The reinforcement of moral norms is particularly effective when church attendance ensures that people are continuously exposed to a moral discourse which repeatedly emphasizes the same values as they were taught by the agents of their primary socialization during childhood. The church (both catholic and protestant) obviously played a central role in the process of moral norm generation and maintenance throughout modern western history. Its impact was all the more significant as (1°) it promised a considerable reward (an eternal life of absolute happiness) for all those who were ready to incur personal sacrifices by behaving in other-regarding ways; and (2°) monitoring costs could be brought to a minimum insofar as God was thought to act as an impartial and free monitoring agent. Regarding the first aspect, the following must be noted: unpleasant experiences of dishonest dealings do not easily discourage believers if they are persuaded that, by continuing to behave morally, they will deserve special attention from God. There is an obvious analogy between this argument and the point made by Kant that ingratitude can stimulate giving, because the benefactor 'may well be convinced that the very disdain of any such reward as gratitude only adds to the moral worth of his benefaction' [Schoeck, 1987: 204—quoted from Elster, 1989a: 259]. As far as the second aspect is concerned, the main effect is that the availability of a free monitoring device allows honesty to be sustained even in the presence of high costs of fraud detection. In the words of Frank:

> Teaching moral values was once the nearly exclusive province of organized religion. The church was uniquely well equipped to perform this task because it had a ready answer to the question. 'Why shouldn't I cheat when

no one is looking?' Indeed, for the religious person, this question does not even arise, for God is *always* looking [Frank, 1988: 250].

Two remarks are in order. First, all (external) manifestations of religiosity and clericalism are not necessarily correlated with co-operative (honest) behaviour or civicness. In certain historical or social settings, engagement in catholic groups and adherence to catholic rituals, for example, has been purely formal and even hypocritical with the result that no genuine commitment towards taking the others' viewpoint into account was implied. Robert Putnam has thus recently argued that in Italy, at least, 'the most devout church-goers are the least civic-minded' [Putnam, 1993: 175–76; see also 107, 130]. In fact, such hypocrisy has sometimes sparked off reactions by non-clerical movements which acted as more genuine defenders of moral tenets.

Second, as has been already illustrated above, norms of generalized morality are not the exclusive province of organized religions. They have also been produced by non-clerical organizations, such as the free masonry. In addition, moral norm reinforcement may come from state agents or political leaders acting as norm reactivators. As a matter of fact, morality and a high sense of public purpose among the rulers are important ingredients of a well-functioning market order not only because they ensure that rules are properly enforced (corruption among state administrators is held in check), but also because of the positive demonstration effect exercised by charismatic leaders with whom people tend to strongly identify. When the public attitude of these leaders exerts a significant impact on people's behaviour, fewer laws are needed and, to the extent that they exist to regulate behaviour, people are more likely to comply. Consequently, less repressive or sanctioning resources are required to ensure their enforceability.

Field experiments actually confirm the great impact of role models on people's behaviour. For example, Horstein et al. (1968) were able to show that the return rate of 'lost' wallets by passers-by in New York city was significantly higher when the subjects of the experiments were exposed to a positive attitude of benevolence on the part of a third party. The interpretation offered by the authors is that the third party served as a role model for the subjects. A related lesson is that feelings or sentiments, not reason, motivate human decisions in situations where our own acts have a significant influence on others' well-being: exposure to different kinds of persons or acts (benevolent or malevolent) evokes particular emotions which drive people to behave in certain ways [Frank, 1988: 216]. Another experiment which confirms the important function of role models (or the fact that altruism or morality is encouraged by the observation of it) is that reported by Singer (1973). A helpless-looking woman was standing near a car with a flat tyre along the road. It was found that drivers passing this woman were more likely to come to her rescue when they previously had the opportunity to observe helping behaviours in a similar type of situation.

Such experiments seem to suggest that role models serve as a signalling device reminding people that there are honest people around. The result would be to enhance people's trust in others' predisposition towards cooperative behaviour. A related explanation is that 'the model, by his behaviour, increases the salience of the relevant norm for the observer, who is consequently more likely to obey this norm' [Darley and Latané, 1970: 85]. Still another interpretation emphasizing the emotional dimension of people's behavior would view role models as privileged agents who reactivate emotional capacities associated with primary socialization processes. In this approach, the display of model behaviour has the effect of increasing—or restoring to previous levels—the values of the payoffs attached by common people to the cooperative outcome. Alternatively, the impact of the role model can be viewed as generating an emotion that makes people undergo only a short-term change of preferences [Elster, 1998: 70]. In the latter two interpretations, and contrary to economists' standard assumption, individual preferences are not considered as stable.

Emphasis on the potential role of the state as a norm-reinforcing agency ought not to deflect our attention from the equally important role that a living and watchful civil society must play to support honest behaviour and to banish economic crime. Of course, the contribution of civil society to norm maintenance is especially significant when the state is wanting in this respect and when its agents are perhaps themselves involved in various sorts of illegal or doubtful practices. A civil society helps to back trust whenever there is a sufficient number of citizens who feel vengeful enough to work towards exposing publicly the illegal acts or malpractices of both private and state agents, and towards bringing enough pressure to sanction them even though such actions entail significant costs to themselves (by denouncing economic crimes they produce a public good). To the extent that the state cannot be relied upon to (re)activate norms of honesty, either because it is itself corrupt or because it has no moral clout or ideological persuasive powers, the existence of an active civil society imbued with moral norms appears as an important condition of efficient exchange.

The argument, it must be pointed out, does not imply that, at every stage of market development, political democracy is absolutely necessary for honest behaviour to be reasonably well sustained. It can therefore accommodate the scepticism recently expressed by Bardhan, for example, about the relationship between democracy and economic growth [Bardhan, 1993]. Nevertheless, inasmuch as the ability of the state to act as a norm supplier (through charismatic leadership and/or through organized ideological persuasion) is subject to erosion over time—leaders pass away and ideologies tend to wear themselves out—, the argument implies that in the long run market expansion and economic growth must be paralleled by the development of civil society and the associated freedoms of political expression.

In the above discussion, emphasis has been placed on the role of organizations, such as churches or states, or of public figures, such as political leaders, for the reinforcement of moral norms. It must be added now that moral norms may also be activated or reinforced in the course of human interaction processes. Solid experimental evidence thus shows that this is the case in small groups where communication (and exchange of promises) takes place, even if only for a short period, between subjects who have met at random for the first time. In such conditions, indeed, communication tends to raise the cooperation rate significantly, especially so if intra-group discussion leads to universal promise-making [see, for example, Dawes, McTavish, and Shaklee, 1977; Dawes and Thaler, 1988]. It would nevertheless be a hasty step to infer from the above results that people are given only to limited-group morality. In point of fact, there is a fundamental difference between deliberately limiting cooperative behaviour to a restricted circle of well-identified persons with whom one has *ex ante* empathy feelings on the one hand, and being *a priori* opened to cooperation with a large number of people provided that some sort of acquainting process occurs during which the 'abstract other' becomes somewhat more familiar, on the other hand.

Communication, it seems, performs three functions. First, it enhances trust in others' predisposition to cooperate with us, especially when communication is accompanied by a verbal exchange of promises and when promise-making is universal (any defection throws doubts on the cohesive ability of the whole group and, therefore, on the credibility of anyone's promise). The fact of the matter is that many people are particularly prone to believe others when the latter say pleasant things or point to attractive prospects. Second, communication stimulates our ability to adopt the others' viewpoint because it enhances our ability to empathize with them. And, third, communication intensifies guilt feelings as a result of the fact that the potential victim of our free riding behaviour has been transformed from a mere stranger into a real person. To sum up, the possibility of communicating with potential (business) partners who are strangers tends to increase our propensity to believe that they can be nice to us and our willingness to show the same kindness to them. In short, communication reinforces people's drive to behave in a reciprocally fair manner.

*A short digression on Japan*

States may not only reinforce norms of generalized morality but may also play a significant role in establishing them. Jean-Jacques Laffont (1975) has thus defended the view that, by means of sustained information campaigns and public display of governmental authority, states may play a major role in inducing people to behave in a 'Kantian way'.[37] For example, 'when the economic development of the Middle Ages required honest practices among merchants, a new ethics appeared, helped by some coercive legislation' (p. 434). The experience of Japan, as interpreted by Mishio Morishima, David Landes, Francis Fukuyama and others, actually offers a good illustration of this possibility as well as of the critical function that a centralized education system can perform in this regard.

According to this account, through a long evolution extending over several centuries, the Japanese people have gradually absorbed and adapted the values of Chinese Confucianism so as to put increasing emphasis on the concepts of loyalty (rather than harmony), filial piety, and wisdom. As a consequence of this ideological process, the Japanese elite came to have special praise for 'law and order' while recognizing their duty to do 'something' for the society [Morishima, 1982: 91–92; Fukuyama, 1995: 179]. In the Tokugawa period, however, values of loyalty and devoted service to the society were still essentially of the limited-group variety and most Japanese peasants and workers 'had scarcely a notion of nation' [Landes, 1998: 383]. During the Meiji period, by imbuing its subjects with a sense of higher duty to emperor and country and by linking this patriotism to work, the imperial state started to initiate a shift from limited-group to (more) generalized or abstract morality.

Confucian morality, above all loyalty to the state, was impressed upon the people by the government as a result of a powerful education system made compulsory not only for the samurai but even for the whole population (end of 19th century).[38] A large share of school time was thus devoted to the study of ethics and, in a country without regular religious instruction and ceremonial, school became 'the temple of virtue and morality' (Landes). In spite of all these efforts, it is not until after the Meiji period that the above values became really widespread and that the Emperor was transformed into the living symbol which commended the loyalty of most Japanese people. Eventually, Japanese Confucian ethics successfully produced a code of abstract (civic) morality reflected in an unremitting spirit of selfless devotion to the country.[39] It also permitted the development of complex hierarchically-structured business organizations (known as *keiretsu*) characterized by a considerable amount of trust between a large number of unrelated people.[40] This picture contrasts with Chinese companies which have always been more strictly based on family or lineage ties [Morishima, 1982: 105, 121, 137, 148–57; Landes, 1998: 383; Fukui, 1992; Fukuyama, 1995: 171–207].

According to another account (personal communication of Yujiro Hayami), however, the role of the Japanese state in fostering universalistic moral norms in modern times should not be overplayed. Indeed, new sects of Confucianism and Zen Bhuddism developed among traders to preach moral values such as honesty, industriousness, and frugality as commercialization progressed in the late Tokugawa period. Before then, both Confucianism and Zen Budhism were the religions and ideologies of the ruling warrior class only. Moral norms would thus have gradually evolved in Japan to foster economic growth when the latter proved possible for other reasons. This said, the essential question remains as to whether and to what extent this decentralized emergence of generalized morality in the Japanese society was itself ultimately conditioned by the ideological climate which political authorities contributed to create through the aforementioned education policy.

## 7.4 LIMITED MORALITY AT WORK

### *Limited morality and the private sector*

A major lesson from Chapter 4 is that rural communities in areas with a long tradition of low population densities have a considerable ability to regulate access to land through informal mechanisms and rules.

This remains true when pressure on land resources increases. Unfortunately, there is a counterpart to this ability of rural communities to successfully address governance problems not easily amenable to market or state solution, namely their parochial character [see, e.g., Bowles and Gintis, 1998: 23]. This parochial character may lead them to adopt protective attitudes and even to give in to chauvinistic tendencies if they feel too much threatened by outsiders or outside forces. Such attitudes and tendencies may take on the form of sheer malpractices and deceit, e.g. double deals directed against strangers, sales of land parcels without informing the (stranger) buyer of the charges weighing on them (mortgage, in particular), etc. In other words, traditional values according to which rural lands ought to remain in the hands of the 'sons of the village' since they are ancestral property give rise to double standards reflected in norms of limited morality. And such norms are the cause of pervasive inefficiencies that result from transaction costs and serious imperfections in land markets but also in other rural factor markets (see *supra*, Chapter 4).

In tribal societies, morals typically differ according to whether one deals with kinspeople or with strangers. This double standard in ethical codes of behaviour is vividly manifested in the following concomitant facts: on the one hand, bargaining or haggling is considered to be aimed at exploiting and cheating the partners and, on the other hand, sheer commercial practices are permitted only with strangers. A merchant always steals, as has been noted with respect to Kapauka Papuans of New Guinea, and that is why trade inside one's tribe is badly looked at while trade conducted with non-kin brings social prestige as well as profit to the successful merchant [Pospisil, 1958: 127]. The fact of the matter is that, in tribal ideology, to cheat one's clan is equivalent to cheating oneself whereas cheating outsiders gives strength to the cheater's clan and weakens the clan of the cheated partner [Massoz, 1982: 87–88]. On the basis of his field observations in Kabylia province, Algeria, Pierre Bourdieu wrote in the same vein:

> Amicable transactions between relatives and allied people contrast with market transactions...and 'the foodstuff or cattle of the fellah' are traditionally opposed to 'the foodstuff or the cattle of the market'; old informants can talk for ever about the guile and deceit commonly observed on the 'big markets', that is, in dealings with strangers. These are stories about mules that run away as soon as they have reached the new purchaser's destination; about oxen that are rubbed with a special plant so as to make them swell up and thereby appear as fatter as what they actually

> are; about related purchasers who collude to propose very low prices... [Bourdieu, 1980: 196—my translation; see also Evans-Pritchard, 1940; Sahlins, 1963, 1968; Polanyi, 1977: 59].

Limited morality is bound to affect the business sector by segmenting the domain of relationships within which business is viable. In the case of Sub-Saharan Africa (SSA), Kennedy has thus observed that there exists 'a marked reluctance' to establish capital-pooling arrangements or business partnerships among non-kinsmen. This reluctance is to be mainly ascribed to 'the widespread fear that partners will cheat in some way or fail to pull their weight', which contributes to create an 'atmosphere of suspicion and pessimism concerning the motivations of others' [Kennedy, 1988: 166]. Such a climate of distrust is highly detrimental to African capitalism in so far as, by preventing the establishment of genuinely corporate forms of business associations, 'it closes one of the most important potential avenues to firm expansion and reduces the likelihood that indigenous companies can become sufficiently competitive to mount an effective challenge to foreign companies' [*ibidem*].

The latter argument, however, is not entirely convincing. As a matter of fact, intense familism combined with distrust of nonkin in traditional China anticipated the business culture of contemporary Taiwan and Hong-Kong [Fukuyama, 1995: 89]. None the less, the fact that many Taiwanese firms are small- and medium-sized largely as a result of their being based on family ties did not prevent them from providing a major impetus to national economic growth, particularly in the export manufacturing sector [Hamilton, 1998]. Something more subtle than sheer size probably accounts for the poor organizational performance of many African firms. Contrary to Chinese enterprises which are controlled by a restricted number of close relatives or members of the lineage, African businesses are generally opened to a large number of kin belonging to the extended family and the tribe of the owner(s). Problems arise because, as explained at length in Chapter 5, relations with kin entail multiple social obligations that may easily cause the ruin of such businesses. Indeed, if tribal ideology, through diffusion of values of limited morality, tends to make kinspeople more trustworthy than strangers, it also tends to discourage accumulation efforts through diffusion of strongly egalitarian social norms. Close monitoring of the successful efforts of a kinsman gives rise to continuous harrassment and to serious strains and tensions if the latter is not considered to be generous and fair enough with his subordinates.

Another crucial difference between SSA and a country like Taiwan lies in the fact that, unlike the former region, the latter country benefits from a host of institutions and informal mechanisms (such as the pervasive business networks mentioned earlier) that have enabled it to establish trust between separate economic entities, e.g., between small-scale family businesses or between them and large-scale upstream or subcontracting firms [Hamilton, Zeile, and Kim, 1990; Hayami and Kawagoe, 1993; Hayami, 1998; Hamilton, 1998]. The unwillingness to share information with other enterprises, which Fafchamps (1996) noted for Ghanaian firms (see *supra*, Chap. 6), is perhaps indicative of the lack of trust and cooperativeness beyond circles of acquaintances in SSA. The only exception, notes Fafchamps in a revealing manner, concerns Accra's women fishmongers whose situation is somewhat peculiar: 'they all belong to a closely knit neighbourhood, they share the same ethnic background, their husbands go to sea together, and they all sell in the same market' [Fafchamps, 1996: 441].

A more general lesson from the same study is that the lack of contractual discipline in Ghana is real and is reflected, *ex post,* in numerous delivery and payment delays. *Ex ante,* it is evident from the fact that firms often resort to unwieldy manners of doing business because they do not want to take the chance of a problem happening. Typically, they fall back on a 'flea market' mode of transacting: 'inspect the good on the spot, pay cash and walk away with it'. In other words, they avoid all transactions that involve delayed obligations that make breach of contract possible [Fafchamps, 1996: 441–44]. A still more recent study using a larger set of survey data collected in several African countries (Burundi, Cameroon, Ghana, Ivory Coast, Kenya, Zambia, and Zimbabwe) has as one of its conclusions that African managed firms face more problems with individuals than other firms, in particular firms run by Asian entrepreneurs, such as Indians in Kenya [Bigsten et al., 1998]. Moreover, firms that buy from family and friends encounter more late delivery problems, suggesting that relations based on family, friendship, or ethnicity/kinship tend to raise the incidence of contract non-performance.[41] At the same time, however, such relations make it easier for firms to solve disputes (through informal channels).

The latter result, however, is no evidence that kin-based or other types of personalized relationships are necessarily more problematic than contractual relationships with strangers. As a matter of fact, it is quite possible that when dealing with the latter, firm managers insist on cash payment upon delivery whereas when dealing with kin, they accept transactions involving delayed obligations. In addition, contractual problems with kin are not necessarily of the moral hazard type: they may reflect genuine difficulties to honour obligations as a result of various contingencies against which family-based mutual aid relationships constitute the best mode of insurance.[42] Alternatively, such problems may arise from the above-noted egalitarian pressures exercised by prevailing family or ethnic norms of sharing.

If the aforementioned empirical studies are useful starters in a field where hard data are conspicuously lacking, the information they provide, albeit undoubtedly interesting, does not allow us to decide which precise factors are at work behind the observed enforcement problems. Also, they do not inform us about selection procedures and organizational problems internal to firms, in particular those of personnel management.[43] Finally, such surveys cannot give us any idea of the entrepreneurial potentialities lost as a result of contractual problems (either with kin or with strangers), since firms which have not been created or have disappeared may not be observed.

### *Limited morality and the public sphere*

Norms of limited morality are bound to affect not only the private but also the public sector. Nepotism and favouritism are often found to be major obstacles on the way to effective functioning of the bureaucracy and public enterprises. Codes of conduct emphasize the strength of ties to close social relations; procedural norms, when they exist, are particularistic; professional standards are low; reward and sanction mechanisms (including litigation) as well as taxation and subsidies are meted out in a specific way so as to make patronage effective instead of promoting economic efficiency and shared growth.

In this respect, the situation of SSA is especially worrying. This region is indeed characterized by the absence of the rule of law understood as a body of clearly formulated rules which everybody has to abide by, including the rulers. As is evident from a series of more or less recent works in political science, the African state is structured by rival networks of politicial factions or cliques articulated around individuals, families, religious, socio-cultural and economic groups, subgroups, sects, castes, etc. These factions are often engaged in merciless struggles for access to power and to the wealth and material privileges which automatically reward the power-holders [Sklar, 1979; Hyden, 1983; Young, 1986; Staniland, 1986; Bienen, 1987; Bayart, 1986, 1989; Kennedy, 1988]. As a matter of fact, once established in key positions of the political power structure (at the level of the presidency, the politico-military hierarchy, the top civil servants, the ruling party officials, etc.), the dominant faction, group or clique hastens to use them in the particular interests of its members, including the 'small men' who draw their livelihood from participating at the lowest level of this structure [Bayart, 1989: 291–93]. The methods used involve clear favouritism in the distribution of divisible goods, such as subsidies for machinery, fertilizer, etc., [Bates, 1981, 1983; Teranishi, 1997], or dubious redistribution and acquisition of wealth through trafficking, racketeering, plundering, and looting [Bayart, 1989].

If African states appear to be strong, it is because their rulers often follow authoritarian modes of conduct to exercise control in a fluid political setup dominated by ethnic and interdistrict competition, factional struggles, personal rivalries, and complicated relations of affection and patronage that cannot be encompassed by class analysis [Hyden, 1986: 66; Ravenhill, 1986; Bienen, 1987: 298–300; Kennedy, 1988: 76; Bayart, 1989: 257–315; Herbst, 1990]. This apparent strength nevertheless conceals their structural fragility and lack of autonomy arising from their being 'generally uninsulated from the particularistic loyalties and "role diffuseness" which prevail in African societies, perhaps precisely to the extent that they have not developed as civil societies' [Booth, 1987: 27].

A plausible reason for the weakness of the African state in many instances is the pervasive presence of exit opportunities which have allowed rural dwellers to escape the grip and taxing power of a proto ruling-class (see *supra*, Chap. 2). Low-population densities and the physical environment of the African continent largely account for this situation. By contrast, as Robert Allen (1997) has recently argued, successful states in the ancient world depended on the ability of the elites to extract a surplus from agricultural and other producers. This ability was greatest when the population was immobile, as evidenced by the success of the Pharaohs in Ancient Egypt. The geography of Egypt, indeed, made the problem of population control simpler than elsewhere—the deserts bordering the Nile meant that habitation was confined to the valley and that farmers could flee tax or rent collectors only along the river— and therefore created a situation where a unified state could be established that lasted for millenia.

South Asian societies differ from African societies in many respects. In particular, in the course of their precolonial histories, they have come to be stratified along an urban-rural divide that brought a high degree of class differentiation in its wake. Moreover, they have inherited the norms of the western legal tradition due to more or less prolonged existence of a colonial state.[44] Even today, however, these societies tend to remain under the strong influence of traditional patterns of social relations such as the principle of the primacy of family and caste relationships. Under these circumstances, it is not surprising that rights and obligations associated with these patterns still tend to predominate over the rules and norms rooted in the abstract individual (as opposed to the concrete person). The Indian psychoanalyst Kakar (1978) has aptly described the essential nature of social relations in contemporary India. He has laid special emphasis on the persisting lack of a common code of generalized morality in the Indian society. I cannot resist the temptation to quote him at some length given the great pertinence of his analysis in the context of this chapter:

> Among those Indians closely identified with the process of modernization, the well-educated urban elite who hold positions of power in modern institutions, the psycho-historical fact of the primacy of relationships, of family loyalties, of *jati* connections, is often a source of considerable emotional stress. For although intellectually the Indian professional or bureaucrat may agree with his western counterpart that, for example, the criterion for appointment or promotion to a particular job must be objective, decisions based solely on the demands of the task and 'merits of the case', he cannot root out the cultural conviction that his relationship to the individual under consideration is the single most important factor in his decision. This conflict between the rational criteria of specific tasks and institutional goals rooted in western societal values, and his own deeply held belief (however ambivalent) in the importance of honouring family and *jati* bonds is typical among highly educated and prominently employed Indians. And among the vast majority of tradition-minded countrymen—whether it be a *bania* bending the law to facilitate the business transaction of a fellow *jati* member, or a *marwari* industrialist employing an insufficiently qualified but distantly related job applicant as a manager, or the clerk accepting bribes in order to put an orphaned niece through school—, dishonesty, nepotism and corruption as they are understood in the West are merely abstract concepts. These negative constructions are irrelevant to Indian psycho-social

> experience, which, from childhood on, nurtures one standard of responsible adult action, and one only, namely, an individual's lifelong obligation to his kith and kin. Allegiance to impersonal institutions and abstract moral concepts is without precedent in individual developmental experience, an adventitious growth in the Indian inner world. Guilt and its attendant inner anxiety are aroused only when individual actions go against the principle of the primacy of relationships, not when foreign ethical standards of justice and efficiency are breached [Kakar, 1978: 125–26—my emphasis].

In Pakistan, reciprocal favours and limited morality are an essential ingredient of bureaucratic practice and they are formalized enough to have a name: *vartan bhanji*. In Baluchistan and the North-West Frontier Province, the two most tribal areas of the country, webs of traditional relationships are still pervasive and run through regional official agencies and municipalities. Thus, in a town like Peshawar, Pathan bureaucrats run their offices like the tribal *jirgas* they have been brought up with [Duncan, 1989: 242–44].

The main contrast here is with East Asia, and Northeast Asia in particular, where the bureaucracy appears remarkably autonomous. There, bureaucrats 'were able to treat the government of their country as if it were the management of a household'. In Korea and Taiwan, for example, political leaders, who ascended from a military background, regarded the building up of their country's industrial power 'as the first order of business', in a context dominated by geopolitical considerations—the strong determination to repossess mainland China for Taiwan, and the need to defend itself in the context of the cold war for Korea [Aoki et al., 1997: 26; see also Luedde-Neurath, 1988; White and Wade, 1988; Wade, 1990]—and influenced by a tradition of centralized governance [Hayami, 1997: 281]. Recent research reveals that the absence of a politically powerful, dominant economic class was an important historical condition that favoured the emergence of effective and dedicated administrations in this part of the world [Woo-Cumings, 1997]. They have been effective in the sense of being relatively little prone to rent-seeking behaviour, and they have been dedicated in the sense of having legitimized their control 'by the equal payment of growth dividends to all economic classes'. Interestingly, this model of 'shared growth' in Northeast Asia 'seems to be a profoundly path-dependent phenomenon that evolved from the unique historical conditions prevailing immediately after the Pacific War' [Aoki et al., 1997: 26–27; Aoki, 1997].

Historical conditions appear to have led Latin America on a different way. In this region, 'personalistic' relationships 'are still the key to much of the political and economic exchange', and maximum effort is devoted to 'getting control of, or influence over, the bureaucratic machinery'. This is the outcome of a long tradition rooted in the Spanish colonial rule [North, 1991: 110–11].

## NOTES

1. As a matter of fact, deductive equilibrium analysis does not explain the process by which decision makers acquire equilibrium beliefs. It is both the strength and the limitation of the deductive equilibrium method that it is able to abstract from the complicated dynamic process that induces equilibrium and from the historical accident that initiated the process. On the contrary, inductive selection principles select equilibrium points based on the history of some pregame, hence these principles are not independent of accident and process [Van Huyck et al., 1990: 234–6].
2. Adam Seligman defines trust as 'some sort of belief in the goodwill of the other, given the opaqueness of other's intentions and calculations' [Seligman, 1997: 43].
3. In Bowles (1998b), the evolutionary modelling of behavioural norms is made on the basis of the assumption that such norms are adopted and abandoned under the influence of both the relative payoffs associated with behaviours and the learning rules constituting the cultural transmission process, and that markets affect both relative payoffs and cultural transmission. It is shown that allocation rules which closely conform to idealized markets 'may support lower equilibrium frequencies of socially beneficial norms and otherwise militate against the prevalence of these norms, by comparison to alternative allocation rules which deviate from the market ideal'. Note that deviations from ideal (Walrasian) market conditions are represented by increasing both the degree of segmentation of the population (see the previous footnote) and the probability of recognizing trade partners (the anonymity condition is relaxed), which implies the possibility of refusing to deal with them if reckoned to be of the wrong type.
4. For instance, the way the (merchant) law provided protection of the *bona fide* purchaser (against the claims of the original owner of stolen or lost goods) from the beginning of the 17. century in England solved an important problem which confronted merchants and hindered trade for many centuries in Europe [North, 1990: 128–29; see also Rosenberg and Birdzell, 1986: Chap. 2].
5. Except for the Champagne fairs, there seems to be little empirical (historical) support for the otherwise ingenious private judge system (personal communication of Avner Greif).
6. There are three types of agents in Kali's model: two types behave mechanistically with regard to cheating, either honestly or dishonestly, while the third type, the opportunists, behave strategically on the basis of cost-benefit considerations.
7. 'Business in present conditions is so complicated and corrupt that reliability and really good contacts are highly valued', said the president of a tourist company from Novosibirsk, Russia [Ledeneva, 1998: 157].
8. As a matter of fact, an increase in network size has two different welfare effects depending on the sphere of the economy. When the network creams off 'good' types (the honest agents and the opportunists who choose to behave honestly) and therefore worsens the pool of agents remaining in the anonymous market, the welfare of people involved in market exchange falls and honesty becomes easier to enforce within the network. The lump-sum entrance fee falls and, as a result, the welfare of the members of the business group is raised. Thus, as the size of the network increases, the welfare of its members rises at the expense of the people operating in the anonymous market. If the network is so large that the fraction of the population remaining

in anonymous market exchange is small, it becomes an economicallly efficient institution. Otherwise, it is inefficient.

9. Another illustration of this possibility is provided by Kranton (1996) who makes the point that personalized exchange can persist even when it is inefficient for the economy. Note that her model is based on the assumption that in reciprocal exchange agents can only obtain the commodity produced by their trading partner.
10. In the words of Ian MacDonald:

    'Under Article 58, Section 12 of the Soviet Criminal Code (1926), failure to denounce anyone guilty of crimes listed in other sections of the Code was punishable by death or imprisonment for an unlimited period. As a corollary of this, the 'duty to inform' was endlessly played upon by the government and the security organs....the practice of denouncing neighbours and even relations out of sheer malice was common, while 'unmasking' one's workmates rapidly became an accepted way of gaining promotion.... Under Khrushchev, the use of civilians to police civilians attained a new sophistication, notably in the form of the *druzhiny* or People's Guards, authorised by the Supreme Soviet in 1959 to rid the streets of 'parasites' and harass anyone generally failing to conform. By exhorting neighbours to spy on each other, sanctioning 'comrades' courts', and encouraging the Komsomol in their traditional role as moral vigilantes, the Soviet authorities mobilised 'the wrath of the People' against the people themselves.... [Eventually] social cohesion had completely collapsed. People no longer trusted each other and love was a rare and improbable bloom hanging on here and there in a landscape of sterile grey.....everyone in Russia was in effect placed in solitary confinement' [MacDonald,1991: 120–23, 220–21].

11. Community norms obtain in situations of repeated encounters. In technical terms, they can be defined as 'stable expectations shared among repeatedly interacting players concerning each other's (penalizing) behaviour in default contingencies—the off-the-path-of-play expectations—that would make a certain standard of behaviour—the on-the-path of play behaviour—self-enforcing' [Aoki, forthcoming: Chap. 1].
12. Just to give one striking example, in their field experiments in New York city (during the spring of 1968), Hornstein and his colleagues found that, in what is typically a one-shot game, an astonishingly high 45 per cent of 'lost' wallets were returned completely intact to their owner by passers-by who came across them [cited from Frank, 1988: 216; for a recent survey, see Ledyard, 1995].
13. In other words, moral norms differ from social norms (e.g., a norm of etiquette) in the sense that they constrain the full-blown pursuit of self-interest in *PD-structured situations*.
14. Note that reciprocal fairness is neither purely egoistic behaviour (since reciprocators incur some personal cost in responding to other people's actions) nor purely altruistic behaviour (since 'gifts are exclusively presented to people who gave something before, or are supposed to give something back later') [Fehr and Tyran, 1996: 134].
15. In numerous experiments with the ultimatum game, it is invariably found that subjects in the position of proposers typically offer something like a seven-three split, and that those in the position of responders typically reject offers of two or less [Elster, 1998: 68].
16. Thus, in the ultimatum game, minimal acceptable offers appear to be lower when the subjects know that the offer has been the result of volition by the person who would be hurt by their rejections [Blount, 1995].
17. Contract choices can obviously be affected by reciprocal behaviour. Firms may thus favour simple, non incentive-compatible labour contracts that induce workers to provide effort beyond the level that is enforceable by incentive compatible devices [Fehr et al., 1997; forthcoming].
18. Of course, players are not rational. Therefore, they do not have a great enough understanding of the situation to do some forward-looking calculations or backward-looking comparisons with others. In particular, they are not able to realize that even if punishing a defection is costly now, it might entail long-term gains by discouraging other defections later [Axelrod, 1986: 58].

19. 'At first, boldness levels fell dramatically due to the vengefulness of the population. Then, gradually, the amount of vengefulness also fell because there was no direct incentive to pay the enforcement cost of punishing a defection. Once vengeance became rare, the average level of boldness rose again, and the norm completely collapsed' [Axelrod, 1986: 64–65].
20. The dynamics are clear in this case too: 'The amount of vengefulness quickly increased to very high levels, and this in turn drove down boldness'. The logic is equally clear: 'At first there was a moderate amount of vengefulness in the population. This meant that a player had a strong incentive to be vengeful, namely, to escape punishment for not punishing an observed defection. Moreover, when each of the players is vengeful out of self-protection, it does not pay for anyone to be bold. Thus the entire system is self-policing, and the norm becomes well-established' [Axelrod, 1986: 54].
21. The internalization mechanism also implies that defection becomes costly rather than rewarding for some of the defectors in the population (bear in mind that Axelrod's base model uses a PD payoff structure).
22. Thus, the dean of a Faculty at the university of Akademgorodok (Russia) expressed his motivation to help by saying that 'If I am asked, I drop everything and help the other person, because I can imagine myself in his place. Indifference or refusal is a psychological trauma' [Ledeneva, 1998: 163].
23. This approach to moral norms is thus radically different from the rational choice approach adopted by Vanberg. For him, indeed, if moral norms help solve PD problems, they are used strategically by the actors. More precisely, if people stick to such norms, it is only because it is difficult to identify situations in which it would not be detrimental to violate them (which happens when violation is undetected) or because of the risk of misidentifying such situations. Given imperfect information, moral routines are therefore rational and morality can be viewed as an 'efficient behavioral technology' [Vanberg, 1988: 3, 21–30]. Quite revealingly, Vanberg has dismissed the true role of emotions in the process of internalization of moral norms, thereby negating the genuine nature of this process. Thus, he writes that 'internal sanctions cannot be considered an autonomous, independent source of moral enforcement. They are a source that ultimately derives from, and ultimately remains dependent on, the direct or indirect experience of external enforcement' [*ibidem*: 31]. For a general critique of the view that norms are merely *ex post* rationalizations of self-interest, see Elster, 1989a: 125–51; 1989b; Hausman and McPherson, 1996: Chap. 5.
24. In psychology, empathy denotes 'an individual's affective experience when it is elicited by social cues which transmit information about the corresponding affective experience of another person' [Aronfreed, 1970: 107]. It refers to 'vicarious emotional experience' [Shott, 1979: 1328]. As initially pointed out by Adam Smith (1759), empathy (called sympathy by him) can be of two sorts according to whether one's emotion arises from the emotion one observes in another (it thus consists of feeling the emotion *the other person* feels) or from the emotion one would feel in another's situation [Shott, *ibidem*]. In fact, the concept has been defined for the first time by David Hume (1740).
25. The reader will find in Frank (1988, Chapter 8) a good summary account of Kagan's theory.
26. The difference between guilt and shame has been aptly put by Robert Frank (1988: 153) in the following terms: 'When a person knows he is responsible for an action that harms others, but no one else knows it, he feels guilt. If others do know, he feels both guilt and shame. If others wrongly believe he has harmed another, he feels only shame'.
27. In the above scheme of analysis, it is worth noting, emotions or passions have a positive role to play in society. This is at variance with the position adopted by Adam Smith in his *Theory of Moral Sentiments*: there, we are told that passions (fear and anger, on the one hand, and 'the love of ease, of pleasure, of applause, and of many other selfish gratifications', on the other hand) are so many drives that are apt to mislead man into mischievous actions while their control enables him 'upon all occasions to act according to the dictates of prudence, of justice, and of proper benevolence' [Smith, 1759: Part VI, Sect. III, 238]. What Smith appears to believe is that, when man reasons coldly and practices self-command, he can think of the long-term or of the social consequences of his behaviour (at least if he is a 'wise' man) while, on the contrary,

when he is given to the urgent drives of passions, he is unable to see beyond his immediate short-term interests and he may thus be sometimes seduced 'to violate all the rules which he himself, in all his sober and cool hours, approves of' [*ibidem*: 237]. What can be argued instead, following a line suggested by Frank (1988), is just the opposite: emotions are susceptible of leading people, almost unconsciously, to overcome the temptation to give in to short-term considerations and to act in accordance with their long-term interests or with public good considerations.

28. In the words of David Hume, the existence of norms 'assures us still more, that the sense of interest has become common to all our fellows, and gives us a confidence of the future regularity of their conduct, and it is only on the expectation of this, that our moderation and abstinence are founded' [Hume, 1740: Book III, Part II, Sect. II, 490].
29. It is interesting to notice that, in socio-psychological experiments simulating games between strangers, high initial rates of cooperation are often followed by a gradual unravelling of cooperation. An oft-adduced explanation for this deteriorating cooperation is that subjects learn to play Nash-equilibrium strategies in the course of the game. An alternative explanation is that reciprocally fair subjects are upset by the defection of a minority of selfish (rational) agents of which they soon become aware. They then respond by retaliating, that is, by reducing their cooperation in order to punish defectors [Fehr and Tyran, 1996: 141–42].
30. For Freudians, the *superego* is precisely formed through such a process of internalization of rules and patterns of conduct that were originally enforced externally, largely by the parents [Darley and Latané, 1970: 84].
31. Note that this depiction of the Italian city-states as integrated communities permeated by pervasive norms and networks of civic commitment somewhat differs from the analysis provided by Greif (see Part I, subsection 4 of this paper).
32. Kriegel has proposed an interesting account of the rise of 'the state and the rule of law' in western Europe. The good fortune of this region, according to her, has been to choose both the tradition of the 'morality of law', based on the Old Testament, and the tradition of 'morality of faith', rooted in the Gospels, when deciding how to use its Judeo-Christian heritage for the building up of modern society. In her own words:

> 'The good fortune of Western Europe was ... to develop a canon that could privatize religion completely in the manner of the Reformation or respect the autonomy of the church in the manner in France, but which escaped the political secularization of faith that would later wreak havoc on nineteenth-century Eastern Europe. The collective political ethos lent its values to a morality of laws, leaving only subjective rights to depend on a morality of faith... Since the Renaissance, all of Western faith, that of the Reformation and that of the Counter-Reformation, has rested on a combination of the Scriptures. In Eastern Europe, by contrast, the Old Testament was largely abandoned... The modern [western European] state repudiated the project of saving society, and of bringing about 'emancipation'; it left to the individual and to the church the task of salvation and concerned itself with justice alone. The mortal god, as Hobbes put it, never sought to displace the immortal; Leviathan refrained from becoming Behemoth. These aspects of the modern state were not adopted suddenly. The triumph of the political morality of law was the culmination of a protracted plurisecular struggle marked by the overturning of a double obstacle: modern political philosophy had to shed both medieval antilegalism in the form of political Augustianism, on the one hand, and classical natural law together with Roman civil law, on the other' [Kriegel, 1995: 53–55].

Note that classical natural law treats legal relations among human beings as essentially similar to relations among things, since it views human beings as one ingredient of nature among others. As for Roman law, its main drawback was that it treats power as a matter of fact, not as an object of law. Roman jurisprudence was founded on private law, which prevented the establishment of modern political right as a rule for the governance of free men and women, for the legal emancipation of the serfs, and for the securing of subjective rights. This is a far cry from the Jewish law which is 'revealed and inscribed in durable lapidary form on tablets', is 'formalistic and literal', and which 'prescribes justice for all and subjects all to the fear of justice': no one is above or outside of the law and 'all are judges, and all may be called before the law' [Kriegel, 1995: 54, 57].

33. In the beginning of the 16th century, as Charles Wilson (1967) noted, the richest and most advanced concentrations of trade, industry, and wealth—Italian cities and the strip of the southern Netherlands that ran from Ypres north-east past Ghent and Bruges up to Antwerp (all located today in Belgium)—were all areas where tradesmen 'had been most successful in emancipating themselves from feudal interference, and in keeping at bay the newer threat of more centralized political control offered by the new monarchies'. The autonomy of city states was brought to an end in the 16. century when a whole complex of technological, organizational, and political changes greatly increased the ability of European princes to mobilize and maintain large armies [Tilly, 1992].
34. For solid evidence to the effect that this emancipation process can be dated back many centuries in the case of England, see Macfarlane (1978).
35. The interruption of Islamic and Chinese intellectual and technological advance at critical times of their history (e.g., the abandonment of the program of great voyages in China during the early 16 century, or the fact that the Confucian doctrine supported and diffused by Chinese rulers abhorred mercantilistic practices) was decided at the highest level in an abrupt and irrevocable fashion and institutionalized in the minutest details [Landes, 1998: 52–55, 96–97, 200; Jones, 1981: 168–69].
36. Note also that moral norms are compatible with inequality as attested, for example, by the norms that teach respect for private property even when such property is unequally distributed, or those that teach hard work, discipline, submission, and temperance to an exploited working class. Thus, to take an example from 19th century England, workers who attended philanthropic religious (protestant) schools known as the Sunday Schools have been found to be more productive and disciplined than those who did not go through such an experience [Howe, 1984: 280; Mathias, 1969: 208; Thompson, 1991: Chap. 6].
37. A moral agent assumes that the other agents will act as he does, and he maximizes his utility function under this new constraint [Laffont, 1975: 430–31].
38. The Imperial Injunction to Soldiers and Sailors of 1882 and the Imperial Rescript on Education of 1890 both used Confucian language to emphasize the virtue of loyalty to the state [Fukuyama, 1995: 179].
39. Tragically, the Emperor could not prevent ultra-rightists from exploiting these intense feelings of nationhood and from leading the country to a disastrous war which was to take a heavy toll of the energies thus mobilized
40. Japan actually came to have one of the lowest percentages of family ownership among the industrialized countries, with only 14 per cent of all equity being owned by families or individuals in 1970 [Fukuyama, 1995: 168].
41. Likewise, Fafchamps and Minten (1998) find that, in Madagascar, having family members in agricultural trade reduce profit margins even after controlling for working capital and equipment, labour, human capital, and management. Yet the authors do not buy the interpretation according to which close relatives burden the respondent's business by tapping into its working capital and by insisting on sharing arbitrage gains. The problem is indeed that, just as relatives might burden the respondent's business, the respondent might burden its relatives' business. In other words, the net effect of having relatives in trade should be zero. More likely are measurement errors arising from the fact that respondents having close relatives in trade have trouble mentally disentangling their business from that of their relatives, and, as a result, they overreport the labour and working capital that is truly theirs.
42. Fafchamps has thus concluded his study on Ghanaian manufacturing by saying that imperfect compliance with contractual obligations does not appear 'to spring from a cultural failure to recognize the need for business predictability', but from the prevailing low level of economic development which gets reflected in all sorts of market imperfections and pervasive uncertainties that call for informal risk-sharing mechanisms [Fafchamps, 1996: 443–45]. Yet, he duly

reckons that these uncertainties open the way for opportunistic tendencies since claims by defaulters that they have been hit by a negative shock are hard to verify.

43. A recent study on the construction sector in Egypt has revealed that workers with equivalent earnings prospects in the craft segment face differential costs of entry depending on their kinship ties, their access to social networks, and, mainly, their region of birth [Assaad, 1997].
44. One may thus think of British India in which the Indian Civil Service and western education have been solidly implanted by the colonial power, a significant event given the profound imprint that these two institutions have left on the elites of the postcolonial societies born of the old British Empire.

# Chapter 8

## NO EASY ANSWER

This last chapter is not intended as a full-fledged conclusion, but rather as the place to discuss the problem of norm evolution and illustrate the resulting existence of multiple path trajectories (Sections 1 and 2). The final section, however, wants to close the book by shortly summarizing the main points that have been presented in the previous chapters.

### 8.1 EVOLUTION OF MORAL NORMS

As has been mentioned earlier, there are reasons to believe that moral norms emphasizing honest behaviour will evolve spontaneously within groups of people who interact frequently. Such endogenous emergence of moral norms is much more problematic, though, when the people concerned are changing partners in anonymous exchanges.

Contrary to what is often believed, Adam Smith identified a serious limitation of the self-regulating capacity of the market system in the proclivity of the merchants and manufacturers to be exclusively concerned about advancing their own short-term selfish interests in whichever way possible. His conclusion was that 'the only guarantee that commercial relations will not shred the moral fabric of society is the creation of an institutional framework which sets bounds upon their self-interested action' [McNally, 1988: 193]. This political task—the constitution and preservation of the moral basis of society—should be undertaken by a select group of virtuous men capable of following the moral ideals of conscience and embodying the civic habits necessary to political stability [*ibidem*: 192–208]. Smith actually believed that there are natural standards of human conduct which are not simply the result of human convention [Young, 1992: 76]. For him, therefore, the social order of the market must be 'manufactured' within the body politic so as to lay down the rules and set up the institutions susceptible of directing self-centered economic appetites into socially desirable channels. In this connection, he stressed the role of the Church in producing and strengthening morality [Colclough, 1991].

Clearly, Smith departed from the line followed by his illustrious predecessor, David Hume, who was persuaded that 'moral sense' would evolve spontaneously with the advent and development of the 'commercial society'. According to him, indeed, moral behaviour depends upon rational considerations and, in an age of cultural and scientific progress, individuals cannot fail to see the necessity for private property, law, and government. Far from contributing to corruption and degeneracy, the development of 'commercial society' can be expected to pave the way for morality, justice, and good government insofar as it goes hand in hand with moral and political progress [McNally, 1988: 167–68].

For Hume, therefore, property, law, and government are the outcome of the evolution of human society. Through the experience derived from their mutual interactions in the (nascent) market economy—and not through the mental representation of abstract principles of duty or the highest good—, individuals come to see the necessity of, and to accept the constraints imposed by, those institutions and conventions which preserve the social order. In the words of Hume, men 'cannot change their natures. All they can do is to change their situation ...' and 'lay themselves under the necessity of observing the laws of justice and equity, notwithstanding their violent propension to prefer contiguous [short-term] to remote [gains]' [Hume, 1740: Book III, Part II, Sect. VII, 537]. 'Public utility' becomes the basis of moral decision and, as pointed out in his *Enquiry concerning the principles of morals,* 'everything which contributes to the happiness of society recommends itself directly to our approbation and good will' [quoted from McNally, 1988: 169].

His ideas developed in the *Treatise of Human Nature* (1740) have been aptly summarized by John McNally in the following way:

> In the *Treatise*, Hume accepts that self-love is the origin of law and government. Nevertheless, since 'the self-love of one person is naturally contrary to that of another', competing and conflicting self-interested passions must 'adjust themselves after such a manner as to concur in some system of conduct and behaviour'. After individuals discover that unbridled selfishness incapacitates them for society, 'they are naturally induced to lay themselves under the restraint of such rules, as may render their commerce more safe and commodious'. As rules of social regulation are developed, they become customary and are passed on to future generations. Eventually people come to cherish the rules which hold society together. They develop a sense of sympathy for those who observe social norms. Moreover, they come to model their behaviour in such a way as to be worthy of the sympathy and approval of others. Through custom and education, then, individuals develop a love of praise and a fear of blame. For Hume, moral

> principles are not innate or providentially inspired. They are practical rules developed in the course of living in society; morality refers to the norms and conventions which prevail there. These norms and conventions can be said to enter into the commonsense view of the world most individuals acquire ... [Sympathy] is a capacity derived from experience and modified as the customary rules of social life change. Sympathy has a rational dimension; it derives from the individual's understanding of the necessity for norms of conduct and behaviour. Thus, although 'self-interest is the original motive to the establishment of justice', as society develops it becomes the case that 'a sympathy with public interest is the source of the moral approbation, which attends that virtue' [McNally, 1988: 168–69].

Because he believes that the ethical reasons justifying moral norms motivate compliance—people want to act on principles that no rational agent could reasonably reject (see *supra*)—, Hume regards the emergence of these norms as a spontaneous process that should not cause major problems.

Some social scientists are inclined to consider that the great monotheistic or transcendental religions (called 'Axial' religions by S.N. Eisenstadt) tended to emerge precisely when existing tribal solidarities began to inhibit the growth of mercantile centers, thereby calling for new codes of (generalized) morality. Thus, for instance, 'Islam emerged and took root in Mecca and Medina in the seventh century, during that period of transition between a pastoral and semi-nomadic mode of social organization and the growth of mercantile centers that saw the emergence of new forms of social organization, of new roles and the redefinition of existing ones at the partial expense of existing tribal solidarities. The emergence of these "Axial" civilizations has indeed been linked to a heightened degree of differentiation among societal units occasioned by the breakdown of tribal communities and their restructuring into broader units often connected to the establishment of the early states in pre-literate societies' [Seligman, 1997: 27–28, partially quoting Eisenstadt, 1986: 20].

When speaking about religions, we must never lose sight of the fact that there is no such thing as an immutable body of religious tenets. The interpretation of monotheistic religions has often changed according to circumstances. For instance, these religions may have been born in times of troubles or of 'cosmological disintegration', as suggested by Eric Voegelin (1956), to be later re-interpreted in a manner suitable to the interests of commercial expansion, perhaps under the impulse of the merchants themselves or their political allies at the height of the social structure and the state apparatus. This latter possibility has been illustrated earlier with specific reference to Confucianism and Zen Buddhism in Japan.

Among today's economists, too, there is a proclivity to look for evolutionary accounts of norm emergence. Thus, reciprocal behaviour is often considered to be genetically determined or the result of long-run social learning processes [Fehr et al., 1996: 134]. The most ambitious attempt, so far, is that of Ken Binmore who does not hesitate to advocate a modern type of social Darwinism to account for the evolution of human morality. In his account, human morality gradually expands, through unthinking imitative behaviour, from extended family circles to wider circles where non-kin interact.[1] The Darwinian perspective adopted does not assume that our genes determine what will be regarded as fair in any given society, but that they determine or constrain the algorithm that a society uses in deciding what is fair [Binmore, 1996b: 154; 1994, 1996a].

Nevertheless, the ambitious attempt by Binmore to provide us with a full theoretical explanation of evolution of human morality is far from convincing. First, the demonstration is about the endogenous propagation of altruistic behaviour (or memes of sympathy)[2] and not of ethical codes based on reciprocal fairness. Second, it relies on successive chains of happy mistakes that are assumed to put manhood on the right track leading to morality. There are two problems here. For one thing, mistakes are supposed to be made by agents belonging to non-kin circles who inadvertently adopt pieces of (altruistic) behaviour evolved within kin-based circles. Yet, strangely enough, mistakes the other way round, which are much less favourable for the evolution of human ethics, are not allowed for in the model. For another thing, assuming accidental mistakes may be an acceptable approach in a very long-term perspective, but not in the more reasonable span of time that matters for social scientists eager to understand differential economic growth performances of human societies over a few centuries or even a few decades.

## 8.2 PATH-DEPENDENT TRAJECTORIES IN EUROPE

### *Path dependence in southern Italy*

A glance at present-day societies should suffice to convince us that the endogenous evolution of universalistic moral norms, as predicted by Hume, has failed to occur in some important instances. In fact, path dependence phenomena appear to be pervasive in the real world and to determine distinct institutional trajectories in different societies (see *supra*). In particular, expectations that developed under peculiar circumstances may self-perpetuate, thus giving rise to a self-enforcing stable system of beliefs and behaviours that has little ability to adjust to welfare-enhancing opportunities.

The case of southern Italy studied by Edward Banfield (1958) and Robert Putnam (1993) and already mentioned in Chapter 3 suggests itself as a good illustration of the possibility for a region to be entrapped in a distrust equilibrium. In the town of Chiaromonte where the first author made his observations, we are told, in a way reminiscent of our analysis of egalitarian norms in Chapter 5, that: 'The parent knows that other families will envy and fear the success of his family and that they are likely to seek to do it injury. He must therefore fear them and be ready to do them injury in order that they may have less power to injure him and his' [Banfield, 1958: 115–16]. In the whole Mezzogiorno, the language used by the people actually testifies to a deep-rooted tradition of distrust. Thus, to be a 'sucker' is known as *fesso*, an Italian term which also means 'cuckolded' [Putnam, 1993: 111–12]. Proverbs likewise point to the pervasive culture of diffidence not just towards the outsider but also within the community, even in small villages. In Calabria, for example, there is the saying that '*chi ara diritto, muore disperato*' ('he who behaves honestly comes to a miserable end'). Other proverbs are: 'Damned is he who trusts another'; 'Don't make loans, don't give gifts, don't do good, for it will turn out bad for you'; 'Everyone thinks of his own good and cheats his companion'; 'When you see the house of your neighbour on fire, carry water to your own' [quoted from Putnam, 1993: 143–44]. It is therefore not surprising that, as a result, southern Italy is permeated by 'defection, distrust, shirking, exploitation, isolation, disorder, and stagnation', all negative features that 'intensify one another in a suffocating miasma of vicious circles' [*ibidem*: 177].

Note carefully that, in such an atmosphere of generalized diffidence, communication and exchange of promises are of no avail. This is because communication does not take place when hostility reigns supreme and/or because deep-rooted suspicion prevents people from re-assuring each other in face-to-face encounters.

In the case of southern Italy, the negative characteristics of pervasive lack of trust, generalized suspicion, exacerbated individualism, and total absence of law-abidingness seem to go back for generations and to have their origin in a tradition of monarchical absolutism dating back to the Norman kingdoms in Sicily and Naples (particularly under Frederick II) and strongly supported by the Catholic church. This autocratic regime went hand in hand with vertical networks of patron-client bonds running through each layer of the local societies, whether urban or rural [Putnam, 1993: Chap. 5]. As we know, this tradition stands in complete contrast with the one which developed in northern and central Italy where communal republicanism allowed for the flourishing of a rich associational life under the form of guilds, neighbourhood associations, parish organizations, confraternities, and the like. True, the northern part of Italy was later to become 'refeudalized' and brought under the control of a succession of centralized sources of authority (many of them foreign), yet 'the republican traditions forged during the Renaissance survived well enough as part of the northern culture to become, in modern times, the source of a higher degree of spontaneous sociability than in the South' [Fukuyama, 1995: 108].

*Path dependence in the ex-Soviet Union*

Another glaring example of path dependence comes from the ex-Soviet Union area. Undoubtedly, many economies of this region exhibit features that are directly inherited from the previous communist regime and cannot be easily transformed because beliefs and the associated behaviours are slow to change: 'This country is not ready for civilized business; there are no laws, no principles, no traditions', said one of the most successful businessmen in present-day Russia [quoted from Ledeneva, 1998: 196].

The communist regime was fundamentally characterized not only by the discretionary power of bureaucrats over subordinates (enforced by the political dictatorship of the communist party), but also by the reputation effects from personal, often informal, long-run ties [Litwack, 1991: 79]. As a matter of fact, such ties used to play a critical role in coordinating economic activity under the planning system since it was impossible to be a successful manager in a Soviet-type economy 'without continually breaking the law and relying on these personal contacts'. On the other hand, vertical relationships between superiors and subordinates also tended to be highly personal, with regular gifts being made by the latter to the former in exchange for various services [*ibidem*: 80–82]. Moreover, as Alena Ledeneva (1998) has recently argued, the Soviet society was permeated by reciprocal help relationships that were more horizontal and less asymmetrical in nature.[3] Most ordinary problems were thus solved by having recourse to the assistance of personal friends and acquaintances without paying much attention to whether the way of solving them was legal or did cause harm to other persons situated out of the circle of *blat* relationships.[4]

Unfortunately, these networks of personalized relationships reinforced by codes of limited morality and evolved to solve scarcity problems during the communist era (since the central planning system did not work) do not seem to have the ability to transform themselves into broader-based economic ties supported by generalized morality. When the planning system was abandoned and economic liberalization became the order of the day, the informal networks inherited from the previous regime persisted. If personalized relationships among common people have the advantage of helping them to make ends meet in harsh transition conditions, those operating in the upper strata of the old society appear to be a largely negative legacy for the development of a market economy. In the words of Ledeneva:

> ...*blat* ... softened the rigid constraints of the command economy and the Soviet political system. It was well adapted to as well as restricted by Soviet morality....Now, with the expansion of the *market* and the concomitant decline of Soviet norms and values, ...*blat* practices stretched beyond their Soviet limits tend to be destructive to the national economy. These patterns which were organically connected to and functional for the Soviet social and political system have been carried over into the post-Soviet era with no control of their negative aspects and no attention to their advantageous sides [Ledeneva, 1998: 182].

If the old system of *blat* relationships was apparently useful for small-scale Russian entrepreneurs who emerged during the years 1988–1991—'the informal contacts and relations of trust formed within *blat* networks were the only guarantee one could rely on', particularly with respect to overcoming financial difficulties [Ledeneva, 1998: 185]—, it proved damaging when the upper echelons of the Soviet bureaucracy or the nomenclatura entered the scene:

> The 'old guard', the nomenclatura—directors of the enterprises and of regional, city, local administration—kept their power and positions in the post-Soviet period. This power and position is now used for private deals. The nomenclatura used to be well connected and they still are. They know each other and are always in touch... It is no wonder that many firms established by the nomenclatura are flourishing.... The dissolution of the

> Communist party and attempts to reduce the influence of the former nomenclatura do not mean that such a strong and well connected apparatus has disappeared... All large-scale operations—financial swindles, non-paid loans, investment projects, in which millions vanished in unknown directions—are mostly based on former connections [Ledeneva, 1998: 187, 211].

When transplanted in the new terrain of a market economy, *blat* methods soon became a formidable weapon in the hands of the old elite: 'The nomenclatura 'started trading their favours: they either want real money in return for favourable decisions or they launch their own businesses' [Ledeneva, 1998: 188]. With respect to the former option, what bears emphasis is the enormous scale of the prevailing corruption: for example, commissions on state loans for private commerce amount to 10 to 50 per cent of the amounts granted [*ibidem*: 208]. As for the latter option, it has led the nomenclatura to indulge in glaring manipulations and malpractices through which they succeeded in appropriating state assets for themselves in the course of dubious privatizations. In the words of a local newspaper (*Izvestiya*), 'our public auctions long ago turned into stage plays with roles assigned in advance. The directors are criminal "authorities" and corrupt bureaucrats' [cited from Ledeneva, 1998: 189]. In a still more striking manner, a Russian expert in commercial law warned that, in his country, owing to the pervasive influence of 'people of the circle', 'banks are not banks, money is not money, and insurance is not insurance' [*ibidem*: 211].

Cases of underhand seizing, or predetermined sales, of state assets are reported daily in the mass media all over Russia, 'where enterprises, land and buildings are privatized in the interests of "people of the circle"' [Ledeneva, 1998: 189]. In such conditions, it is not surprising that many instant millionaires in Russia were 'powerful communist insiders who profited from the Soviet era', yet were more limited in their ability to accumulate wealth when socialist restraints were still in force [*ibidem*: 186]. These people were part of genuine mafias with formidable power to establish their own, limited version of law and order, and ready to use any suitable method, including those of gangsterism, to achieve quick enrichment [Simis, 1982; Timofeyev, 1992; Vaksberg, 1991; Handelman, 1994; Follain, 1995].[5] In this way, the transition in post-Soviet Russia turned into a nightmare full of organized crime and racketeering, such as the one described below:

> These criminal businesses are by no means the kind of property owners who intend to boost production. Their objective is to buy cheap and sell for

> many times what they paid. For this reason, one of the gangs intended to acquire controlling blocks of shares in 53 major enterprises undergoing privatization in St Petersburg and Murmansk in 1993. The 'expropriation' of controlling blocks was planned and carried out like a combat operation... A genuine intelligence network (including bought-off bureaucrats and bankers) was set up, and it reported to 'headquarter'. Then Khomschuk's gang 'bullyboys' would show up at a plant: 'We are distributing humanitarian aid'. 'Give us the addresses of your retired workers!' After that, a call would be paid to every retiree, and, for a symbolic sum of money or after a brief intimidation session, the shares to which he was entitled would migrate into Khomschuk's coffers [quoted from Ledeneva, 1998: 190].

It has been argued that, by selling protection and defending property rights in the context of vanishing central political power, mafia-type organizations can perform a useful function in society [Gambetta, 1988a, 1993; Catanzaro, 1992; Anderson, 1995].[6] However, the possibility that they deliberately create chaos to justify their own interventions cannot be ruled out *a priori*. In other words, 'it is hard to tell whether a gang is using its monopoly power as a means of providing the benefits of enforcement of property rights or to extort a reward from the agents in its territory. In the extreme case, the Mafia may ask for tribute and offer in return "protection" from the Mafia itself—the case of pure extortion' [Konrad and Skaperdas, 1997: 51–52]. For example, we are told that all those who run kiosks in Russia have to face demands of payment for protection if they want to ensure against the risk of their kiosks being attacked or burnt overnight [Ledeneva, 1998: 191]. But who is actually threatening of attacking and burning kiosks? The question is particularly apposite in regard of private enterprises three quarters of which are reportedly forced to pay 10–20 per cent of their earnings to criminal gangs. Note that 150 of these gangs control some 40,000 private and state run companies, including most of the country's 1,800 commercial banks [*ibidem*]. Under these circumstances, it is not surprising that Russian and non-Russian companies increasingly hire private western security firms that are usually run by former soldiers and intelligence people, thus setting off a process of foreign colonization of the country [The Economist, 1998: 35–36].

Even assuming away this difficulty, a serious problem arises from the fact that mafias themselves contribute to weaken the central state by infiltrating it and exercising strong lobbying pressures on its agents with a view to advancing their own particularistic interests.[7] As attested by the Russian and south Italian experiences, mafias may largely succeed in 'swallowing' the state. To this decisive shortcoming must be added the fact that they are a very costly way of establishing trust in so far as protection purchased from one mafia network can always be denied by another network, as a result of mafia struggles to conquer new terrain. Gangs and mafias, after all, are known for fierce territorial wars [Skaperdas and Syropoulos, 1995: 69; Konrad and Skaperdas, 1997: 55]. They may, of course, attempt to establish peace among themselves by means of collusive agreements aimed at carefully delimiting their respective operating territories. The difficulty remains that such peaceful agreements are generally reached after protracted periods of violent confrontation, sometimes extreme brutality, are often unstable, and have the effect of fragmenting the economic space, thereby reducing the scope of trade opportunities and potential gains from exchange.

Clearly, norms of generalized morality may fail to emerge when needed. In addition, they may erode without any countervailing effect arising in time to arrest the decay of an economy.[8] This is exemplified by the decline of the Roman Empire as documented and interpreted by McMullen (1988).

## 8.3 CONCLUDING REMARKS

As pointed out in Chapter 3, getting amoral societies out of their distrust equilibrium requires an external intervention. After having argued, on the basis of the Italian experience, that 'A region's chances of achieving socioeconomic development during this century have depended less on its initial socioeconomic endowments than on its civic endowments', or that 'perhaps civics helps to explain economics, rather than the reverse' [Putnam, 1993: 154, 157], Putnam stresses that bringing new formal institutions into being (e.g., through decentralization reforms such as they were implemented in the whole of Italy) is liable to change political and social practices with the result that institutional and economic performances can be improved. Yet, in regions with a bad civic record, even if formal institutional changes are adequate, history will move slowly and the efficiency of the economic exchanges will improve only over decades [*ibidem*: 184].

In the case of SSA, Marcel Fafchamps, Paul Collier and others have similarly emphasized the need to bring institutional innovations to improve contract enforcement mechanisms. Establishing a system of credit rating to disseminate information about credit repayment performance among firms (so that they can better screen their potential business partners) or to enable banks and financial institutions to better assess the creditworthiness of their clients; instituting special judges or legal officers to impound assets and accounts to serve clearly identifiable commercial debt instruments; favouring private arbitration; promoting specialized commercial courts with simplified judicial and asset recovery procedures; improving the audit system so as to permit a more correct valuation of enterprises, are all interesting examples of what such innovations could be [Collier, 1994; Fafchamps, 1996].

What is not said, however, is how judges will be made impartial and non-corrupt (which necessitates, among other things, that political authorities stop interfering with the judicial system), or how falsification of credit rating records will be prevented when powerful businesses-people will be designated as loan delinquants, or how the auditing of accounts will be made sufficiently independent to be reliable. So far at least, economists have had little to say on these vexed questions which are all the more difficult to solve as they tend to arise simultaneously.

To return to the case of Russia, a country with a protracted history of authoritarianism, the full dimension of the present challenge confronting her can only be grasped if one is ready to listen to parliamentary deputy Vladimir Lepyokhin when he says: 'Society doesn't exist. What society is there in Russia? Have you seen one? How does it express itself? What does it look like? I don't see one. You can see some weak political parties. You can see authorities. That's it. There aren't any other institutions' [*Guardian,* 20 September 1995—quoted from Ledeneva, 1998: 212]. The challenge actually consists of undoing a strong legacy of centralized power, absence of civil society, command economy, and morality limited to restricted circles of people [Yergin and Gustavson, 1994]. In countries of SSA, the legacy to be defeated is one of absence of a strong state, an independent and effective bureaucracy, and a civil society differentiated along class lines rather than on the basis of highly segmented ethnic and other traditional affiliations.

In the cases of both these regions, it is worth pondering over the critique raised by the Hungarian historian Julius Szekfü (as synthesized by Andrew Janos) against superficial and abrupt transplantations of liberalism into unprepared soils, such as has occurred in his own country in the beginning of this century:

> The results of this transplantation were not only grotesque, they were outright harmful, because the gap between form and substance could only be

> closed by corrupting the electoral process in politics and by perverting the market mechanism in economics. In turn, the prevailing methods of corruption—the purchase of votes by the government, and the purchase of favours by the entrepreneur—had a deeply corrosive effect on nationale morale. They undermined the self-respect of the elites and the legitimacy of the nation state, and in this manner they paved the way for the revolutions of 1918–1919, and for the 'national tragedy' of the peace treaty [Janos, 1982: 267].

In short, the problem is that 'the market is embedded in society rather than conversely' [Bromley, 1989: 64]. In western Europe, it took its roots in a society where the political morality of modern law had triumphed after a protracted plurisecular struggle that unrolled within the confines of a deep-rooted tradition pervaded by a few specific, yet conflicting philosophies of law [Kriegel, 1995: Chap. 4—see *supra*]. Elsewhere, the social terrain may not be as congenial to the kind of public morality that the market requires. Consequently, establishing the formal institutions of the market by a single act of will cannot solve the problem of the market order on its own. In other words, when some essential features liable to produce generalized trust, (including a state abiding by the rule of the law) are absent, the social fabric of a society may not be easily adjusted to accommodate the market mechanism. History does matter, not a surprising fact given that it embodies the social norms prevailing in an particular society and that such norms are an indispensable concomitant of formal laws and regulations. True, societies may undergo profound changes and depart from previous trajectories under the influence of new-economic opportunities and the presence of new constraints imposed by economic and political forces operating on the national, regional or international level. The question nevertheless remains as to whether endogenous changes in societal fabrics are rapid enough to meet present-day challenges effectively.

On the other hand, as the first part of this book has reminded us, market development, including the emergence of private property rights, and the expansion of labour division depend to a significant extent on population density—which is determined by demographic forces as well as by settlement patterns and migratory flows—, and on the degree of opening to outside economic opportunities—which is partly conditioned by geographical factors and partly by economic policy. In particular, incentive problems are more difficult to surmount when populations are thinly spread over a territory than when they are highly concentrated. Moreover, in the characteristic tribal surroundings of low density countries, egalitarian norms are liable to make capital accumulation more difficult. As a result, economic growth tends to be retarded until people learn to gradually circumvent or undermine these norms.

Finally, population density and geographical configurations do not only impinge on market development but also condition the rise of a modern and effective state understood as a centralized apparatus able to impose its authority over an unified area of sufficient size; to devise, implement and legitimate development-oriented policies; to use the services of a bureaucracy independent enough of peculiar interests (including those of the rulers); and to codify and enforce all the rules and institutions required for such tasks. To the extent that these relationships are valid, low population densities that presently obtain or that were characteristic of a not-too-distant past and have helped shape a country's development path tend to create serious obstacles on the way to rapid economic growth.

In the end, what comes out is a broad perspective on development that pays attention not only to economic policy factors, but also to structural forces comprising demographic, geographical, political and socio-cultural features of human societies. This perspective is akin to the classical approach followed by the great pioneers in development economics, from David Hume to John Stuart Mill, through Adam Smith, John McCulloch, Thomas-Robert Malthus and John Rae to whom the preseent author is greatly indebted.

## NOTES

1. The evolutionary process envisioned by Binmore can be summarized as follows. Since siblings share genes and therefore sympathize with each other's reproductive aspirations, they build a direct concern for the welfare of their relatives in their personal utility functions. This leads them to follow rules of Kantian or semi-Kantian ethics (maximize your payoff on the assumption that your siblings will choose the same strategy as yourself, or that they will do it half of the time). Moral behaviour is then expanded from the extended family to the world at large 'through players misreading signals from their environment and so mistakenly applying a piece of behaviour or a way of thinking that has evolved for use within some inner circle to a larger set of people or to a new game.... But playing the outer-circle game as though it were the inner-circle game will sometimes result in the players co-ordinating on an equilibrium of the outer-circle game. The group wiill then have stumbled upon an *equilibrium selection device* for the outer-circle game...Nature therefore did not need to invent some entirely new mechanism to bridge the gap between altruism within the family and fairness between strangers'. In other words, because people sometimes take a technique used within one circle of social problems and unthinkingly apply it to a wider domain of problems, they may sometimes succeed in co-ordinating behaviour on a Pareto-improving equilibrium of the wider game, 'whereupon group selection will move the evolutionary ratchet one further notch forward' [Binmore, 1996b: 167–68, 170].

2. A meme is the social equivalent of a gene, that is, 'an idea, a rule-of-thumb, a norm, or anything else that can be replicated from one head to another by imitation or education' [Binmore, 1996b: 152].
3. The proverb 'Do not have 100 roubles, have 100 friends' was an apt one in this period [Ledeneva, 1998: 197].
4. I cannot agree when Ledeneva when she contends that in Soviet times 'helping out by *blat* was often exercised at the expense of state property' as though no other citizen was harmed in the process [Ledeneva, 1998: 179]. Jumping the queue for a rationed good (whether a consumption good, a job, or a registration in the university) thanks to the deliberate intervention of a 'friend' obviously causes harm to other concrete persons.
5. According to information from law enforcement agencies, 'as much as 70 per cent of the real estate put up for sale at auctions winds up in the hands of individuals who are agreed upon beforehand. Before a public auction begins, the information is conveyed to everyone that an "authority" is interested in this piece of property, and that if anyone takes the risk of competing for it, he shouldn't complain later that he wasn't warned' [Ledeneva, 1998: 189].
6. Rumanian informants told me in the early eighties that Russian goods exported to Rumania by road were accompanied by armoured vehicles.
7. For an analytical elaboration of the competition between the government and the mafia as providers of protection, see Grossman, 1995.
8. For a discussion of the possible causes of an erosion of moral norms in advanced capitalist societies, see Platteau, 1994b: 791–94.

# REFERENCES


ABB (Association Belge des Banques), 1989, 'Le crédit à la consommation aujourd'hui—Objections à une centrale de risques positive', *Aspects et Documents*, No. 96, Bruxelles.

ABREU, D., 1988, 'On the Theory of Infinitely Repeated Games with Discounting', *Econometrica*, Vol. 56, No. 2, pp. 383–396.

ACHESON, J.M., 1972, 'Territories of the Lobstermen', *Natural History*, Vol. 81, No. 1, pp. 60–69.

ACHESON, J.M., 1989, 'Management of Common-Property Resources', in Plattner, S. (ed.), *Economic Anthropology*, Stanford, Cal.: Stanford University Press, pp. 351–378.

AGARWAL, B., 1991, 'Social Security and the Family: Coping with Seasonality and Calamity in Rural India', in Ahmad, E., J. Drèze, J. Hills, and A. Sen (eds.), *Social Security in Developing Countries*, Oxford: Clarendon Press, pp. 171–244.

AGELL, J., and P. LUNDBERG, 1995, 'Theories of Pay and Unemployment: Survey Evidence from Swedish Manufacturing Firms', *Scandinavian Journal of Economics*, Vol. 97, No. 1, pp. 295–308.

AHMED, R., and N. RUSTAGI, 1984, 'Marketing and Price Incentives in African and Asian Countries: A Comparison', in: Dieter, E. (Ed.), *Agricultural Marketing Strategy and Pricing Policy*, Washington, DC: The World Bank.

AHMED, R., and C. DONOVAN, 1992, 'Issues of Infrastructural Development: A Synthesis of the Literature', Washington, D.C: International Food Policy Research Institute.

AKERLOF, G., 1976, 'The Economics of Caste and of the Rat Race and Other Woeful Tales', *Quarterly Journal of Economics*, Vol. 90, No. 4, pp. 599–617.

AKERLOF, G., 1984, *An Economic Theorist's Book of Tales*, Cambridge: Cambridge University Press.

ALCHIAN, A., and H. DEMSETZ, 1973, 'The Property Right Paradigm', *Journal of Economic History*, Vol. 33, No. 1, 16–27.

ALDERMAN, H., and C.H. PAXSON, 1992, 'Do the Poor Insure? A Synthesis of the Literature on Risk and Consumption in Developing Countries', Policy Research Working Papers, WPS 1008, Washington, DC: The World Bank.

ALEXANDER, P., 1982, *Sri Lankan Fishermen: Rural Capitalism and Peasant Society*, Canberra: Australian National University Press.

ALLEN, R., 1992, *Enclosure and the Yeomen*, Oxford: Oxford University Press.

ALLEN, R., 1997, 'Agriculture and the Origins of the State in Ancient Egypt', in *Explorations in Economic History*, Vol. 34, No. 1, pp. 135–154.

ALSTON, L.J., G.D. LIBECAP, and R. SCHNEIDER, 1996, 'The Determinants and Impact of Property Rights: Land Titles on the Brazilian Frontier', *The Journal of Law, Economics, and Organization*, Vol. 12, No. 1, pp. 25–61.

AMBEC, S., 1998, 'An Income-Sharing Norm Mutually Enforced by Social Status', Département des sciences économiques, Université de Montréal, Montréal (mimeo).

ANDERSON, A., 1995, 'Organised Crime, Mafia and Governments', in Fiorentini, G., and S. Peltzman (eds.), *The Economics of Organised Crime*, Cambridge: Cambridge University Press, pp. 33–54.

ANDERSON, P., 1974, *Lineages of the Absolutist State*, London & New York: Verso.

ANDRE, C., 1989, *Evolution des systèmes d'exploitation et des droits fonciers: le cas du Rwanda*, unpublished master thesis, Faculté des Sciences Economiques et Sociales, Namur, Belgium.

ANDRE, C., and J.P. PLATTEAU, 1998, 'Land Relations Under Unbearable Stress: Rwanda Caught in the Malthusian Trap', *Journal of Economic Behavior and Organization*, Vol. 34, No. 1, pp. 1–47.

ANTLE, J.M., 1983, 'Infrastructure and Aggregate Agricultural Productivity: International Evidence', *Economic Development and Cultural Change*, Vol. 31, No. 3, pp. 609–619.

AOKI, M., 1997, 'Unintended Fit: Organizational Evolution and Government Design of Institutions in Japan', in Aoki, M., H.K. Kim, and M. Okuno-Fujiwara (eds.), *The Role of Government in East Asian Development—Comparative Institutional Analysis*, Oxford: Clarendon Press, pp. 233–253.

AOKI, M., forthcoming, *Towards a Comparative Institutional Analysis*, MIT Press.

AOKI, M., K. MURDOCK, and M. OKUNO-FUJIWARA, 1997, 'Beyond the East Asian Miracle: Introducing the Market-Enhancing View', in Aoki, M., H.K. Kim, and M. Okuno-Fujiwara (eds.), *The Role of Government in East Asian Development—Comparative Institutional Analysis*, Oxford: Clarendon Press, pp. 1–37.

ARDENER, E., 1970, 'Witchcraft, Economics and the Continuity of Belief', in Douglas, M. (ed.), *Witchcraft Confessions and Accusation*, London: Tavistock Publications, pp. 141–160.

ARNOLD, J.E.M., and J.G. CAMPBELL, 1986, 'Collective Management of Hill Forests in Nepal: The Community Forestry Development Project', in National Research Council, *Proceedings of the Conference on Common Property Resource Management*, Washington, D.C.: National Academy Press, pp. 425–454.

ARNOLD, J.E.M., forthcoming, 'Devolution of Control of Common-Pool Resources to Local Communities: Experiences in Forestry', in A. de Janvry, G. Gordillo, J.P. Platteau, and E. Sadoulet (eds), *Access to Land, Rural Poverty, and Public Action,* Oxford: Clarendon Press.

ARONFREED, J., 1968, *Conduct and Conscience: The Socialization of Internalized Control Over Behavior*, New York: Academic Press.

ARONFREED, J., 1969, 'The Concept of Internalization', in Goslin, D.A. (ed.), *Handbook of Socialization—Theory and Research*, Chicago: Rand-McNally.

ARONFREED, J., 1970, 'The Socialization of Altruistic and Sympathetic Behavior: Some Theoretical and Experimental Analyses', in Macaulay, J. and L. Berkowitz (eds.), *Altruism and Helping Behavior*, New York, San Francisco & London: Academic Press, pp. 103–126.

ARROW, K., 1971, 'Political and Economic Evaluation of Social Effects and Externalities', in Intriligator, M. (ed.), *Frontiers of Quantitative Economics*, Amsterdam: North-Holland, pp. 3–25.

ARROW, K., 1973, *Information and Economic Behavior*, Stockholm: Federation of Swedish Industries.

ARYEETEY, E., 1997, 'Rural Finance in Africa', in *Proceedings of the World Bank Annual Conference on Development Economics—1996*, Washington, DC: World Bank.

ASADA, Y., Y. HIRASAWA, and F. NAGASAKI, 1983, 'Fishery Management in Japan', *FAO Fisheries Technical Paper*, No. 238, Rome: FAO.

ASHTON, T.S., 1955, *An Economic History of England—The Eighteenth Century.*

ASSAAD, R., 1997, 'Kinship Ties, Social Networks, and Segmented Labor Markets: Evidence from the Construction Sector in Egypt', *Journal of Development Economics*, Vol. 52, No. 1, pp. 1–30.

ATKINS, F., 1988, 'Land Reform: A Failure of Neoclassical Theorization?', *World Development*, Vol. 16, No. 8, pp. 935–946.

ATWOOD, D.A., 1990, 'Land Registration in Africa: The Impact on Agricultural Production', *World Development*, Vol. 18, No. 5, pp. 659–671.

AUKRUST, O., 1959, 'Investment and Economic Growth', *Productivity Measurement Review*, No. 16, pp. 35–50.

AULT, D.E., and G.L. RUTMAN, 1979, 'The Development of Individual Rights to Property in Tribal Africa', *Journal of Law and Economics*, Vol. 22, No. 1, pp. 163–182.

AUMANN, R.J., 1964, 'Markets with a Continuum of Traders', *Econometrica*, Vol. 32, No. 1–2, pp. 39–50.

AUSTEN, R., 1987, *African Economic History*, London: James Currey & Portsmouth NH: Heinemann.

AUSTIN, G., 1993, 'Indigenous Credit Institutions in West Africa, c.1750–c.1960', in Austin, G., and K. Sugihara (eds.), *Local Suppliers of Credit in the Third World, 1750–1960*, New York: St. Martin's Press, pp. 93–159.

AXELROD, R., 1984, *The Evolution of Cooperation*, New York: Basic Books.

AXELROD, R., 1986, 'An Evolutionary Approach to Norms', *American Political Science Review*, Vol. 80, No. 4, pp. 1095–1111; reprinted in Axelrod, R., 1997, *The Complexity of Cooperation—Agent-Based Models of Competition and Collaboration*, Princeton, New Jersey: Princeton University Press, pp. 44–68.

BADIANE, O., 1992, 'National Policies For Integrated Regional Markets in West Africa', Washington, DC: International Food Policy Research Institute.

BADIANE, O., and G.E. SHIVELEY, 1998, 'Spatial Integration, Transport Costs, and the Response of Local Prices to Policy Changes in Ghana', *Journal of Development Economics*, Vol. 56, No. 2, pp. 411–431.

BADINI, A., 1994, *Naître et grandir chez les Moosé traditionnels*, Paris-Ouagadougou: Sépia-A.D.D.B.

BADOUIN, R., 1971, *Economie rurale*, Paris: Armand Colin.

BAGCHI, A., 1992, 'Riding the Free Rider—A Lesson From Barrackpore', *Economic and Political Weekly*, Vol. 27, No. 34, pp. 1778–1780.

BALAND, J.M., and J.P. PLATTEAU, 1996, *Halting Degradation of Natural Resources—Is There a Role for Rural Communities?*, Oxford: Clarendon Press.

BALAND, J.M., and J.P. PLATTEAU, 1997, 'Wealth Inequality and Efficiency in the Commons—Part I: The Unregulated Case', Vol. 49, No. 4, pp. 451–482.

BALAND, J.M., and J.P. PLATTEAU, 1998a, 'Wealth Inequality and Efficiency in the Commons—Part I: The Regulated Case', Vol. 50, No. 1, pp. 1–22.

BALAND, J.M., and J.P. PLATTEAU, 1998b, 'Dividing the Commons—A Partial Assessment of the New Institutional Economics of Property Rights', *American Journal of Agricultural Economics*, Vol. 80, August, pp. 644–650.

BALAND, J.M., and J.P. PLATTEAU, 1999, 'The Ambiguous Impact of Inequality on Local Resource Management', *World Development*, Vol. 27, No. 5.

BALAND, J.M., and P. FRANCOIS, 1997, 'Commons as Insurance and the Welfare Impact of Privatization', University of Namur, Dept. of Economics, mimeo.

BALAND, J.M., and F. MANIQUET, 1998, 'Welfare Implications of the Privatization of the Commons', University of Namur, Dept. of Economics, mimeo.

BALAND, J.M., F. GASPART, F. PLACE, and J.P. PLATTEAU, 1999, 'Poverty, Tenure Security and Access to Land in Central Uganda: the Role of Market and Non-market Processes', Cahiers de Recherche, Faculté des sciences économiques, sociales et de gestion, Development series, University of Namur (Belgium).

BALIBAR, E., and I. WALLERSTEIN, 1988, *Race, Nation, Classe: les identités ambigües*, Paris: Editions La Découverte.

BANFIELD, E.C., 1958, *The Moral Basis of a Backward Society*, Chicago: The Free Press.

BARDHAN, P.K., 1984, *Land, Labour and Rural Poverty: Essays in Development Economics*, New York: Columbia University Press (or New Delhi: Oxford University Press).

BARDHAN, P.K., 1985, 'Marxist Ideas in Development Economics—A Brief Evaluation', *Economic and Political Weekly*, Vol. 20, No. 13, pp. 550–555.

BARDHAN, P.K., 1989, 'Alternative Approaches to the Theory of Institutions in Economic Development', in Bardhan, P. (ed.), *The Economic Theory of Agrarian Institutions*, Oxford: Clarendon Press, pp. 3–17.

BARDHAN, P.K., 1993, 'Symposium on Democracy and Development', *Journal of Economic Perspectives*, Vol. 7, No. 3, pp. 45–49.

BARRETT, C., and M.R. CARTER, 1999, 'Microeconomically Coherent Agricultural Policy Reform in Africa', in Paulson, J. (ed), *African Economies in Transition, Vol. 2: The Reform Experience, London: Macmillan Press,* pp. 288–347.

BARRO, R.J., 1991, 'Economic Growth in a Cross Section of Countries', *Quarterly Journal of Economics*, Vol. 106, No. 2, pp. 407–433.

BARRO, R.J., 1997, *Determinants of Economic Growth—A Cross-Country Empirical Study*, Cambridge, MA. & London: The MIT Press.

BARROWS, R., and M. ROTH, 1989, 'Land Tenure and Investment in African Agriculture: Theory and Evidence', Land Tenure Center, LTC Paper No. 136, University of Wisconsin-Madison.

BARTH, F., 1967, 'Economic Spheres in Darfur', in Firth, R. (ed.), *Themes in Economic Anthropology*, London: Tavistock Publications, pp. 149–174.

BARTHEZ, A., 1982, *Famille, travail et agriculture*, Paris: Economica.

BARZEL, Y., 1989, *Economic Analysis of Property Rights*, Cambridge: Cambridge University Press.

BASSETT, T.J., 1993a, 'Introduction: The Land Question and Agricultural Transformation in Sub-Saharan Africa', in Bassett, T.J., and D.E. Crummey (eds.), *Land in African Agrarian Systems*, Madison, Wisconsin: The University of Wisconsin Press: pp. 3–31.

BASSETT, T.J., 1993b, 'Land Use Conflicts in Pastoral Development in Northern Cote d'Ivoire', in Bassett, T.J., and D.E. Crummey (eds.), *Land in African Agrarian Systems*, Madison, Wisconsin: University of Wisconsin Press, pp. 131–154.

BASSETT, T.J., and D.E. CRUMMEY, 1993 (eds.), *Land in African Agrarian Systems*, Madison, Wisconsin: The University of Wisconsin Press.

BASU, K., 1986a, 'One Kind of Power', *Oxford Economic Papers*, Vol. 38, No. 2, pp. 259–282.

BASU, K., 1986b, 'Markets, Power and Social Norms', *Economic and Political Weekly*, Vol. XXI, No. 43, October, pp. 1893–1896.

BASU, K., 1986c, 'The Market for Land—An Analysis of Interim Transaction', *Journal of Development Economics,* Vol. 20, No. 1, pp. 163–77.

BASU, K., 1997, *Analytical Development Economics—The Less Developed Economy Revisited*, Cambridge, Mssts & London: the MIT Press.

BASU, K., E. JONES, and E. SCHLICHT, 1987, 'The Growth and Decay of Custom: The Role of the New Institutional Economics in Economic History', *Explorations in Economic History*, Vol. 24, No. 1, pp. 1–21.

BATES, R.H., 1981, *Markets and States in Tropical Africa: The Political Basis of Agricultural Policies*, Berkeley: University of California Press.

BATES, R.H., 1983, *Essays on the Political Economy of Rural Africa*, Cambridge: Cambridge University Press.

BATES, R.H., 1989, *Beyond the Miracle of the Market—The Political Economy of Agrarian Development in Kenya*, Cambridge: Cambridge University Press.

BAUER, P.T., and B.S. YAMEY, 1957, *The Economics of Under-Developed Countries*, Cambridge: Cambridge University Press.

BAYART, J.F., 1986, 'Civil Society in Africa', in Chabal, P. (ed.), *Political Domination in Africa—Reflections on the Limits of Power*, Cambridge: Cambridge University Press, pp. 109–125.

BAYART, J.F., 1989, *L'Etat en Afrique*, Paris: Fayard.

BECK, T., 1994, 'Common Property Resource Access by Poor and Class Conflict in West Bengal', *Economic and Political Weekly*, Vol. 29, No. 4, pp. 187–97.

BELL, C., and M. Zusman, 1976, 'A Bargaining Approach to Cropsharing Contracts', *American Economic Review*, Vol. 66, No. 4, pp. 578–588.

BELSHAW, C., 1965, *Traditional Exchange and Modern Markets*, Englewood Cliffs, NJ: Prentice-Hall.

BENDOR, J., D. MOOKHERJEE, and D. RAY, 1994, 'Aspirations, Adaptive Learning and Cooperation in Repeated Games', *Ruth Pollack Working Papers Series on Economics*, No. 27, Dpt of Economics, Boston University.

BENOIT, J.P., and V. KRISHNA, 1985, 'Finitely Repeated Games', *Econometrica*, Vol. 53, No. 4, pp. 905–22.

BERGER, P., and T. LUCKMANN, 1967, *The Social Construction of Reality*, Harmondsworth: Penguin Books.

BERGSTEN, G.S., 1985, 'On the Role of Social Norms in a Market Economy', *Public Choice*, Vol. 45, No. 1, pp. 113–137.

BERKES, F., 1986, 'Local-Level Management and the Commons Problem—A Comparative Study of Turkish Coastal Fisheries', *Marine Policy*, Vol. 10, July, pp. 215–29.

BERKES, F., 1987, 'Common-Property Resource Management and Cree Indian Fisheries in Subarctic Canada', in McCay, B.J., and J.M. Acheson (eds.), *The Question of the Commons: The Culture and Ecology of Communal Resources*, Tucson, Ariz.: University of Arizona Press, pp. 66–91.

BERRY, S., 1984, 'The Food Crisis and Agrarian Change in Africa: A Review Essa', *African Studies Review*, Vol. 27, No. 2, pp. 59–112.

BERRY, S., 1988, 'Concentration Without Privatization? Some Consequences of Changing Patterns of Rural Land Control in Africa', in Downs, R.E., and S.P. Reyna (eds.), *Land and Society in Contemporary Africa*, Hanover and London: University Press of New England, pp. 53–75.

BERRY, S., 1993, *No Condition is Permanent*, Madison: University of Wisconsin Press.

BERTHELEMY, J.C. and C. MORRISSON, 1987, 'Manufactured Goods Supply and Cash Crops in Sub-Saharan Africa', *World Development*, Vol. 15, No. 10/11, pp. 1353–1367.

BEVAN, D., P. COLLIER, and J.W. GUNNING, 1989, *Peasants and Governments—An Economic Analysis*, Clarendon Press: Oxford.

BESLEY, T., 1995a, 'Savings, Credit and Insurance', in Behrman, J., and T.N. Srinivasan (eds.), *Handbook of Development Economics—Vol. 3A*, Amsterdam: Elsevier, 2123–2207.

BESLEY, T., 1995b, 'Nonmarket Institutions for Credit and Risk Sharing in Low-Income Countries', *Journal of Economic Perspectives*, Vol. 9, No. 3, pp. 115–127.

BESLEY, T., 1995c, 'Property Rights and Investment Incentives: Theory and Evidence from Ghana', *Journal of Political Economy*, Vol. 103, No. 5, pp. 903–937.

BEVERIDGE, A.A., and A.R. OBERSCHALL, 1979, *African Businessmen and Development in Zambia*, Princeton, NJ: Princeton University Press.

BEYNON, J. (ed.), 1992, 'Market Liberalization and Private Sector Response in Eastern and Southern Africa', Working Paper No. 6, Oxford: Food Studies Group, International Development Centre.

BIENEN, H., 1987, 'Domestic Political Considerations for Food Policy', in Mellor, J., C. Delgado, and M. Blackie (eds.), *Accelerating Food Production in sub-Saharan Africa*, London and Baltimore: The Johns Hopkins University Press, pp. 296–308.

BIGSTEN, A., P. COLLIER, S. DERCON, M. FAFCHAMPS, B. GAUTHIER, J.W. GUNNING, A. ODURO, R. OOSTENDORP, C. PATILLO, M. SODERBOM, F. TEAL, and A. ZEUFACK, 1998, 'Contract Flexibility and Conflict Resolution: Evidence from African Manufacturing', Washington: The World Bank (mimeo).

BINMORE, K., 1992, *Funs and Games: A Text on Game Theory*, Cambridge, Mass.: D.C. Heath & Co.

BINMORE, K., 1994, *Playing Fair: Game Theory and the Social Contract I*, Cambridge, Mass.: MIT Press.

BINMORE, K., 1996a, *Just Playing: Game Theory and the Social Contract II*, Cambridge, Mass.: MIT Press.

BINMORE, K., 1996b, 'Evolution of Fairness Norms', *Nordic Journal of Political Economy*, Vol. 23, No. 2, pp. 151–173.

BINSWANGER, H.P., 1990, 'The Policy Response of Agriculture', in *Proceedings of the World Bank Annual Conference on Development Economics—1989*, Washington, D.C.: The World Bank, pp. 231–258.

BINSWANGER, H.P., 1991, 'Brazilian Policies that Encourage Deforestation in the Amazon', *World Development*, Vol. 19, No. 7, pp. 821–29.

BINSWANGER, H.P., and M. ROSENZWEIG, 1986, 'Behavioural and Material Determinants of Production Relations in Agriculture', *Journal of Development Studies*, Vol. 22, No. 3, pp. 503–39.

BINSWANGER, H., and J. McINTIRE, 1987, 'Behavioural and Material Determinants of Production Relations in Land-Abundant Tropical Agriculture', *Economic Development and Cultural Change*, Vol. 36, No. 1, pp. 73–99.

BINSWANGER, H., J. McINTIRE, and C. UDRY, 1989, 'Production Relations in Semi-Arid African Agriculture', in Bardhan, P. (ed.), *The Economic Theory of Agrarian Institutions*, Oxford: Clarendon Press, pp. 122–144.

BINSWANGER, H.P., Y. MUNDLAK, M.C. YANG, and A. BOWERS, 1987, 'On the Determinants of Cross-Country Aggregate Agriculture Supply', *Journal of Econometrics*, Vol. 36, No. 1, pp. 111–131.

BINSWANGER, H.P., S. KHANDKER, and M.R. ROSENZWEIG, 1993, 'How Infrastructure and Financial Institutions Affect Agricultural Output and Investment in India', *Journal of Development Economics*, Vol. 41, No. 2, pp. 337–66.

BINSWANGER, H.P., K. DEININGER, and G. FEDER, 1995, 'Power, Distortions, Revolt and Reform in Agricultural Land Relations', in Behrman, J. and T.N. Srinivasan (eds.), *Handbook of Development Economics—Vol. 3B*, Amsterdam: Elsevier, pp. 2659–2772.

BINSWANGER, H.P., and K. DEININGER, 1997, 'Explaining Agricultural and Agrarian Policies in Developing Countries', *Journal of Economic Literature*, Vol. 35, No. 4, pp. 1958–2005.

BLISS, C.J., and N.H. STERN, 1982, *Palanpur*, Oxford: Oxford University Press.

BLOCH, P.C., 1993, 'An Egalitarian Development Project in a Stratified Society: Who Ends Up With the Land?', in Bassett, T.J., and D.C. Crummey (eds.), *Land in African Agrarian Systems*, Madison, Wisconsin: University of Wisconsin Press, pp. 222–243.

BLOCK, S.A., 1994, 'A New View of Agricultural Productivity in Sub-Saharan Africa', *American Journal of Agricultural Economics*, Vol. 76, No. 3, pp. 619–24.

BLOUNT, S., 1995, 'When Social Outcomes Aren't Fair: The Effect of Causal Attributions on Preferences', *Organizational Behavior and Human Decision Processes*, Vol. 63, No. 2, pp. 131–144.

BOEHM, C., 1993, 'Egalitarian Behavior and Reverse Dominance Hierarchy', *Current Anthropology*, Vol. 34, No. 3, pp. 227–254.

BOND, M.E., 1983, 'Agricultural Responses to Prices in Sub-Saharan Africa', *International Monetary Fund Staff Papers*, Vol. 30, No. 4, pp. 703–726.

BOSERUP, E., 1965, *The Conditions of Agricultural Growth: The Economics of Agrarian Change under Population Pressure*, London: Allen and Unwin.

BOSERUP, E., 1981, *Population and Technology*, Oxford: Basil Blackwell.

BOONE, C., 1992, *Merchant Capital and the Roots of State Power in Senegal 1930–1985*, Cambridge: Cambridge University Press.

BOOTH, D., 1987, 'Alternatives in the Restructuring of State-Society Relations: Research Issues for Tropical Africa', *IDS Bulletin*, Vol. 18, No. 4, pp. 23–30.

BOOTH, A., and R.M. SUNDRUM, 1985, *Labour Absorption in Agriculture*, Oxford: Oxford University Press.

BOSERUP, E., 1965, *The Conditions of Agricultural Growth: The Economics of Agrarian Change under Population Pressure*, London: Allen and Unwin.

BOSERUP, E., 1981, *Population and Technology*, Oxford: Basil Blackwell.

BOURDIEU, P. 1963, 'La société traditionnelle: Attitude à l'égard du temps et conduite économique', *Sociologie du travail*, Vol. 5, No. 1, pp. 24–44.

BOURDIEU, P., 1977, *Algérie 60: Structures économiques et structures temporelles*, Paris: Les éditions de Minuit.

BOURDIEU, P., 1980, *Le sens pratique*, Paris: Les éditions de Minuit.

BOURDIEU, P., and A. SAYAD, 1964, *Le déracinement—La crise de l'agriculture traditionnelle en Algérie*, Paris: Editions de Minuit.

BOUTILLIER, J.L., 1963, 'Les rapports du système foncier toucouleur et de l'organisation sociale et économique traditionnelle—leur évolution actuelle', in Biebuyck, D. (ed.), *African Agrarian Systems*, London: Oxford University Press, pp. 116–133.

BOWLES, S., 1996, 'Markets as Cultural Institutions: Equilibrium Norms in Competitive Economies', Working Paper 1996–5, Dept. of Economics, University of Massachusetts.

BOWLES, S., 1998a, 'Endogenous Preferences: The Cultural Consequences of Markets and other Economic Institutions', *Journal of Economic Literature*, Vol. 36, No. 1, pp. 75–111.

BOWLES, S., 1998b, 'Mandeville's Mistake: The Evolution of Norms in Market Environments', Dept. of Economics, University of Massachusetts (mimeo).

BOWLES, S., and H. GINTIS, 1998, 'The Moral Economy of Communities: Structured Populations and the Evolution of Pro-Social Norms', *Evolution and Human Behavior*, Vol. 19, No. 1, pp. 3–25.

BOYER, R., and A. ORLEAN, 1991, 'Why Are Institutional Transitions so Difficult?', Centre de Recherches en Epistémologie Appliquée (CREA), Ecole Polytechnique (Paris), Rapport No. 9105A.

BRASSELLE, A.S., F. GASPART, and J.P. PLATTEAU, 1998, 'Land Tenure Security and Investment Incentives: Further Puzzling Evidence from Burkina Faso', Cahiers de recherche, CRED (Centre de Recherche en Economie du Développement), Department of Economics, University of Namur, Belgium.

BRAUN, R., 1978, 'Early Industrialization and Demographic Change in the Canton of Zürich', in Tilly, C. (ed.), *Historical Studies of Changing Fertility*, Princeton: Princeton University Press, pp. 289–334.

BRAY, F., 1983, 'Patterns of Evolution in Rice-Growing Societies', *Journal of Peasant Studies*, Vol. 11, No. 1, pp. 3–33.

BRIGHTMAN, R.A., 1987, 'Conservation and Resource Depletion: The Case of the Boreal Forest Algonquians', in McCay, B.J., and J.M. Acheson (eds.), *The Question of the Commons: The Culture and Ecology of Communal Resources*, Tucson, Ariz.: University of Arizona Press, pp. 121–41.

BRITO, D.L., M.D. INTRILIGATOR, and E. SHESHINSKI, 1997, 'Privatization and the Distribution of Income in the Commons', *Journal of Public Economics*, Vol. 64, No. 2, pp. 181–205.

BROMLEY, D.W., 1986, 'Closing Comments at the Conference on Common Property Resource Management', in National Research Council, *Proceedings of the Conference on Common Property Resource Management*, Washington, D.C.: National Academy Press, pp. 593–98.

BROMLEY, D., 1989, *Economic Interests and Institutions—The Conceptual Foundations of Public Policy*, Oxford: Basil Blackwell.

BROMLEY, D., and D. CHAPAGAIN, 1984, 'The Village Against the Centre: Resource Depletion in South Asia', *American Journal of Agricultural Economics*, Vol. 66, No. 5, pp. 868–873.

BROWN, M., 1988, *Adam Smith's Economies—Its Place in the Development of Economic Thought*, London: Croom Helm.

BRUCE, J.W., 1986, 'Land Tenure Issues in Project Design and Strategies for Agricultural Development in Sub-Saharan Africa', Land Tenure Center, LTC Paper No. 128, University of Wisconsin-Madison.

BRUCE, J.W., 1988, 'A Perspective on Indigenous Land Tenure Systems and Land Concentration', in Downs, R.E., and S.P. Reyna (eds.), *Land and Society in Contemporary Africa*, Hanover and London: University Press of New England, pp. 23–52.

BRUCE, J.W., 1993, 'Do Indigenous Tenure Systems Constrain Agricultural Development?', in Bassett, T.J., and D.E. Crummey (eds.), *Land in African Agrarian Systems*, Madison, Wisc.: University of Wisconsin Press, pp. 35–56.

BRUCE, J.W., and L. FORTMANN, 1989, 'Agroforestry: Tenure and Incentives', Land Tenure Center, LTC Paper No. 135, University of Wisconsin-Madison.

BRUCE, J.W., S.E. MIGOT-ADHOLLA, and J. ATHERTON, 1994, 'The Findings and their Policy Implications: Institutional Adaptation or Replacement?', in Bruce, J.W., and S.E. Migot-Adholla (eds.), *Searching for Land Tenure Security in Africa*, Dubuque, Iowa: Kendall/Hunt Publishing Cy, pp. 251–265.

BRUCE, J.W., and S.E. MIGOT-ADHOLLA (eds.), 1994, *Searching for Land Tenure Security in Africa*, Dubuque, Iowa: Kendall/Hunt Publishing Cy.

BRUTON, H.J., 1965, *Principles of Development Economics*, Englewood Cliffs, N.J. & Prentice-Hall.

BUCHANAN, J.M., 1975, *The Limits of Liberty—Between Anarchy and Leviathan*, Chicago and London: The University of Chicago Press.

BUREAU, R., 1996, *Le peuple du fleuve—Sociologie de la conversion chez les Douala*, Paris: Karthala.

CALDWELL, J.C., 1991, 'The Soft Underbelly of Development: Demographic Transition in Conditions of Limited Economic Change', *Proceedings of the World Bank Annual Conference on Development Economics—1990*, Washington, DC: The World Bank, pp. 207–253.

CALDWELL, J.C., and P. CALDWELL, 1987, 'The Cultural Context of High Fertility in sub-Saharan Africa', *Population and Development Review*, Vol. 13, No. 3, pp. 409–437.

CALDWELL, J.C., and P. CALDWELL, 1990, 'High Fertility in Sub-Saharan Africa', *Scientific American*, May, pp. 82–89.

CAMERER, C., and R. THALER, 1995, 'Ultimatums, Dictators and Manners', *Journal of Economic Perspectives*, Vol. 9, pp. 209–19.

CARRIER, J.G., 1987, 'Marine Tenure and Conservation in Papua New Guinea', in McCay, B.J., and J.M. Acheson (eds.), *The Question of the Commons: The Culture and Ecology of Communal Resources*, Tucson, Ariz.: University of Arizona Press, pp. 142–67.

CARTER, M., 1991, 'Risk, Reciprocity and Conditional Self-Insurance in the Sahel: Measurement and Implications for the Trajectory of Agricultural Development in West Africa', Dept of Agricultural Economics Staff Paper No. 333, University of Madison-Wisconsin.

CARTER, M.R., 1997, 'Environment, Technology, and the Social Articulation of Risk in West African Agriculture', *Economic Development and Cultural Change*, Vol. 45, No. 3, pp. 557–590.

CARTER, M. and D. MESBAH, 1990, 'Economic Theory of Land Markets and its Implications for the Land Access of the Rural Poor', Dept of Agricultural Economics, University of Wisconsin-Madison, mimeo.

CARTER, M.R., and K. WIEBE, 1990, 'Access to Capital and Its Impact on Agrarian Structure and Productivity in Kenya', *American Journal of Agricultural Economics*, Vol. 72, December, pp. 1146–50

CARTER, M.R., K.D. WIEBE, and B. BLAREL, 1994, 'Tenure Security for Whom? Differential Effects of Land Policy in Kenya', in Bruce, J.W., and S.E. Migot-Adholla (eds.), *Searching for Land Tenure Security in Africa*, Dubuque, Iowa: Kendall/Hunt Publishing Cy, pp. 141–168.

CARTER, M.R., and F. ZIMMERMAN, 1993, 'Mediating Risk Through Markets, Rational Cooperation, and Public Policy: Institutional Alternatives and the Trajectories of Agrarian Development in the West African Sahel', Department of Economics, University of Wisconsin, Madison (mimeo).

CARTER, Mt.R., D. FLETSCHNER, and P. OLINTO, 1997, 'Do the "Poor but Efficient" Survive in the Land Market? Capital Access and Land Accumulation in an Inegalitarian Agrarian Economy', Department of Agricultural and Applied Economics, University of Wisconsin, Madison (mimeo).

CASHDAN, E., 1983, 'Territoriality Among Human Foragers: Ecological Models and an Application to Four Bushman Groups', *Current Anthropology*, Vol. 24, No. 1, pp. 47–66.

CASHDAN, E., 1985, 'Coping with Risk: Reciprocity Among the Basarwa of Northern Botswana', *Man*, Vol. 20, No. 3, pp. 454–74.

CASHDAN, E. (ed.), 1990, *Risk and Uncertainty in Tribal and Peasant Economies*, Boulder, San Francisco & London: Westview Press.

CATANZARO, R., 1992, *Men of Respect: A Social History of the Sicilian Mafia*, New York: The Free Press.

CAVERIVIERE, M., et M. DEBENE, 1988, *Le droit foncier sénégalais*, Paris: Berger-Levrault.

CHHIBBER, A., 1989, 'The Aggregate Supply Response—A Survey', in Commander, S. (ed.), *Structural Adjustment and Agriculture—Theory and Practice in Africa and Latin America*, London: Overseas Development Institute (ODI), pp. 55–68.

CLEAVER, K., and G. SCHREIBER, 1992, 'The Population, Agriculture and Environment Nexus in Sub-Saharan Africa', *Agriculture and Rural Development Series No. 1*, Technical Department, Africa Region, Washington, D.C.: The World Bank.

COATE, S., and M. RAVAILLON, 1993, 'Reciprocity Without Commitment: Characterization and Performance of Informal Insurance Arrangements', *Journal of Development Economics*, Vol. 40, No. 1, pp. 1–24.

COHEN, A., 1969, *Custom and Politics in Urban Africa*, London: Routledge and Kegan Paul.

COHEN, A., 1971, 'Cultural Strategies in the Organization of Trading Diasporas', in Meillassoux, C. (ed.), *The Development of Indigenous Trade and Markets in West Africa*, London: Oxford University Press, pp. 266–81.

COHEN, G.A., 1978, *Karl Marx's Theory of History: A Defence*, Oxford: Oxford University Press.

COHEN, J., 1980, 'Land Tenure and Rural Development in Africa', in Bates, R.H., and M.F. Lofchie, (eds.), *Agricultural Development in Africa—Issues of Public Policy*, New York: Praeger, pp. 349–400.

COHEN, J.S., and M.L. WEITZMAN, 1975, 'A Marxian Model of Enclosures', *Journal of Development Economics*, Vol. 1, No. 1, pp. 287–336.

COLCHESTER, M., 1994, 'Sustaining the Forests: The Community-based Approach in South and South-East Asia', *Development and Change*, Vol. 25, No. 1, pp. 69–100.

COLCLOUGH, C., 1991, 'Structuralism Versus Neo-Liberalism: An Introduction', in Colclough, C., and J. Manor (eds.), *States or Markets? Neo-Liberalism and the Development Policy Debate*, Oxford: Clarendon Press.

COLDHAM, S., 1978, 'The Effect of Registration of Title upon Customary Land Rights in Kenya', *Journal of African Law*, Vol. 22, No. 2, pp. 91–111.

COLEMAN, J.S., 1987, 'Norms as a Social Capital', in Radnitzky, G., and P. Bernholz (eds.), *Economic Imperialism. The Economic Method Applied Outside the Field of Economics*, New York: Paragon House Publishers, pp. 133–153.

COLEMAN, J.S., 1988, 'Social Capital in the Creation of Human Capital', *American Journal of Sociology*, Vol. 94, No. 1, pp. S95–S12O.

COLEMAN, J.S., 1990, *Foundations of Social Theory*, Cambridge, Mssts & London: The Belknap Press of Harvard University Press.

COLLIER, P., 1983, 'Malfunctioning of African Rural Factor Markets: Theory and a Kenyan Example', *Oxford Bulletin of Economics and Statistics*, Vol. 45, No. 2, pp. 141–171.

COLLIER, P., 1994, 'The Marginalisation of Africa', Centre for the Study of African Economies, Oxford University (mimeo).

COLLIER, P., and J. GUNNING, 1999, 'Explaining African Economic Performance', *Journal of Economic Literature,* Vol. 37, No. 1, pp. 64–111.

COLSON, E., 1974, *Tradition and Contract: The Problem of Order*, Chicago: Aldine Publishing Cy.

CONGLETON, R., 1980, 'Competitive Process, Competitive Waste, and Institutions', in Buchanan, J., R. Tollison, and G. Tullock (eds.), *Toward a Theory of the Rent-Seeking Society*, Texas A&M Press.

COQUERY-VIDROVITCH, C., 1985, *Afrique noire—Permanences et ruptures*, Paris: Payot.

CORDELL, J.C., and M.A. McKEAN, 1986, 'Sea Tenure in Bahia, Brazil', in National Research Council, *Proceedings of the Conference on Common Property Resource Management*, Washington, D.C.: National Academy Press, pp. 85–112.

CROOK, R., and MANOR, J., 1994, 'Democratic Decentralization in South Asia and West Africa', Final Report to ESCOR, London: Overseas Development Administration.

CROUSSE, B., 1986, 'Logique traditionnelle et logique d'Etat', in Crousse, B., E. Le Bris, et E. Le Roy, (eds.), *Espaces disputés en Afrique noire*, Paris: Karthala, pp. 199–215.

CROUZET, F., 1985, *De la supériorité de l'Angleterre sur la France: l'économique et l'imaginaire aux XVII-XXèmes siècles*, Paris: Perrin.

CRUISE O'BRIEN, D.B., 1971, *The Mourides of Senegal: Political and Economic Organization of an Islamic Brotherhood*, Oxford: Oxford University Press.

CRUZ, W.D., 1986, 'Overfishing and Conflict in a Traditional Fishery: San Miguel Bay, Philippines', in National Research Council, *Proceedings of the Conference on Common Property Resource Management*, Washington D.C.: National Academy Press, pp. 115–133.

DAHLMAN, C.J., 1980, *The Open Field System and Beyond: A Property Rights Analysis of an Economic Institution*, Cambridge: Cambridge University Press.

DARLEY, J.M., and B. LATANE, 1970, 'Norms and Normative Behaviour: Field Studies of Social Interdependence', in Macaulay, J., and L. Berkowitz (eds.), *Altruism and Helping Behaviour—Social Psychological Studies of Some Antecedents and Consequences*, New York, San Francisco & London: Academic Press, pp. 83–101.

DASGUPTA, P., 1988, 'Trust as a Commodity', in Gambetta, D. (ed.), *Trust-Making and Breaking Cooperative Relations*, Oxford: Basil Blackwell, pp. 49–72.

DASGUPTA, P., 1993, *An Inquiry into Well-Being and Destitution*, Oxford: Clarendon Press.

DASGUPTA, P.S, 1995, 'The Population Problem: Theory and Evidence', *Journal of Economic Literature*, Vol. XXXIII, No. 4, pp. 1879–1902.

DASGUPTA, P.S., and G.M. HEAL, 1979, *Economic Theory and Exhaustible Resources*, Cambridge: Cambridge University Press.

DASGUPTA, P., and K.-G. MÄLER, 1990, 'The Environment and Emerging Development Issues', The Development Economics Research Programme, No. 28, STICERD, London School of Economics and Political Science.

DASGUPTA, P., and K.-G. MÄLER, 1995, 'Poverty and the Environmental Resource Base', in Behrman, J., and T.N. Srinivasan (eds.), *Handbook of Development Economics*, Vol. IIIA, Amsterdam: Elsevier, pp. 2371–2463.

DAS GUPTA, M., 1987, 'Informal Security Mechanisms and Population Retention in Rural India', *Economic Development and Cultural Change*, Vol. 36, No. 1, pp. 101–120.

DAVID, C.C., and K. OTSUKA, 1995, *Modern Rice Technology and Income Distribution in Asia*, Boulder: Lynne Rienner.

DAVIS, L.E., and D.C. NORTH, 1971, *Institutional Change and American Economic Growth*, Cambridge: Cambridge University Press.

DAWES, R.M., and R.H. THALER, 1988, 'Anomalies Cooperation', *Journal of Economic Perspectives*, Vol. 2, No. 3, pp. 187–197.

DAWES, R.M., J. McTAVISH, and H. SHAKLEE, 1977, 'Behavior, Communication, and Assumptions About Other People's Behavior in a Commons Dilemma Situation', *Journal of Personality and Social Psychology*, Vol. 35, No. 1, pp. 1–11.

DE ALESSI, L., 1980, 'The Economics of Property Rights: A Review of the Evidence', *Research in Law and Economics*, Vol. 2, No. 1, pp. 1–47.

DEATON, A., 1992a, 'Household Saving in LDC's: Credit Markets, Insurance, and Welfare', *Scandinavian Journal of Economics*, Vol. 94, No. 1, pp. 253–273.

DEATON, A., 1992b, 'Saving and Income Smoothing in the Côte d'Ivoire', *Journal of African Economies*, Vol. 1, No. 1, pp. 1–24.

DEBREU, G., and H. SCARF, 1963, 'A Limit Theorem on the Core of an Economy', *International Economic Review*, Vol. 4, No. 3, pp. 235–46.

DE HAAN, L.J., 1995, 'Local Environmental Management in North Benin: Bright Spots in the Local Impasse', in Van Den Breemer, H.P.M., C.A. Drijver, and L.B. Venema (eds.), *Local Resource Management in Africa*, New York: John Wiley & Sons, pp. 129–146.

De JANVRY, A., M. FAFCHAMPS, and E. SADOULET, 1991, 'Peasant Household Behavior with Missing Markets: Some Paradoxes Explained', *Economic Journal*, Vol. 101, pp. 1400–1417.

De LAME, D., 1996, *Une colline entre mille ou le calme avant la tempête—Transformations et blocages du Rwanda rural*, Musée Royal de L'Afrique Centrale, Annales Sciences Humaines, Vol. 154, Tervuren (Belgium).

DELGADO, C.L., 1992, 'Why Domestic Food Prices Matter to Growth Strategy in Semi-Open West African Agriculture', *Journal of African Economies*, Vol. 1, No. 3, pp. 446–471.

DELGADO, C.L., 1996, 'Agricultural Transformation: the Key to Broad-Based Growth and Poverty Alleviation in Africa', in Ndulu, B., and N. van de Walle (eds.), *Agenda for Africa's Economic Renewal*: New Brunswick and Oxford: Transaction Publishers, pp. 151–178.

DELGADO, C.L. and J.W. MELLOR, 1984, 'A Structural View of Policy Issues in African Agricultural Development', *American Journal of Agricultural Economics*, Vol. 66, No. 3, pp. 665–70.

DELGADO, C.L., and C. RANADE, 1987, 'Technological Change and Agricultural Labor Use', in Mellor, J., and M. Blackie (eds.), *Accelerating Food Production in Sub-Saharan Africa*, Baltimore, Md. & London: Johns Hopkins, pp. 118–34.

DE MEZA, D., and J.R. GOULD, 1987, 'Free Access versus Private Property in a Resource: Income Distributions Compared', *Journal of Political Economy, Vol. 95, No. 6, pp. 1317–25.*

DEMSETZ, H., 1967, 'Toward a Theory of Property Rights', *American Economic Review*, Vol. 57, No. 2, pp. 347–359.

DENISON, E.F., 1962, *The Sources of Economic Growth in the United States and the Alternatives Before Us*, New York: Committee for Economic Development.

DENISON, E.F., 1967, *Why Growth Rates Differ*, Washington, DC: The Brookings Institute.

DENZAU, A.T., and M. MUNGER, 1986, 'Legislators and Interest Groups: How Unorganized Interests Get Represented', *American Political Science Review*, Vol. 80, No. 1, pp. 89–106.

DERCON, S., 1995, 'On Market Integration and Liberalisation: Method and Application to Ethiopia', *Journal of Development Studies*, Vol. 32, No. 1, pp. 112–143.

DERCON, S., 1998, 'Wealth, Risk and Activity Choice: Cattle in Western Tanzania', *Journal of Development Economics*, Vol. 55, No. 1, pp. 1–42.

DERCON, S., and P. KRISHNAN, 1996, 'Income Portfolios in Rural Ethiopia and Tanzania: Choices and Constraints', *Journal of Development Studies*, Vol. 32, No. 6, pp. 850–875.

DE ROSNY, E., 1981, *Les yeux de ma chèvre. Sur les pas des maîtres de la nuit en pays douala*, Paris: Plon.

DE ROSNY, E., 1992, *L'Afrique des guérisons*, Paris: Editions Karthala.

DES OMBIAUX, 1986, *Le Maugré*, Bruxelles: Editions Labor.

DE VILLE, P., 1990, 'Comportements concurrentiels et équilibre général: de la nécessité des institutions', *Economie Appliquée*, tome 43, No. 3, pp. 9–34.

DE ZEEUW, F., 1997, 'Borrowing of Land, Security of Tenure and Sustainable Land Use in Burkina Faso', *Development and Change*, Vol. 28, No. 3, pp. 583–595.

DIEMER, G., and E. VAN DER LAAN, 1987, *L'irrigation au Sahel—La crise des périmètres irrigués et la voie haalpulaar*, Paris & Wageningen: Karthala and CTA.

DIOP, A.B., 1981, *La société Wolof—Tradition et changement*, Paris: Karthala.

DIXIT, A.K., 1996, *The Making of Economic Policy: A Transaction-Cost Politics Perspective*, Cambridge, Mass & London, England: The MIT Press.

DOMAR, E., 1970, 'The Causes of Slavery or Serfdom: A Hypothesis', *Journal of Economic History*, Vol. 30, No. 1, pp. 18–32.

DOORNBOS, M.R., 1975, 'Land Tenure and Political Conflict in Ankole, Uganda', *Journal of Development Studies*, Vol. 12, No. 1, pp. 54–74.

DORNER, P., and B. SALIBA, 1981, 'Interventions in Land Markets to Benefit the Poor', Land Tenure Center, LTC Paper No. 74, University of Wisconsin-Madison.

DOROSH, P., and R. BERNIER, 1994, 'Staggered Reforms and Limited Success: Structural Adjustment in Madagascar', in Sahn, D.E. (ed.), *Adjusting to Policy Failure in African Economies*, Ithaca & London: Cornell University Press, pp. 332–65.

DOWNS, R.E., and S.P. REYNA (eds.), 1988, *Land and Society in Contemporary Africa*, Hanover & London: University Press of New England.

DRIJVER, C.A., and Y.J.J. VAN ZORGE, 1995, 'With a Little Help from Our Friends: The Gouzda Case of Local Resource Management in Cameroon', in Van Den Breemer, H.P.M., C.A. Drijver, and L.B. Venema (eds.), *Local Resource Management in Africa*, New York: John Wiley & Sons, pp. 147–160.

DUBUISSON, D., 1998, 'Dynamique des marchés fonciers informels dans des conditions de valorisation de la terre—le cas des périmètres irrigués de Yalogo (Burkina Faso)', Faculté des Sciences Economiques, Sociales et de Gestion (mimeo).

DUBUISSON, J.F., 1998, *Evolution du régime foncier et intensification de l'agriculture en Afrique sub-saharienne: le cas d'un village du Sud Bénin*,, M.A. Thesis, Faculté des Sciences économiques, sociales et de gestion, University of Namur, Belgium.

DUNCAN, E., 1989, *Breaking the Curfew—A Political Journey Through Pakistan*, London: Michael Joseph.

DYSON-HUDSON, R., and E.A. SMITH, 1978, 'Human Territoriality: An Ecological Reassessment', *American Anthropologist*, Vol. 80, No. 1, pp. 21–41.

EASTER, K.W., and K. PALANISAMI, 1986, 'Tank Irrigation in India: An Example of Common Property Resource Management', in National Research Council, *Proceedings of the Conference on Common Property Resource Management*, Washington, D.C.: National Academy Press, pp. 215–230.

ECONOMIST, 1995, 'Out of Africa, a smoother ride', *The Economist*, June 10th-16th..

ECONOMIST, 1998, 'Western Man's Burden', *The Economist*, December 12th-18th.

EGGERTSSON, T., 1990, *Economic Behavior and Institutions*, Cambridge: Cambridge University Press.

EICHER, C., 1984, 'Facing Up to Africa's Food Crisis', in Eicher, C., and J.M. Staatz (eds.), *Agricultural Development in the Third World*, Baltimore & London: The Johns Hopkins University Press, pp. 453–79.

EICHER, C.K., and D.C. BAKER, 1982, 'Research on Agricultural Development in Sub-Saharan Africa: A Critical Survey', MSU International Development Paper No. 1, Dept of Agricultural Economics, Michigan State University.

EISENSTADT, S.N., 1966, *Modernization: Protest and Change*, New Jersey: Englewood Cliffs, N.J. & Prentice-Hall.

EISENSTADT, S.N., 1986 (ed.), *The Origins and Diversity of the Axial Age Civilizations*, Albany: State University of New York Press.

EISER, J.R., 1978, 'Cooperation and Conflict Between Individuals', in Tajfel, H., and C. Fraser (eds.), *Introducing Social Psychology*, Harmondsworth: Penguin Books.

ELLIS, S., and J.Y. FAURE, 1995, *Entreprises et entrepreneurs africains*, Paris: Karthala-ORSTOM.

ELLICKSON, R.C., 1991, *Order Without Law- How Neighbors Settle Disputes*, Cambridge, Mass. and London: Harvard University Press.

ELLSWORTH, L., 1988, *Mutual Insurance and Non-market Transactions Among Farmers in Burkina Faso*, University of Wisconsin-Madison, Unpublished Ph. D. Thesis.

ELSTER, J., 1985, *Making Sense of Marx*, Cambridge: Cambridge University Press.

ELSTER, J., 1989a, *The Cement of Society—A Study of Social Order*, Cambridge: Cambridge University Press.

ELSTER, J., 1989b, 'Social Norms and Economic Theory', *Journal of Economic Perspectives*, Vol. 3, No. 1, pp. 99–117.

ELSTER, J., 1998, 'Emotions and Economic Theory', *Journal of Economic Literature*, Vol. 36, No. 1, pp. 47–74.

ENGELHARD, P., and T. BEN ABDALLAH, 1986, *Enjeux de l'après-barrage—vallée du Sénégal*, Dakar: ENDA et République Franc[,]aise, Ministère de la Coopération.

ENKE, S., 1963, *Economics for Development*, Englewood Cliffs, NJ and Prentice-Hall.

ENSMINGER, J., 1990, 'Co-Opting the Elders: the Political Economy of State Incorporation in Africa', *American Anthropologist*, Vol. 92, pp. 662–75.

ENSMINGER, J., 1992, *Making a Market—The Institutional Transformation of an African Society*, Cambridge: Cambridge University Press.

ESWARAN, M., and A. KOTWAL, 1985, 'A Theory of Contractual Structure in Agriculture', *American Economic Review*, Vol. 75, No. 3, pp. 352–367.

ETZIONI, A., 1988, *The Moral Dimension—Toward a New Economics*, New York and London: The Free Press.

EVANS-PRITCHARD, E.E., 1937, *Witchcraft, Oracles and Magic among the Azande*, Oxford & New York: Oxford University Press.

EVANS-PRITCHARD, E.E., 1940, *The Nuer: A Description of the Modes of Livelihood and Political Institutions of a Nilotic People*, Oxford: Clarendon Press.

EVANS-PRITCHARD, E.E., 1964, *Closed Systems and Open Minds*, Chicago: Aldine Publishing Co.

FAFCHAMPS, M., 1991, 'The Rural Community, Mutual Assistance, and Structural Adjustment', Food Research Institute, Stanford University, mimeo.

FAFCHAMPS, M., 1992, 'Solidarity Networks in Preindustrial Societies: Rational Peasants with a Moral Economy', *Economic Development and Cultural Change*, Vol. 41, No. 1, pp. 147–174.

FAFCHAMPS, M., 1994, 'Risk Sharing, Quasi-credit and the Enforcement of Informal Contracts', Stanford University (mimeo).

FAFCHAMPS, M., 1996, 'The Enforcement of Commercial Contracts in Ghana', *World Development*, Vol. 24, No. 3, pp. 427–448.

FAFCHAMPS, M., C. UDRY, and K. CZUKAS, 1998, 'Drought and Saving in West Africa: Are Livestock a Buffer Stock?', *Journal of Development Economics*, Vol. 55, No. 2, pp. 273–305.

FAFCHAMPS, M., and B. MINTEN, 1998, 'Returns to Social Capital Among Traders', Department of Economics, Stanford University (mimeo).

FALLOUX, F., 1987, 'Land Management, Titling and Tenancy', in Davis, T.J., and I.A. Schirmer, (eds.), *Sustainability Issues in Agricultural Development-Proceedings of the Seventh Agricultural Sector Symposium*, Washington: the World Bank, pp. 190–208.

FAO, 1986, *African Agriculture: The Next 25 Years* (Main Report + 5 Technical Annexes), Rome: The Food and Agriculture Organisation of the United Nations.

FAO, 1995, *The State of Food and Agriculture 1995*, Rome: The Food and Agriculture Organization of the United Nations.

FAY, C., 1990a, 'Sacrifices, prix du sang, 'eau du maître': fondation des territoires de pêche dans le delta central du Niger (Mali)', in Verdeaux, F. (ed.), *La pêche—Enjeux de développement et objet de recherche*, Paris: Editions de l'ORSTOM, pp. 159–76.

FAY, C., 1990b, 'Systèmes halieutiques et espaces de pouvoirs: transformation des droits et des pratiques de pêche dans le delta central du Niger (Mali), 1920–80', in Verdeaux, F. (ed.), *La pêche—Enjeux de développement et objet de recherche*, Paris: Editions de l'ORSTOM, pp. 213–36.

FEDER, E., 1977, 'Agribusiness and the Elimination of Latin America's Rural Proletariat', *World Development*, Vol. 5, No. ..., pp. 559–571.

FEDER, E., 1979, 'Agricultural Resources in Underdeveloped Countries: Competition Between Man and Animal', *Economic and Political Weekly*, Vol. 14, August, pp. 1345–1366.

FEDER, G., 1987, 'Land Ownership Security and Farm Productivity: Evidence from Thailand', *Journal of Development Studies*, Vol. 24, No. 1, pp. 16–30.

FEDER, G., 1993, 'The Economics of Land and Titling in Thailand', in: Hoff, K., A. Braverman, and J.E. Stiglitz (eds.), *The Economics of Rural Organization—Theory, Practice, and Policy*, New York: Oxford University Press (Published for the World Bank), pp. 259–68.

FEDER, G., T. ONCHAN, Y. CHALAMWONG, and C. HONGLADAROM, 1988, *Land Policies and Farm Productivity in Thailand*, Baltimore: Johns Hopkins University Press (for the World Bank).

FEDER, G., and D. FEENY, 1991, 'Land Tenure and Property Rights: Theory and Implications for Development Policy', *The World Bank Economic Review*, Vol. 5, No. 1, pp. 135–53.

FEDER, G., and A. NISHIO, 1997, 'The Benefits of Land Registration and Titling—Economic and Social Perspectives', Washinton, D.C.: The World Bank (mimeo).

FEDER, G., and R. NORONHA, 1987, 'Land Rights Systems and Agricultural Development in Sub-Saharan Africa', *Research Observer*, Vol. 2, No. 2, pp. 143–169.

FEENY, D., 1988, 'The Development of Property Rights in Land: A Comparative Study', in Bates, R., (ed.), *Toward a Political Economy of Development*, Berkeley, Los Angeles & London: University of California Press, pp. 272–299.

FEENY, D., 1989, 'The Decline of Property Rights in Man in Thailand, 1800–1913', *Journal of Economic History*, Vol. 49, No. 2, pp. 285–296.

FEHR, E., and J.R. TYRAN, 1996, 'Institutions and Reciprocal Fairness', *Nordic Journal of Political Economy*, Vol. 23, No. 2, pp. 133–144.

FEHR, E., S. GAECHTER, and G. KIRCHSTEIGER, 1997, 'Reciprocity as a Contract Enforcement Device. Experimental Evidence', *Econometrica*, Vol. 65, No. 4, pp. 833–860.

FEHR, E., G. KIRCHSTEIGER, and A. RIEDL, 1998, 'Gift Exchange and Reciprocity in Competitive Experimental Markets', *European Economic Review*, Vol. 42, No. 1, pp. 1–34.

FEHR, E. et al., forthcoming, 'When Social Norms Overpower Competition—Social Exchange in Experimental Labor Markets', *Journal of Labor Economics*.

FERNANDEZ, R., and D. RODRIK, 1991, 'Resistance to Reform: Status Quo Bias in the Presence of Individual Specific Uncertainty', *American Economic Review*, Vol. 81, No. 5, pp. 1146–1155.

FIELD, A.J., 1981, 'The Problem with Neoclassical Institutional Economics: A Critique with Special Reference to the North/Thomas model of pre-1500 Europe', *Explorations in Economic History*, Vol. 18, No. 1, pp. 174–198.

FIELD, A.J., 1984, 'Microeconomics, Norms, and Rationality', *Economic Development and Cultural Change*, Vol. 32, No. 4, pp. 683–711.

FINNEY, B.R., 1972, 'Big-men, Half-men and Trader-chiefs: Entrepreneurial Styles in Australian New Guinea and French Polynesia', in Epstein, T.S., and D.H. Penny (eds.), *Opportunity and Response—Case Studies in Economic Development*, London: C. Hurst & Company, pp. 114–130.

FIRMIN-SELLERS, K., 1996, *The Transformation of Property Rights in the Gold Coast—An Empirical Analysis Applying Rational Choice Theory*, Cambridge: Cambridge University Press.

FISIY, C., and P. GESCHIERE, 1991, 'Sorcery, Witchcraft and Accumulation: Regional Variations in South and West Cameroon', *Critique of Anthropology*, Vol. 11, No. 3, pp. 251–278.

FLEURET, A., 1988, 'Some Consequences of Tenure and Agrarian Reform in Taita, Kenya', in Downs, R.E., and S.P. Reyna (eds.), *Land and Society in Contemporary Africa*, Hanover & London: University Press of New England, pp. 136–158.

FONG, C., 1998, 'Economic Experience, Endogenous Beliefs, and Public Generosity', Washington University (unpublished), Washington, DC.

FOLLAIN, J., 1995, *A Dishonoured Society*, London: Little & Brown.

FOSTER, A.D., and M.R. ROSENZWEIG, 1995, 'Imperfect Commitment, Altruism and the Family: Evidence from Transfer Behavior in Low-Income Rural Areas', Department of Economics, University of Pennsylvania (mimeo).

FOSTER, A.D., and M.R. ROSENZWEIG, 1996, 'Financial Intermediation, Transfers and Commitment: Do Banks Crowd Out Private Insurance Arrangements in Low-Income Rural Areas?', Department of Economics, University of Pennsylvania (mimeo).

FRANK, R., 1988, *Passions Within Reason: The Strategic Role of Emotions*, New York: Norton.

FRANK, R., 1995, *The Winner-Take-All Society*, New York: Martin Kessler Books at the Free Press.

FRANK, R., 1996, 'Social Norms as Positional Arms Control Agreements', Paper presented at the Conference on the Economics of Values and Institutions, Yale University, New Haven, April 19–21.

FREUDENBERGER, M.S., and P. MATHIEU, 1993, 'The Question of the Commons in the Sahel', Land Tenure Center, University of Wisconsin-Madison (mimeo).

FRIEDMAN, J.W., 1990, *Game Theory with Applications to Economics*, New York & Oxford: Oxford University Press (2d edition).

FRIEDMAN, J., E. JIMENEZ, and S.K. MAYO, 1988, 'The Demand for Tenure Security in Developing Countries', *Journal of Development Economics*, Vol. 29, No. 2, pp. 185–198.

FROMM, E., 1949, 'Psychoanalytic Characterology and Its Applications to the Understanding of Culture', in Sargent, S.S., and M.W. Smith (eds.), *Culture and Personality*, New York: The Viking Fund.

FUKUI, H., 1992, 'The Japanese State and Economic Development: A Profile of a Nationalist-Paternalist Capitalist State', in Appelbaum, R.P., and J. Henderson (eds.), *States and Development in the Asian Pacific Rim*, Newbury Park, CA: Sage, pp. 199–225.

FUKUYAMA, F., 1995, *Trust—The Social Virtues and the Creation of Prosperity*, London: Hamish Hamilton.

GABSEWICZ, J., and B. SHITOVITZ, 1992, 'The Core in Imperfectly Competitive Economies', in Aumann, R.J., and S. Hart (eds.), *Handbook of Game Theory, Volume 1*, Elsevier Science Publishers, pp. 460–83.

GAMBETTA, D., 1988a, 'Mafia: The Price of Distrust', in Gambetta, D. (ed.), *Trust-Making and Breaking Cooperative Relations*, Oxford: Basil Blackwell, pp. 158–175.

GAMBETTA, D., 1988b, 'Can We Trust Trust?', in Gambetta, D. (ed.), *Trust-Making and Breaking Cooperative Relations*, Oxford: Basil Blackwell, pp. 213–237.

GAMBETTA, D., 1993, *The Sicilian Mafia: the Business of Private Protection*, Cambridge, Mass.: Harvard University Press.

GASPART, F., 1996, 'Vulcans and Klingons: Simulating an Evolutionary Game with Random Matching and Adjustable Expectations', Cahiers de la faculté des sciences économiques et sociales, No. 169, University of Namur, Namur.

GASPART, F., 1998, 'Simulating an Evolutionary Game with Random Matching and Adjustable Expectations', Faculty of Economics, University of Namur (mimeo).

GASTELLU, J.M., 1982, 'Droit d'usage et propriété privée', in Le Bris, E., E. Le Roy, and F. Leimdorfer, (eds.), *Enjeux fonciers en Afrique noire*, Paris: ORSTOM and Karthala, pp. 269–279.

GAVIAN, S., and M. FAFCHAMPS, 1996, 'Land Tenure and Allocative Efficiency in Niger', *American Journal of Agricultural Economics*, Vol. 78, pp. 460–471.

GEERTZ, C., 1970, *Agricultural Involution: the Process of Ecological Change in Indonesia*, Berkeley & Los Angeles: University of California Press.

GEERTZ, C., 1979, 'Suq: The Bazaar Economy in Sefrou', in Geertz, C., H. Geertz, and L. Rosen, *Meaning and Order in Moroccan Society*, Cambridge: Cambridge University Press.

GENTIL, D., and Y. FOURNIER, 1993, *Les paysans peuvent-ils devenir banquiers? Epargne et crédit en Afrique*, Paris: Syros.

GERSOVITZ, M., 1987, 'Some Sources and Implications of Uncertainty in the Senegalese Economy', in Waterbury, J., and M. Gersovitz (eds.), *The Political Economy of Risk and Choice in Senegal*, London: Frank Cass and Co.

GESCHIERE, P., 1994, 'Parenté et argent dans une société lignagère', in Bayart, J.F. (ed.), *La réinvention du capitalisme*, Paris: Karthala, pp. 87–113.

GESCHIERE, P., 1995, *Sorcellerie et politique en Afrique—La viande des autres*, Paris: Editions Karthala.

GIBBONS, R., 1992, *Game Theory for Applied Economists*, Princeton, N.J.: Princeton University Press.

GILLES, J.L., and K. JAMTGAARD, 1981, 'Overgrazing Pastoral Areas: the Commons Reconsidered', *Sociologica Ruralis*, Vol. 21, No. 2, pp. 129–141.

GIRI, J., 1983, *Le Sahel demain*, Paris: Karthala.

GLAZIER, J., 1985, *Land and the Uses of Tradition Among the Mbeere of Kenya*, Lanham, MD: University Press of America.

GODELIER, M., 1974, 'Anthropologie et économie. Une anthropologie économique est-elle possible?', in Godelier, M. (ed.), *Un domaine contesté: l'anthropologie économique*, Paris: Mouton, pp. 285–345.

GOHEEN, M., 1988, 'Land Accumulation and Local Control: The Manipulation of Symbols and Power in Nso, Cameroon', in Downs, R.E., and S.P. Reyna (eds.), *Land and Society in Contemporary Africa*, Hanover & London: University Press of New England, pp. 280–308.

GOLAN, E.H., 1990, 'Land Tenure Reform in Senegal: An Economic Study from the Peanut Basin', Land Tenure Center, LTC Paper No. 101, University of Madison-Wisconsin.

GOLDMAN, A., and J. SMITH, 1995, 'Agricultural Transformations in India and Northern Nigeria: Exploring the Nature of Green Revolutions', *World Development*, Vol. 23, No. 2, pp. 243–263.

GOUROU, P., 1991, *L'Afrique tropicale: nain ou géant agricole?*, Paris.

GRANOVETTER, M., 1985, 'Economic Action and Social Structure: The Problem of Embeddedness', *American Journal of Sociology*, Vol. 91, No. 3, pp. 481–510.

GRAVELLE, H., and R. REES, 1992, *Microeconomics*, London and New York: Longman (2d edition).

GRAYZEL, J., 1988, 'Land Tenure and Development in Mauritania: The Causes and Consequences of Legal Modernization in a National Context', in Downs, R.E., and S.P. Reyna (eds.), *Land and Society in Contemporary Africa*, Hanover & London: University Press of New England, pp. 309–339.

GREEN, J.K., 1987, 'Evaluating the Impact of Consolidation of Holdings, Individualization of Tenure, and Registration of Title: Lessons from Kenya', Land Tenure Center, LTC Paper No. 129, University of Wisconsin-Madison.

GREIF, A., 1989, 'Reputation and Coalitions in Medieval Trade: Evidence on the Maghribi Traders', *Journal of Economic History*, Vol. 49, No. 4, pp. 857–882.

GREIF, A., 1992a, 'Institutions and International Trade: Lessons from the Commercial Revolution', *American Economic Review*, Papers and Proceedings, Vol. 82, No. 2, pp. 128–133.

GREIF, A., 1992b, 'Institutional Infrastructure and Economic Development: Reflection from the Commercial Revolution', Department of Economics, Stanford University (mimeo).

GREIF, A., 1993, 'Contract Enforceability and Economic Institutions in Early Trade: the Maghribi Traders' Coalition', *American Economic Review*, Vol. 83, No. 3, pp. 525–548.

GREIF, A., 1994a, 'Cultural Beliefs and the Organization of Society: A Historical and Theoretical Reflection on Collectivist and Individualist Societies', *Journal of Political Economy*, Vol. 102, No. 5, pp. 912–950.

GREIF, A., 1994b, 'Trading Institutions and the Commercial Revolution in Medieval Europe', in Aganbegyan, A., O. Bogomolov, and M. Kaser (eds.), *Economics in a Changing World—Vol. 1*, London: Macmillan, pp. 115–125.

GREIF, A., 1997, 'Microtheory and Recent Developments in the Study of Economic Institutions Through Economic History', in Kreps, D.M., and K.F. Wallis (eds.), *Advances in Economic Theory—Vol. II*, Cambridge: Cambridge University Press, pp. 79–113.

GREIF, A., 1998, 'Historical and Comparative Institutional Analysis', *American Economic Review*, Vol. 88, No. 2, pp. 80–89.

GREIF, A., forthcoming, *Genoa and the Maghribi Traders—Historical and Comparative Institutional Analysis*, Cambridge: Cambridge University Press.

GREIF, A., P.R. MILGROM, and B.R. WEINGAST, 1992, 'The Merchant Gild As a Nexus of Contracts', Department of Economics, Stanford University (mimeo).

GREGERSEN, H., S. DRAPER, and D. ELZ, (eds.), 1989, *People and Trees—The Role of Social Forestry in Sustainable Development*, Washington, D.C.: The World Bank.

GREGORY, C.A., 1982, *Gifts and Commodities*, London and New York: Academic Press.

GRIFFITH, W.B., and R.S. GOLDFARB, 1991, 'Amending the economist's "rational egoist" model to include moral values and norms', in Koford, K.J., and J.B. Miller (eds.), *Social Norms and Economic Institutions*, Ann-Arbor: University of Michigan Press, pp. 39–84.

GROSSMAN, H., 1995, 'Rival Kleptocrats: The Mafia versus the State', in Fiorentini, G., and S. Peltzman (eds.), *The Economics of Organised Crime*, Cambridge: Cambridge University Press, pp. 143–160.

GRUENAIS, M.-E., 1986, 'Territoires autochtones et mise en valeur des terres', in Crousse, B., E., Le Bris, et E. Le Roy, *Espaces disputés en Afrique noire*, Paris: Karthala, pp. 283–98.

GUHA, R., 1985, 'Scientific Forestry and Social Change in Uttarakland', *Economic and Political Weekly*, Vol. 20, Nos 45–46–47, Special Number, pp. 1939–52.

GULBRANDSEN, O., 1990, 'Material and Symbolic Aspects of Changing Property Relations in a Tswana Society', in Baxter, P., and R. Hogg (eds.), *Property, Poverty and People: Changing Rights in Property and Problems of Pastoral Development*, Manchester: University of Manchester, Dept. of Social Anthropology and International Development Centre.

GUTH, W., and H. KLIEMT, 1994, 'Competition or Co-operation? On the Evolutionary Economics of Trust, Exploitation and Moral Attitudes', University of Frankfurt (mimeo).

HAGEN, E.E., 1962, *The Theory of Social Change: How Economic Growth Begins*, Homewood, Ill.

HAGEN, E.E., 1975, *The Economics of Development*, Homewood, Ill.: Richard D. Irwin.

HAHN, F., 1982, 'Reflections on the Invisible Hand', *Lloyds Bank Review*, No. 144, April, pp. 1–21.

HALLPIKE, C.R., 1988, *The Principles of Social Evolution*, Oxford: Clarendon Press.

HAMILTON, G.G., 1998, 'Culture and Organization in Taiwan's Market Economy', in Hefner, R.W. (ed.), 1998, *Market Cultures—Society and Morality in the New Asian Capitalisms*, Boulder, Col.: Westview Press, pp. 41–77.

HAMILTON, G.G., W. ZEILE, and W.J. KIM, 1990, 'The Network Structure of East Asian Economies', in Clegg, S.R., and S.G. Redding (eds.), *Capitalism in Contrasting Cultures*, Berlin: Walter de Gruyter, pp. 105–129.

HANDELMAN, S., 1994, *Comrade Criminal: The Theft of the Second Russian Revolution*, London: Michael Joseph.

HARRISON, P., 1992, 'What Is Going Right with African Agriculture?', in Obasanjo, O., and H. d'Orville (eds.), *The Challenges of Agricultural Production and Food Security in Africa*, Washington, D.C.: Crane Russak, pp. 129–138.

HAUGERUD, A., 1983, 'The Consequences of Land Tenure Reform among Smallholders in the Kenya Highlands', *Rural Africana*, No. 15–16, Winter-Spring, pp. 65–89.

HAUGERUD, A., 1989, 'Land Tenure and Agrarian Change in Kenya', *Africa*, Vol. 59, No. 1, pp. 62–90.

HAUSMAN, D.M., and M.S. McPHERSON, 1996, *Economic Analysis and Moral Philosophy*, Cambridge: Cambridge University Press.

HAYAMI, Y., 1997, *Development Economics—From the Poverty to the Wealth of Nations*, Oxford: Clarendon Press.

HAYAMI, Y., (ed.), 1998, *Toward the Rural-Based Development of Commerce and Industry—Selected Experiences from East Asia*, EDI Learning Resources Series, Washington, DC: The World Bank.

HAYAMI, Y., and V. RUTTAN, 1985, *Agricultural Development—An International Perspective*, Baltimore & London: The Johns Hopkins University Press.

HAYAMI, Y., and M. KIKUCHI, 1981, *Asian Village Economy at the Crossroads*, Tokyo: University of Tokyo Press, and Baltimore: Johns Hopkins University Press.

HAYAMI, Y., and T. KAWAGOE, 1993, *The Agrarian Origins of Commerce and Industry: A Study of Peasant Marketing in Indonesia*, London: Macmillan and New York: St. Martin's Press.

HAYAMI, K., and K. OTSUKA, 1993, *The Economics of Contract Choice—An Agrarian Perspective*, Oxford: Clarendon Press.

HAYEK, F., 1948, *Individualism and Economic Order*, London: Routledge & Kegan Paul.

HAYEK, F., 1960, *The Constitution of Liberty*, London: Routledge & Kegan Paul.

HAYEK, F., 1973, *Law, Legislation, and Liberty*, Vol. 1: *Rules and Order*, Chicago: University of Chicago Press.

HAYES, J., M. ROTH, and L. ZEPEDA, 1997, 'Tenure Security, Investment and Productivity in Gambian Agriculture: A Generalized Probit Analysis', *American Journal of Agricultural Economics*, Vol. 79, No. 2, pp. 369–382.

HEFNER, R.W. (ed.), 1998, *Market Cultures—Society and Morality in the New Asian Capitalisms*, Boulder, Col.: Westview Press.

HENRY, A., G-H TCHENTE, and P. GUILLERME-DIEUMEGARD, 1991, *Tontines et banques au Cameroun—Les principes de la Société des amis*, Paris: Karthala.

HERBST, J., 1990, 'The Structural Adjustment of Politics in Africa', *World Development*, Vol. 18, No. 7, pp. 949–958.

HICKS, J., 1969, *A Theory of Economic History*, Oxford: Clarendon Press.

HIGGINS, B. 1968, *Economic Development—Problems, Principles and Policies*, New York: W.W. Norton & Cy [first edition 1959].

HILL, P., 1963, *The Migrant Cocoa-Farmers of Southern Ghana*, Cambridge: Cambridge University Press.

HINE, J. and RIZET, C., 1991, 'Halving Africa's Freight Transport Costs: Could It Be Done?', International Symposium on Transport and Communications in Africa, Brussels: The Royal Academy of Overseas Sciences.

HIRSCHMAN, A.O., 1958, *The Strategy of Economic Development*, New Haven & London: Yale University Press.

HO, S.P.S., 1978, *Economic Development in Taiwan: 1860–1970*, New Haven: Yale University Press.

HO, S.P.S., 1979, 'Decentralized Industrialization and Rural Development: Evidence from Taiwan', *Economic Development and Cultural Change,* Vol. 28, No. 1, pp. 77–96.

HOBEN, A., 1988, 'The Political Economy of Land Tenure in Somalia', in Downs, R.E., and S.P. Reyna (eds.), *Land and Society in Contemporary Africa*, Hanover & London: University Press of New England, pp. 192–220.

HODDER, R., 1996, *Merchant Princes of the East—Cultural Delusions, Economic Success and the Overseas Chinese in Southeast Asia*, NewYork: John Wiley & Sons.

HOMANS, G., 1950, *The Human Group*, New York: Harcourt Brace.

HOMANS, G., 1958, 'Social Behavior as Exchange', *American Journal of Sociology*, Vol. 65, pp. 597–606.

HORNSTEIN, J., E. FISCH, and M. HOLMES, 1968, 'Influence of a Model's Feelings About His Behavior and His Relevance as a Comparison Other on Observers' Helping Behavior', *Journal of Personality and Social Psychology,* Vol. 10, pp. 220–26.

HOSELITZ, B.F., 1960, *Sociological Factors in Economic Development*, Chicago: Free Press.

HOSKING, G., 1997, *Russia—People and Empire, 1552–1917*, London: Harper Collins Publishers.

HOWARD, M.C., and J.E. KING, 1975, *The Political Economy of Marx*, Harlow, Essex & New York: Longman.

HOWE, A., 1984, *The Cotton Masters, 1830–1860*, Oxford: Clarendon Press.

HOWE, J., 1992, 'Aspects of Rural Transport Infrastructure in Ethiopia', International Institute for Infrastructural, Hydraulic and Environmental Engineering, IHE Working Paper IP-1, Delft: The Netherlands.

HOWE, J., 1993, 'The Bicycle in Africa: Luxury or Necessity?', International Institute for Infrastructural, Hydraulic and Environmental Engineering, IHE Working Paper IP-3, Delft: The Netherlands.

HOWE, J., 1994, 'Enhancing Non-Motorised Transport Use in Africa—Changing the Policy Climate', International Institute for Infrastructural, Hydraulic and Environmental Engineering, IHE Working Paper IP-5, Delft: The Netherlands.

HUME, D., 1740, *A Treatise of Human Nature*, (ed. L.A. Selby-Bigge), Oxford: Clarendon Press (1888).

HUNTER, G., 1969, *Modernizing Peasant Societies: A Comparative Study in Asia and Africa*, New York & London: Oxford University Press.

HVIDING, E., and G.B.K. BAINES, 1994, 'Community-based Fisheries Management, Tradition and the Challenges of Development in Marovo, Solomon Islands', *Development and Change*, Vol. 25, No. 1, pp. 13–39.

HYDE, W.F., G.S. AMACHER, and W. MAGRATH, 1996, 'Deforestation and Forest Land Use: Theory, Evidence, and Policy Implications', *The World Bank Research Observer*, Vol. 11, No. 2, pp. 223–48.

HYDEN, G., 1983, *No Shortcuts to Progress—African Development Management in Perspective*, Berkeley & Los Angeles: University of California Press.

HYDEN, G., 1986, 'African Social Structure and Economic Development', in Berg, R.J. and J.S. Whitaker (eds.), *Strategies for African Development,* Berkeley, Calif.: University of California Press.

JAEGER, W.K., 1992a, 'The Causes of Africa's Food Crisis', *World Development*, Vol. 20, No. 11, pp. 1631–45.

JAEGER, W.K., 1992b, 'The Effects of Economic Policies on African Agriculture', World Bank Discussion Papers, Africa Technical Department Series, Washington, DC: The World Bank.

JANOS, A., 1982, *The Politics of Backwardness in Hungary, 1825–1945*, Princeton, NJ: Princeton University Press.

JAYARAMAN, T.K., 1981, 'Farmers' Organizations in Surface Irrigation Projects: Two Empirical Studies from Gujarat', *Economic and Political Weekly*, Vol. 16, No. 39, pp. A89–A98.

JEAY, A.M., 1984, 'Droits traditionnels versus législation moderne et recommandations pour une gestion rationnelle des ressources de la pêche—le cas des Somono du Moyen Niger (Mali)', Université Montpellier III (France).

JESSUP, T.C., and N.L. PELUSO, 1986, 'Minor Forest Products as Common Property Resources in East Kalimantan, Indonesia', in National Research Council, *Proceeding of the Conference on Common Property Resource Management*, Washington, D.C.: National Academy Press, pp. 501–531.

JEWSIEWICKI, B., 1993, *Naître et mourir au Zaïre—Un demi-siècle d'histoire au quotidien*, Paris: Karthala.

JODHA, N.S., 1986, 'Common Property Resources and Rural Poor in Dry Regions of India', *Economic and Political Weekly*, Vol. 21, No. 27, pp. 1169–1182.

JODHA, N.S., 1992, 'Common Property Resources—A Missing Dimension of Development Strategies', *World Bank Discussion Papers*, No. 169, Washington: The World Bank.

JOHNSON, R.N., and G.D. LIBECAP, 1982, 'Contracting Problems and Regulation: The Case of the Fishery', *American Economic Review*, Vol. 72, pp. 1005–1022.

JOHNSON, O.E.G., 1972, 'Economic Analysis, the Legal Framework and Land Tenure Systems', *Journal of Law and Economics*, Vol. 15, No. 1, pp. 259–76.

JOHNSTON, M., 1981, 'Indonesia: Traditions on the Move', *RRDC Bulletin*, University of Reding, November.

JOHNSON, R.N., and G.D. LIBECAP, 1982, 'Contracting Problems and Regulation: The Case of the Fishery', *American Economic Review*, Vol. 72, pp. 1005–1022.

JOHNSTON, B.F., 1986, 'Governmental Strategies for Agricultural Development', in Berg, R.J., and J.S. Whitaker (eds.), *Strategies for African Development*, Berkeley, Cal.: University of California Press, pp. 155–83.

JONES, E.L., 1981, *The European Miracle: Environments, Economies and Geopolitics in the History of Europe and Asia*, Cambridge: Cambridge University Press.

JONES, S.R.G., 1984, *The Economics of Conformism*, Oxford: Basil Blackwell.

JUL-LARSEN, E., 1993, 'The Micro-state of the Popo in Pointe Noire. An Analysis of Local Governance, State-Society Relations and Access to Ressources', Centre for Development Studies, University of Bergen Norway (mimeo).

KAGAN, J., 1984, *The Nature of the Child*, New York: Basic Books.

KAHNEMANN, D., J.L. KNETSCH, and R. THALER, 1986, 'Fairness as a Constraint on Profit Seeking: Entitlements in the Market', *American Economic Review*, Vol. 76, No. 4, pp. 728–41.

KAKAR, S., 1978, *The Inner World*, Delhi: Oxford University Press.

KALI, R., 1998, 'Endogenous Business Networks', Department of Business Administration, Instituto Tecnologico Autonomo de Mexico, Mexico (mimeo).

KANBUR, R., 1992, 'Heterogeneity, Distribution, and Cooperation in Common Property Resource Management', Policy Research Working Papers, WPS 844, Washington, D.C.: The World Bank.

KANDORI, M., 1992, 'Social Norms and Community Enforcement', *Review of Economic Studies*, Vol. 59, pp. 63–80.

KAO, C., 1991, 'Personal Trust in the Large Businesses in Taiwan: A Traditional Foundation for Contemporary Economic Activities', in Hamilton, G. (ed.), *Business Networks and Economic Development in East and Southeast Asia*, Hong Kong: Centre of Asian Studies, University of Hong Kong, pp. 234–273.

KARANTH, G.K., 1992, 'Privatisation of Common Property Resources—Lessons from Rural Karnataka', *Economic and Political Weekly*, Vol. 27, Nos 31–32, pp. 1680–88.

KAUL, M.C., 1996, *Common Lands and Customary Law: Institutional Change in North India over the Past Two Centuries*, Oxford: Oxford University Press.

KENNEDY, P., 1988, *African Capitalism—The Struggle for Ascendency*, Cambridge: Cambridge University Press.

KERNER, D.O., 1988, 'Land Scarcity and Rights of Control in the Development of Commercial Farming in Northeast Tanzania', in Downs, R.E., and S.P. Reyna (eds.), *Land and Society in Contemporary Africa*, Hanover & London: University Press of New England, pp. 159–191.

KEVANE, M., 1996, 'Agrarian Structure and Agricultural Practice: Typology and Application to Western Sudan', *American Journal of Agricultural Economics*, Vol. 78, No. 1, pp. 236–45.

KIAMBA, M., 1989, 'The Introduction and Evolution of Private Landed Property in Kenya', *Development and Change*, Vol. 20, No. 1, pp. 121–147.

KIKUCHI, M., and Y. HAYAMI, 1980, 'Inducements to Institutional Innovations in an Agrarian Community', *Economic Development and Cultural Change*, Vol. 29, No. 1, pp. 21–36.

KIMBALL, M.S., 1988, 'Farmers' Cooperatives as Behavior Toward Risk', *American Economic Review*, Vol. 78, No. 1, pp. 224–32.

KLUCKHOHN, C., 1944, *Navaho Witchcraft*, Papers of the Peabody Museum, Harvard University.

KOCHERLAKOTA, N.R., 1994, 'Efficient Bilateral Risk Sharing without Commitment', Department of Economics, University of Iowa (mimeo).

KOEHN, P., 1983, 'State Land Allocation and Class Formation in Nigeria', *Journal of Modern African Studies*, Vol. 21, No. 3.

KOEHN, P., 1984, ' 'Development' Administration and Land Allocation in Nigeria', *Rural Africana*, Vol. 18, Winter, pp. 59–75.

KOHNERT, D., 1996, 'Magic and Witchcraft: Implications for Democratization and Poverty-Alleviating Aid in Africa', *World Development*, Vol. 24, No. 8, pp. 1347–1355.

KONE, F.A., 1985, 'Traditional Fishing Rights in the Central Delta of the Niger and the Lake Region: Conflicts and Recommendations With a View to Equitable and Rational Management of Fishery Resources', FAO Fisheries Report, No. 360, Rome: FAO.

KONRAD, K.A., and S. SKAPERDAS, 1997, 'Backing Up Words with Deeds. Information and Punishment in Organized Crime', *Nordic Journal of Political Economy*, Vol. 24, No. 1, pp. 51–63.

KRANTON, R., 1996, 'Reciprocal Exchange: A Self-Sustaining System', *American Economic Review*, Vol. 86, No. 4, pp. 830–851.

KREPS, D.M., 1990, *A Course in Microeconomic Theory*, New York: Harvester Wheatsheaf.

KREPS, D.M., 1997, 'Intrinsic Motivation and Extrinsic Incentives', *American Economic Review*, Papers and Proceedings, Vol. 87, No. 2, pp. 359–364.

KREPS, D.M., and R. WILSON, 1982, 'Reputation and Imperfect Information', *Journal of Economic Theory*, Vol. 27, No. 2, pp. 253–279.

KREPS, D.M., P. MILGROM, J. ROBERTS, and R. WILSON, 1982, 'Rational Cooperation in the Finitely Repeated Prisoners' Dilemma', *Journal of Economic Theory*, Vol. 27, No. 2, pp. 245–252.

KRIEGEL, B., 1995, *The State and the Rule of Law*, Princeton, New Jersey: Princeton University Press.

KRUGMAN, P., 1997, *Development, Geography, and Economic Theory*, Cambridge, MA & London: The MIT Press.

KUMAR, B.G., 1990, 'Ethiopian Famines, 1973–1985: A Case Study', in Drèze, J., and A.K. Sen (eds.), *The Political Economy of Hunger, Vol. II: Famine Prevention*, Oxford: Clarendon Press, pp. 173–216.

KUMAR, D., 1992, *Land and Caste in South India—Agricultural Labour in the Madras Presidency During the Nineteenth Century*, New Delhi: Manohar.

KURAN, T., 1987, 'Preference Falsification, Policy Continuity, and Collective Conservatism', *Economic Journal*, Vol. 97, No. , pp. 642–65.

KURAN, T., 1988, 'The Tenacious Past: Theories of Personal and Collective Conservatism', *Journal of Economic Behavior and Organization*, Vol. 10, No. , pp. 143–71.

KURAN, T., 1995, *Private Truths, Public Lies—The Social Consequences of Preference Falsification*, Cambridge, Mssts & London: Harvard University Press.

KURIEN, J., 1978, 'Entry of Big Business into Fishing—Its Impact on Fish Economy', *Economic and Political Weekly*, Vol. 13, No. 36, pp. 1557–1665.

KUZNETS, S., 1966, *Modern Economic Growth*, New Haven: Yale University Press.

KUZNETS, S., 1968, *Toward a Theory of Economic Growth*, New York: W.W. Norton & Cy.

LAFFONT, J.J., 1975, 'Macroeconomic Constraints, Economic Efficiency and Ethics: an Introduction to Kantian Economics', *Economica*, Vol. 42, No. 168, pp. 430–437.

LANDES, D., 1998, *The Wealth and Poverty of Nations—Why Some Are So Rich and Some So Poor?*, London: Little, Brown and Cy.

LANE, R.E., 1991, *The Market Experience*, Cambridge: Cambridge University Press.

LANGLOIS, R., 1986, 'The New Institutional Economics: An Introductory Essay', in Langlois, R. (ed.), *Economics as a Process—Essays in the New Institutional Economics*, Cambridge: Cambridge University Press, pp. 1–25.

LAURENT, P.J., 1998, *Une association de développement en pays mossi*, Paris: Karthala.

LAURENT, P. J., MATHIEU, P. and M. TOTTE, 1994, 'Migrations et accès à la terre au Burkina Faso', *Cahiers du Cidep*, No. 20, Louvain-la-Neuve.

LAURENT, P-J, 1995, 'Les pouvoirs politiques locaux et la décentralisation au Burkina Faso', *Cahiers du Cidep*, No. 26, University of Louvain-la-Neuve.

LAWRY, S.W., 1989a, 'Tenure Policy and Natural Resource Management in Sahelian West Africa', Land Tenure Center, University of Wisconsin-Madison, Research Paper No. 130.

LAWRY, S.W., 1989b, 'Tenure Policy Toward Common Property Natural Resources', Land Tenure Center, University of Wisconsin-Madison, Research Paper No. 134.

LAWRY, S.W., 1993, 'Transactions in Cropland Held Under Customary Tenure in Lesotho', in T.J. Bassett and D.E. Crummey (eds.), *Land in African Agrarian Systems*, Madison, Wisconsin: The University of Wisconsin Press, pp. 57–74.

LEDENEVA, A.V., 1998, *Russia's Economy of Favours—Blat, Networking and Informal Exchange*, Cambridge: Cambridge University Press.

LEDYARD, J.O., 1995, 'Public Goods: A Survey of Experimental Research', in Kagel, J.H., and A.E. Roth (eds.), *The Handbook of Experimental Economics*, Princeton, NJ: Princeton University Press, pp. 111–194.

LELART, M., 1990, *La tontine—Pratique informelle d'épargne et de crédit dans les pays en voie de développement*, London & Paris: John Libbey (Published for UREF).

LELE, U., and S.W. STONE, 1989, 'Population Pressure, the Environment and Agricultural Intensification—Variations on the Boserup Hypothesis', MADIA Discussion Paper 4, Washington, D.C.: The World Bank.

LE ROY, E., 1979, 'Réforme foncière et stratégique du développement—Réflexion à partir de l'exemple sénégalais', *African Perspectives*, Vol. 1, pp. 67–81.

LE ROY, E., 1985, 'La loi sur le domaine national a vingt ans: joyeux anniversaire?', *Mondes en Développement*, Tome 13, No. 52, pp. 667–685.

LESERVOISIER, O., 1994, *La question foncière en Mauritanie—Terres et pouvoirs dans la région du Gorgol*, Paris: Editions L'Harmattan.

LESTHAEGHE, R., G. KAUFMANN, D. MEEKERS, and J. SURKYN, 1994, 'Post-Partum Abstinence, Polygyny, and Age at Marriage: A Macro-Level Analysis of Sub-Saharan Societies', in Bledsoe, C., and G. Pison (eds.), *Nuptiality in Sub-Saharan Africa—Contemporary Anthropological and Demographic Perspectives*, Oxford: Clarendon Press, pp. 25–54.

LEVI, M., 1988, *Of Rule and Revenue*, Berkeley: The University of California Press.

LEVIEIL, D.P., 1987, *Territorial Use Rights in Fishing and the Management of Small-Scale Fisheries: The Case of Lake Titicaca (Peru)*, Unpublished Ph.D. Thesis, University of British Columbia (Vancouver).

LEVINE, H.B., 1984, 'Controlling Access: Forms of "Territoriality" in Three New Zealand Crayfishing Villages', *Ethnology*, Vol. 23, No. 2, pp. 89–99.

LEWIS, W.A., 1955, *The Theory of Economic Growth*, London: George Allen & Unwin Ltd.

LI, T.M., 1998, 'Constituting Capitalist Culture—The Singapore Malay Problem and Entrepreneurship Reconsidered', in Hefner, R.W. (ed.), 1998, *Market Cultures—Society and Morality in the New Asian Capitalisms*, Boulder, Col.: Westview Press, pp. 147–172.

LIBECAP, G.D., 1989a, *Contracting for Property Rights*, Cambridge: Cambridge University Press.

LIBECAP, G.D., 1989b, 'Distributional Issues in Contracting for Property Rights', in *Journal of Institutional and Theoretical Economics*, Vol. 145, No. 1, pp. 6–24.

LIBECAP, G.D., 1996, 'Economic Variables and the Development of the Law: the Case of Western Mineral Rights', in Alston, L.J., T. Eggertsson, and D.C. North (eds.), *Empirical Studies in Institutional Change*, Cambridge: Cambridge University Press, pp. 34–58.

LINDBECK, A., S. NYBERG, and J.W. WEIBULL, 1996, 'Social Norms, the Welfare State, and Voting', Institute for International Economic Studies, Seminar Paper No. 608, Stockholm University.

LIPTON, M., 1985, 'Indian Agricultural Development and African Food Strategies: A Role for EC?', in Callewaert, W.M., and R. Kumar (eds.), *EEC-India: Towards a Common Perspective*, Leuven: Peeters, pp. 45–85.

LITWACK, J.M., 1991, 'Legality and Market Reform in Soviet-Type Economies', *Journal of Economic Perspectives*, Vol. 5, No. 4, pp. 77–89.

LONG, N., 1970, 'Rural Entrepreneurship and Religious Commitment in Zambia', *Internationales Jahrbuch für Religionssoziologie*, Vol. VI: 142–57.

LONG, N., 1977, *An Introduction to the Sociology of Rural Development*, London & New York: Tavistock Publications.

LOPEZ, R., and A. VALDES, 1997, 'Chile: Poverty and Income Distribution in a High Growth Economy, 1987–1995', Washington, DC: The World Bank.

LOW, B.S., 1990, 'Human Responses to Environmental Extremeness and Uncertainty: A Cross-Cultural Perspective', in Cashdan, E. (ed.), *Risk and Uncertainty in Tribal and Peasant Economies*, Boulder, San Francisco & London: Westview Press, pp. 229–255.

LTC (Land Tenure Center), 1990, *Security of Tenure in Africa*, University of Madison-Wisconsin.

LUEDDE-NEURATH, R., 1988, 'State Intervention and Export-Oriented Development in South Korea', in White, G. (ed.), *Developmental States in East Asia*, London: Macmillan, pp. 68–112.

MacDONALD, I., 1991, *The New Shostakovich*, Oxford: Oxford University Press.

MACFARLANE, A., 1978, *The Origins of English Individualism*, Oxford: Basil Blackwell.

MACGAFFEY, J., 1987, *Entrepreneurs and Parasites: The Struggle for Indigenous Capitalism in Zaïre*, New York: Cambridge University Press.

MACKENZIE, F., 1993, '"A Piece of Land Never Shrinks": Reconceptualizing Land Tenure in a Smallholding District, Kenya', in Bassett, T.J., and D.E. Crummey (eds.), *Land in African Agrarian Systems*, Madison, Wisconsin: University of Wisconsin Press, pp. 194–221.

MACKIE, J., 1998, 'Business Success Among Southeast Asian Chinese—The Role of Culture, Values, and Social Structures', in Hefner, R.W. (ed.), *Market Cultures—Society and Morality in the New Asian Capitalisms*, Boulder, Col.: Westview Press, pp. 129–146.

MAHAR, D., 1988, 'Government Policies and Deforestation in Brazil's Amazon Region', World Bank Environment Department, Working Paper No. 7.

MAHDI, M., 1986, 'Private Rights and Collective Management of Water in a High Atlas Berber Tribe', in National Research Council, *Proceedings of the Conference on Common Property Resource Management*, Washington, D.C.: National Academy Press, pp. 181–98.

MAIGA, M., 1995, *Le fleuve Sénégal et l'intégration de l'Afrique de l'Ouest en 2011*, Dakar: Codesria & Paris: Karthala.

MALARNEY, S.K., 1998, 'State Stigma, Family Prestige, and the Development of Commerce in the Red River Delta of Vietnam', in Hefner, R.W. (ed.), *Market Cultures—Society and Morality in the New Asian Capitalisms*, Boulder, Col.: Westview Press, pp. 268–289.

MALINOWSKI, B., 1920, 'Kula: Circulating Exchange of Valuables in the Archipelagoes of Eastern New Guinea', *Man*, July.

MALINOWSKI, B., 1922, *Argonauts of the Western Pacific*, London: Routledge and Kegan Paul.

MARRIS, P., and A. SOMERSET, 1971, *African Businessmen*, London: Routledge & Kegan Paul.

MARX, K., 1859, *A Contribution to the Critique of Political Economy*, Marx-Engels Werke, Vol. 13 (English translation published by Progress Publishers, Moscow, 1979; and taken over by Lawrence and Wishart, London, Vol. 1 of the complete edition of Marx-Engels works).

MAS-COLELL, A., 1992, 'The Cournotian Foundations of Walrasian Equilibrium Theory: An Exposition of Recent Theory', in Hildenbrand, W. (ed.), *Advances in Economic Theory*, Cambridge: Cambridge University Press, pp. 183–224.

MASSOZ, M., 1982, *Le Congo de Papa*, Liège: Editions Dricot.

MATHEW, S., 1990, *Fishing Legislation and Gear Conflicts in Asian Countries*, Samudra Monographs, Brussels: Samudra Publications.

MATHIAS, P., 1969, *The First Industrial Nation*, New York: Charles Scribner & Sons.

MATHIEU, P., 1987, *Agriculture irriguée, réforme foncière et stratégies paysannes dans la vallée du fleuve Sénégal, 1960–1985*, Unpublished Ph.D. thesis, Fondation Universitaire Luxembourgeoise, Arlon (Belgium).

MATHUR, P.N., 1991, *Why Developing Countries Fail to Develop?*, London: Macmillan.

MATLON, P., 1994, 'Indigenous Land Use Systems and Investments in Soil Fertility in Burkina Faso', in in J.W. Bruce and S.E. Migot-Adholla (eds.), *Searching for Land Tenure Security in Africa*, Dubuque, Iowa: Kendall/Hunt Publishing Cy, pp. 41–69.

MATTHEWS, R.C.O., 1986, 'The Economics of Institutions and the Sources of Growth', *The Economic Journal*, Vol. 96, No. 384, pp. 903–918.

MAYNARD SMITH, J., 1982, *Evolution and the Theory of Games*, Cambridge: Cambridge University Press.

McCARTHY, N., A. DE JANVRY, and E. SADOULET, 1998, 'Land Allocation Under Dual Individual-Collective Use in Mexico', *Journal of Development Economics*, Vol. 56, No. 2, pp. 239–264.

McCLOSKEY, D.N., 1972, 'The Enclosure of Open Fields: Preface to a Study of Its Impact on the Efficiency of English Agriculture in the Eighteenth Century', *Journal of Economic History*, Vol. 32, No. 1, pp. 15–35.

McCLOSKEY, D.N., 1976, 'English Open Fields as Behavior Towards Risk', in Uselding, P. (ed.) *Research in Economic History*, Vol. 1, Greenwhich, Conn.: JAI Press, pp. 124–171.

McEVOY, A.F., 1986, *The Fisherman's Problem—Ecology and Law in the California Fisheries, 1850–1980*, Cambridge: Cambridge University Press.

McKEAN, M.A., 1986, 'Management of Traditional Common Lands (Iriaichi) in Japan', in National Research Council, *Proceedings of the Conference on Common Property Resource Management*, Washington, D.C.: National Academy Press, pp. 533–589.

McLELLAN, D., 1977, *Karl Marx—Selected Writings*, Oxford: Oxford University Press.

McMULLEN, R., 1988, *Corruption and the Decline of Rome*, New Haven, Conn.: Yale University Press.

McNALLY, D., 1988, *Political Economy and the Rise of Capitalism—A Reinterpretation*, Berkeley, Cal & London: University of California Press.

MEEK, C.K., 1949, *Land, Law and Custom in the Colonies*, 2nd edition, London: Oxford University Press (Reprint, London: Frank Cass, 1968).

MEIER, G.M., and R.E. BALDWIN, 1957, *Economic Development*, New York: John Wiley & Sons.

MELARD, C., J.P. PLATTEAU and H. WATONGOKA, 1998, *Etude des incidences socio-économiques de l'introduction de la technique de pêche au filet maillant au lac Kivu*, FUCID (Fondation Universitaire pour la Coopération Internationale au Développement), University of Namur, Belgium.

MELLOR, J. and C. DELGADO, 1987, 'Food Production in Sub-Saharan Africa', Food Policy Statement No. 7, Washington, DC: IFPRI.

MESSERSCHMIDT, D.A., 1986, 'People and Resources in Nepal: Customary Resource Management Systems of the Upper Kali Gandaki', in National Research Council, *Proceedings of the Conference on Common Property Resource Management*, Washington, D.C.: National Academy Press, pp. 455–80.

MIGEOTTE, F., 1995, *Innovation institutionnelle et tensions sociales: le cas de l'intensification de l'élevage sur une colline rwandaise*, Musée Royal d'Afrique Centrale, Tervuren (Belgium).

MIGOT-ADHOLLA, S.E., P. HAZELL, B. BLAREL, and F. PLACE, 1991, 'Indigenous Land Rights Systems in Sub-Saharan Africa: a Constraint on Policy?', *World Bank Economic Review*, Vol. 5, No. 1, pp. 155–175.

MIGOT-ADHOLLA, S.E., G. BENNEH, F. PLACE, and S. ATSU, 1994a, 'Land, Security of Tenure, and Productivity in Ghana', in J.W. Bruce and S.E. Migot-Adholla (eds.), *Searching for Land Tenure Security in Africa*, Dubuque, Iowa: Kendall/Hunt Publishing Cy, pp. 97–118.

MIGOT-ADHOLLA, S.E., F. PLACE, and W. OLUOCH-KOSURA, 1994b, 'Security of Tenure and Land Productivity in Kenya', in J.W. Bruce and S.E. Migot-Adholla (eds.), *Searching for Land Tenure Security in Africa*, Dubuque, Iowa: Kendall/Hunt Publishing Cy, pp. 119–40.

MILGROM, P., D.C. NORTH, and B. WEINGAST, 1990, 'The Role of Institutions in the Revival of Trade: the Medieval Law Merchant', *Economics and Politics, Vol. 2, No. 1, pp. 1–23.*

MILGROM, P., and J. ROBERTS, 1992, *Economics, Organization and Management*, Englewood Cliffs, N.J.: Prentice-Hall International.

MILL, J.S., 1848, *Principles of Political Economy—with some of their applications to social philosophy*, Reprints of Economic Classics, Augustus M. Kelley, New-York (1965).

MINNAAR, A., D. OFFRINGA, and C. PAYZE, *To Live in Fear: Witchburning and Medicine Murder in Venda*, HSRC.

MOOR, G.M., 1996, 'Tenure Security and Productivity in the Zimbabwean Small Farm Sector: Implications for South Africa', Department of Agricultural Economics, University of Natal, Pietermaritzburg.

MOORE, M., 1988, 'Economic Growth and the Rise of Civil Society: Agriculture in Taiwan and South Korea', in White, G. (ed.), *Developmental States in East Asia*, London: Macmillan, pp. 113–152.

MOORE, M., 1993, 'Declining to Learn from the East? The World Bank on "Governance and Development"', IDS Bulletin, Vol. 24, No. 1, pp. 39–50.

MOORE, M., 1994, 'How Difficult is it to Construct Market Relations? A Commentary on Platteau', *Journal of Development Studies*, Vol. 30, No. 4, pp. 818–830.

MOORE, M., 1997, 'Societies, Polities and Capitalists in Developing Countries: A Literature Survey', *Journal of Development Studies*, Vol. 33, No. 3, pp. 287–363.

MOORE, W.E., 1963, *Social Change*, New Jersey: Englewood Cliffs and New York: Prentice-Hall.

MORDUCH, J., 1995, 'Income Smoothing and Consumption Smoothing', *Journal of Economic Perspectives*, Vol. 9, No. 3, pp. 103–114.

MORISHIMA, M., 1982, *Why Has Japan 'Succeeded'?—Western Technology and the Japanese Ethos*, Cambridge: Cambridge University Press.

MOULIN, H., 1995, *Cooperative Microeconomics—A Game-Theoretic Introduction*, London & New York: Prentice Hall and Harvester Wheatsheaf.

MUELLER, D.C., 1989, *Public Choice*, Cambridge: Cambridge University Press.

MUGANGU MATABARO, S., 1997, *La gestion foncière rurale au Zaïre—Réformes juridiques et pratiques foncières locales (Cas du Bushi)*, Paris: Editions L'Harmattan et Bruxelles: Academia Bruylant.

MUKWAYA, A.B., 1953, *Land Tenure in Buganda: Present Day Tendencies*, Kampala: Eagle Press.

MURSHID, 1997, 'Generalised Morality and the Problem of Transition to an Impersonal Exchange Regime: A Response to Platteau', *Journal of Development Studies*, Vol. 33, No. 5, pp. 693–713.

MYERSON, R.B., 1991, *Game Theory—Analysis of Conflict*, Cambridge, Mssts & London: Harvard University Press.

MYINT, H., 1971, 'The "Classical Theory" of International Trade and the Underdeveloped Countries', in Myint, H., *Economic Theory and the Underdeveloped Countries*, London & Toronto: Oxford University Press, pp. 118–46 (originally published in *The Economic Journal*, June 1958, pp. 317–37) .

NABLI, M.K., and J.B. NUGENT (eds.), 1989a, *The New Institutional Economics and Development: Theory and Applications to Tunisia*, Amsterdam: North-Holland.

NABLI, M.K., and J.B. NUGENT, 1989b, 'The New Institutional Economics and Its Applicability to Development', *World Development*, Vol. 17, No. 9, pp. 1333–1347.

NAGATA, J., 1979, *Malaysian Mosaic*, Vancouver: University of British Columbia Press.

NAQVI, N., and F. WEMHONER, 1995, 'Power, Coercion and the Games Landlords Play', *Journal of Development Economics*, Vol. 47, No. 1, pp. 191–205.

NELSON, R.R., and S.G. WINTER, 1982, *An Evolutionary Theory of Economic Change*, Cambridge, Mass.: Harvard University Press.

NETTING, R. McC., 1972, 'Of Men and Meadows: Strategies of Alpine Land Use', *Anthropological Quarterly*, Vol. 45, pp. 132–144.

NETTING, R. McC., 1976, 'What Alpine Peasants Have in Common: Observations on Communal Tenure in a Swiss Village', *Human Ecology*, Vol. 4, pp. 135–146.

NETTING, R., McC., 1981, *Balancing on an Alp*, Cambridge: Cambridge University Press.

NETTING, R., 1982, 'Territory, Property and Tenure', in Adams, R., N.J. Smelser, and D.J. Treiman (eds.), *Behavioural and Social Science Research: A National Resource, Part II*, Washington, DC: National Academy Press.

NORONHA, R., 1985, *A Review of the Literature on Land Tenure Systems in Sub-Saharan Africa*, Research Unit of the Agriculture and Rural Development Department, Report No: ARU 43, Washington: The World Bank.

NORONHA, R., 1997, 'Common-Property Resource Management in Traditional Societies', in Dasgupta, P., and K-G. Mäler (eds.), *The Environment and Emerging Development Issues*, Vol. 1, Oxford: Clarendon Press, pp. 48–69.

NORTH, D.C., 1981, *Structure and Change in Economic History*, New York: Norton.

NORTH, D.C., 1990, *Institutions, Institutional Change and Economic Performance*, Cambridge: Cambridge University Press.

NORTH, D.C., 1991, 'Institutions', *Journal of Economic Perspectives*, Vol. 5, No. 1, pp. 97–112.

NORTH, D.C., and R.P. THOMAS, 1973, *The Rise of the Western World—A New Economic History*, Cambridge: Cambridge University Press.

NUGENT, J.B., and N. SANCHEZ, 1993, 'Tribes, Chiefs, and Transhumance: A Comparative Institutional Analysis', *Economic Development and Cultural Change*, Vol. 42, No. 1, pp. 87–113.

OKOTH-OGENDO, H.W.O., 1976, 'African Land Tenure Reform', in Hayer, J., J.K. Maitha, and W.M. Senga (eds.), *Agricultural Development in Kenya: An Economic Assessment*, Nairobi: Oxford University Press, pp. 124–142.

OKOTH-OGENDO, H.W.O., 1993, 'Agrarian Reform in Sub-Saharan Africa: An Assessment of State Responses to the African Agrarian Crisis and Their Implications for Agricultural Development', in Bassett, T.J., and D.E. Crummey (eds.), *Land in African Agrarian Systems*, Madison, Wisconsin: The University of Wisconsin Press, pp. 247–273.

OLSON, M., 1965, *The Logic of Collective Action*, Cambridge, Mass.: Harvard University Press.

OLSON, M., 1982, *The Rise and Decline of Nations*, New Haven and London: Yale University Press.

OPP, K.D., 1979, 'The Emergence and Effects of Social Norms. A Confrontation of Some Hypotheses of Sociology and Economics', *Kyklos*, Vol. 32, Fasc. 4, pp. 775–801.

OPP, K.D., 1982, 'The Evolutionary Emergence of Norms', *British Journal of Social Psychology*, Vol. 21, pp. 139–149.

ORTIZ, S., 1967, 'The Structure of Decision-making among Indians of Columbia', in Firth, R. (ed.), *Themes in Economic Anthropology*, London: Tavistock Publications, pp. 191–228.

ORTIZ, S., 1973, *Uncertainties in Peasant Farming. A Columbian Case*, London: The Athlone Press.

OSTROM, E., 1990, *Governing the Commons: the Evolution of Institutions for Collective Action*, Cambridge: Cambridge University Press.

OSTROM, E., R. GARDNER, and J. WALKER, 1994, *Rules, Games, and Common-Pool Resources*, Ann Arbor: The University of Michigan Press.

OTSUKA, K., M. KIKUCHI, and Y. HAYAMI, 1986, 'Community and Market in Contract Choice: Jeepney in the Philippines', *Economic Development and Cultural Change*, Vol. 34, No. 2, pp. 279–298.

OTSUKA, K., H. CHUMA, and Y. HAYAMI, 1992, 'Land and Labor Contracts in Agrarian Economies: Theories and Facts', *Journal of Economic Literature*, Vol. 30, No. 4, pp. 1965–2018.

OTSUKA, K., and C.L. DELGADO, 1995, 'New Technologies and the Competitiveness of High- and Low-Potential Rural Areas in Asia and Africa', in Peters, G.H., and D.D. Hedley (eds.), *Agricultural Competitiveness: Market Forces and Policy Choice*, Dartmouth Publishing Company, pp. 364–376.

PAGDEN, A., 1988, 'The Destruction of Trust and its Economic Consequences in the Case of Eighteenth-century Naples', in Gambetta, D. (ed.), *Trust-Making and Breaking Cooperative Relations*, Oxford: Basil Blackwell, pp. 127–141.

PARKIN, D.J., *Palm, Wine and Witnesses*, London: Intertext Books.

PENDER, J.L., and J.M. KERR, 1994, 'The Effect of Transferable Land Rights on Credit, Land Investment and Use: Evidence from South India', Provo, Utah: Brigham Young University, Department of Economics.

PETERS, P.E., 1994, *Dividing the Commons—Politics, Policy, and Culture in Botswana*, Charlottesville & London: The University Press of Virginia.

PETERSON, W.L., 1979, 'International Farm Prices and the Social Cost of Cheap Food Policies', *American Journal of Agricultural Economics*, Vol. 61, No. 1, pp. 12–21.

PHELPS, E., 1975, 'Introduction', in Phelps, E. (ed.), *Altruism, Morality, and Economic Theory*, New York: Russell Sage Foundation, pp. 1–9.

PIKETTY, T., 1995, 'Social Mobility and Redistributive Politics', *Quarterly Journal of Economics*, Vol. CX, Issue 3, pp. 551–584.

PINCKNEY, T.C., and P.K. KIMUYU, 1994, 'Land Tenure Reform in East Africa: Good, Bad, or Unimportant?', *Journal of African Economies*, Vol. 3, No. 1, pp. 1–28.

PINGALI, P.L., and H.P. BINSWANGER, 1984, 'Population Density and Farming Systems: The Changing Locus of Innovations and Technical Change', Working Paper No. ARV 24, Washington, D.C.: The World Bank.

PINGALI, P., Y. BIGOT, and H.P. BINSWANGER, 1987, *Agricultural Mechanization and the Evolution of Farming Systems in Sub-Saharan Africa*, Baltimore & London: The Johns Hopkins University Press.

PINGALI, P.L., and H.P BINSWANGER, 1986, 'Population Density, Market Access and Farmer-Generated Technical Change in Sub-Saharan Africa', Research Unit of the Agricultural and Rural Development Dept, Washington, D.C.: The World Bank.

PIPES, R., 1995, *Russia under the Old Regime*, London: Penguin Books.

PIPES, R., 1999, *Property and Freedom*, New York: Alfred Knopf.

PLACE, F., and P. HAZELL, 1993, 'Productivity Effects of Indigenous Land Tenure Systems in Sub-Saharan Africa', *American Journal of Agricultural Economics*, Vol. 75, No. 1, pp. 10–19.

PLACE, F., and S.E. MIGOT-ADHOLLA, 1998, 'Land Registration and Smallholder Farms in Kenya', *Land Economics*, Vol. 74, No. 3, pp. 360–373.

PLATONOV, S.F., 1985, *The Time of Troubles—A Historical Study of the Internal Crisis and Social Struggle in Sixteenth- and Seventeenth-Century Muscovy*, Lawrence: University Press of Kansas.

PLATTEAU, J.P., 1978, *Les économistes classiques et le sous-développement*, Paris: Presses Universitaires de France (2 vols).

PLATTEAU, J.P., 1990, 'The Food Crisis in Africa: A Comparative Structural Analysis', in Drèze, J. and A. Sen (eds.), *The Political Economy of Hunger, Vol. 2: Famine Prevention*, Oxford: Clarendon Press, pp. 279–387.

PLATTEAU, J.P., 1991, 'Traditional Systems of Social Security and Hunger Insurance: Past Achievements and Modern Challenges', in Ahmad, E., J. Drèze, J. Hills, and A.K. Sen (eds.), *Social Security in Developing Countries*, Oxford: Clarendon Press, pp. 112–70.

PLATTEAU, J.P., 1992, *Land Reform and Structural Adjustment in Sub-Saharan Africa: Controversies and Guidelines*, FAO Economic and Social Development Paper No. 107, Rome: FAO (324 pp).

PLATTEAU, J.P., 1994a, 'Behind the Market Stage Where Real Societies Exist—Part I: The Role of Public and Private Order Institutions', *Journal of Development Studies*, Vol. 30, No. 3, pp. 533–577.

PLATTEAU, J.P., 1994b, 'Behind the Market Stage Where Real Societies Exist—Part II: The Role of Moral Norms', *Journal of Development Studies*, Vol. 30, No. 4, pp. 753–817.

PLATTEAU, J.P., 1995a, 'The Food Crisis in Africa: A Comparative Structural Analysis', in Drèze, J., A.K. Sen and A. Hussain (eds.), 1995, *The Political Economy of Hunger—Selected Essays*, Oxford: Clarendon Press, pp. 445–553.

PLATTEAU, J.P., 1995b, 'A Framework for the Analysis of Evolving Patron-Client Ties in Agrarian Economies', *World Development*, Vol. 23, No. 5, pp. 767–786.

PLATTEAU, J.P., 1995c, 'An Indian Model of Aristocratic Patronage', *Oxford Economic Papers*, Vol. 47, No. 4, pp. 636–662.

PLATTEAU, J.P., 1996a, 'Physical Infrastructure as a Constraint on Agricultural Growth: the Case of Sub-Saharan Africa', *Oxford Development Studies*, Vol. 24, No. 3, pp. 189–219.

PLATTEAU, J.P., 1996b, 'Comments on Aryeetey's "Rural Finance in Africa"', *Proceedings of the World Bank Annual Conference on Development Economics—1996*, Washington, DC: The World Bank.

PLATTEAU, J.P., 1996c, 'The Evolutionary Theory of Land Rights As Applied to Sub-Saharan Africa: A Critical Assessment', *Development and Change*, Vol. 27, No. 1, pp. 29–86.

PLATTEAU, J.P., 1997, 'Mutual Insurance as an Elusive Concept in Traditional Rural Communities', *Journal of Development Studies*, Vol. 33, No. 6, pp. 764–796.

PLATTEAU, J.P., and A. ABRAHAM, 1987, 'An Inquiry into Quasi-Credit Contracts: The Role of Reciprocal Credit and Interlinked Deals in Small-Scale Fishing Communities', *Journal of Development Studies*, Vol. 23, No. 4, pp. 461–90.

PLATTEAU, J.P., and J. NUGENT, 1992, 'Share Contracts and their Rationale: Lessons from Marine Fishing', *Journal of Development Studies*, Vol. 28, No. 3, pp. 386–422.

PLATTEAU, J.P., and Y. HAYAMI, 1998, 'Resource Endowments and Agricultural Development: Africa vs. Asia', in Aoki, M., and Y. Hayami (eds.), *The Institutional Foundation of Economic Development in East Asia*, London: Macmillan, pp. 357–410.

PLATTEAU, J.P., and E. SEKI, 2000, Coordination and Pooling Arrangements in Japanese Fisheries', in M. Aoki and Y. Hayami, (eds.), *Market, Community and Economic Development*, Oxford: Clarendon Press.

POEWE, K., 1989, *Religion, Kinship, and Economy in Luapula, Zambia*, Lewiston, N.Y.: Edwin Mellen.

POLANYI, K., 1957, *The Great Transformation*, New York: Rineholt.

POLANYI, K., 1968, 'Ports of Trade in Early Societies', in Dalton, G. (ed.), *Primitive, Archaic and Modern Economies*, New York: Doubleday.

POLANYI, K., 1977, *The Livelihood of Man*, New York and London: Academic Press.

POLANYI, K., C.W. ARENSBERG, and H.W. PEARSON (eds.), 1957, *Trade and Market in the Early Empires*, New York: Free Press, and London: Collier-Macmillan.

POSNER, R., 1981, *The Economics of Justice*, Caınbridge, Mssts and London: Harvard University Press.

POSPISIL, L., 1958, *Kapauka Papuans and their Law*, New Haven, Conn.: Yale University Press.

PUTNAM, R.D.,1993, *Making Democracy Work—Civic Traditions in Modern Italy*, Princeton, NJ: Princeton University Press.

PUTTERMAN, L., 1995, 'Economic Reform and Smallholder Agriculture in Tanzania: A Discussion of Recent Market Liberalization, Road Rehabilitation, and Technology Dissemination Efforts', *World Development*, Vol. 23, No. 2, pp. 311–326.

RABIN, M., 1993, 'Incorporating Fairness into Game Theory and Economics', *American Economic Review*, Vol. 83, No. 5, pp. 1281–1302.

RABIN, M., 1998, 'Psychology and Economics', *Journal of Economic Literature*, Vol. 36, No. 1, pp. 11–46.

RAEFF, M., 1984, *Understanding Imperial Russia*, New York: Columbia University Press.

RAO, C.H.H., 1971, 'Uncertainty, Entrepreneurship, and Sharecropping in India', *Journal of Political Economy*, Vol. 79, pp. 578–595.

RAO, V.M., 1972, 'Land Transfers: Findings in a Ryotwari Region', *Economic and Political Weekly*, Vol. 7 (Review of Agriculture), 30 Sept.

RASMUSEN, E., 1989, *Games and Information—An Introduction to Game Theory*, Oxford: Blackwell.

RAVENHILL, J. (ed.), 1986, *Africa in Economic Crisis*, London: Macmillan.

RAYNAUT, C., 1976, 'Transformation du système de production et inégalité économique: le cas d'un village haoussa (Niger)', *Revue canadienne des études africaines*, Vol. 10, No. 2, pp. 279–306.

REARDON, T., C. DELGADO, and P. MATLON, 1992, 'Determinants and Effects of Income Diversification Amongst Farm Households in Burkina Faso', *Journal of Development Studies*, Vol. 28, No. 2, pp. 264–296.

REPETTO, R., 1988, 'Economic Policy Reform for Natural Resource Conservation', World Bank Environment Department, Working Paper No. 4.

RIASANOVSKY, N.V., 1993, *A History of Russia*, New York & Oxford: Oxford University Press (5th edition).

RICHARDS, P., 1985, *Indigenous Agricultural Revolution—Ecology and Food Production in West Africa*, London & Boulder, Col: Hutchinson and Westview Press.

RICHARDS, P., 1995, 'Saving the Rain Forest: Contested Futures in Conservation', in Wallman, S. (ed.), *Contemporary Futures*, London: Routledge, pp. 138–53.

RIDDELL, J.C., J.W. SALACUSE, and D. TABACHNICK, 1987, 'The National Land Law of Zaire and Indigenous Land Tenure in Central Bandundu, Zaire', Land Tenure Center, LTC Paper No. 92, University of Wisconsin-Madison.

RIKER,W.H, and I. SENED, 1991, 'A Political Theory of the Origin of Property Rights: Airport Slots', *American Journal of Political Science*, Vol. 35, pp. 951–969.

RIVERSON, J., J. GAVIRIA and S. THRISCUTT, 1991, 'Rural Roads in Sub-Saharan Africa—Lessons from World Bank Experience', World Bank Technical Paper No. 141, Africa Technical Department Series, Washington, DC: The World Bank.

ROBERTSON, A.F., 1987, *The Dynamics of Productive Relationships—African Share Contracts in Comparative Perspective*, Cambridge: Cambridge University Press.

ROEMER, J.E., 1989, 'A Public Ownership Resolution of the Tragedy of the Commons', *Social Philosophy and Policy*, Vol. 2, No. 6, pp. 74–92.

ROGERS, E., 1969, *Modernization Among Peasants—The Impact of Communications*, New York: Holt, Rinehart and Winston.

RONDINELLI, D.A. (ed.), 1993, *Development Projects as Policy Experiments—An Adaptive Approach to Development Administration*, London & New York: Routledge.

ROSENBERG, N., and L.E. BIRDZELL, 1986, *How the West Grew Rich*, New York: Basic Books.

ROSENZWEIG, M.R., H.P. BINSWANGER, and J. McINTIRE, 1988, 'From Land Abundance to Land Scarcity—The Effects of Population Growth on Production Relations in Agrarian Economies', in Lee, R.D., W. Brian Arthur, A.C. Kelley, G. Rodgers, and T.N. Srinivasan (eds.), *Population, Food and Rural Development*, Oxford: Clarendon Press, pp. 77–100.

ROSTOW, W.W., 1960, *The Stages of Economic Growth*, Cambridge: Cambridge University Press.

ROSTOW, W.W., 1963, *The Economics of Take-Off into Sutained Growth*, New York: St. Martin's Press.

ROTH, M., 1993, 'Somalia Land Policies and Tenure Impacts: The Case of the Lower Shebelle', in Bassett, T.J., and D.E. Crummey (eds.), *Land in African Agrarian Systems*, Madison, Wisconsin: The University of Wisconsin Press, pp. 298–325.

ROTH, A.E., 1988, 'Laboratory Experimentation in Economics: A Methodological Overview', *Economic Journal*, Vol. 98, No. 393, pp. 974–1031.

ROTH, A.E., 1995, 'Bargaining Experiments', in Roth, A.E., and J.H. Kagel (eds.), *Handbook of Experimental Economics*, Princeton, NJ: Princeton University Press, pp. 253–348.

ROTH, A.E., V. PRASNIKAR, M. OKUNO-FUJIWARA, and S. ZAMIR, 1991, 'Bargaining and Market Behavior in Jerusalem, Ljubljana, Pittsburgh, and Tokyo: An Experimental Study', *American Economic Review*, Vol. 81, pp. 1068–95.

ROTH, M., J. COCHRANE, and W. KISAMBA-MUGERWA, 1994a, 'Tenure Security, Credit Use, and Farm Investment in the Rujumbura Pilot Land Registration Scheme, Uganda', in J.W. Bruce and S. Migot-Adholla (eds.), *Searching for Land Tenure Security in Africa*, Dubuque, Iowa: Kendall/Hunt Publishing Cy, pp. 169–198.

ROTH, M., J. UNRUH, and R. BARROWS, 1994b, 'Land Registration, Tenure Security, Credit Use, and Investment in the Shebelle Region of Somalia', in J.W. Bruce and S. Migot-Adholla (eds.), *Searching for Land Tenure Security in Africa*, Dubuque, Iowa: Kendall/Hunt Publishing Cy, pp. 199–230.

ROTH, M., A.M. KHAN, and M.C. ZULU, 1994c, 'Legal Framework and Administration of Land Policy in Zambia', in Roth, M., and S.G. Smith (eds.), *Land Tenure, Land Markets, and Institutional Transformation in Zambia*, Land Tenure Center, Madison: University of Wisconsin.

ROWLANDS, M., and J.P. WARNIER, 1988, 'Sorcery, Power, and the Modern State in Cameroon', *Man*, Vol. 23, No. 1, pp. 118–132.

RUDDLE, K., 1987, 'Administration and Conflict Management in Japanese Coastal Fisheries', *FAO Fisheries Technical Paper*, No. 273, Rome: FAO.

RUNGE, C.F., 1984, 'Strategic Interdependence in Models of Property Rights', *American Journal of Agricultural Economics*, Vol. 66, No. 5, pp. 807–813.

RUNGE, C.F, 1986, 'Common Property and Collective Action in Economic Development', *World Development*, Vol. 14, No. 5, pp. 623–635.

RUTHENBERG, H., 1980, *Farming Systems in the Tropics*, Oxford: Clarendon Press (3rd edition).

RUTTAN, V., and Y. HAYAMI, 1984, 'Toward a Theory of Induced Institutional Innovation', *Journal of development Studies*, Vol. 20, No. 4, pp. 203–223.

SADOULET, E., and A. de JANVRY, 1995, *Quantitative Development Policy Analysis*, Baltimore & London: The John Hopkins University Press.

SAHLINS, M., 1963, 'On the Sociology of Primitive Exchange', in Banton, M. (ed.), *The Relevance of Models for Social Anthropology*, London: Tavistock Publications, pp. 139–227.

SAHLINS, M., 1968, *Tribesmen*, Englewood Cliffs, New Jersey: Prentice-Hall.

SAMUELSON, P.A., 1974, 'Is the Rent Collector Worthy of his Full Hire?', *Eastern Economic Journal*, Vol. 1, No. 1, pp. 1–7.

SANDERS, J.H., J.G. NAGY, and S. RAMASWAMY, 1990, 'Developing New Agricultural Technologies for the Sahelian Countries: the Burkina Faso Case', *Economic Development and Cultural Change*, Vol. 39, No. 1, pp. 1–22.

SANTORUM, A. and A. TIBAIJUKA, 1992, 'Trading Responses to Food Market Liberalization in Tanzania', in Beynon, J. (ed.), *Market Liberalization and Private Sector Response in Eastern and Southern Africa*, Working Paper No. 6, Oxford: Food Studies Group, pp. 21–22 (also published in *Food Policy*, Vol. 17, December 1992).

SARAP, K., 1996, 'Land Market Transactions in Rural Haryana', *Economic and Political Weekly*, Vol. 31, No. 39, pp. A-106–115.

SAUL, M., 1988, 'Money and Land Tenure as Factors in Farm Size Differentiation in Burkina Faso', in Downs, R.E., and S.P. Reyna (eds.), *Land and Society in Contemporary Africa*, Hanover & London: University Press of New England, pp. 243–279.

SAUL, M., 1993, 'Land Custom in Bare: Agnatic Corporation and Rural Capitalism in Western Burkina', in Bassett, T.J., and D.E. Crummey (eds.), *Land in African Agrarian Systems*, Madison, Wisconsin: The University of Wisconsin Press, pp. 75–100.

SAXENA, N.C., 1997, *The Saga of Participatory Forest Management in India*, CIFOR Special Publication, CIFOR (India).

SCHIFF, M. and C. MONTENEGRO, 1993, 'Aggregate Agricultural Supply Response in Developing Countries: Critical Survey and Empirical Analysis', Policy Research Department, Trade Policy Division, World Bank: Washington, DC.

SCHOECK, H., 1987, *Envy*, Indianapolis, Ind.: Liberty Press.

SCHOTTER, A., 1981, *The Economic Theory of Social Institutions*, New York: Cambridge University Press.

SCHOTTER, A., 1986, 'The Evolution of Rules', in Langlois, R. (ed.), *Economics as a Process—Essays in the New Institutional Economics*, Cambridge: Cambridge University Press, 117–33.

SCHOTTER, A., A. WEISS, and I. ZAPATER, 1996, 'Fairness and Survival in Ultimatum and Dictatorship Games', *Journal of Economic Behavior and Organization*, Vol. 31, No. 1, pp. 37–56.

SCHROEDER, L., 1994, 'Provision and Production of Rural Roads in Developing Countries: A Synthesis of Research Findings', Decentralisation: Finance and Management Project (DFM), Associates in Rural Development, Inc., Document prepared for the U.S. Agency for International Development, Global Bureau democracy Center.

SCHULTZ, T.S., 1961, 'Economic Prospects of Primary Products', in Ellis, H.S. (ed.), *Economic Development for Latin America*, London: Macmillan, pp. 308–331.

SCOTT, J.C., 1976, *The Moral Economy of the Peasant—Rebellion and Subsistence in Southeast Asia*, New Haven & London: Yale University Press.

SEABRIGHT, P., 1993, 'Managing Local Commons: Theoretical Issues in Incentive Design', *Journal of Economic Perspectives*, Vol. 7, No. 4, pp. 113–134.

SELIGMAN, A.B., 1997, *The Problem of Trust*, Princeton, New Jersey: Princeton University Press.

SEN, A.K., 1967, 'Isolation, Assurance and the Social Rate of Discount', *Quarterly Journal of Economics*, Vol. 81, No. 1, pp. 113–124.

SENED, I., 1997, *The Political Institution of Private Property*, Cambridge: Cambridge University Press.

SEPPÄLÄ, Pekka, 1993, *The Changing Generation—The Devolution of Land Among the Babukusu in Western Kenya*, The Finnish Anthropological Society, Transaction No. 35, Helsinki.

SETHI, R., and E. SOMANATHAN, 1996, 'The Evolution of Social Norms in Common Property Use', *American Economic Review*, Vol. 86, No. 4, pp. 766–88.

SHAPLEY, L.S., and M. SHUBIK, 1977, 'Trade Using One Commodity as a Means of Payment', *Journal of Political Economy*, Vol. 85, No. 5, pp. 937–968.

SHARMA, N. and J. DREZE, 1996, 'Sharecropping in a North Indian Village', *Journal of Development Studies*, Vol. 33, No. 1, pp. 1–39.

SHIPTON, P., 1988, 'The Kenyan Land Tenure Reform: Misunderstandings in the Public Creation of Private Property', in Downs, R.E., and S.P. Reyna (eds.), *Land and Society in Contemporary Africa*, Hanover & London: University Press of New England, pp. 91–135.

SHOTT, S., 1979, 'Emotion and Social Life: A Symbolic Interactionist Analysis', *American Journal of Sociology*, Vol. 84, No. 6, pp. 1335–1360.

SHUBIK, M., 1986, 'A Game Theoretic Approach to the Theory of Money and Financial Institutions', Cowles Foundation Discussion Paper No. 805, Yale University.

SKINNER, Q., 1974, 'Some Problems in the Analysis of Political Thought and Action', *Political Theory*, Vol. 2, No. 1, pp. 277–303.

SIMIS, K., 1982, *The Corrupt Society*, New York: Simon and Schuster.

SIMS, H., 1988, *Political Regimes, Public Policy and Economic Development—Agricultural Performance and Rural Change in Two Punjabs*, New Delhi: Sage Publications.

SINGER, P., 1973, 'Altruism and Commerce: a Defence of Titmuss against Arrow', *Philosophy and Public Affairs*, Vol. 2, pp. 312–320.

SINGH, I., L. SQUIRE, and J. STRAUSS (eds.), 1986, *Agricultural Household Models: Extensions, Application and Policy*, Baltimore: The John Hopkins University Press.

SJAASTAD, E., and D.W. BROMLEY, 1997, 'Indigenous Land Rights in Sub-Saharan Africa: Appropriation, Security, and Investment Demand', *World Development*, Vol. 25, No. 4, pp. 549–562.

SJAASTAD, E., 1998, *Land Tenure and Land Use in Zambia—Cases from the Northern and Southern Provinces*, PHD. Thesis, Agricultural University of Norway, As (mimeo).

SKAPERDAS, S., and C. SYROPOULOS, 1995, 'Gangs as Primitive States', in Fiorentini, G., and S. Peltzman (eds.), *The Economics of Organised Crime*, Cambridge: Cambridge University Press, pp. 61–82.

SKLAR, R.L., 1979, 'The Nature of Class Domination in Africa', *Journal of Modern African Studies*, Vol. 17, No. 4, pp. 531–552.

SMELSER, N.J., 1963, 'Mechanism of Change and Adjustment to Change', in Hoselitz, B.F., and W.E. Moore, *Industrialization and Society*, The Hague: Mouton.

SMITH, Adam, 1759, *The Theory of the Moral Sentiments*, (ed. by D.D. Raphael and A.L. Macfie) Indianapolis: Liberty Classics (1982).

SMITH, T.C., 1959, *The Agrarian Origins of Modern Japan*, Stanford, Cal.: Stanford University Press.

SMITH, J., A.D. BARAU, A. GOLDMAN, and J.H. MARECK, 1994, 'The Role of Technology in Agricultural Intensification: The Evolution of Maize Production in the Northern Guinea Savanna of Nigeria', *Economic Development and Cultural Change*, Vol. 42, No. 3, pp. 537–54.

SOLOW, R., 1957, 'Technical Change and the Aggregate Production Function', *The Review of Economics and Statistics*, Vol. 29, No. 3.

SPENCER, D.S.C., 1986, 'Agricultural Research: Lessons of the Past, Strategies for the Future', in Berg, R.J., and J.S. Whitaker (eds.), *Strategies for African Development*, Berkeley, Cal.: University of California Press, pp. 215–41.

SPENCER, D.S.C., 1994, 'Infrastructure and Technology Constraints to Agricultural Development in the Humid and Subhumid Tropics of Africa', Environment and Production Technology Division Discussion Paper No. 3, Washington, DC: International Food Policy Research Institute.

STAGE, O., 1995, 'Putting the Pieces Together—A Study of the Zambezia Infrastructure Project in Lugela District', Report prepared for IBIS by T&B Consult, Copenhagen (mimeo).

STANFIELD, D., 1990, 'Rural Land Titling and Registration in Latin America and The Caribbean: Implications for Rural Development Programs', Land Tenure Center, Unversity of Wisconsin-Madison.

STANILAND, M., 1986, 'Democracy and Ethnocentrism', in Chabal, P. (ed.), *Political Domination in Africa—Reflections on the Limits of Power*, Cambridge: Cambridge University Press, pp. 52–70.

STARR, R.M., 1986, 'Decentralized Trade in a Credit Economy', in Heller, W.P., R.M. Starr, and D.A. Starrett, *Equilibrium Analysis—Essays in honor of Kenneth Arrow, Volume II*, Cambridge: Cambridge University Press, pp. 105–120.

STEINHERR, A., and J. THISSE, 1979, 'Are Labor-Managers Really Perverse', *Economic Letters*, Vol. 2, No. 2, pp. 137–141.

STIGLITZ, J.E., 1989, 'Rational Peasants, Efficient Institutions, and a Theory of Rural Organization: Methodological Remarks for Development Economics', in Bardhan, P. (ed.), *The Economic Theory of Agrarian Institutions*, Oxford: Clarendon Press, pp. 18–29.

STRINGER, R., 1989, 'Farmland Transfers and the Role of Land Banks in Latin America', Land Tenure Center, LTC Paper No. 131, University of Madison-Wisconsin.

SUGDEN, R., 1984, 'Reciprocity: The Supply of Public Goods Through Voluntary Contributions', *Economic Journal*, Vol. 94, pp. 772–787.

SUGDEN, R., 1986, *The Economics of Rights, Co-operation and Welfare*, Oxford: Basil Blackwell.

SUGDEN, R., 1989, 'Spontaneous Order', *Journal of Economic Perspectives*, Vol. 3, No. 4, pp. 85–97.

SWALLOW, B., (ed.), 1994, 'Evaluating the Relationship Between Property Rights, Risk, Technology and Productivity in Sub-Saharan Africa', Socio-Economics and Policy Research, Working Document No. 18, International Livestock Centre for Africa, Addis Ababa.

SWYNNERTON, R.J.M., 1954, *A Plan to Intensify the Development of African Agriculture in Kenya*, Nairobi: Government Printer.

SYLLA, A., 1994, *La philosophie morale des Wolof*, IFAN, Université de Dakar.

SZANTON, D.L., 1998, 'Contingent Moralities—Social and Economic Investment in a Philippine Fishing Town', in Hefner, R.W. (ed.), *Market Cultures—Society and Morality in the New Asian Capitalisms*, Boulder, Col.: Westview Press, pp. 251–267.

TANG, S.Y., 1991, 'Institutional Arrangements and the Management of Common-Pool Resources', *Public Administration Review*, Vol. 51, No. 1, pp. 42–51.

TANG, S.Y., 1992, *Institutions and Collective Action—Self-Governance in Irrigation Systems*, San Francisco: ICS Press.

TANG, S.Y., 1994, 'Institutions and Performance in Irrigation Systems', in Ostrom, E., R. Gardner, and J. Walker, *Rules, Games, and Common-Pool Resources*, Ann Arbor: The University of Michigan Press, pp. 225–45.

TAYLOR, L., 1987, '"The River Would Run Red With Blood": Community and Common Property in an Irish Fishing Settlement', in B.J. McCay and J.M. Acheson (eds.), *The Question of the Commons: The Culture and Ecology of Communal Resources*, Tucson, Ariz.: University of Arizona Press, pp. 290–307.

TAYLOR, M., 1987, *The Possibility of Cooperation*, Cambridge: Cambridge University Press.

TERANISHI, J., 1997, 'Sectoral Resource Transfer, Conflict, and Macrostability in Economic Development: A Comparative Analysis', in Aoki, M., H.K. Kim, and M. Okuno-Fujiwara (eds.), *The Role of Government in East Asian Development—Comparative Institutional Analysis*, Oxford: Clarendon Press, pp. 279–322.

THOMAS, K., 1973, *Religion and the Decline of Magic*, Harmondsworth: Penguin Books.

THOMAS, J.P., and T. WORRALL, 1994, 'Informal Insurance Arrangements in Village Economies', Department of Economics, University of Warwick (mimeo).

THOMPSON, E.P., 1991, *Customs in Common*, Harmondsworth: Penguin Books.

THOMSON, J.T., D.H. FEENY, and R.J. OAKERSON, 1986, 'Institutional Dynamics: The Evolution and Dissolution of Common Property Resource Management', in National Research Council, *Proceedings of the Conference on Common Property Resource Management*, Washington, D.C.: National Academy Press, pp. 391–424.

TIFFEN, M., 1976, *The Enterprising Peasant: Economic Development in Gombe Emirate, North Eastern State, Nigeria, 1900–1968*, London: H.M. Stationary Office.

TIFFEN, M., M. MORTIMORE, and F. GICHUKI, 1994, *More People, Less Erosion—Environmental Recovery in Kenya*, New York: John Wiley & Sons.

TIFFEN, M., and M. MORTIMORE, 1994, 'Malthus Controverted: The Role of Capital and Technology in Growth and Environment Recovery in Kenya', *World Development*, Vol. 22, No. 7, pp. 997–1010.

TILLY, C., 1992, *Coercion, Capital, and European States—AD 990–1992*, Cambridge, MA & Oxford: Blackwell.

TIMOFEYEV, L., 1992, *Russia's Secret Rulers*, New York: Alfred A. Knopf.

TOUFIQUE, K.A., 1977, 'Some Observations on Power and Property Rights in the Inland Fisheries of Bangladesh', *World Development*, Vol. 25, No. 3, pp. 457–467.

TOWNSEND, R.M., 1994, 'Risk and Insurance in Village India', *Econometrica*, Vol. 62, No. 3, pp. 539–91.

TOWNSEND, R.M., 1995, 'Consumption Insurance: An Evaluation of Risk-Bearing Systems in Low-Income Economies', *Journal of Economic Perspectives*, Vol. 9, No. 3, pp. 83–102.

TRIVERS, R.L., 1971, 'The Evolution of Reciprocal Altruism', *Quarterly Journal of Biology*, Vol. 46, pp. 35–57.

TYLER, T.R., 1990, *Why People Obey the Law*, New Haven & london: Yale University Press.

UDRY, C., 1989, 'Rural Credit in Northern Nigeria—Testing the Role of Credit as Insurance', Dept of Economics, Yale University, mimeo.

UDRY, C., 1990, 'Credit Markets in Northern Nigeria: Credit as Insurance in a Rural Economy', *World Bank Economic Review*, Vol. 4, No. 3, pp. 251–269.

UDRY, C., 1991, 'A Competitive Analysis of Rural Credit: State-contingent Loans in Northern Nigeria', Yale University Economic Growth Center Discussion Paper No. 630.

UDRY, C., 1994, 'Risk and Insurance in a Rural Credit Market: An Empirical Investigation in Northern Nigeria', *Review of Economic Studies*, Vol. 61, pp. 495–526.

UNDP (United Nations Development Programme) and WORLD BANK, 1992, *African Development Indicators*, Washington, DC: The World Bank.

VAIZEY, J., 1964, *The Residual Factor and Economic Growth*, Paris: OECD Publications.

VAKSBERG, A., 1991, *The Soviet Mafia*, New York: St. Martin's Press.

VANBERG, V., 1988, *Morality and Economics—De Moribus Est Disputandum*, The Social Philosophy and Policy Center, Original Papers No. 7, New Brunswick and London: Transaction Books.

VAN DE LAAR, A., 1980, *The World Bank and the Poor*, Boston & The Hague: Martinus Nijhoff.

VAN DEN BERG, 1997, *Land Right, Marriage Left—Women's Management of Insecurity in North Cameroon*, CNWS Publications, Leiden.

VAN DEN BREEMER, H.P.M., R.R. BERGH, and G. HESSELING, 1995, 'Towards Local Management of Natural Resources in Senegal', in Van Den Breemer, H.P.M., C.A. Drijver, and L.B. Venema (eds.), *Local Resource Management in Africa*, New York: John Wiley & Sons, pp. 97–110.

VAN HUYCK, J.B., R.C. BATTALIO, and R.O. BEIL, 1990, 'Tacit Coordination Games, Strategic Uncertainty, and Coordination Failure', *American Economic Review*, Vol. 80, No. 1, pp. 234–248.

VERDEAUX, F., 1990, 'Généalogie d'un phénomène de surexploitation: lagune Aby (Côte d'Ivoire), 1935–82', in Verdeaux, F. (ed.), *La pêche—Enjeux de développement et objet de recherche*, Paris: Editions de l'ORSTOM: pp. 191–211.

VISWANATH, C.K., 1997, 'Adivasis: Protesting Land Alienation', *Economic and Political Weekly*, Vol. 32, No. 32, pp. 2016–2017.

VOEGELIN, E., 1956, *Order and History*, Vol. 1: *Israël and Revelation*, Baton Rouge: Louisiana State University Press.

VON BRAUN, J., 1991, 'Social Security in Sub-Saharan Africa: Reflections on Policy Challenges', in Ahmad, E., J. Drèze, J. Hills, and A. Sen (eds.), *Social Security in Developing Countries*, Oxford: Clarendon Press, pp. 395–414.

VON BRAUN, J., and P.J.R. WEBB, 1989, 'The Impact of New Crop Technology on the Agricultural Division of Labor in a West African Setting', *Economic Development and Cultural Change*, Vol. 37, No. 3, pp. 513–534.

VROMEN, J.J., 1995, *Economic Evolution—An Enquiry into the Foundations of New Institutional Economics*, London & New York: Routledge.

WADE, R., 1988, *Village Republics—Economic Conditions for Collective Action in South India*, Cambridge: Cambridge University Press.

WADE, R., 1990, *Governing the Market*, Princeton: Princeton University Press.

WADHWA, D.C., 1989, 'Guaranteeing Title to Land. A Preliminary Study', *Economic and Political Weekly*, Vol. 24, No. 41, pp. 2323–2334.

WALKER, T.S., and J.G. RYAN, 1990, *Village and Household Economies in India's Semi-Arid Tropics*, Baltimore, MD: Johns Hopkins University Press.

WASSERMAN, G., 1976, *Politics of Decolonization—Kenya Europeans and the Land Issue, 1960–1965, Cambridge: Cambridge University Press* .

WATTS, M.J., 1993, 'Idioms of Land and Labor: Producing Politics and Rice in Senegambia', in Bassett, T.J., and D.E. Crummey (eds.), *Land in African Agrarian Systems*, Madison, Wisconsin; University of Wisconsin Press, pp. 157–193.

WEBB, P., J. VON BRAUN, and Y. YOHANNES, 1991, 'Famine in Ethiopia: Policy Implications of Coping Failure at National and Household Levels, IFPRI, Washington DC, (mimeo).

WEBER, M., 1951, *The Religion of China: Confucianism and Taoism*, Glencoe: Free Press.

WEBER, M., 1970, *The Protestant Ethic*, London: George Allen and Unwin.

WEBER, M., 1971, *Economie et société*, Paris: Plon [English version: *Economy and Society*, Berkeley: University of California Press, 1978].

WEBER, M., 1981, *General Economic History*, New Brunswick: Transaction Press.

WEBSTER, A., 1990, *Introduction to the Sociology of Development*, London: Macmillan Press.

WEIGEL, J.Y., 1982, *Migration et production domestique des Soninké du Sénégal*, Paris: ORSTOM.

WEISSING, F., and E. OSTROM, 1992, 'Irrigation Institutions and the Games Irrigators Play: Rule Enforcement on Government- and Farmer-Managed Systems', in Scharpf, F.W. (ed.), *Games in Hierarchies and Networks: Analytical and Empirical Approaches to the Study of Governance Institutions*, Frankfurt: Campus; Boulder: Westview.

WEITZMAN, M., 1974, 'Free Access vs. Private Ownership as Alternative Systems for Managing Common Property', *Journal of Economic Theory*, Vol. 8, No. 2, pp. 225–234.

WEITZMAN, M., 1993, 'Economic Transition—Can Theory Help?', *European Economic Review*, Vol. 37, No. ..., pp. 549–555.

WHITEHEAD, A., 1990, 'Rural Women and Food Production in Sub-Saharan Africa', in Drèze, J., and A.K. Sen (eds.), *The Political Economy of Hunger, Vol. 1: Entitlement and Well-Being*, Oxford: Clarendon Press.

WIESSNER, P., 1982, 'Risk, Reciprocity and Social Influences on! Kung San Economics', in Leacock, E., and R.B. Lee (eds.), *Politics and History in Band Societies*, Cambridge: Cambridge University Press, 61–84.

WHITE, D.M., 1977, *Social Organization and the Sea: A Gulf Coast Shrimp Fishery*, Unpublished Ph.D. thesis, Southern Methodist University (USA).

WHITE, G., and R. WADE, 1988, 'Developmental States and Markets in East Asia: an Introduction', in G. White (ed.), *Developmental States in East Asia*, London: Macmillan, pp. 1–29.

WIESSNER, P., 1982, 'Risk, Reciprocity and Social Influences on! Kung San Economics', in Leacock, E., and R.B. Lee (eds.), *Politics and History in Band Societies*, Cambridge: Cambridge University Press, pp. 61–84.

WIGGINS, S., 1995, 'Changes in African Farming Systems Between the mid-1970s and the mid-1980s', *Journal of International Development*, Vol. 7, No. 6, pp. 807–48.

WIJAYA, M.L., 1996, *Voluntary Reciprocity as an Informal Social Insurance Mechanism—A Game Theoretic Approach*, PhD Thesis, No. 108, Faculty of Economics and Business Management, Katholieke Universiteit, Leuven (Belgium).

WILLIAMSON, O.E., 1985, *The Economic Institutions of Capitalism*, New York: Free Press.

WILSON, C.W., 1967, 'Trade, Society, and the State', in *The Cambridge Economic History of Europe, Vol. IV: The Economy of Expanding Europe in the Sixteenth and Seventeenth Centuries*, Cambridge: Cambridge University Press.

WILSON, P.N., and G.D. THOMPSON, 1993, 'Common Property and Uncertainty: Compensating Coalitions by Mexico's Pastoral *Ejidatorios*', *Economic Development and Cultural Change*, Vol. 41, No. 2, pp. 299–318.

WITTFOGEL, K.A., 1957, *Oriental Despotism. A Comparative Study of Total Power*, New Haven: Yale University Press.

WOLF, E.R., 1955, 'Types of Latin American Peasantry: A Preliminary Discussion', *American Anthropology*, Vol. 57, June.

WOLF, E., 1982, *Europe and the People Without History*, Berkeley: University of California Press.

WOO-CUMINGS, M., 1997, 'The Political Economy of Growth in East Asia: A Perspective on the State, Market, and Ideology', in Aoki, M., H.K. Kim, and M. Okuno-Fujiwara (eds.), *The Role of Government in East Asian Development—Comparative Institutional Analysis*, Oxford: Clarendon Press, pp. 323–341.

WOOLSEY-BIGGART, N., and G. HAMILTON, 1992, 'On the Limits of Firm-Based Theory to Explain Business Networks: the Western Bias of Neo-Classical Economics', in Nitin, N., and R.G. Eccles (eds.), *Networks and Organizations*, Harvard Business School Press.

WORLD BANK, 1989, *Sub-Saharan Africa—From Crisis to Sustainable Growth*, Washington, D.C.

WORLD BANK, 1990, *Proceedings of the World Bank Annual Conference on Development Economics—1989*, Washington, D.C.: The World Bank.

WORLD BANK, 1991, *Rwanda—Agricultural Strategy Review*, Report No. 8704-RW, Agriculture Operations Division, Africa Region, Washington, DC: The World Bank.

WORLD BANK, 1993, *World Bank Development Report—1993*, Washington, DC: The World Bank.

WORLD BANK, 1996, *World Bank Development Report—1996*, Washington, DC: The World Bank.

YERGIN, D., and T. GUSTAVSON, 1994, *Russia 2010*, London: Nicholas Bradley.

YOUNG, C., 1986, 'Africa's Colonial Legacy', in Berg, R.J., and J.S. Whitaker, (eds.), *Strategies for African Development*, Berkeley: University of California Press, pp. 25–51.

YOUNG, H.P., 1993a, 'The Evolution of Conventions', *Econometrica*, Vol. 61, No. 1, pp. 57–84.

YOUNG, H.P., 1993b, 'An Evolutionary Model of Bargaining', *Journal of Economic Theory*, Vol. 59, No. 1, pp. 145–68.

YOUNG, H.P., 1994, *Equity—In Theory and Practice*, Princeton, N.J.: Princeton University Press.

YOUNG, H.P., 1996, 'The Economics of Convention', *Journal of Economic Perspectives*, Vol. 10, No. 2, pp. 105–122.

YOUNG, H.P., 1998, *Individual Strategy and Social Structure—An Evolutionary Theory of Institutions*, Princeton, N.J.: Princeton University Press.

YOUNG, J.T., 1992, 'Natural Morality and the Ideal Impartial Spectator in Adam Smith', *International Journal of Social Economics,* Vol. 19, Nos. 10/11/12. pp. 71–82.

ZIMMERMAN, F., and M.R. CARTER, 1997, 'Rethinking the Demand for Institutional Innovation: Land Rights and Land Markets in the West African Sahel', Staff Paper Series, No. 400, Department of Agricultural and Applied Economics, University of Wisconsin, Madison.

ZUBAIR, M.A., 1987, 'The Administration of Land, Water and Grazing Rights under Sokoto Caliphate of Northern Nigeria: An Islamic Legal Viewpoint', in *Land and Water Rights Issues in Irrigated Schemes in Sub-Saharan Africa and Madagascar*, Paris: Centre d'études juridiques comparatives, pp. 122–135.

ZUFFEREY, F.S., 1986, 'A Study of Local Institutions and Resource Management Inquiry in Eastern Central District', Land Tenure Center, LTC Paper No. 88, University of Wisconsin-Madison.

# Index

Lightning Source UK Ltd.
Milton Keynes UK
UKOW041935100412

190439UK00007B/48/A

9 789058 230584